ARCHITECTURE OF THE AFTERLIFE:

THE FLIPSIDE CODE

Discovering the Blueprint for the Great Beyond

By

Richard Martini

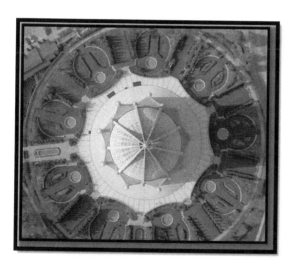

ARCHITECTURE OF THE AFTERLIFE:

THE FLIPSIDE CODE Discovering the Blueprint for the Great Beyond By Richard Martini

Cover Art: The Duomo in Florence by Brunelleschi. To date no one knows how he was able to get thousands of bricks to defy gravity in the largest free standing dome built since antiquity. The secret apparently lies in the weeks he spent in Rome scouring through the ceiling of the structure of architect Hadrian's "Pantheon" in Rome to learn his secret.

Above: Aerial view of the Bahai Temple in Wilmette, Illinois. As a young architect with Holabird and Root in Chicago, my father R. Charles Martini designed the windows of the Bahai Temple. Every time I pass it I think of him, but this is the first time I've ever seen the Temple from his "current perspective." (From YouTube)

CONTENTS

FOREWORD

I began to examine the flipside a few years ago, but in an indirect way. I'm not a medium, not a psychic, not a hypnotherapist; just a filmmaker who has written for magazines, trade publications and a handful of "bestselling" (Amazon kindle in their genre) books about the afterlife. For those aware of my books - "Flipside: A Tourist's Guide on How to Navigate the Afterlife," "It's a Wonderful Afterlife; Further Adventures in the Flipside," "Hacking the Afterlife: Practical Advice from the Flipside" or "Backstage Pass to the Flipside: Talking to the Afterlife with Jennifer Shaffer" - you're well aware of what I've been up to.

But for those of you who aren't; in a nutshell, I've been filming people under deep hypnosis for over a decade (more than 50 cases so far) and have compared their answers to the thousands of cases of Dr. Helen Wambach and Michael Newton. This book has excerpts of about 50 interviews with people *not under hypnosis* who say the same things about the journey.

What people say is both consistent and reproducible. I've done six of my own deep hypnosis sessions, and made a documentary about the research of hypnotherapist Michael Newton and others using deep hypnosis ("Flipside: A Journey into the Afterlife" available on Amazon and Gaia). The film contains excerpts from a dozen hypnotherapy sessions.

Dr. Helen Wambach (her books are "Reliving Past Lives" and "Life Before Life") was a clinical psychologist who did PTSD therapy for Viet Nam veterans in the 1970's. During her sessions, she found people would go further than she imagined they would or could. In order to study whether or not their memories of past lives could be accurate, she applied a scientific approach to her research.

She didn't ask people to "go to" a specific past life memory, but recruited groups of people and gave them options of different time periods to explore. 100 years ago, 250 years ago, 500, etc. The people doing the session made the choice of what lifetime if any they would explore. Then she would conduct four "two hour sessions" (eight hours per day) where she would do a group hypnosis sessions and have them report whatever they remembered.

She tossed out results that appeared biased. She focused on people who remembered how they lived, what their houses looked like, what kind of clothing they wore and what kind of tools they used, including their eating utensils.

She did this, because there are historical records regarding these items, and they aren't often examined while under hypnosis. She could compare what people "remembered" versus the scientific record of that era. So if a person was using a two pronged fork, a fork with three tines, or four and it matched the time and era, they wouldn't be eliminated from the study. She focused on architecture, how houses were built, clothing was manufactured, the kinds of foods people ate, etc. That way, she could compare what they remembered with the actual, verifiable historical record.

She found that only 1% of her clients could be eliminated for reasons she felt didn't hold up and the rest fell into different categories. From these datasets, she reported 2000 clients who could recall previous lifetimes, could compare their reports and see the consistencies in relation to historical facts.

In Michael Newton's work, he estimated 7000 subjects over his 40 year career and four books. First publishing in 1994, he used a direct approach, asking people to recall a "lifetime that had some influence on their current lifetime." He then mapped out what they said about the journey, compared it to the thousands of cases he had gathered. What he found was that his clients' comments were consistent about the journey, and what I found by comparing Wambach's data with Newton's reports – was they matched in terms of hallmarks of the so called "afterlife."

"So called" because people consistently say we're "fully conscious" prior to incarnation, that we choose our lifetimes, bring about a third of our conscious energy to that lifetime, so we are semiconscious while on the planet, and then when the body fails, that conscious energy returns "back home" (the term they all use) to reconnect with the conscious energy left behind.

I've spent over ten years filming people saying the identical things, and have put some of those transcripts into my first four books.

Somewhere along the line, I met Jennifer Shaffer, and the past five years I've been conducting direct interviews with mediums like Jennifer to access people on the flipside who are no longer on the planet. I try to focus on hearing or learning "new information" from them – details only people on the flipside would know, then afterwards see if I can verify the details. We have a series of books about our conversations; "Backstage Pass to the Flipside: Talking to the Afterlife with Jennifer Shaffer." Jennifer also appears in the film "Backstage Pass to the Flipside: Talking to Bill Paxton" on Gaia.

One could say that I've become familiar with the architecture of the afterlife.

One thing I've noticed is that when I ask people to recall a vivid experience, like a near death experience, once they began to talk about the "memory" of the event, they can shift from *past tense to present tense and learn new information about the experience.*

For example, asking "So what did you see, if anything?" may result in "I saw a bright light, a bright white light." I'll then ask "Can you see it now, as you remember it?" If they can, I'll say "Try to walk closer to that light and tell me what that feels like?" By doing so, I've shifted from past tense to present tense, and they begin to refer to these memories as if they're in front of them. It's a subtle shift, but I do it consciously.

In the book "The Holographic Universe" Michael Talbot introduced the idea the universe is holographic. If one breaks a piece of a hologram, that small piece retains all the information of the original hologram. I've found that any recalled memory is holographic as well.

If I can get a person to remember a vivid detail – could be from a dream, from an 'other worldly event' – could be from a near death experience, out of body experience, or something they saw while under deep hypnosis – we can visit that event again, and learn new things from it.

One would think that wouldn't be possible; I've found that it is.

The reason for this, on a physical level, appears related to something I was told during an interview with Jennifer Shaffer in the book "Backstage Pass to the Flipside: Talking to the Afterlife with Jennifer Shaffer." Jennifer and I were having a discussion with a scientist who is no longer on the planet, and I was asking him about an event that happened during his lifetime.

Stephen Hawking had recently passed. Jennifer was describing him and I asked him about something I had seen on the Stephen Colbert "Late Show" the night before.

It was a story told by the actor Hank Azaria.

Hank, the actor who plays Apu as well as other characters in "The Simpsons," said "One of the funniest things he'd ever heard while working on "The Simpson's" was during a "table read" waiting for Stephen Hawking to appear." Hawking was late, all the actors were waiting and Azaria recounted how comedian Harry Shearer had said "the funniest adlib he'd ever heard."

I asked Stephen Hawking via Jennifer Shaffer if he knew what that adlib was that Harry Shearer had made at the table read.

Jennifer said "He said "The man has no sense of time."

Which is precisely what Azaria said that Harry Shearer had said. (Jennifer had not seen the show, nor knew who Hank or Harry were).

So I asked Hawking directly, through Jennifer: "How do you access that information? I assume you either heard it after the fact, because you weren't there when it happened, or were you watching the Late Show last night? How did you know what Harry Shearer said?"

He said "Think of time like a packet. A packet *of time.* Or a CD that contains that event... and when you want to access an event that occurred, you take out that CD and access all the information from the event." He said "It's all math, just the way that information is stored on a CD, and you just need to access the math of the event that you're trying to report."

Stephen Hawking, *Mr. Time,* said from the flipside, "the way to access memory, or events in the past is to think of them as packets of time, and then, like a hologram, we can access them and learn new information."

I thought that was pretty interesting.

In this book you're going to hear some pretty fantastical things regarding time, regarding consciousness. In the case of mediums, we'll meet some who are adept at "accessing frequencies" or seeing, hearing or sensing things that "aren't there" (i.e., dogs can smell cancer, bees can see UV rays, just because we cannot does not mean they cannot). So in light of their ability to sense or see things, I began to interview various people about event that occurred in their life that are "packets of time."

I'm not trying to convince anyone people have the ability to access people no longer on the planet *or* that there are packets of time – I'm trying to understand the nature of how things work *over there*. It's not my theory, belief or opinion they can – I've been filming or recording them do so for years. This is the first time I've had the chance to transcribe some of these interviews that began some years ago.

In this discussion of the architecture of the afterlife, and for those familiar with my books, in the transcripts of deep hypnosis sessions, people remember a previous lifetime, then are able to access the between lives realm to understand "why" they chose that particular lifetime, why they chose this current lifetime, and what the two may have in common.

That technique was developed by Michael Newton, and the members of the Newton Institute are the people I recommend seeking out to do this kind of work. It's in-depth process, and with the help of licensed, trained guides, one can learn profound lessons about their life, or previous lifetimes. They can learn why a person has chose those lifetimes, why they chose this one, as well as the process that was included in coming to be on the planet.

I've done six of these sessions myself. I've visited classrooms, libraries, met guides and teachers in my sessions. And when I was filming the 50 or so cases, they too met their guides and teachers, as well as their "council of elders."

That's the term that Michael Newton used to coin the idea that we all had a "council" of teachers that helped us to review or go over our lifetime. In Michael's 7000 cases, he focused on this aspect as well as others, and in my case, when I began this film, I too had an experience of "visiting my council." In most of the accounts, the council is a small group of people who are tasked to help a person go over what they've done during a lifetime.

The first time I heard about a council outside this research was reviewing the life and death of the Olympic wrestler Dave Schultz. His father Phillip gave a poignant eulogy when his son died, which included the following detail: he said when the Olympic champion was five, he had come to him and said "Dad, can I tell you a secret?" Phillip said Dave walked him into the woods behind their home and said "I spoke to my council before I came here. They were old men with beards and they said that I could come here to teach a lesson in love, but I won't be here for very long."

Apparently, everyone has a council. We all visit them twice; once before we come to our incarnation so they can go over what we promised to accomplish or learn during our journey here, and then once again when we return "home" after a lifetime.

People talk about the afterlife, but don't call it that or heaven – in all the cases I've filmed people use the word *"home"* to refer to where they go after a lifetime. It's what people consistently say when asked while under hypnosis "Where do you go after this lifetime you just remembered?" When they first said "I went home" I was confused. Did they mean the home from the lifetime they'd just remembered, or the home from this lifetime they're currently living? As it turns out they meant *neither.*

"Home" is the term *they* use for the afterlife.

So if we allow that for a moment, people report that on our way home, we often take a detour to visit our "council." The councils are generally from 3-15 individuals – sometimes more, sometimes less. But I'm getting ahead of this story – we'll get to councils in a bit.

I just wanted to introduce the reader to the idea.

Once I discovered people could access these packets of memory when they were fully conscious, I realized they could also visit their guides and council as well. In the Michael Newton model of these sessions, people visit councils, recount life reviews but generally don't ask them any questions.

I started asking questions to members of the councils because I was curious. "Who are you?" "Why are you on this council?" "Have you ever incarnated?" "Can you show this person your planet or universe?" Some of them were reluctant to speak (some refuse to reply) but others are forthcoming, happy to share their own stories.

But we'll get there.

At this point, I often say "Buckle up. You're in for a bumpy ride." But I won't – we begin with mediums and their rides, so it's easier to assume they operate with a different set of physics... but then we'll get to average folks who are able to access their councils and are able to hear profound messages from them.

So sit back, relax, and turn off your disbelief key. What you're about to read or hear was filmed first, transcribed, edited and is now in front of you or in your ears. No harm can come of learning this information – only healing. Enjoy.

Welcome to the Martini zone.

My pals who help me access the flipside; Luana Anders and Jennifer Shaffer

INTRODUCTION:

THE MARTINI METHOD

Near Mt. Kailash with a shopkeeper from Darchen I'd met a week earlier. Robert Thurman is over her shoulder; Mt. Kailash is behind us. I had just made a trip around the sacred mountain in Western Tibet.

When I started filming people under deep hypnosis, I thought "Wow, what a novel way to gain insight into the human condition." I sat in the corner of the room, often just listening, while the camera did all the work. I didn't want to disrupt what people were doing – the hypnotherapist preparing the client, the person coming in for a private intimate session – and me with my cameras and microphones to catch every breath.

At first I thought that might be impossible. After all, who can forget when a camera is pointed at your face and a microphone is under your nose? But as it turns out, most people suddenly disappear, and their subconscious takes over.

These hypnotherapy sessions typically last from four to six hours. I've filmed sessions with Jimmy Quast, Paul Aurand, Pete Smith, Lyn Blankenship, Scott De Tamble and others and the hallmarks are the same. No matter who is asking the questions, no matter who is lying on the couch – these people say relatively the same things about the afterlife. All while under hypnosis.

They talk about a past life memory, the end of that lifetime, how they were often met by a guide or guides, went to visit their soul group or fellow classmates who normally incarnate with them – some visit libraries, classrooms, many visit their "councils" etc. For fans of "Flipside" and my other books they're familiar with what I'm saying.

However; "Science doesn't consider hypnosis a valid tool of science." I heard that from Dr. Bruce Greyson at the University of Virginia.

I was staying at his home, he brought me in to meet the fellow scientists of the Department of Perceptual Studies, Ed and Emily Kelly, Dr. Jim Tucker, etc, and I presented what I'd learned from the twelve deep hypnosis sessions to date. (Since then I've filmed over 50). Ian Stevenson, who founded DOPS was adamant that hypnosis wasn't a valid tool of science (which I debate in "It's a Wonderful Afterlife" and won't belabor here) but as I pointed out to the scientists; "Even if you don't consider it a valid tool of science, the consistent reports of what people say while under hypnosis is consistent across the globe. So that alone deserves further study."

I introduced them to the work of Michael Newton and I've heard since then they've done their own research into what people say under deep hypnosis.

In "Flipside" there's the dramatic memory of a woman dying in Auschwitz, but she gave her name and the town she was from. I was able to find a number of Ana or Anna Pachinskys who died at Auschwitz, who were from Poland.

But each time a person recalls a previous lifetime, I use the details given to do a deep dive into the forensics of that memory. In "Flipside" I was able to verify a number of details about previous lifetimes, as well as in "It's a Wonderful Afterlife" and "Hacking the Afterlife." In "Hacking" we got "new information" from someone no longer on the planet (Amelia Earhart) that I was able to forensically find out to be accurate – six months after the session.

In other words, she told us details (via Jennifer Shaffer) no one knew, is not public knowledge, could not be cryptomnesia[i] – a detail about her life I didn't know, even though I've worked on two Hollywood films about her. And I was later able to forensically verify this "new information" that I heard from her during this "interview."

Again, when we access a packet of time, we can learn "new information." Every event, every memory is a packet of time.

One doesn't have to be consciously aware of that packet of time – or have to be aware that packet of time is accessible. I've found if one has a memory of anything – a dream, a visitation, a near death event, a past life memory, any "consciousness altered experience" – a person can use that packet of time as a gateway. As a portal to the flipside.

They don't need to be under hypnosis... at all.

By interviewing mediums, I realized asking direct question to people no longer on the planet was a possibility. For the past five years, every week I get together with medium Jennifer Shaffer and we access people on the flipside and ask them about their journey.

Filming people I knew, or whom my friends on the other side knew, giving us new information about their journey and existence without any hypnosis whatsoever. As it turns out one doesn't have to be a medium to access this same information.

If people were "making up memories" the memories would be "all over the map." Those memories, the ones of the flipside, would be based on their beliefs; if they are believers in a religion, or religious figures, they should have an experience that's congruent with those beliefs. If they have no beliefs whatsoever, or believe in science, it follows they would not have an experience at all.

But that ain't what I'm hearing.

So – simply put – without any hypnosis, just by asking a series of questions, I'm getting the same results from people who are not under hypnosis at all.

In this book I have transcribed sessions done on Skype, sessions done in public in front of an audience, sessions done on a radio show, sessions I've done with complete strangers I've never met, people that I know well in noisy cafe's. It doesn't matter; they all recall details about previous lifetimes, as well as the same structural hallmarks of the afterlife.

I've spoken directly to "council members" on the flipside – that is, a person is visiting their council and I interview the various council members about who they are, where they come from, how many councils they sit on, what their reason is for being on this council, whether or not they approve of my asking them these questions, and what the lottery numbers are.

Yes, I always ask, and yes, I always get a laugh.

But the point of this exercise is that *evidence of something that is beyond our comprehension is here* – people saying that they can talk to their councils without ever having heard that there is such a thing as a council. People talk to their guides, without ever having met them before. Their guides tell me things about my own life via a person I've never met, has zero knowledge about me, but their council members are aware of exactly what I'm doing.

This book is nothing short of a revelation of another alternate universe that we exist in.

I'm going to walk you into this universe, show you how easy it is to get there, and give every hypnotherapist whoever did this kind of work a shortcut on how to do the same thing with their clients, their patients. I'm also going to show everyone reading this book how simple it is for them to do it on their own – without help.

Some have asked me "why is it important to know this when we haven't known it as a species since the dawn of mankind?"

The answer I hear is "Because we are in danger of losing this planet."

There's no other way to put it. The reason I'm able to access this information is because those on the flipside know that we can always incarnate on some other planet, but it's taken a long time to make earth habitable, and if we're going to return to it in the future, we need to find a way to alert people to leave behind fresh air, water and earth for not only their children, but our own possible return.

Again, I'm only a reporter here – I ask leading questions decidedly, I cajole and bug people to ask their guides to show up – and when they do, they take us in all kinds of unusual directions.

But they allow me to badger, cajole them, ask these impertinent questions not because they find me amusing (some do, some don't) but because they are aware we are at a crucial point in the history of mankind. The reason our consciousness is expanding to be aware that our loved ones don't die, they're all accessible, so that we can become aware of how and why we incarnate, how we sometimes incarnate on other planets, in other realms, and how and why there is no such a thing as an "alien" when we are all "aliens" in the sense of "choosing to incarnate as a human on this planet."

There, now you don't have to read this book. You know what I'm aiming at, you can get a refund, return it to whomever gave it as a gift. "No thanks, not interested." But I'm warning the dear reader, that if you turn the page, you'll hear an alternate version of reality. And somewhere in your higher conscious mind will be the odd realization that what I'm reporting is not only accurate, but important to realize.

And that's just the introduction.

CHAPTER ONE:

TALKING TO BILL PAXTON

Mr. Bill (Wikimedia)

To start this journey, as "proof of concept" I'm going to go to my pal and leadoff hitter from the flipside bench; Bill Paxton. For those who've read "Backstage Pass to the Flipside: Talking to the Afterlife with Jennifer Shaffer," they'll find part one of this three part interview in that book. I asked three different mediums the same questions to ask my friend, who had passed suddenly while having routine heart surgery.

I knew Bill when he first began his career; we met when he was a member of a band called "Martini Ranch" (no relation) and he helped me rewrite my script "You Can't Hurry Love." He was initially going to star in my first film but that didn't happen.

At that point he had been in a couple of James Cameron films, ("Aliens" hadn't been released yet) and we found common ground in laughter and story telling. In this chapter, Kimberly Babcock accesses him (without knowing who he is or was) and described him perfectly as one who "knows no stranger" – a guy that lights up a room when he enters it and can talk to anyone about anything. He had the gift of gab, a great storyteller, and a unique and uncanny ability to make people feel at ease and connected to him from that point forward.

We met in a pub in London. His soon to be wife was friends with a neighbor of mine Lori from my hometown near Chicago, and my friend and her husband were living in London. I was in transit from visiting my friend and mentor Charles Grodin on the set of "Ishtar" in Morocco, and brought a case of food poisoning from a sandwich I had at the Morocco airport. I spend a day flat out on a cot in Lori and John Gresty's London flat, and after a couple of days was able to feebly join them at a London pub.

My pals introduced me to their new friend "Bill." I didn't recognize his name but when I heard Bill's laugh I recognized it from the film "Weird Science" directed by my hometown's own John Hughes. (Fellow *"Shermerville"* native) I shared stories with Bill about going to school with John, how he had eloped with the best friend of my sister in law, and Bill shared tales of filmmaking in Chicago over a pint or three of Guinness. He was in London making a film, he said, the "sequel to Alien" shooting on sound stages in Pinewood. He was someone you could fall in love with instantly.

That led to our hanging out in Santa Monica where we both lived, then various locales worldwide, including the Cannes film festival, and staying in random touch over the phone. Last time I heard his laugh, he stopped in to see a screening of my film "Cannes Man" in Santa Monica – the funny thing is that I again recognized that laugh immediately just as I had in the pub. "Bill's here!"

His career skyrocketed, family and fame made it hard to see him, but I always felt like we were one sentence away from our next laugh. I was disconcerted to hear he had passed, but was equally amazed and pleased that he started showing up during interviews I was doing with mediums.

I include these three interviews here to introduce the audience to the idea our loved ones are accessible. I don't feel the need to prove that our loved ones still exist, I've been doing that since "Flipside." But for those who may need a refresher or a taste of what's to come, I offer these three interviews with the one and only Bill Paxton.

INTERVIEW VIA MEDIUM JENNIFER SHAFFER

"It's fun. I can fly"

Bill Paxton and his father John. Photo: Wikimedia

This interview was conducted in the office of medium Jennifer Shaffer (*JenniferShaffer.com*). As an experiment, I said I wanted to speak to my friend "Bill" to see if she might figure out who he is based on her ability to "see" or "hear" things from the flipside. My questions are *in italics,* her replies are **in bold.** "Luana" is a reference to the actress Luana Anders, who fans of "Flipside" will know, has been my mentor or comrade in helping access people on the other side. She also knew and was a fan of Billy's.

Rich: We have a mutual friend who passed away recently, his name is Bill. Can Luana bring him forward?

Jennifer: They just danced.

Who just danced?

Bill and Luana did a little tango thing.

(Note: Luana acted in over 30 feature films and 300 television shows. She died in 1996, and was the person who introduced me to the flipside by showing up in my apartment both in Santa Monica in New York. At some point I thought "Well, if she can visit me, where is she?" I report that extensively in "Flipside," and Luana has been instrumental in the structure of how I speak to people on the flipside via Jennifer Shaffer. Luana helps people "over there" to "slow down their frequency" and put answers in Jennifer's mind as images or sounds – and Jennifer is able to translate what they're trying to say. Luana knew Bill, was a fan of his work and I wasn't surprised to hear she brought him forward.)

Does Bill want to talk to us?

He just showed me him filing his nails... (Like "Yeah, what is it?" Bill and my relationship was always poking fun at each other.)

He's here? (Not quite believing it myself)

He says, "He's shampooing his hair, getting ready."

Tell us what it's like over there.

"It's fun," he says. He says, "I can fly" and that he likes scaring people.

Who was the first person to greet you when you crossed over?

"His dad."

(Note: Bill's father John did precede him and as we'll hear from another medium, he says the same answer.)

Was that a happy reunion?

He says, "It was shocking... because that meant that he had died." He said "Yes, at first, it was shocking, but then that subsided." He said, "At first, he was startled. It wasn't scary," he says. "It was like a recognition of both worlds." He showed me them (being) together.

Was this an "exit point" for you? Something that you planned to have happen? Was this the right or wrong time for your exit?

(Note: "Exit points" are something we've learned in these interviews. People say that we generally stay here to accomplish what we've set out to do, but "exit ramps" or "exit points" sometimes appear, and we wind up leaving earlier than we thought we would.)

He's saying, "It was the wrong time for his physical body, it was the right time for his soul."

You once talked about going to visit the Titanic. What was that like?

(Jennifer stops, makes a face, eyes wide.) Is this the Billy that was in the movie "Titanic?" He showed me a picture of that guy who just passed. I'm so confused.

Well, let's ask him. Is that picture that Jennifer is seeing of a person, is that a picture of you? If it isn't, give her a thumbs down.

He gave me a thumbs up. This is him? I saw him here, in the office when we met the other day... Oh, I love him, I had no idea...(that we would speak to him).

Bill, take Jennifer down with you in that capsule when you went to see the Titanic.

(Note: Jim Cameron took Bill in his submersible to see the Titanic for a number of trips.)[1]

(Staring into the distance, Jennifer shivers.) **I got scared because of the water rushing** (past) **but then he grabbed my hand and he calmed my heart down.** (Jennifer pauses) **He's taking me to a corner, he's showing me the boat. If you had a blueprint of the boat we're going to the farthest right corner of the Titanic... okay...** (To Bill) **Go slower. He just told me, "You don't have to hold your breath."**

Describe what you're seeing and feeling.

I'm feeling a sense of peace. I'd be really scared to ever go into something like that. He's taking me down to the right of the bow... that's below on the bottom, in the front, and there's a hole in the front – he showed me an explosion... an explosion that caused that hole. It's in the front.

(Note: Ding! This is accurate. Jim Cameron has taken 33 trips to visit the Titanic. National Geographic did an extensive survey of the wreck, and it does include a hole where she's describing it. Knowing Jennifer as well as I do I'm confident she's not referring to something that she's seen, but something that she is "seeing.")

They hit the iceberg on the right side.[2]

---

[1] Oddly enough, in April 2017, a few weeks after this interview, a "locket" from the Titanic was found on the ocean floor in a bag.

Jennifer aside: I didn't know that.

Okay, thanks Billy. Let's move on to some other questions.

It's funny; I feel like I'm decompressing now.

Bill, have you seen John Hughes since you got back?

(Jennifer laughs) He says, "He's really busy."

Anything you want to say to Jim Cameron?

"Thank you." He said it again, "Thank you."

Anything more specific?

He said, "He knows where it is."

Where what is?

Something they were looking for? Jewelry?

I don't know. I thought that was made up. Where is it Billy? Is he showing you a jewel?

He's saying to be quiet. He showed me you, interrupting him... he says, "I'm trying to talk."

Sorry.

He's saying it's something that was lost on the ship. (Oddly enough, a few weeks after this, they found more artifacts near the ship, including jewelry) **He's showing me a future project with Jim... Might be a movie, something they talked about.**

Is that something you were going to be involved with?

He's showing me looking at papers, but I don't know.

Well, I can't really call up Jim and ask him, but Billy, you know how to whisper in his ear.

"I know how to scare him," he said.

---

2   http://www.dailymail.co.uk/news/article-2118217/New-Titanic-images-doomed-ship-youve-seen-before.html

That's allowed. Let's talk about other stuff. What do we look like to you? How do you communicate with us?

(Jennifer laughs.) **He says so many funny things. He just showed me an image of my** (backless) **dress and said, "I can almost feel it." I'm asking, "Are you kidding around, or just being Bill?" He said, "I'm being Bill." He showed me the aerial view of being above us, your head, he says he sees eyes because they're windows...**

Windows of the soul?

That works best, the eyes, that's what he sees.

Can you physical manifest something over here? Like move a napkin, or make a splash in water?

He says, "You'd have to be Einstein."

(Note: This is a reference to the math involved. What people consistently say is that in order to create an image over there, it's a math equation that they work on and learn how to do. He's saying, in order to "manifest" over here, which includes appearances, etc, it would require "higher math.")

Bill, you also said your experience over there was that you were learning how to fly. Can you show Jennifer how you can fly from one place to the next?

He's showing me (visually) **before I can really process it. He's going to all these corners really fast, then he showed me how many things are going on in the interim. Then he slowed it down, super slow and showed me how things move here - but he's going faster than that.**

You mean like a super fast game of Pong or tag? And he slowed it down so you only see four or five touches?

"Yes."

Describe what do we look like to you; how do you communicate to us?

He showed me the aerial view from above us, he showed me your head. He said, "What works best is the eyes, as they're the windows to the soul."

If you were going to pick some aspects of life on the planet that you might miss, or wish you could live again?

He showed me a pistol, chewing tobacco, horses...

He misses chewing tobacco?

No, he's showing me like another lifetime.

Where was that?

In Texas. Near Austin. Feels like after the civil war... after 1879.

(Note: Bill goes on to describe in detail a former lifetime, details of which I was able to verify through research. It involved a small group of Mormon settlers who lived near Austin, and he was showing her a lifetime where he was the leader of that group.)

Bill any of your old girlfriends I need to reach out to tell them you said hello?

"I had no old girlfriends. I only had eyes for my wife."

That was just a test buddy.

He's laughing.

What can we ask you that an average person might ask? What's your day like? Do you sleep?

"There's no sleeping here."

Do you have a place that you like to hang out?

He's showing me on a white beach.

For relaxation?

"Yeah. To think."

What do you think about?

"How he wants his next life to be."

Tell us, what will it be? Any idea?

He says he wants the world to be a better place.

How can you help effect that?

He showed me someone like Elon Musk, someone who knows how to get things done or made.

So how do you create your white beach? How do you create objects over there?

He said, "It's by using mathematics and science." He says, "He puts an equation together that gets him the right (visual or) **taste of whatever you want to drink or experience. Whatever you're looking for."**

So when you want to experience a white beach it's a mathematical equation?

"It is, but you don't have to take it to that extent. It just happens."

Billy, is there anything you want me to pass along to your family and friends?

"Reach out to them," he says.

Who wants to hear from some dude who claims he's talking to your loved one?

"Get over it," he says.

Give me something to say that your friends and family would know comes from you.

"When one of them has a dream about him, that's him trying to get through. There are changes, or decisions being made, and he wants them to know whenever they ask him questions, he's there trying to help out."

So your message is; "Listen?"

"Bingo. Whatever it takes; it's important."

Thanks Billy.

....

INTERVIEW WITH BILL VIA MEDIUM KIMBERLY BABCOCK

The man of the hour. (Wikimedia)

Oddly enough, as I was editing this chapter, Bill came through (via an interview with Jennifer) to say **"You need to *punch up* this portion."** He said to Jennifer that **"his chapter was in three parts"** (ding! It is) and told me to work on the second part (as I'm doing now, thanks to the *editor over my shoulder*.)

Jennifer could not know the interview was in "three parts" and would never use the term that I should "punch something up." (I've never heard anyone on the flipside use this term, but it is something Bill would have used as a filmmaker.)

The way this interview came about was I got a call from Dr. Elisa Medhus whose son Erik took his own life some years ago. She wrote a book about it, and I met her at the LA Times book fair. She told me she prior to her son's passing, she didn't believe in the afterlife, but one day her cellphone rang; it was an anonymous call but she answered it – and she heard her deceased son Erik's voice saying "Mom, I'm okay!" She told me that she got a call from a medium in Atlanta (Jamie Butler) a few days later, who said "Your son has shown up in my living room and refuses to leave until I call you."

That began a working relationship between Dr. Medhus, her son Erik on the flipside (his book "My Life After Death" is worth reading) and various mediums who answer questions posed by Dr. Medhus. (ChannelingErik.com) I know Dr. Medhus to be a straightforward heartfelt person, who despite being walloped by this unfathomable tragedy, has found a way to help others by demonstrating she can learn "new information" from her son and their interviews. Dr. Medhus asked me to meet up with medium Kimberly Babcock as she was about to do some readings with her son Erik, and wanted to hear what I thought about her ability.

Kimberly is a minister, medium and intuitive and is from Ohio. We met at Hugo's restaurant in West Hollywood. After the first part of the interview, Bill popped into my mind; I hadn't planned on asking questions about him but took the opportunity to do so. My questions are *in italics,* Kimberly's replies are **in bold.** I did not plan to "talk to Bill," had told no one I might – but he popped into my mind.

Rich: Oh, by the way, a friend of mine passed recently. Can you bring my friend "Bill" forward?

Kimberly: "Bill has been waiting for you."

Hi Bill. What do you want to say to your family or friends?

Was he not able to say goodbye before he passed?

That's correct.

He's showing me it must have been quick or there was no closure when he passed.

Well, this is a way of helping give closure; what would you like to say?

That's it; "That I have closure and that "I'm at peace." He says, "He knows he didn't get to say goodbye... that they (his family) still have that wound, because there was no closure before he passed because he didn't get to say goodbye before he passed."

What does he look like to you?

I don't see him at all. I just sense him. Did he have issues with his chest? I'm feeling like his passing was very quick. He said, "I'm sorry."

To whom?

"To them." Was he on medication or something with medicine?

He was getting an operation; they were working on his heart.

I think it's more than that; medicine was involved with his health and his passing. He's showing me a pill bottle, as if they were giving him medicine.[3]

Okay. So now you're back home – are you there with your soul group? Who greeted you when you crossed over?

His dad. I see the word "dad" written in the air.

(Note: Same answer to my earlier question to Jennifer Shaffer. His father John, who had passed some years earlier.)

Last time we were together was at screening of my film "Cannes Man." I didn't talk to you, but I heard your distinct laugh in the audience. How'd you like that film?

When you said, "I didn't talk to you" he said, *"I did talk to you."*

Oh. Yeah, you're right. That's correct, yes, when I called you up to invite you to the screening. (Ding!) We did speak on the phone. Sorry, I forgot.

When you said, "How'd you like the film?" He feels so much like - you and he wanted to do something similar or that you did similar work – it seems like he saw himself in it.

(Note: As noted, Bill and I tried to work together on my film "You Can't Hurry Love." It eventually starred Bridget Fonda and David Packer. When Bill made "A Simple Plan" he called to say "I finally got to work with Bridget!" "Cannes Man" was about a hapless delivery boy who attends the film festival, and using hype, a film producer (Seymour Cassel) turns him into the "flavor of the moment." Bill and I also spent a few flavor filled evenings in Cannes. He would have been great in the part.)

Rich: He should have been in it.

Kimberly: He feels like it (the story) **represents him...**

Agreed. Billy, my friend, I just wanted to open this door, I thought this would be a fun chance to say hi.

---

[3]   https://www.mirror.co.uk/3am/celebrity-news/weeks-before-bill-paxtons-death-9934233

He says... (Kimberly aside) It's funny it feels like he's such a smart aleck! He says, "You always have a chance to say "Hi" Rich - you don't need her." He's very funny.

Let me ask, so were you impressed when we spoke to Jesus a few moments ago?

(Note: Just prior to my asking questions, I asked Kimberly about when she has seen Jesus during mediumship sessions, and Jennifer described him in detail. That interview appears later in the book.)

He's razzing you. He says... um, he's like "What are you talkin' about bro? Jesus and I go way back, what are you talking 'bout?" He's like "Who are you?" He's kind of beating you up.

(Note: She could not possibly know that's our relationship. Glad to hear he's still enjoying the razzing.)

So Billy, when you're looking at us in this restaurant in West Hollywood, what do you see?

He looks at watch, he's like looking at his watch... did he smoke?

I don't remember. He may have.

It's like he's got a cigar, something bigger than a cigarette.

(Note: This is accurate. Looking at his watch can only mean one thing; "C'mon Rich, get on with the questions!" I'm emotional at this moment, because I realize it actually is him.)

Tell him he's very missed.

He feels like the kind of guy... it's like "He knows no stranger," that kind of person (well loved).

That's accurate. So what's the biggest thing you learned passing over?

"That there is no time, there is no death." He didn't realize how much fear he had until he died, until he came here. "There is no fear; there is no time."

Did you have your past life review already?

He says, "A long time ago."

(Note: A "past life review" is something people report during near death experiences and while under hypnosis. During a "visit to the council" they get to review all the good or bad things they've done in their lifetime. The comment *"There is no time"* relates to the experience of being "in the afterlife." We are "outside of time" and it feels as if "time doesn't exist." He repeats it – "there is no time, there is no fear, there is no death.")

Any of the highlights... (laughs) or low lights you want to share? Anything you were surprised to see?

(Kimberly aside) Wow, that's an interesting perspective. He says that he realizes... he says... I'll just say it verbatim as if I'm him; "I'll say this. I realize the fear that I carried within myself planted fear in others and for that I shed remorse. I acknowledge my remorse and I know I have to heal in that way." He's showing (me) the collateral damage he did, he's giving an example; here's an example; "If we walk around (during our lifetime) saying "I'm so worried," like "I'm so worried about my heart (or other fears) because then we believe in our fears." And it created this collateral damage. He didn't realize how much he did that. Like he "Just worried about stuff that was minute," he says.

How'd you like your memorial service?

He stood up and did a salute.

Some of your friends have written some wonderful tributes on Facebook. Are you aware of them?

"No." It feels (like he has) no connection. He says to tell you that "He can connect emotionally to his friends, but when it goes to social media it has an emotional imprint... But it's almost invisible to them (on the flipside)."

Is there any one thing you want me to tell you friends and fans?

(Kimberly aside) He's funny. I really like his personality; he's one of those people who's going to give you a little bit... just enough to make you want more. When you said, "Is there anything you want me to tell your friends and family?" He literally said, "I can fly." (Kimberly laughs) He's playing the song "I can fly, I can fly"

(Sings the Peter Pan version). He's laughing because it's like, "I know they want more... but this is what I'll give them: I can fly."

(Note: This is the same thing he said to Jennifer Shaffer. <u>Literally</u>.)

Can you tell Kim your last name?

Kimberly laughs. (Kimberly to Bill: "Why?" She then gestures with a "zipped lip.") That's what he did. I said, "Are you sure?" He's checking his pockets (as if looking for a wallet.) He said "Nope." He zipped his lip and then pointed to you.

I have other friends named Billy who are on the other side, just to be sure, tell her which one of my Billy's is this? (I was trying to trick him into revealing it to her.)

He said, "Whichever one had the heart issues." Now he's pulled his energy back.

(Note: There's only one who had heart issues.)

We ended the interview, and then moments later Kim's father called from Ohio to see how she was doing on her trip out West. She asked him what he was doing and she later said; "He told me he was watching this old film called "Twister."

At that point I told her who **Bill Paxton** was, and how he was the star of that film. How Bill and I had met early in our careers, and I always considered him a close friend, even when his career sky-rocketed away from mine. She was surprised, but not as much as I was at the clever way he revealed his identity to her. I mean "What are the odds?"

All I can say is "Well played, Bill. Well played."

INTERVIEW WITH BILL VIA MEDIUM RAYLENE NUNES

The director holding a DVD of his film. (From YouTube)

For those that might think bias is involved with these interviews, because a medium might be "reading my mind" (good trick, that) this is an example of a third party interview.

I was not in the room. I supplied the questions and someone else asked the medium for the answers. The medium had no idea who was going to be interviewed, and knew little if anything about the subject.

This interview was conducted by Dr. Elisa Medhus. As noted, Dr. Medhus can be found at "ChannelingErik.com" I have excerpted a few of her sessions for my books and one day she called and offered to "talk to someone on the flipside" for me, using her choice of a medium and her son Erik to assist.

I suggested an interview with Bill and supplied her with the questions. This interview is excerpted from the full session (at Dr. Medhus' website: "Channeling Erik.") Dr. Medhus' questions are *in italics,* and Raylene's answers are **in bold**. (The film version of this interview is available at MartiniProds on YouTube or via Gaia.com "Talking to Bill Paxton." Raylene can be found at *angelmedium7.com*)

Dr. Medhus: Hey Ms. Raylene, how are you doing?

Raylene: I'm doing fantastic Elisa, how about yourself?

I'm doing excellent and I guess our boy is there. Erik, (Dr. Medhus' son Erik assists, as Luana does for us.) I love you so much!

He is here, he says "Hello mama, I love you very much too." He's excited.

We're going to bring in a good buddy of my friend, Rich Martini, a filmmaker – it's Bill Paxton, a movie star, who was in "Twister" and some other things; died way too young. Erik can you go get him?

He's here already. (Listens) He says that one was of the movies I really enjoyed creating was "Titanic," that was one of my favorites.

You were in that?

(Note: I know that Dr. Medhus doesn't know the breadth and depth of Bill's career, so that makes her an ideal candidate to conduct this interview. Not many folks recognized Bill in "Titanic" as the leader of the underwater expedition. I'm also noting Dr. Medhus doesn't know anything about Bill's career outside of "Twister" and neither did Raylene, a busy mom as well as a talented medium.)

"Yeah," he says "He worked awful hard on it."

What was your favorite other than that?

He says "Twister."

I loved that. Do you mind if we ask you some questions? I have questions from your friend Rich, but I have some spiritual questions that might be a learning opportunity for the viewers.

He says "He's ready for this and thank you for the opportunity to get his voice across."

Do you any messages for your buddy Rich?

He's sitting down and he says "Rich was more than a buddy to me; he was a really close friend who I loved dearly." He says "My departure has been hard for him and extremely hard for my family." He says "I want everyone to know I am happy and healthy." He's showing me that his heart is the reason why he passed over. "I had heart complications with an operation. I didn't expect to die and nobody expected me to die so this was sudden for

people, for my family members too." He's telling Rich to be patient he says because there are going to be big changes with regard to his career in the film industry.

(Note: I print this interview not to hear my old pal pat me on the back, I certainly loved him and was a fan like everyone. He's a generous soul, and I feel almost like he's saying some of this to make me feel good about digging into his life, perhaps bringing added grief to those who loved him by opening this door. I offer this transcript as verbatim information; I would be less than honest if I said I wasn't mind boggled to hear him saying these things through someone else.)

Will Rich get involved with our website, Channeling Erik?

He said his (my) work now is focused on spirituality, almost like investigating the afterlife is what he's going to be doing. He's showing me documentaries and documentaries turned into something else. He's showing me a poster board, like a poster board for a movie.

Can you explain that?

"He does good when he puts things all together like a poster board or a collage, and this is how he figures out what his next step is."

(Note: I learned that technique from a writing class where Francis Coppola demonstrated his "3x5" story board with different colored cards. When Bill helped me work on the script for "You Can't Hurry Love," we used the same technique, which I'd forgotten about until I typed up this sentence.)

(Reading one of my questions) Who was there to greet you Bill?

He's being a smart ass. He says "God." He says "My first family member was my grandmother on my mother's side of the family, who helped him to transition." His transition was really shocking for him, he says "I didn't realize that I was dead."

Anyone else meet you around the same time as your grandmother?

Yes, he's showing me a man – his father.

(Neither Raylene or Dr. Medhus could know that Bill said the same thing to both Kimberly Babcock and Jennifer Shaffer; that "his father (John) was there to greet him.")

So it was a heart complication that occurred?

He said, "He had a stroke during surgery and that's why he passed away. It wasn't expected, he had heart complications when he was alive." He says, "It was part of his contract to leave when he did." He's mentioning his daughter and his son who are currently living right now – (says) "They're not struggling as much as they were; his daughter is having experiences with him and he wants her to know it's real and she's not losing her mind; it is her dad coming to visit her."

(Question) "Why did you die so young?"

He says "The first and foremost part... of the mission... of my contract was to come in and shed light on humanity on Earth. I wanted to bring laughter... a lot of people are born without humor or have a foot up their ass."

(Note: I know this isn't Raylene's way of expressing herself, but it sure as hell was Bill's. He said it often, with his Texas twang. Funny to hear him say it here as well. "Foot up their ass" is very Bill.)

"My movies were to enlighten (lighten up) the world. The reason I left was to help my loved ones with the experience of loss. I wasn't expecting it as people don't." (Raylene looks, smiles) He's showing me his hair, a head full of hair, he's pointing out his hair is in really good condition – and he's proud of his hair (on the flipside.)

(Note: What he says here is in line with the research of people under deep hypnosis talking about previous lifetimes. Sometimes a person passes away early because of reasons that don't become apparent for many lifetimes. Sometimes they experience things here to help "teach" lessons in life, including loss, including sorrow. It's part of the whole package of the classroom we sign up to experience.)

Well, you were very good looking.

He says "I didn't realize my looks were good when I was alive – I had self-confidence issues. I didn't realize I was as good looking as I was. So thank you."

Why did you have self-esteem issues?

He's saying "They come in from previous lifetimes. I'd look in the mirror and I didn't see prettiness or handsomeness. I'd see humor and a good person; which is why I went into this industry."

(Another one of my questions). Rich asked "If the doctors made a mistake or was this meant to be?"

(Note: I always ask a version of "was your passing known to you in advance, was it part of your life's plan or some kind of accident?" I don't know any of the particulars of what happened during Bill's surgery but Dr. Medhus is a licensed Doctor, and she asked my question in her own words.)

He says, "There was no mistake that the doctor made; it was my choice to go, because it was time. There's no..." (Listens) He says, "There's nothing that could have prevented this from happening."

So it wasn't the doctor's fault?

He said "The doctor did everything to try and save me. The doctor is still living with pain." He says "The doctor performed thousands of operations – something connected to the valves in his heart... and this doctor still has residual pain over this."

(Another question) "So who are you hanging out with over there?"

"I hang out with quite a bit of people and I'm learning from your son Erik, who is teaching me how to manipulate energy. I'm learning how to manipulate electronics, lights, TVs. When things malfunction, you'll know that I'm around." He says "Rich, you'll know what I'm talking about."

(Note: Unfortunately, I do.)

Who else are you hanging out with?

"His father, his grandmother... Paul Walker the actor." He's hanging out with... (Listens, asks) Who is that? He says "They're

not human, more like ETs, he's communicating with other terrestrial beings... he says, "Since I've come over here, this is what I'm interested in; multi-dimensional beings." He says, "He wants to put more awareness to people .. he's going to help Rich to put this out there."

(Note: This isn't the science fiction portion of the interview. For further context, continue reading this book. There's no other way to describe people who "incarnate off planet" or whom have had lifetimes on other planets and present themselves as "E.T.s." But I don't want to skip ahead, plenty of these reports to come.)

Is Rich is being helpful?

"He will and he should; he's a key component, both in the book and filming."

Any other actors you're hanging out with besides Paul Walker?

"Prince."

(Note: Prince shows up often in my work with Jennifer Shaffer, I know he's shown up in Raylene's sessions as well as a frequent contributor to Dr. Medhus' website. He appears throughout the books with Jennifer Shaffer as part of our "classroom" which includes Robin Williams and Bill. But it's an unusual observation, as the question was "*actors*" but the answer is the same.)

Who else?

Two gentlemen coming forward. One's an actor. I can't think of the name of that movie – (Raylene aside) I just suck at names.

What's the movie name?

It's a combat movie. I'm asking Erik to help with the name. It's someone he's worked with and created movies with – a business partner. Do you know the movies "Aliens?" It's like that.

(One of my questions) "In other interviews someone said you were hanging out with Harry Dean Stanton."

(Note: When my old friend Harry Dean passed away, Bill came with him for his interview in the book "Backstage Pass to the Flipside:

Talking to the Afterlife with Jennifer Shaffer." Harry Dean Stanton was in the first "Alien" film (and died in the story). Bill was in the sequel "Aliens" but they costarred in "Big Love" together. Six degrees of Luana Anders.)

That's the second gentleman (who is) over here (Harry Dean Stanton.)

(Note: Harry Dean has two chapters in "Backstage Pass to the Flipside" because he gave me verifiable proof that it was him reaching out to us. He gave me personal and private messages for his friends, that I passed along at his memorial service a week after we spoke to him. Each detail was completely accurate, and the people I spoke with had not shared those details with anyone. Further, when I asked Harry "What do you want me to say at your Memorial?" He said *"Tell them to believe in the afterlife."* I laughed and said "Harry you were a famous skeptic. None of your pals will believe I spoke with you." He said *"Then tell them to believe in the possibility of an afterlife. Then they won't waste a minute of their life, like I did, arguing about it."*)

(My question) "What do you miss about being on the planet if anything?"

Physical touch – and smelling things. He says "You can't really experience the smell of flowers, grass... (Raylene looks at him "really?") Poop... the dirty stuff. You miss those smells you don't produce them anymore, you can create smells and food, but it's not tangible."

(Note: Bill was hilarious when telling a self effacing story about some odd smell or some physical experience he had. (Getting worms from a trip to Mexico comes to mind.) He had zero embarrassment in talking about human functions.)

Where do you hang out over there?

"I'm in-between roles."

(Note: That's too funny to pass up. When we are off the planet, we are all in-between roles. Didn't get this joke until editing it.)

"A lot of times I am in the dimensions where humans are. I have young kids so I haven't crossed over fully. I do not choose to be

completely over (here) as I choose to be part of my family's life." (Listens) He really likes to ride in cars.. and a motorcycle... He's showing me a different type of bike – it's really loud. He says, "These are the types of things I miss; his food, his tasting, he likes Italian food, he's missing noodles" and things like that.

(Note: This is another example; I had asked Jennifer what he missed, and he described a "dish of noodles" that his wife would make. I tried to get him to name it, but the most I could get from him was "like a goulash but made with noodles." He couldn't remember the name, and while editing this chapter, I remembered the comment.)

When you do create a landscape what's your favorite to create?

"A racing track, cars going around it. And he has created it instantaneously... he says "At the snap of the finger there's a racetrack in front of me."

Anywhere else? (Referring to my question)

He loves water, he's showing me ocean, he enjoys the water more than mountains. He would often find himself finding his own thoughts when he was out in nature out near the water, this is where he would sense what was going to happen.

(Note: This was like his previous comment to Jennifer that he "liked to create white sandy beaches so he could go and contemplate his journey.")

Were you able to tap into your intuition near water?

He said "I wasn't really connected to spirituality before he passed away." He says "He knew there was life before death, but he didn't know there was this; you assume your body wasn't going to live on, but you still carry what the physical body can carry with it. I was able to put myself into a different place .. by thinking. I wasn't expecting it to be this!" He's snapping his fingers. "I can be anywhere I want without any stress coming to me."

(Another question) Do you have any regrets?

"I wish I would have spent more time with my children, it took time away from my family to be an actor. I wish I had more time with them. But I don't regret my life or anything I've done – I wish I had more time."

Any messages for anyone in your family?

He gets quite emotional when he talks about his family. He says "I want them to know I'm happy and I don't want anyone to stress over legal matters."

He says, "He's visiting them in dreams, his daughter is getting a clear knowing that he's there, he planted a seed and he's open." He said his son as well. He says "He's more logic minded, so he's having harder time to get through via a dream because the logic is holding him down."

He's saying his family should play his movies – his laughter and personality will help them to connect to them. He's saying that "He's telling his loved ones they couldn't have done anything; no one could have." He's saying, "No testing would have prevented this."

Anything for your wife?

He's getting emotional. He's sitting down – he says "She was the love of my life; she is the love of my life. I will continue to wait for her, I feel the grief that she has." He says "It's okay for you to be happy." He says "He's going to be there to help guide her."

(Note: He said the same things to Jennifer about assisting her to move on with her life, but that "he will always be there by her side.")

Anything for Rich Martini? How did you became pals?

He's showing me that they became friends through the film business. "Neither were well known when they starting inter-acting with each together." It looks like the movie "Alien" – that's what he's showing me - it's in connection to that.

(Note: *Ding!* Doesn't get much more accurate. As noted, we met in a pub in London when he was making the film "Aliens" (if Raylene had known that, she would have said "Aliens" instead of "Alien" – as the sequel has the S in the title))

"That kind of sparked the relation to him, that's when our relationship really grew – the interest in the paranormal, the stuff that unexplainable is why Rich and I connected. Rich is a soul-mate, someone I've lived multiple lives with." He's saying "Go where your thoughts are putting you, stick to one road, and go with it, and you will see change that will happen." He's talking about finances changing for Rich, there's some kind of documentary that Rich is working on that he needs to finish this is going to help him turn it into a movie or series.

(Note: "From your lips to God's ear, Billy.")

He says "(Rich) You need to work on yourself, you need to take care of your health." He says he's not throwing you under the bus... but he's looking at health issues for you. He'll know what I'm talking about." He says, "I'm really happy you found your way into Rich's life; he's saying it's not by coincidence, it's been something that's been contracted... Rich is supposed to know you (Dr. Medhus) because of this work that you're doing with Erik."

What were you here to accomplish and did you accomplish that?

"I did... and accomplished much more than was in my contract. One thing I want to tell people is that you have free will. You can do anything you want to, and you can change a contract; you have free will and you can change anything. You put something in your mind, and you can shoot for the stars. I put so much doubt in my mind..." He says "I wasn't supposed to be as famous as I got."

(Note: Bill is saying the same things that the people say under hypnosis, both in Wambach's work and Newtons, and the 50 people I've filmed. We all have contracts, but we have free will, to both screw them up or outdo what we set out to do to begin with. The future is not set, there are likely outcomes that some can observe, but in terms of "shooting for the stars" Bill is the perfect example of how a funny kid from Texas can become an icon and a beloved movie star.)

What insights did you get when you transitioned?

He says it was more of "Oh shit, I'm dead." He says, "It was a shock, not fear, a shock because I was no more part of the human life and my body was gone."

"I wasn't afraid, I felt safe, you know how you're with your mom and feel safe? I just felt shocked. The light wasn't right; I looked around the hospital room in front of me, and it was from there I was pulled into another room, everything around was amplified. I could see light but it's not like the bright light of the sun – it was a warm and welcoming light... along with that I had my grandmother and my father there to greet me."

"We weren't communicating by mouth, just with our minds. Just knowing the information that was coming to me as I was looking at my family members." After that he went into a room that had a table, kind of reminds me of like a judge scene – like (a council of) higher people.

He went into this room that has that authority or knowledge... They sat him down and they let him know that he was going (to go) through a life review.

He says "It felt like it was going to take forever and when I came out, there were many more people than I could see (during the interview). We had a celebration.

(Note: The reader is going to visit quite a few councils in this book, but this is one that isn't coming from someone under hypnosis, or chatting over coffee – this is someone on the flipside, giving us a really detailed memory of what happened when he arrived on the flipside. As we'll see, it is identical to many other people's experience – either when reporting a near death event, or while under hypnosis.)

Anything you can share about you that nobody knows?

He's showing me an army flag (?) – a little piece of fabric; given to him from someone who was in service, "This is with me."

What are you doing in the afterlife right now?

He says "I'm still learning how to communicate more and condense my energy so my family can connect with me. On top of that I'm learning how to communicate with other beings."

Anything that we can tell people?

"Be yourself, be authentic. Don't try and be someone you're not. Because if you do, you're not doing what you came here to do. My advice is to be authentic to yourself."

Is it difficult adjusting to the afterlife?

He says "No, it's (just) something you learn to adjust to. It's energy based; like if you think of electricity and you put your finger in the socket it'll shock you? I've learned not to put my finger in the socket so quickly, because I can travel at the speed of thought."

(Note: Wow.)

Anything else you want to share?

Bill is thanking you for the time and opportunity and is thanking you for this as well Elisa. He says "Thank you to all the viewers and to his fans, really grateful for you all."

.....

Thanks Bill for opening this book about the architecture of the afterlife, demonstrating it's possible to ask and receive information from people no longer on the planet.

Portrait of an artist as a young man.

CHAPTER TWO:

"WANT TO TAKE A RIDE?"

FROM "MIDNIGHT IN THE DESERT" AND "THE KINGDOM OF KNYE" WITH HEATHER WADE (Photo: Heather Wade)

TALKING TO ART BELL ON THE FLIPSIDE

I got a call from radio personality Heather Wade some years before these interviews. Heather worked long and hard for Art Bell, the famous radio DJ from Pahrump Nevada, who created the show "Coast to Coast" some years ago. Heather is not a medium, not a psychic, does not claim to have any abilities whatsoever in terms of accessing the afterlife. It just so happened that in the middle of our "live on air interview" she revealed that she had a near death experience earlier in her life.

As noted, I've found that people who've had a "consciousness altered event" can access that event later in life, no matter when it occurred. By simply asking questions like "What happened next?" they appear to be able to relive the event (without any of the stress associated with experiencing it.)

Heather was working as a producer for Art Bell's radio call in show when she called to say that Art had heard me on a "Coast to Coast with George Noory" episode and wanted to have me on his show. I said I was all for it – but didn't hear back for a couple of years.

Heather then took over for Art Bell behind the microphone for a number of years, and re-invited me on the show. Art was still alive, producing, Heather was on air, recording.

I had never tried to do an experiment "on air" with someone to specifically "see where we could go" (working in show business, I know what "dead air" sounds like – an anathema to radio broadcasts – which might occur while a person is "trying to figure out what it is they're seeing.") But something in Heather's persona and voice made me feel that it was worth the effort to try.

My comments *are in italics,* Heather's answer are **in bold.**

We begin our discussion and Heather asks me about my journey into this research. I end it with;

Rich: All I can say is, I'm not offering a belief, theory or philosophy, I'm just reporting what people said consistently while under deep hypnosis. We pass away however that transpires, some people stick around because they want to hang around. Since time is different over there – relatively different – it's not a big deal to stick around for ten years or 100.

Heather: Time has no feeling over there. I had an NDE (near death experience) once.

What do you recall about it?

Well, during my NDE, I didn't see a tunnel or a light, it felt like I was traveling in space. I didn't meet a council – can't say I understand all of this, it's what I know happened to me – I had a life review, and I felt all the pain and emotion I had ever given another human being and it was virtually all at once.

(Note: Near death experiences often have a "tunnel" or some experience with moving through a door of light – but not all do.)

Rich: I've learned that you can access this information in real time – find new information or reexamine it. Would you like to do that?

Heather: That's incredible. Yes.

Okay, everyone pull up a chair, let's see where we go, as we didn't plan this...

No, this is as spur of the moment as it gets.

I'm interested in what happened during your NDE during the travel thru space moment – can you get a freeze frame from it? Just prior to the past life review part. Are you with me?

Yes, yes... okay.

Go to that moment prior. Do you feel as if you're moving through space?

Yes. It feels like there should be wind and there's no wind.

Are you moving up, across or down?

Up and then across... and I'm getting out of the Earth's atmosphere into space incredibly fast. And the thing I'm asking myself is, "Why is there no wind? I'm not in a vehicle."

What's the next visual you see?

Tiny pin lights, going by incredibly fast... and then all of a sudden, there's an abrupt slowing down. And now I know I'm somewhere - it's still is dark and it's still in space.

Are there any pin lights around you?

Yes and what looks like a colorful cloud.

Let's just go over to the cloud – in your mind's eye, go over to the cloud.

Okay.

What are the colors?

It's .. beautiful. Almost like a fire that has just stopped. That is still in time. It's bright bright oranges, reds, yellows, whites, all of these colors.

(Note: I've never heard any such description, but I am used to asking questions without knowing where we are going.)

Walk into the cloud of light or put your hand into it. What's that feel like, if anything?

I feel pressure and very warm – I know that I can go inside the thing.

Let's do that – go on in.

It's very very warm – incredibly warm.

Emotional or physical warmth?

Both. There's a contentment there...

That's interesting; what does that mean?

(Note: I know what contentment means, I'm asking as it might clarify her experience.)

I feel like I've been here before but I'm not sure... It's like a memory from when you were one years old, it feels like I've been here before. It feels like a very hot summer day that I would not be able to survive in a body – it's like 150 degrees, but for some reason that feels good.

There's a feeling of remembrance?

Yes.

Let's move through this cloud, what do you see on the other side?

It's not that I see something... but I feel a presence there.

Male or female, neither or both?

Male.

How old is this presence? I mean like old old, or a younger person?

Gosh, it's impossible to know; but it feels as if this presence has always been there and always been here when I come to this place.

(Note: When we meet a guide, or one of our "teachers," people report it's as if they've "known them forever" despite consciously meeting them for the first time. Heather is saying "I feel like I've always known this person" which as we'll learn, is the case.)

Let's ask this presence to appear in human form, can you do that?

I'm getting an image, Richard, a very distinct image of a man. He's very tall and he has long white hair and looks very, very Chinese.

Try not to judge this. Allow for a second we're playing a game – don't take this too seriously, I'm saying this to your audience, this is a person in your mind's eye – about how tall is this fella?

(Note: I say this because Heather has agreed to do this exploration live on the air, she has an audience tuned in, and it might freak some out for her to be saying "I see someone here!")

He's about six feet tall.

Can I ask a name we can use for him to have this conversation?

C... H... O... W... N.

Mr. Chown?

I have no idea what this means. This is a little bit weird in this... I wish we didn't have to take a break but I'm due to take a station break.

Before we take a break – let me say "Mr. Chown, thanks for showing up and thanks for allowing us to talk to you, and please hang around until after the break."

(Note: We took the two or three minute break. When off the air, the guest has "dead air." So I have no idea if she's still got her guide in her mind.)

Okay, we're back. (On air)

Heather, allow me to point out that you're fully conscious – you're not under any hypnosis.

Well, you certainly are doing something different than hypnosis, a different type, I don't think I've ever been in hypnotic state – I'm glad that by now, my running the show is a muscle memory so that's a good thing. Richard I gotta tell you I have this strong strong image of this man... who looks like a cross between Pai Mei (the white haired Sensei from the "Kill Bill" films) and a laughing Buddha – he laughed at me during the break.

In your mind's eye try to take his hands in yours. Can you do that?

Yes. Yes. Well, I feel they're very, very warm – he's got incredible life, almost like touching a living person.

You feel that coming from his hands?

Yes, it does. He has soft hands, of an older person, definitely feels like human hands.

Imagine stepping around behind his shoulder and looking back at you – what do you look like to him?

Oh my god! I'm just light... it's a peach colored light.

Take a closer look at it. Is it solid or vibrating?

It's pulsing rather slowly. Yes.

(Note: I ask this question often – sometimes people see themselves as they are now, sometimes as a younger person; in this case, a pure pulsating energy. The reason I ask is when they see something they've never seen before; it can't be something they're creating. It's likely coming from whomever they're accessing.)

*As you look at yourself from his point of view, realize that this is how **he sees you**. If I may, this is new information - this is something you've never considered – the idea of seeing yourself as light. You're able to see yourself as he sees you. Now back to holding his hands. What color are his eyes?*

Black actually, but very shiny, this guy is incredibly happy. He's laughing and something I heard was "Why didn't you ask me to do this before, it would have been so much easier!"

I love that – he's teasing you for not doing this earlier. Hey, Mr. C, don't beat her up, we have you now live on air. Put in her mind what you think of her journey Mr. Chow.

All I can do is give a response that I'm getting. He says "Well, she didn't want to, but now that she's on the path, she's having a much better time."

Let me ask; have you ever incarnated on the planet with her?

He says, "No."

Have you incarnated on the planet?

He says, "Yes."

Put in her mind's eye when that was – roughly a year and a place, where were you?

He says, "It was so long ago it would be hard to know a year. It would be before history."

Were you a human, an animal or some other lifeform?

He says, "Human."

Before history, I see – let me ask you, Mr. Chow; are you her guide? Is that the term we should consider you?

He says, "Yes."

Are you a member of her soul group or is that separate?

He says, "A separate group."

How many are in that group?

"18."

(Note: Heather is not familiar with my books or Michael Newton's books. In his research, Newton found that people report to have 3 to 25 people in their "soul group" with the average being around 15. That is – "people who normally incarnate with us from life to life.")

Mr. Chown can you take her to visit her council?

Oh now... this is really weird, really strange – it's like an outdoor area, but it's in space.

How many people are there in this council?

I can count right quick; seems like a dozen beings there.

How are they arrayed?

It's a completed circle and I'm in the middle.

May we talk to the spokesperson for the council?

There's a female with a book; it looks like she's in charge.

Stand in front of her and describe what she looks like.

She also looks Chinese to me – she also has long white hair, she's wearing white clothes that reflect up on to her face... she looks sort of ageless, but I could guess in her 30s.

Go over and offer your hand as if you can take her hand in yours.

Ah...gosh, it's strange because I can feel the crease in her hand where she was holding onto the book. Her hand is soft and she's smiling at me and she's saying "It's been a long time."

Can we ask her name?

Her name? "Chen."

Ms. Chen would you show our friend here the book you're looking at?

Oh. There's my name... there's pictures.

How is your name written? In script? What's the typeface?

This is very strange - it's not in any language I'm familiar with here in the waking world, it's different, looks like it's made up of different characters but I can read it.

(Note: This is a bit unusual. It appears to be a book of Heather's life. I know it's odd to hear her say that she can read the language on the book and see that it means her name - after all, it's an etheric book, as this is an energetic construct.)

Describe what you see inside the book; are there pages and can you turn them?

Yes, there are pages and I can turn the pages.

Please turn to a page Ms. Chen would like you to look at.

Okay, she's opening up the book, it's going back deep into the book. So now, I don't know, it's like three quarters of the way into this book - I'm just guessing - and I see a picture of a house.

Does this house look familiar?

Yeah, it does, looks like the house where I live. Oh my god, (I see) I'm sitting on the porch and now I have white hair, and I'm rocking in this chair and I'm sort of staring out and uh... -ok this is weird it looks like a photograph (in the book) but the picture is moving, I'm in this rocking chair and if I look out, you can see the wind in the trees and everything... it's like a moving photograph.

Ms. Chen, because we're doing this live on the air, would you please give her what message this passage represents? Can you put words in Heather's mind to explain?

I don't want people to get the impression that I'm channeling.

I'm asking Miss Chen to talk to you and you interpret it as best you can.

"Things seem so large and so immediate.... but things pass, and the pain is not what matters. It's the love that matters. And it's how you talk to each other that matters." And I'm asking (her) for more and she's shaking her head.

Okay that's fine, that's plenty.

(Note: It's worth repeating; "What appears large and immediate is not. Things pass, pain is not what matters. (It's temporary). What matters is love and how you speak to each other." A profound message of love and respect from the flipside.)

Ms. Chen would you take hold of Heather's hand and you mentioned the word love can you give her a sensation in her body so when you mention love she can experience that?

Now she's laughing; she thinks this is really funny. Richard, I've got to tell you – I'm in an air conditioned room and I'm getting this sensation that feels like when you take Niacin – you get this hot flush that makes you feel you're 5 degrees hotter from the inside out.

Like a flush?

Then goosebumps all over.

Thank you Miss Chen. This sensation is to let you know she's connected to you, to know she's always keeping an eye on you – no matter how difficult your life may ever be; they're there to hold you up and greet you upon their return.

It's not just for me (this is occurring) "Every soul has this." that's my understanding I'm getting... I don't know how to express this, but there is non-verbal information... and "Everybody has this. People who feel that they're alone are never alone."

Is there anything anyone in your council or your guide wants to impart in this method?

"Don't stay with the pain."

Is there anyone there that can give heather a feeling of unconditional love?

Oh wow. They've all stood up – wow. This is a very strange sensation! A very very strange feeling! It almost feels like... Here I am in this studio, I'm in a room with nobody, and I suddenly feel like there's a bunch of people here (with me) and the temperature in the room has gone up. I often joke around that this is cold in here, but it's not now!

Wow. I asked about a feeling of unconditional love. Ms. Chen seems like the spokesperson in the group... anything about her appearance?

I see where... that there are certain areas.... her ears and hands and neck have sparkles.

What quality does she represent in terms of your journey?

"Courage."

Was that for a previous lifetime, something Heather was able to overcome?

"That's for this lifetime."

Thank you. If you don't mind, put into Heather's mind how you think she's doing now ... and if this is important work she is doing on the radio?

"Almost the same answer as before; she didn't want to but now that she's doing this .. Yes. It's a little slow for our taste, but yes."

Okay, thanks. You like what she's doing, but it could be a little faster. Interesting answer.

Wow. Richard, this is really odd, odd experience. It is so strange; I almost feel as if I'm in two places at once... and so I'm here talking to you on the air and...

Visually you're somewhere in deep space. Let's ask Miss Chen, is this space you're in now part of our universe?

"When it's time for you, this is where you'll come."

I just want to point out to your audience, this place is accessible to all of us – sometime we dream about it, sometimes we don't. It's new information; "unconditional love is always the key."

TWO YEARS LATER

As I was preparing this book for print, I reached out to Heather and sent her this chapter. She told me she had a new radio program "The Kingdom of Nye" and asked me to appear.

Since our last on-air chat, her mentor and friend Art Bell had passed away. When Heather asked me to appear, I casually said "Hey, maybe we can talk to Art."

I had no idea if she wanted to do that, could do that – but threw it out there as a possibility. I don't know Heather personally, I find her an excellent interviewer, and I'm amazed at her ability to speak openly and honestly on the air. Not many can do that. We go out on a limb in this interview, I offer it verbatim.

HEATHER WADE TALKS TO ART BELL ON THE FLIPSIDE

Part Two - August 2019. Transcript from live broadcast.

Heather: Welcome my friend and fantastic guest to the show, Rich Martini. I can't believe this moment is here.

Rich: Wow, what a wonderful introduction. I had such fun talking to you the last time; as I transcribed the program, it was mind blowing – I know your audience doesn't know where we went – but it was to another realm. We talked about a near death experience you once had and we were off and running.

The beauty of that was that it was so spontaneous, you just said, "Do you want to go back to that place now?" and I said "why not?" It was so not planned, so spontaneous. It made such an impression – I could close my eyes and visualize the spirit guide, my council. I can picture it again, kind of see it again – that's why my heart's pounding because I know we're going there again.

In my mind's eye they're all tapping their watches right now. Let's talk to your guide first. Do you remember him?

I do; it was a funny look, which made me think I was making this up. He looked like a Chinese martial arts master, white hair, moustache, trimmed; what you would imagine if you climbed a hill to find the guru.

Let's shift from past to present tense. Can you see him now?

Yes, it looks like he has darker robes on; dark blue, long white scarf around his neck over these dark blue robes.

I want to thank him and ask if it's okay to ask him questions.

He's nodding his head and saying "Yes, be my guest."

What shall we call you today?

He's laughing and saying, "You know what my name is, I'm Chown."

We spoke a couple of years ago – what does that time frame feel like to you?

First answer is "Why has it taken so long? I've been here this entire time, why have you struggled, why have you not contacted me at a moment's notice?"

He's not saying that I forgot to call him, but that you forgot, correct?

He's confused about that, he says "You've been going through this struggle," and he's saying "I'm right here."

(Note: This is pretty amazing, and I want to take a moment to acknowledge it. I have not spoken to Heather in two years, it took me two years to transcribe our session, and prior to this moment, I had sent it along a few weeks prior. Her guide is referring to her struggles after her mentor and friend Art Bell passed away; she went through some difficulty over that, (none of which I was aware of) as we'll soon hear. But her guide is speaking directly to her; saying *"I was here when you were struggling. Why didn't you call upon me?"*)

Mr. Chown was this part of her journey that she signed up to experience? These difficulties you are referring to?

He says "It's part of the deal."

She had a mentor who passed away; is this the right time to bring him forward?

"He's here – he's on his way. He's not standing by me now but if you want to go see him, we can go and see him."

Why don't we do that? You made the suggestion Mr. Chown; let's meet with her mentor. Put him in Heather's mind's eye. About how old does he look?

I'm getting a number .. 55.

How old was your mentor when he passed?

He was 72. (Suddenly excited) I can see him Rich. I can see him! I can see him right now, I can see his hair, salt and pepper hair, longer than I remember. He's wearing a green polo shirt without a logo. It has a little pocket; he has some jeans on and those shoes he always wore. He says "Don't make fun of my shoes; they're comfortable."

(Note: I wasn't sure when the right time would be to bring up Art Bell's passing, but her guide mentioned him. Everything she's saying is live on the air, what she's seeing while not under any hypnosis.)

Can you go up and take hold of his hands? What's that feel like?

Oh God. He's smiling at me. He's saying, "It's about time."

Tell us about his hands.

It's very strange, I can feel my physical body, at the same time I can feel my energy body. I can feel his hands – like (in real) life. I can feel his big, strong hands.

Let's ask him this, what do you look like to him? How does he see you?

He's seeing me in an old outfit that I once wore for some reason – short sleeves, black shirt and a long skirt with diagonal lines – I don't know why.

I ask because this is his *image of you; not your own. If you were creating it, it might have been just what you are wearing now, but it's different. (Which I can't see). What color eyes does he have?*

They're dark brown.

Can I ask you some questions?

"Go right ahead;" he's very relaxed.

Would you put in Heather's mind what your name is?

"Why you know who I am, this is Art. I'm your friend, Art."

I didn't want to say his name, but to let his old friend say it. Art, who was there to greet you when you crossed over?

He says "Lots of cats... Ramona... his mom, some friends. Um.. (Heather laughs) Believe it or not some people he remembers from his show... Father Martin was there.

(Note: I didn't know "Ramona" referred to one of Art's wives. I had no idea who Father Martin was. Wikipedia: "Malachi Martin was an Irish Catholic priest and writer on the Catholic Church" and a frequent guest on Art's show.)

That's cool – was that a surprise?

He says "It was a great comfort because he was scared."

Scared of cats or people?

He says "I looked down and there were cats running up to my feet; a very strange thing to see."

Many people say an animal is the first thing to meet them – puts them at ease. It's often someone they loved, puts them in a mindset as to what comes next. So it didn't take you long to adjust?

As soon as he saw Ramona, and then here comes Father Martin; he says, "It was a great shock, I didn't expect to find myself here and I didn't understand that there was a *here*."

I'm sorry we never spoke when you were on the planet.

He loves being on the radio – he knows he's on the radio!

Art, you've been standing by to talk to Heather haven't you?

He says "I needed someone to help her... Heather is struggling with this so hard." He's saying "We needed a third party to help bridge it." He's getting a huge, huge kick out of this. I gotta tell you this Rich; he's getting a huge kick out of this."

I'm glad to hear it. Art, let me ask you some mundane questions. What do you miss about being on the planet?

(Heather laughs) "Smoking, and eating, yeah and being able to talk to people... and he wants to call people and he can't call any people!"

I tell people to take out a photo, say their loved one's name and ask questions. "When they hear an answer before they can form the question, then they know they have a connection." Is that correct?

He says "Heather does that. She's got a picture (of me); I'm trying to answer her, but she doesn't always hear me. I'll answer five, six seven times in a row. She doesn't hear me." Rich, he wants me to ask you; "How can I help her hear me? How can I help Heather to hear me because it's very frustrating!"

Well, one way is to give her an image instead of sound. You're used to communicating by voice, it's quite hard to create sound; easier to create images that might appear in her mind. One way would be for you, Art, to use an image as metaphor, use the images in her mind to tap on that picture she carries in her memory. What have you tried, Art? Dreams?

"Oh, everything, I talk to her when she's sleeping, I try to... I tamper with electronics in her house; I nudge her, I bump her, I mess with the blankets, all kinds of stuff. Half the time she answers... and half of the time she doesn't." (Heather aside:) He's so entertained by this. I don't know how you do this... Rich, it's amazing. We've got to take a break....

Well, obviously, he's been waiting to talk to you Heather; so allow me to say it for you; "We'll be back with Art Bell after the break."

I told you Rich was one of the coolest people – I want to reiterate, I'm not a channeler. This is Rich and his technique, we'll be right back, with this conversation, with this out of this world conversation. I'm Heather Wade.

(Note: I find this hilarious that Art would ask me a question from the flipside. That has to be a first. What a treat for me to say "We'll be right back with Art Bell on the flipside." There is a commercial break, when we come back:)

Back with my friend Richard Martini. I want everyone to keep in mind that you can do this also. We are using me as an example to show what's possible. It's just as wild for me as it is for you people to hear it. Rich, during the break Art was still talking to me. I'm overwhelmed with the most incredible sensation of joy. I can't remember feeling this must joy, I feel like a lightbulb up all the way.

What did he say during the break?

He was saying "Aren't there going to be any more questions?"

Well of course, yes, sir – Art you were the master of the interview, I heard you do interviews and know how good you are at digging deeper, so I'm going to ask you some standard questions and see where they take us. Who are you hanging out with over there?

I can see a picture of Ramona. She was his soul mate – that's what he's saying... He says, "We're together here, that's what makes it so much easier to be here." She's got long dark black hair and a very friendly expression on her face.

(Note: Art had married again, had a loving family, and people might wonder "Why is he not saying something to his family?" (He does mention them later). Heather is reporting what she's seeing in response to my questions. I'm sure he's reaching out to his loved ones as much or more than he says he's been doing with Heather.)

How do you occupy your time Art? What do you do over there?

"I watch people."

How do you do that?

He says he "gets into the home" – into the room and he'll observe people. When that gets boring, he'll go to places around the planet he wants to see and he'll watching things happening. That's entertaining. He's now saying something unusual about the landscape; he says, "There are places to go (over) here, places to go here." It's "outdoor landscapes of the spirit world," he's calling it, "there are other spirits and intelligences and he tries to learn from them."

Let's put one in Heather's mind now – if it's inside or outside, what's it look like?

I'm seeing trees, but they're not normal; they're orange and red. They look... it's weird... like pine trees, oak trees, rolling hills landscape with scattered houses.

Art, I'm going to do something unusual – I want you to walk her over to one of these trees. can you do that?

Okay, I seem to be going down and now I'm sort of looking through the eyes of my energy body – I can still feel his hand, he was holding onto it through the whole break. And we're in front of a sequoia; it's green, bright orange and red.

If you can, put her arms around this tree and describe the feeling.

It feels sort of rough... but it's weird, it's like I can put my hand through it.

Because it's etheric, more of a mental construct. But let's do that, put your arm inside the tree. What do you feel if anything?

I can push through it and then it feels very dense and... oh my god... this thing has thoughts. It's alive.

That's why I asked you to do so, as I've done this in the past. I want you to address this entity – this tree. Is it a male or female presence, neither or both?

I'm picking up a bit of both, but more male.

For the sake of this conversation, can you give us a name to address you with?

You're going to laugh – I heard "Call me John."

May I ask you some direct questions, John?

"Yeah, if you want."

How is it that you're an energy in the tree. Do all trees have individual energy, or do you represent all trees?

"I wanted to be this, here."

Are you also incarnated somewhere else as we speak?

"No, I'm here."

Were you incarnated on Earth at some point?

"Yes."

How many Earth years did you live?

I'm getting an exact figure; it's 643 years.

So John this is an opportunity for your voice to be heard, and we are live on the air speaking to many people. How can we help our planet?

"Talk to us."

Did humans used to be able to communicate with you?

"You used to try."

Was there a time in our history when humans could talk to you?

"When you did, you tried; we were here and listened. Now you're not talking and you're not listening."

In a session just a month ago, I asked a tree, the entity within a tree, what the best method for humans to help the planet and he said "Plant a trillion trees; it would bring the temperature down and bring balance to carbon and oxygen."

"Yes, please, we need more of us."

(Note: "More of us trees." This isn't the first time I've heard "you used to try." Odd detail that I've heard often from people who don't know each other, haven't read my books.)

He's telling me something odd; he wasn't always a tree. He says he was a human who wanted to be this (form) in the spiritual landscape. He's saying "Yes – more of us means that we can listen to you."

Us being able to communicate to hear you, is that what you mean?

Yes; to care for the planet earth, he's saying "There are too many humans. You need more plants of all kinds."

You had an incarnation at some point? You were human at some point? When was that?

"Yes." What I see is armor; he was kind of fighting man, (Heather aside:) I don't know all my history, but he's got an axe, not for trees – like an axe for war.

Do you mean like a Viking kind of weapon?

It's curved like that; he looks tired and dirty like he's been fighting and he's saying "I used to kill (others) and trees don't kill."

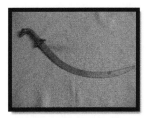

(Sword with Ram's head. From Viking Sword com)

What year did you have this existence as warrior?

I'm hearing an exact number; 1249.

Where on the planet where you?

"In the north where it was cold."

Was this in the Viking era?

"If that's what you call it."

I just wanted to open up this door, trees are sentient, and more and more science is confirming that they communicate with each other, but I wasn't aware that we used to be able to communicate with them but no longer can.

That is just so wild! Just to feel that connection. That was crazy.

So Art let's go back to you; you said you like to travel around. Describe that to us – how do you travel? Is how you travel physical or mental?

He says "It's mental he can think and he is there – he can think about traveling there and experience it if he wants to."

(Note: I've heard this consistently from people on the flipside. That they travel at the speed of thought. As Bill Paxton put it; "Tell them I can fly.")

Where might be a place on the planet you like to go?

He says "Cities... like Paris, London, Dubai.

Does anyone there notice you? Pets or animals?

He says "Once in a while a dog or a cat may notice, once in a while children..." But he doesn't really like that.

If you could project yourself to someplace where you would be seen, how do you do that? What's that mental process to try to be seen or felt while someone's sleeping??

He says he tries to remember what it's like to be solid and he's still learning ... and this is very difficult and that frustrates him. He

says he "tries to remember what it's like to be solid and present resistance to objects so he could stand on a floor."

Who have seen over there you were surprised to see?

Brad Steiger. Art wrote a book with Brad – "The Source" Art says, "He was one of my favorite guests." He loved Brad and they were friends, and he ran into him.

(Note: Art wrote "The Source: Journey through the Unexplained" with Brad. Brad wrote a number of books about the paranormal, and both men died a month apart from each other in 2018).

Were you surprised to see him?

He was glad to find somebody he could make sense of all this with!

I have a question – do you do any physical activities over there?

"Walking. Lots of walking."

Describe that; where would you go?

"Over land. Some place where there's lots of people... and I'll find a path that's kind of clear, start walking around. There's no pain and no body, so I can walk around and watch people for as long as I like.

Do you hear any music over there?

He says he plays music. He's got a rec room – he made himself a radio room. He says "I can't be without no radio room!" So he built himself a radio room and he gets in there, he plays music, he says "I can't not broadcast!"

How does that work, do you have people listening in to a broadcast?

He says "Oh yes, they're starting to more and more."

So how do you construct a radio studio? What's the blueprint – what's the math? When you create it, is it 100% there or a smaller percentage of it exists?

There's nothing there at first; I had to find a place. Then I had to imagine each thing, one at a time; the walls, floor, roof, windows, doors, and had to imagine everything one item at a time. The desk,

chair, then had to remember specific components, that he needs on the desk, down to every cable. And then to hook that stuff up.

And then you broadcast?

He says "No, no, no." He says "It's not a broadcast out; they're all around me and they hear it. He's like, "I have a studio audience, they're all around me listening."

(Note: Think about that for a moment; whenever he feels like being on the radio, he goes to this room he's mentally constructed, like prisoners of war in solitary confinement creating imaginary chess matches in their cells. Imagine the math involved – it's like playing 5D chess in your mind, the matrix playing this incredible game in his mind. We spoke to Garry Shandling in an interview and said he was "golfing." When asked if he was playing 36 holes, he said "No, two. The tees are very far apart.")

You said you play music? What's the method? Are you accessing your memory or pulling it from somewhere else?

He says "I don't need CD's anymore!" He says "He's got to really remember it, he operates the same buttons, and out here comes the sound."

What would be a band or musical style you like to listen to?

It's 1950s and 60s; he's really getting into that. "And a lot of Elvis."

Have you met Elvis?

"I can't find him yet, but I have a lot of time to do so."

(Note: For fans of my books "Backstage Pass to the Flipside: Talking to the Afterlife with Jennifer Shaffer" we did speak to Elvis.)

Art, come with us, we're going to walk Heather in to see her council. We're going to talk to her council and have some fun, will you come along with us?

He says he will and says "Don't let her miss a break." I don't know how you are able to do this Rich, where my mind is able to differentiate where we are. God and I thought this was going to painful; this is a lot of fun! This is wild right now – it's like having an out of body experience while I'm doing a radio show – as soon as we come back with Rich Martini.

(After a break)

I'd like to bring Richard Martini back onto the show. Such a gift you have to be able to do this with people to demonstrate it on live radio. I'm not someone easily hypnotized and you take me there in an effortless way.

Well it's not me; this is about people connecting with their loved ones on the flipside.

This is as *woo woo* as I've ever gotten; it's so personal that I can't sit here and say this isn't rehearsed or a performance; it's what's coming through and it doesn't get any more real than this. Art is saying that Rich has established a stronger link... is that correct?

Well, I just try to explore what I'm hearing based on what I've heard. Let's take a look at your council. When I say "Look at your council" what do you see?

I find myself the energy body appears to be traveling through a dark area, looks like space, distant points of light; it must be stars.

We did this same journey the last time we visited your council. Let's ask your guide, Mr. Chown if we can walk in and visit them. Are we inside or outside?

We're outside in a sense, there is a table, a half circle table, a group of people there; they seem impatient.

Of course, they're tapping their wrists! Sorry to laugh, I know you council members are busy, and you've got other work to do. How many do you see in front of you?

Twelve. Six and six.

Art, stay with us; how do you think Heather's doing?

He says "She's keeping the studio clean, I appreciate that – things seem to be working and I'm very proud at what she's done. She's done more than I ever thought you could."

I'm going to ask your guide, who does she need to speak to? Last time we spoke to council member Ms. Chen – you described her as Asian, and she possessed a particular kind of emotion or quality you'd earned over a lifetime. So who wants to speak to us?

He's pointing out Miss Chen at the table – but he says "If you're here you need to speak with David. He's pointing to an older gent. He's towards the right of the table, third from the end. He's wearing loose fitting clothes, not robes, has on a beige shirt, laces up the center of the chest. He has long baggy pants, and he's got beads. He has brown hair and little bit of a beard; not too long.

(Note: We met with two of her council members the previous trip, but this time, someone she's never heard of, never met before, wants to speak to her.)

David is it okay for us to talk to you?

"Well I've been waiting."

Sorry we had a detour, we talked to a tree. Heather, can you hold his hands?

He's very kind but says "I've been waiting." His hands feel very warm and soft, he's very welcoming. He's got blue eyes and shaggy hair and a four inch beard – he says "He's not trying to have a beard, just not shaving."

What's a quality do you represent on her council?

"The latter part of her spiritual path."

You've been waiting patiently – how is Heather doing?

"There is more to go," he says. And "You got off the path and now your back on, thank goodness. You came to your senses now you're back on track and we need to keep you there.

What was up with this event – this consciousness altering moment? (Heather had told me about falling, waking up on the floor with a broken leg.)

Oh my God, Rich. I'll just say it. He says we did that to her because she needed to learn a lesson. She was thinking about... and this...

okay this is going to get into sensitive material, he says "She was contemplating ending her life, and we're not going to let that happen. She doesn't get to make that choice."

(Note: I had no idea. I understand what she's saying, and I have heard others say the same kind of thing. I try to point out in these sessions that we are never alone, we are always connected to our guides and teachers, and it's important to repeat that, as I do here.)

For those listening in... it's important to hear that we are never alone. Thank you for sharing that Heather. Allow me to ask, David is everyone tethered to their council? (Meaning we are never ever "alone." We always can ask for help from our guides.)

He says "We're always here, if you can get through to talk to us, we're always here."

In terms of people who might be thinking about that path – what's the most effective way for them to connect with you?

"All you have to do is just quiet the mind - quiet the mind and go deep into your mind you'll find us if you keep looking and asking, you'll find we're right there."

Have you incarnated on the planet?

"Yes, a long time ago."

How many councils to you sit on, David?

"Six."

You've been with her for many lifetimes?

"Nine lives so far; this would be the ninth."

In terms of her path and journey – put it in her mind how she's doing.

"She's doing better now, almost slipped off the path in a bad way but we set that right, and now we're pretty sure she's going to do what we set in place..." He's showing me that I agreed to this path "before she came here."

How far away are you from council member Miss Chen?

Five over.

Miss Chen, you showed Heather an image of herself in the future looking at a book on a porch. What was that about?

"That was to show her she's still going to be alive, even after all of this dance with death, she's still going to be alive, and that book is in her house right now."

I just wanted to clarify that Heather saw herself in the future, alive and in a rocking chair on her porch, reading a book; it's important to put that in your mind as well. So David, why did you allow her to come in and talk to you today?

"She needs protection too many things to knock her off the path, she needs guidance, she's got to know to keep going, and you keep going and what is supposed to happen for her is now on its way."

Who put the thought in my head to reach out to heather?

"Art."

Can I ask David, are you familiar with what I'm doing?

"Oh, we know you Richard."

May I ask how? Were you guys sitting around the council water cooler?

"You just keep showing up in councils, they recognize your voice, you've guided so many souls, there are councils members on many different councils, four of my council members are on other councils for other souls, councils for groups of souls, you've talked to so many souls, that now they recognize your voice when they show up."

If I may, what's your opinion of what I'm doing – not for my own benefit, but for the people in the audience who wonder what the value of speaking to councils might be.

For the betterment of all the souls, they're all intertwined. There's more to this.. Okay, I'm trying to hear; "When you are guiding one soul to the right thing, that branches other souls onto the right path for the right thing. There are plans for everyone and when we don't follow them it causes damage, there's a collective spirit and

when one soul is not on the proper track it disrupts that field..."
(Heather aside) I don't understand that, I'm just passing this on.

I do, I understand this is Dave and not Heather speaking. He's saying "We're all connected, when one of us is able to access our guides, teachers, it influences everyone because the field becomes easier to navigate. Once a person masters something, it's no longer a mystery – if our consciousness is connected to others, then if someone learns how to speak to the flipside, perhaps they all do." David, is this accurate?

He's talking about you Rich; he's saying "You are on your right path and you're helping souls here and over there and that's helping the whole field to be less disturbed. What you are doing is putting souls on the right path." He says, "You're able to help heal souls that are over there that aren't quite sure what to do over there." (Heather aside) I'm getting a warm wave of emotion from the entire council as I say this; they consider you a friend.

Well, my friends I'd like to get the lottery numbers for this Friday? If you don't mind...

Ha ha ha... oh that's funny, I'm getting a chorus of numbers thrown around from all of them.. "99, 87, 12, 6!" They're saying, "You just need to listen!" We have to take a break, but I have all these intelligences bouncing around my brain, and it's enjoyable actually.

My god what a wild night, Rich Martini taking me to places it seems only he knows how to take me. You can do this yourself, get a partner and do this, you need a good jumping off point to take you in the rest of the way – and wow. I mean I feel like I'm just floating a couple of feet off the Earth right now .. we'll come right back and get more of this going on.... I'm Heather Wade on this plane on this planet. Ha, ha, ha! (After a break)

Rich, I keep asking them "So what is it? Tell me what the thing is that's supposed to happen for me in the future?" I'm expecting some tangible answer, the answer I get is "You have to do this to help other souls."

Well, that sounds like a very specific answer to me. You've got this venue, going on the air, and you're sharing your experiences. You have many guests who talk about life and love, the fact that you can help a soul – They're saying "You are going to help souls with your work."

Oh yeah. David has been nodding his head, saying "Yes that's exactly what it's about; it's about making connections between souls." He's saying about this field – he's saying "You don't get this yet, but there's a field created with all the souls on earth, if you can help one, you help them all." He's showing me when you reach out to help one person in pain, the shape of their energy body is smaller, hollow, hurting; when another soul comes to help or comforts, the energy body grows and people are able to carry on with their mission which helps the whole big picture. This is what we're supposed to be doing. We're supposed to light each other's candle." That's his words.

Wow. I've never heard anything quite like that – beautiful. I'm thinking our friend Art may have things he wants to talk about.

Oh yeah, he's not done.

What have you learned since you've been on the flipside that you can share?

"That this a place, souls carry on, this is a place after..." – this was a big question for Art – he thought it was going to be all blackness. "It was all kinds of things, that was very shocking." He says it was a shock to the spirit, what he thought it was, what people told him in life (it would be), was not what he found when he got there.

What's your opinion of aliens and UFOs?

"They're real."

Should we drop the term alien because we all incarnate, choose to come to the planet; so technically we're all aliens?

Yes, we are. Our souls go from planet to planet.

Have you ever incarnated on another planet Art?

"He says he knows that now, yes."

Art, could you put this in Heather's mind? Where was it? In our universe or another one?

"It was in our galaxy and the sky looked different – looked purple there."

In our galaxy The Milky Way? What would we know this by?

"We wouldn't know it; nothing we recognize, no."

What's the terrain look like?

"There's a little moon and two larger ones in the sky, there are clouds that are white, but the sky looks a deep lavender purple; looks like a desert landscape, I can see a tree line way out there – looks like civilization. I can tell there's lights out there, a civilization out there."

Take her to the place you normally reside.

"We're inside. It's a very large and open structure – a house – there are huge windows; a lot of light coming in. It's very comfortable, not sparsely furnished – wide open spaces in the building, a little cleaner than a home on earth would be."

Any chairs?

"They don't have a back on them, they have like a wide cushion; you could have 12 people sitting there. There's a tray on the table, a pitcher of a green drink; a couple of glasses. It's a place to sit down and look out the window."

So do that; sit down and take a sip of this drink. What do you look like?

"I got tall, thin, a very pale tone to the skin, almost white. Not quite all the way white, but also white hair, incredibly long and tall and white and his clothes are a brightly colored pattern. It's a pattern on the shirt and pants with some sort of triangle pattern on it. The pattern is green and orange, which is a visual contrast to the skin and hair. He has eyes and a nose – the nose is not so prominent; the eyes are quite large, and the mouth isn't very prominent because the head is a bit bigger than ours, not huge – He's saying "(that's because) we use our mind.""

Take a hold of his hands. What do they feel like?

"They're smooth and kind of cold. He has longer fingers, very long, very very long fingers, four fingers and a thumb."

Has Heather had a lifetime on your planet, Art?

"No, not here."

You mean she has? Somewhere else?

"Yes."

Should we access that, Heather?

If you want to go.

Sure, let's. Art, come with us, please, put it in her mind's eye where this planet is – is it in our galaxy, universe or another one?

It's in our galaxy. (Hesitates) God. Oh God, Rich. You're not going to believe this. It's Mars.

Try not to judge what you're feeling. What makes you think it's Mars?

I can see the earth. I'm looking in the sky and I see the Earth.

Describe the terrain from this place that seems like Mars; any people there?

Well there are adobe structures – not a barren landscape at all. There's trees there, the soil is reddish, reminds me of the sierra foothills.

Describe yourself.

I have arms and legs, wearing something very tight fitting starting at my wrist, it goes down to my ankles – I'm a female in very good shape.

When did this memory occur?

This is way in the past. Far in the past.

What happened to these lifeforms on Mars. I've heard life on Mars can't work because of the lack of a shield from the sun.

There was a sickness, a pandemic and also famine. It was getting harder and harder to grow food.

From lack of passing laws to stop climate change? Sorry, couldn't resist.

It wasn't that, the soil was being depleted, we kept moving from place to place to grow food.

How did it work out you abandoned Mars? What happened?

Oh. I see explosions. Oh god, these are great explosions - I see... we built ships, we got ourselves out there; I can't tell if it's a war or we got attacked. There are people running, screaming, people with weapons; it's chaos.

(Note: I know how odd this sounds, but I try to focus on the details. Again, this could be a "Mars" in another galaxy, another time frame. However, I have had at least one other person claim to have "witnessed" a "war on Mars." During Jennifer Shaffer's deep hypnosis session (as reported in "Hacking the Afterlife") Jennifer also recalled being in a conflagration on Mars.)

Try to shift your consciousness aboard the crafts escaping; how many are on these ships?

Three to four thousand people.

Let's see if we can speak to the captain or pilot of the ship. What's he look like?

He's got a real air of authority, I'm intimidated by him – he's noticing me there, and he's turning around.

Sir, I have a question for you – what happened to your planet?

"We were attacked, I don't know by who."

Who attacked you? People from another planet?

"They could not have been from here; a bomb came from the sky."

Are they from our universe?

"Yes, but we don't know where."

This will sound weird. Heather, shift your consciousness to one of the people dropping the bombs. Who is this person?

Oh God, I've got so much anger, so much anger! I'm angry, I'm infuriated.

Okay, hold on Mr. Infuriated. Is this being a male or female? What's he look like?

He's humanoid. His skin is light green, has scales on it.

Like a lizard guy, reptilian?

That's what it looks like.

Take a good look at him – without stress or fear – let's ask; why are you attacking this planet?

"Because it was once ours. How dare you take what was once ours?" (Heather aside:) Wow.

Take it easy dude. Don't get pissed at me. Ultimately you wanted to destroy this planet?

"Yes to show who was in charge."

Let me ask about your planet is it in our universe?

"It's in this galaxy."

Is this a planet that looks like Mars or was Mars?

"This is what you know as your red planet."

Why have you stayed away from earth all these years? Have you incarnated on earth since then?

"No; we'd never sink ourselves that low."

That's funny. Are you familiar with what I'm doing?

"No. I don't understand what this is."

Imagine yourself watching a television show. Have you had other lifetimes less angry?

"Yes, we have peace on our world."

So you destroyed this planet while you now have peace on your world?

"We had to show that this is our home, we're trying to clear out the infestation."

Well, we can see you were successful because no one lives on Mars now. Let's turn back to your council and David. What was the point of letting us experience that? Why did you let her experience that?

"You're leading her. She's very open."

Was that accurate about the destruction of Mars?

"It is accurate, and we wanted to show her the soul is timeless."

(Note: As you can see, I probe to see if there was any possible alternate reason for this memory. If we can disprove a detail in her session, then it follows we can toss all to "imagination." But when someone is this adamant about a memory – knowing that I'm asking questions about alternate versions, I can only offer that the Earth is estimated to be 4.5 billion years old, Mars is 4.6 billion years old – so perhaps a couple billion years ago, there was a group of individuals who inhabited Mars, and pissed off their neighbors. It sounds a bit like "Planet of the Apes" at this point, so when someone finally does spend time on Mars, they may found a Statue of Liberty buried somewhere.... But I digress. Plus there's another mention of "life on Mars" in a later session in this book.)

Is this kind of apocalyptic event ever going to occur on our planet?

"Only if you do it to yourselves."

Thank you David. For the audience out there; don't be stressed – Oh my god! Martians!

You had me in such a state at that moment, you're asking me these questions; I didn't feel like I was sitting in this chair. I could smell things. I gotta tell you, I have to ask this – how do we know this isn't my imagination?

It is. We have to remember how our senses work. In terms of this story about Mars, anyone could suggest it was something you read, or saw in a film...

There were things that I saw – in all of these places that I wouldn't know, there were things there I wouldn't have in my imagination and it felt real. I could feel that – it's amazing.

What is memory other than an experience that happened? It's one thing when you dream about something, yet another when you remember something – you remember the physical experiences and aspects of that place and time.

I'm sure some people listening tonight are saying "Oh c'mon!" But I went into this interview tonight with a simple self directive, "Just trust the information that's all you have to do – open up and trust the information, whether it makes sense to me or not." I didn't know where it was coming from that I could talk to David on the council. I can feel his kind and warm energy and I know what this man looks like now. That to me is absolutely amazing... God where are the words? Such a transcendent experience! I feel like I came into my studio tonight, Art would joke around and say "Wanna take a ride?" You have taken me for an absolutely insane, wonderfully crazy ride. I cannot thank you enough.

I appreciate the compliment, if people know me well enough, they'd tell you, Rich didn't do anything – the talent I have, if it's a talent, is that I just ask the questions and not judge the answers.

It's because you care about what you're doing. You had an experience awhile ago and are now helping us having an experience for ourselves – you don't need acid with this, I'm kidding, but wow. Art is tapping me on the shoulder; another thing he wants to tell us, "You guys wouldn't believe this, but in the afterlife he's able to have scenarios and talk to people still living."

That makes sense, as people claim we only bring about a third of our conscious energy to a lifetime, and two thirds of us is always "back home" – or where Art currently resides. So he can access people that are still on the planet without them being aware of it here.

Yes, when you were talking about the two thirds, he's saying "He's able to have scenarios; he can recall a specific situation from his living life, and be there in that moment, and talk to those people whether they are alive or dead. He can recall these things." He's telling me "If I wanted to remember having Sloppy Joes with you, I can go back to the dinner table, and recall that event – anything that I lived, I can relive those moments on the other side. He's laughing, "I bet you didn't think it was like that did you?"

(Note: What Art is saying is that he goes to an event in his past – as was explained to me in a session with a scientist, he said that "Memories of events are like CD's. They contain all the information and data from that event. They're time packets." (Stephen Hawking interview in "Backstage Pass to the Flipside")

Who has Art talked to that's over here still?

He says, "He's talking to his family, his friends." He says "I try to whisper in people's ears at night." I can see him right there, anybody he wished he would have talked to, he's saying "There's a conversation he wanted to have with Whitley (Streiber) and I can go to Whitley's house and talk to him here and somehow that reaches into Whitley's soul – it will seem like a dream or a meditation (to him) but over there it's as real as us talking over here."

(Note: Whitley Streiber was a screenwriter who had an alien encounter and wrote about it in "Communion." What Art is saying, is that he can have a live conversation with Whitley while he's asleep – and Whitley may not consciously remember it, but his higher self will.)

Art, let me ask, in terms of Whitley's experience being abducted. Is it that he was physically brought up to the spacecraft, or was it his etheric or energy body that made that trip, being brought up by people he already knew?

He says "Yes, sometimes (they are) people you know, sometimes they are souls (the aliens) that you have not known but it's time for you to meet." "Yes," he's emphatically saying "Yes, yes, yes; it's the etheric body and not the physical body."

I've asked this to people before, just like we've done. If they had a UFO encounter and have forgotten it, I ask them to go aboard the ship, and ask if we can speak to the pilot. I ask questions like "Are you just driving by, or is this person someone you know, recognize or a stranger?" They all have reported that they recognize them, that when prompted, they'll see the planet where they knew them from. They may have had many lifetimes here as humans, and they're gathering information for their friends back on their planet. Not that it's a cookbook – "How to Serve Man" but to understand how to open up the consciousness of humans. (Twilight Zone reference)

I'm just marveling at what you're describing; what you're telling us is that there is a bigger picture here that involves each of us, every soul matters – every soul weaves the tapestry of all that is. It is just mind blowing... When you take people in their minds to these places - my brain is exploding with so much information. I feel like our way of speaking verbally is so much slower. I've never thought in a million years I'd be saying these kinds of things... talking to our reptilian pilot!

People who have near death experiences or out of body experiences sometimes talk about seeing an etheric energetic thread that connects the energy body to their body. Perhaps that's what connects all of us.

This is what blows me away; when you make a connection with a soul like that, there's so much information coming in, verbally communicating is slow for this kind of "meeting of souls." When you answered the question from Art about how to communicate, and you said, "He should try images," I got a flood of information. He was showing me images of my own self in my house! Showed me lying on the couch with my foot elevated after I broke it.

He says "I was standing by the couch with my hand over your foot. I was trying to do this healing thing but I don't really know how to do that." But from my perspective, I remember that moment I was lying there and remember feeling (tingling) sensations; I thought it was my nerves going haywire; it felt like fingertips rolling down my foot. I thought it was "in my mind." And he's saying, "I'm just no good at the healing thing." As soon as you told him "try images," here came the flood of like 25 images of me struggling in the studio, struggling with people, struggling with my emotions... and he can give me that perspective of where he is!

Wow to all that. Couple of things to observe – as much as we can say anyone can try this; most people visit their council they have from 3 to 12 people; the reason you have so many council members is that you've lived many lifetimes; you've earn each of their roles on your council. Dave said he's been with you for 9 lifetimes; you've had many lifetimes; you just are not consciously aware of them.

You have taken me to places I didn't know I had a lifetime on another planet, it's so amazing to learn.

Many people spend time debating with their conscious mind what's real or imaginary – it's all okay. Try to allow – write down what you observe, go about your day and sometime later, ask the questions again. But important to remember we're here to live life, not necessarily look in the rear view mirror.

I know the audience would like to reach out to you – but we're out of time. Anything else?

"Keep talking to your guides, they're waiting to talk to you."

. . . .

On a final note – as thrilled as I was to have Heather talk to Art Bell, I got a some really off the wall comments from his fans. After this show, his fanatics wrote to say they heard a "female voice" (on air) feeding Heather the answers... claimed it was my friend, the medium Jennifer Shaffer giving her these answers. (Really? Just think about that for half a second. You're saying "someone else" was chatting with Art Bell and giving her answers about seeing herself?)

I didn't know Art. I don't know Heather. But as you'll see from this book she went the same places others have gone, only with a lot of clarity, insight and passion. With Art to guide her. My favorite line from this interview, my saying "We'll be right back after this break with more of Art Bell on the flipside."

Milky Way; NASA

CHAPTER THREE:

"A TRIP DOWN MEMORY LANE"

Tony Stockwell gazing into the flipside at Paramount Studios.

WITH MEDIUM TONY STOCKWELL

Some years ago, the medium Jennifer Shaffer asked if I knew one of her favorite mediums, Tony Stockwell, who was appearing in Los Angeles. (For those familiar with *"Hacking the Afterlife"* Jennifer does some amazing readings of her own, and as I've noted, has assisted law enforcement agencies nationwide with missing person cases.) I had not heard of Tony, but she made me aware of his talent.

As mentioned, mediumship was not something I had explored or examined in my work about the flipside; I had confined my earlier research to eyewitness reports of people who had a near death experience or a between life event through deep hypnosis where they saw or experienced "other worldly events." This "between life" technique was pioneered by psychologist Michael Newton ("Journey of Souls") and I've written about it extensively in my books.

Gary Schwartz PhD, who wrote the foreword to "Flipside" has focused much of his research on mediumship and the science behind how it was possible for people to receive messages from those no longer on the planet. (Gary had a paranormal event while at Harvard Medical school where a "voice" called out to warn him of an impending car accident;

he credits the voice specifically telling him to put on his seat belt that saved his and his then wife's lives.)[4] He's on the cutting edge of paranormal research when it comes to mediumship at his lab at the University of Arizona.

I had always felt that mediumship was about an individual whose "tuning" or energetic energy somehow aligned with folks on the flipside. Somehow, they could sense, feel, or experience events that the rest of us cannot; it was up to the interpretive expertise of the medium to be able to convey what the meaning of a symbol might be.

Some are very good at it. As I mentioned in "Flipside," Charles Grodin arranged for James Van Praagh to appear on his show while I was one of the producers of his show at CNBC. In both shows James appeared, we did an experiment James was not aware of, but both Charles and I were. Our dear friend Luana Anders had passed away around that time, and I had caught James on CNN talking to people who'd crossed over. I mentioned him to Chuck, and avowed skeptic, he suggested we have him on the show and try a live experiment.

I called in from my home in Santa Monica, and Chuck arranged it so that he could put me live on the air; James was not aware I was calling in. He was sitting with Chuck on air when they connected me and James asked me for my "loved one's name." I said, "My friend's name is Luana." James said, "She's showing me you were holding her hand when she died (I was) and she has a wonderful laugh, a great sense of humor. She's talking about your cocktail glass collection in your kitchen (with a name like Martini I get a few as gifts) and she says; "There's a photograph on your refrigerator that is the essence of your relationship."

I was stunned. I do have a photograph of her on the refrigerator of the two of us in Rome, having cappuccinos and laughing. And it's the only time in my life where when I posted a photograph I said, aloud "Oh look. The essence of our relationship. Cappuccinos and laughs."

---

[4] Gary Schwartz PhD, Dr. Schwartz is Professor of Psychology, Medicine, Neurology, Psychiatry and Surgery. After receiving his doctorate from Harvard University, he served as a professor of psychology and psychiatry at Yale University, director of the Yale Psychophysiology Center, and co-director of the Yale Behavioral Medicine Clinic. Dr. Schwartz has published more than four hundred scientific papers, edited eleven academic books, is the author of several books including The Afterlife Experiments, The Truth About Medium, The G.O.D. Experiments, and The Energy Healing Experiments.

Charles didn't know that, and to this day I don't think I could convey how much that sentence "the essence of your relationship" made me realize he was speaking directly to her. It wasn't until I tried between life hypnosis some years later that I had the experience of holding her hand and talking to her, laughing again, but that's covered elsewhere. (James Van Praagh tours with Tony Stockwell, and they've done multiple events together.)

Another medium I was aware of, was John Edward. I've spoken in public about the woman who worked me on the feature film "Salt"[5] who said, she got a call "out of the blue" from John. He explained over the phone who he was and said, that her father was "coming through" during his sessions and was bugging him to contact her.

A skeptic, she had not heard of John Edward or his work as a medium, and when John invited her to his office, she brought her boyfriend to ensure this wasn't a crazed fan of her acting career trying to meet her.

She told me she got to his office in Brooklyn and John said, "Your father has been trying to reach you and I got your phone number through the Screen Actor's Guild. He tells me he wants you to give your mother a call." She did, calling her mom back in the Midwest, who knew very well who John Edward is. "Why is John calling me?" The daughter said that her father wanted her to find something in the house. John directed her over the speaker phone, and the mother went downstairs to look for a "red folder."

The daughter told me John would correct her – "not that room" – until she got on a ladder, reached up and pulled down a red family album that had photographs of their family. John said, "your father wants you to see those photographs, taken before his depression, before he killed himself" (The actress had never told anyone about her father's suicide). The photos were of a happy man, and a happy family. John said,; "That's how he is now, and that's how he wants you to remember him."

Then at some point, John added, "Oh and your father wants you to marry your boyfriend, because you're pregnant with his baby." This was a detail the actress did not know, and indeed discovered she was – she took her father's advice from the flipside, married her boyfriend and they have a child. I met her on the set of "Salt" just a few years

[5] Directed by Phillip Noyce, starring Angelina Jolie and Liev Shreiber

after this event which she told me in privacy, and as far as I can tell; has shared with no one.

For those keeping a scorecard, this is an example of several things:

1. "New information" from the flipside. A father revealing a detail that John nor the daughter or the boyfriend new. Could not be cryptomnesia, ("Cryptomnesia occurs when a forgotten memory returns without its being recognized as such by the subject, who believes it is something new and original." Wikipedia) fantasy, imaginary, or any other part of the usual arguments skeptics make. (I know, I was one of them).

2. This is an example of someone from the flipside contacting someone over on this side to bring them a detail – but this woman did not know who John Edward was, had never heard of him, and was not seeking any kind of confirmation for a detail that she'd never revealed before; that her father had killed himself.

3. Further, the moment featured a phone call between the father, John Edward, the mother and daughter. Where the father directed the mother were to find something that he could clearly see from his perspective on the flipside. Only the father on the flipside knew its location – something that he directed his widow to find. And further,

4. This story has never been told by John Edward as far as I know – she was not a client, she did not pay to speak to her father, she did not have any idea whatsoever why this medium was calling her – and took her boyfriend as security in case he might be a stalker.

At some point in my research I realized that mediumship was just another method of communication between the flipside and here. If people could see, speak to, visit with people no longer on the planet during a near death experience (as happens in several cases, according to Dr. Greyson's Research during near death events)[6] then perhaps there's a way of examining the process of mediumship independently of a reading.

---

[6] "The Handbook of Near-Death Experiences – thirty years of investigation." Edited by Janice Miner Holden, EdD, Bruce Greyson, MD and Debbie James, RN/MSN. Praeger Publishers. Pg 186 "Veridical Experiences."

I began to include interviews with mediums in my research. But my interviews were not to "prove" or "disprove" their ability to do the kind of work they do – the interviews were a result of someone being recommended to me by someone who knew their work well. My interest was to ask them about how they were led to this work. What was the inciting incident that told them they might have an ability to see beyond our realm? What was their first conscious memory of being able to do so?

Enter Tony Stockwell.

Imagine my chagrin when my old friend Chuck Tebbetts suggested I meet Tony, who was going to be in town. Jennifer Shaffer had raved about him, and this was the same Chuck Tebbetts in London who introduced me to Robert Beer, the Oxford professor and artist, who ultimately introduced me to the work of Michael Newton and led me down this path for my flipside adventure. (When Chuck suggests I should meet someone, I know there's probably a spiritual adventure involved.)

Tony's bio in part reads: "Tony Stockwell's career as a medium began at the age of 16 when he was invited to a local Spiritualist church by a friend to see another medium at work. After this experience, Tony decided that he wanted to become a medium. In his early years, he practiced mediumship at the Spiritualist Association of Great Britain.

Tony has worked extensively in the media and has had three television series: The Psychic Detective, Street Psychic, and Psychic School, two TV specials: Street Psychic San Francisco and The National ESP Challenge. He has appeared on The Three Mediums, The Best of British Mediumship and guested on Sixth Sense with Colin Fry. In 2009, he toured the UK with the American medium James Van Praagh.

In addition to his tours and media appearances, Tony has written four books about his experiences as a Spiritualist medium, and released four audio CDs on communication with spirits, angels, and spirit guides. He also runs a training school for aspiring mediums."

I caught up with him just after one of his training sessions for mediumship in Hollywood. Since we were close to Paramount Studios, I wrangled a pass onto the lot. It has an other worldly ambience about it, and our hour-long discussion about the Flipside was filmed in front of the old commissary, where the ghosts of Cecil B. DeMille, Mary Pickford, Adolph Zuckor lurk, and yards from the ghost of my acting career, where in my "Laverne & Shirley" TV debut, I played a pizza delivery guy who was always mysteriously missing a few slices.[7]

Tony is a renowned medium who appears worldwide, has done a number of shows in the UK, and often appears with James Van Praagh in mediumship events worldwide.

Rich: Tell me your first conscious memory of being able to talk to spirit.

Tony: I probably was about 8; aged 7 or 8. I had a box-bed – it was like a bunk bed, but rather than two beds, it was a cupboard bed. I'd get in that little cupboard when I should have been asleep, and I could see a little boy in the corner of the cupboard.

He had a dark face, a sooty face. It was a random thing; I knew he was a chimney sweep from some era... I'd have these simple conversations with him. I'd get out, get back into bed, this happened on or off for long time. (He was) like an imaginary friend, but it felt more real than that.

I have memories of my name being called in the house when no one was there, or people who were there promised they weren't calling me... but it was an ethereal quality to the voice. (I've had) simple feelings and thoughts, but I couldn't honestly say spirits come at me.

Have you ever run into this sooty faced boy since?

No.

Let me ask if you have you ever had - I'm sure you're aware of your guides or guide – do you have more than one?

I think so.

---

[7] Alas, the episode had Harry Dean Stanton singing in it – his songs went long, my part didn't make the final cut, but the residuals still appear like ghosts in my mailbox. (You could say I've always been a few slices shy of a full pizza.) Interview with Tony Stockwell. Paramount Lot. June 28, 2017

Have you ever had a conversation with them about how they came into your life and journey?

No, I've never had a conversation with them about that.

All right, so do you want to?

To have a "conversation" with them? It doesn't really happen (that way) for me...

Well, hang on, I'm asking if you want to.

I'd love to speak with them.

Let's see where we go. But I'd like you to start with the kid. Because this is someone you remember.

I have no other reference for him other than that he was a kid.

Well, let's see if we can speak with the "sooty faced fellow." Can you see him now, in your mind's eye?

(Looks into the distance.) Yeah.

How tall is he?

He's a child.

About how old?

My age at the time, eight.

What color eyes?

It's too dark to see him; he has pale skin, dark hair, a cap, round face. He's smaller than me at the time, very thin... in that image...where it comes from I don't know... I think spirit comes for a reason.

Try to reach out and take his hands in yours. What do his hands feel like? Rough?

No, smooth.

Walk backwards with him, bring him into the light; what color are his eyes?

Blue.

Can we ask him some questions directly?

Give it a go.

What's your name, mate?

Will. William.

Thanks for showing up today. William, what's your last name?

Collins.[8]

Do they call you Will or Bill?

"I'm like a Billy."

So, Billy Collins, thank you for sharing that with us. What year were you alive?

"1861."

Let me ask you Billy, do you know our friend Tony here?

"Yes."

Are you mates or friends?

"Yeah."

Will you put in his mind where you guys knew each other from?

(Tony, as an aside) It's very interesting you're doing this, because it does feel very real... (Looks into the distance; answering the question) Like a workhouse environment.

Describe that to me, what does that mean?

Old Victorian house in London where the poor live.

Where the poor live? I'm sorry, what year was this again? 18....

---

[8] Many William Collins in London at the time, including many orphans from a variety of British wars and cholera epidemic of 1854 in London. **https://en.wikipedia.org/wiki/1854_Broad_Street_cholera_outbreak** and Ancestry's – with a search for William Collins died 1861 yields over 2k results.

1861.

And are we in London?

"Yes."

What section of London are we in?

"North London."

Would you show Tony a happier moment when you guys were together? Maybe sharing a meal, goofing around?

(long pause. Shakes his head) "There were no happy moments."

I'm sorry. Okay, let's show him another moment then – what was your relationship? Friends?

"No, we were brothers."

Can you show Tony the room that you slept in?

"It's a big room with lots of people who slept in the same space."

What did you do during the day?

"Worked. Sweeping. Floors. Everywhere, bedrooms, hallways."

Of this big house?

"Yeah."

So, there are a lot of people in this house. Is this an orphanage?

"Adults and children."

I see, so it's a poor house?

"Yeah, like a poor house."

Victorian Workhouse (Wikipedia)

(*Note:* From a Victorian History of London in 1861: *"Its broad closets and chambers are filled with ragged children who share their rough beds with coals, coke, wood, and few cooking utensils. Its dark wainscotings, scratched and chipped are hung with damp yellow clothes, its passages strewn with oyster-shells, broken tobacco-pipes; its fore-court filled with ashes, broken saucepans, sometimes a dead cat - the playthings of dirty children, who roll about on its hard, black earth... Scores of such houses containing forty, fifty, or even sixty human beings.. ")* [9]

Can you show Tony some proud moment in your life?

(A pause) "There wasn't one."

Can you show Tony the last day of your life?

I can see it. He's on the floor. Ill. About eight years old.

Describe what happens.

"I'm sick. Feverish." (Tony) I feel I'm there watching him. Older by two years.

(*Note:* There's a shift during these experiences, sometimes in the same sentence from "first person" to "third person." It appears to be part of the process of visualizing an event.)

Will, take a look at your brother. Describe what he looks like.

"Looks the same (as me). The same. Blue eyes. Dark hair. (They look) Like brothers."

[9]   From   "Ragged   London"   1861   by   John   Hollingshead
http://www.mernick.org.uk/thhol/raglon01.html#introduction

Is his face dirty like yours?

"Yeah."

Let's go to the moment after you've crossed over Will. Are you standing, are you floating? Are you moving?

"Standing."

Can you see yourself on the ground?

"No. No ground. White."

Who's the first person you see after the white?

Feels very much like his father.

So, Tony's father as well?

"Yes."

Can his father come forward to answer some questions for us? Would that be okay?

(After a pause, shakes his head.) "That doesn't feel right."

Will, I want you to go forward after your father comes through – who else is there to greet you or help you? Or do you stick around, is that why you were hanging out with Tony?

It's a weird feeling. I don't think I do stay there. I don't stay there very long at all.

Where do you go?

Back.

(*Note:* When he says "back" I assume he means "back home" as he says in a while.)

Describe what that journey is like.

Quick. Fast. Smooth.

When you get where you're going, what does it look like? What's the sensation you have?

Being sad again and being afraid again.

(*Note:* Some people report staying with the emotion and trauma of their previous life for awhile, but eventually break out of it. Part of the process of reintegrating is to examine and learn from the lessons of that previous lifetime.)

I would think there'd be some fear associated with being there by yourself... but not now... there's no fear you have now, is there? This is a memory of fear, isn't it?

Hmm. (as if considering that.)

Try to go the moment where you get back to wherever back is – is there anyone around who can help us? A male or female?

I appreciate what you're saying – but it doesn't feel right. It feels like he's alone, my conscious mind is coming in and trying to make some sense of it - but I feel like he's alone, and suspended. He's waiting for people to join him as opposed to anyone else being there waiting for him, other than his father - who doesn't feel like there's a connection there. He doesn't know this man... it's like someone just told him that he's his father.

Okay, so Will, can you go forward in time to the point when someone does come forward to help you?

(after a pause) No, that's not available to me. (Speaking as Tony) It's weird. It's not available. It's like it's... (after a beat) It's all gone... (recovering) It's very interesting... when you evoke that sense of memory, it does open it up for me...

(Note: At this point, we could have stopped. "Will" had reached a suspended point in his journey as if he could not access what happened next. I tried another path.)

Will, I understand you can't go forward, but we're going to let you go for a moment... If you don't mind. Let's go back to Will's brother. What is Will's brother's name? The guy that was watching him die.

"Tom."

Let's focus for a moment on Tom, can we? So, Tom, your brother has died. What happens to you? Does Tom have a happy moment in this life?

"No, the whole thing feels quite depressing really."

Does Tom get married?

"No."

Does Tom find any love?

"No. Doesn't feel that way."

All right, let's go forward in Tom's life. His brother is gone. What happens to Tom? Does he stay in this home?

"He dies in this home. The same (as Will). I think it's almost directly after..."

Like they all caught a cold or something?

"Yes, like some illness. Tom lasts another day, another week, it's very quickly soon after."

Wow. What a tough life. Let's follow Tom for a minute, can we?

Okay.

Tom's last day on the planet. Where are we?

"Poor house."

Standing, sitting?

"Same spot as his brother."

Wow. So very Dickens... 1860's? Very Oliver Twist. (Which was written in 1837) Before Tom crosses over, he's lying on the floor, let's ask him to rise up and move out of the house and into the street. What street was this poor house on? What name comes to mind?

"A name does come to mind. It's Coopers' Lane.[10]"

---

[10] **http://www.geopunk.co.uk/NW1-2/Cooper's-Lane** Cooper's Lane is in North London.

(*Note:* This is historically accurate. From John Hollingshead's: "Ragged London in 1861" *"Not far from this place… under the shadow of the large engineering premises is a reproduction of the worst features of a back settlement in Manchester, Bolton, or Birmingham. In no part of the overcrowded parish that probably contains nearly one hundred and seventy thousand people are there any streets more badly built, more neglected, or more hopelessly filthy and miserable than Jurston Street,* **Cooper Street,** *and their adjacent thoroughfares."*

Looking up Cooper's Lane, I found it was the center of the poor house district in 1861. London took a census in 1861, which includes several references to both Tom and William Collins – and a likely cause of their parents missing in action could have been the War in Crimea for the father, or the great cholera outbreak of 1854.)[11]

Okay, Tom just wander down Cooper's Lane now – no need to worry about being seen in public; take us to your most favorite place in London.

The only impression I have is a pub.

What's the name of this pub?

Don't know... (near) St. Mary's...[12]

What's the pub look like inside?

"Smoky, dark..."

Does it cater to wealthy people?

"Poor people."

Could you get a pint?

"I'm too young. I'm here because it's warm."

Is there anyone that knows you in here?

---

[11] https://www1.udel.edu/johnmack/frec682/cholera/

[12] The city was separated into "Parishes" where the local church took care of the poor or recorded their lives. St. Mary's Parish was in Highgate in 1861. **https://en.wikipedia.org/wiki/St_Mary_Matfelon**

"No. Doesn't feel like that – it's almost a place you sneak into for the warmth... a place just to remain dry and warm in a space."

Tom, look at the name of the pub in the mirror above the bar... or written above the door.

"Feels like "Nell Gwynne."[13]

(Note: This is accurate, see footnote below.)

This is 1862?

"1861."

There's a reason you're in here other than warmth. Are you able to escape from your dreary day?

"Feels like the only respite you could have – just by trying to hide under a table or something."

Any friends in here? Anybody that sees you?

"No."

(Trying to keep it light) Or a bar man who says, "Get out kid, or I'm going to name a drink after you?"

The Nell Gynne from TripAdvisor.com

---

[13] The Nell Gwynne was originally the Bull pub in 1650. It became the Nell Gwynne in the 1830's. There were a number of barefist boxing saloons in London, the Gwynne is 7 miles from Cooper Street. https://londonunveiled.com/2012/07/07/nell-gwynne-tavern/

"No. It feels like there's bareknuckle boxing or something in here. (I'm here) Just to be allowed to help catch and carry things, to facilitate this boxing, gambling...."

Do they give you tips?

"Food."

Do me a favor and go back to one of these matches... what do you see?

"Weirdly – blood. I see blood and aggressions."

Does it splatter on you?

"No. It's not good. It's not a nice feeling. None of it's nice. The whole experience is uncomfortable. It's dark."

Here's what I'm going to ask you Tom and you know the answer to this, before we ask your guides... why did you choose this lifetime?

(long pause) "To appreciate kindness."

So, the lack of kindness allows you to appreciate what kindness is?

"Plus, you're trying to bring your own kindness in small ways... even when it's hard."

Go to a moment where you felt you learned something about kindness.

"Yeah. I shared the food with other people."

With whom?

"Just children, women."

Bringing back food from the pub?

"Yeah, bringing it back... to the poorhouse and to another poorhouse. This is a slightly different place."

Can you remember your mom?

"She died years before."

And your dad was not in the picture at all?

"No."

Okay, let's go to the last day of Tom's life. Now he's going back somewhere, as we said; who's there to greet him when he's crosses over?

"Bill."

How's that feel to see Bill?

"It's nice."

What happens next?

"Just Bill."

I want Tom to go forward in time... somewhere... does he go to a place?

Yeah, like a pasture, like a field.

I want you to describe this field to me.

It undulates. It's English, and its... hard to describe.

This kind of setting is often referred to as a "place of healing..." I'm going to guess this is where your guide - he or she - would take you to this place of healing.

I see meadows.

Are there any trees close by?

Yes, trees, streams.

What does it feel like to put your foot in the stream?

Clean.

Go to the nearest tree – can you? What does it look like?

It feels alive. Trees are alive. Being alive.

Put your arms around the tree. What do you feel?

Home.

(*Note:* For those familiar with my research, this word is often spoken when people describe this between lives realm. It's consistently reported when people are asked "where would you like to go now?"

and they say "Home." Tony has not read any of my books, nor has had any between life hypnotherapy)

What does "home" mean?

Centered, safe.

Do me a favor, if you can, put your hand inside the tree... What's the sensation you feel, if any?

Complete. Allowed. Safe. Accepted.

A feeling of love?

Yes.

Unconditional love in a way?

Yeah, I get that.

Look around this pasture, this meadow and if your guide could come forward, and talk to us now I'd appreciate it – who do you see, male or female?

(A long pause. He shakes his head.) I don't.

I'm going to ask your guide to come forward. What's he like?

A male. I can see him.

How tall is he, what's he look like?

Short. 5 foot 4. No hair. Dark eyes.

Is he Caucasian, Asian?

He's Tibetan.

(Greeting him in Tibetan) Taishe delek! Thank you so much for coming... what is your name?

I know it; Zintar Lunga.

Zintar Lunga, thank you so much. Lunga means wind in Tibetan by the way.

(Note: Tony shrugs. I wasn't conscious of its meaning either yet I say "It's means *wind in Tibetan*." Lunga is not a word I'm consciously familiar with but "knew" what it meant when he said it. "Lung (Tibetan: རླུང rlung) means wind or breath. It is a key concept in the Vajrayana traditions of Tibetan Buddhism and has meanings (*Wikipedia*) that include "Oral transmission of knowledge from teacher to student." *"Tsongkhapa" 2019, Thubten Jinpa pg 53)/*

Mr. Wind, thank you for showing up. Can we ask you some questions that you can answer on behalf of Tony?

(Long pause. Slight nod.)

Very good. When he was Tom, and now he's in this field, did you bring him here?

"It's unrelated." (He waves his hands to demonstrate two places)

Show Tony where the place of healing is that he goes to in-between lives.

"It's both. It's on a mountain top. Like a building without walls, but high, very, very high. You never walked there - it's almost the weirdest feeling of, that you have to fly (to get) there."

Describe what that feeling like when Tony is there, between lives? Is it similar to what Tom was feeling; "safety?"

"Safe. Yes. Safe."

Is that a monastery up there??

"Like a monastery."

How is Tony doing in your mind's eye in this life?

(shrugs, simply:) "Well."

Have you ever incarnated with Tony?

"Yes, in Tibet. In the mountains."

What color robes did you wear?

"Red."

What role does Lunga have in this Tibetan lifetime?

"He's a healer. He uses herbs and is a doctor."

What is Tony's name in this lifetime in Tibet?

"Tem. Or Tems... something like that.[14]"

What is your role in your relationship with Lunga in this lifetime?

"Just to follow."

Do you work with him?

"Yes. "

Do you collect the medicine?

(Note: Tibetan medicine uses herbs and flowers crushed together with a pistil to create pills that affect the health. It's an ancient practice that originated in the Ayurvedic medicine in India, and later spread from Tibet to China. An attendant would be well versed in what flowers are needed.)

"Yes. I feel like I'm a child. I'm 12 years old."

Is he also teaching you about Buddhism and does he seem like a good teacher?

"Oh very."

If you were going to ride a donkey to the capital city of Lhasa – how many days would that take?

"Nine days."

(*Note:* Having been across Tibet, and based on the monastery being high up in the mountains, and a donkey traveling 20-30 miles per day, the monastery would be roughly 180 to 270 miles from Lhasa.)

The abbot of your monastery, is he a venerated lama? Or is it your guide?

"My guide."

---

[14] "Ma-tem" means threshold or sill in Tibetan. "A Tibetan-English Dictionary, with Special Reference to the Prevailing Dialects: Heinrich August Jäschke January 1, 1881

Show Tem to a happy moment in this lifetime. Something you did you were proud of.

(Nods.) "It feels like it's the day I'm being given to him; I'm very small, 3 or 4 years old."

(Note: That's the typical age when a child enters the monastery.)

Take a look at your parents. What do they look like? Was this a happy day for them?

(Nods.) "It's a big honor..."

How many in your family?

"I had nine brothers and sisters. "

Go ahead in this lifetime. Do you become a Geshe or a Buddhist teacher?

"No, he dies. From a fall from the mountain on a path."

Go to that day. What happens after the fall?

"Just light, white light..."

Beyond the light?

"Just more crystal light. "

Is there anyone to greet you?

My guide is there to greet me.

Why did he choose that life or why did you help him to choose that life?

(a pause) "Service."

Lunga, would you take Tony to visit his council? Would you tell me, are we inside or outside?

Inside. There are eight in a circle.

Let's go around to the eight different people. Approach the first person on your far left. Is this person a male or female?

Female. Young.

What color is her hair? Or what is she wearing?

White.

Does she mind if I ask her some questions? What would Tony call you?

"Mother."

Very good. About how old is mother?

About 20.

Is she wearing any ornament or something around her neck?

Gold.

What does the gold represent to Tony and his spiritual evolvement? What did he earn to gain your participation on his council?

Feels like "tolerance of intolerance."

Thank you, Mother. Next person down the row – is that male or female?

Androgynous. Dark skinned. Green eyes.

Let's ask their name.

Funny thing, but it sounds like "Mira."

Mira... which means "to look; what is he or she wearing?

"It's not important."

Any jewelry?

"Wood. (He holds his shirt, as if holding onto something.) It's a bear carved from wood. A carved bear."

Mira, please tell Tony what that bear represents. What did he do to earn that bear?

(Long pause.) "It goes with bravery and standing up for what you believe in. Courage."

So the bear represents courage to stand up for what you believe in. So far, we have tolerance, courage, we've also heard that Tony has earned service, and kindness... let's go to your lead council person. Is it a male or female?

More masculine.

Describe this person to me.

Not Earthly.

Is there a name we can use to address him?

It sounds random... but it sounds like Moishe...

Can I ask Moishe direct questions about Tony?[15]

(Nods.)

We've found four characteristics that he earned in different lifetimes – what are four others? Besides kindness, service, tolerance, courage...

I can't access it.

Moishe put a feeling in Tony's body ... you've met him before, haven't you?

(Nods.)

Why did he choose this life?

"Just because it was needed. He responded to the need."

Yes, but he has a particular skill set; maybe Lunga can answer this... is Lunga part of your council?

(Nods.)

Let me ask you Lunga; have all these lifetimes helped put Tony into a space where all of these lessons contribute to his being able to help heal people during this lifetime?

"Yes."

What does Tem look like to you in spirit form?

---

[15] I find these names are never as "random" as they seem. I doubt Tony is aware of this, but "Moishe" means "delivered from the water" Origin of Moishe: Yiddish variation of Moses, Egyptian. https://nameberry.com/babyname/Moishe

"Light. White. Like a pearlized, blue and pink and gold within the white."

What does the blue represent?

"Peace."

What does the pink represent?

"Love."

What does the gold represent?

"Majesty of the soul."

Can you put a sensation in his body that he'll recognize as a direct message from you... whenever he feels that?

I feel it in my hands.

Does your lead council member Moishe have any object on his clothing?

A star... it's small... like on his chest.

What's it made of?

It's light... that moves. It's attached...

What's the sensation you get from touching his hands?

Family.

Take a look at the star... is a pointy, like a symbol, or an actual star?

It's a star... just light.

What does this star represent in terms of spiritual evolvement?

It's a way of accessing a space or an area... we don't go to.

Who's "we?"

I don't know. It's a portal of some kind.

You say "we" don't normally go there but it's a portal. Is that correct? Okay, so are we allowed to go there?

(He shakes his head, no.)

So, can you allow Tony to put his hand inside your star and transport him to that place?

"No."

Why not?

"It's just... he's not ready."

Look, I'm a curious guy, what does the portal represent? Is that a place that's of higher consciousness from a different realm?

"It's a totally different realm."

Like, if where we are sitting on earth is the 5th realm... and where we're having this conversation where you are is the 7th realm; how far does this portal go to?

"Way higher."

Once someone goes through that portal, do they experience unconditional love there?

"You're still working towards that."

Are you saying, without using the word God – God was once described to me as "opening your heart to all things" - is that something of what's inside that portal?

"It's hard to put it into words. It feels like... it's everything."

All encompassing?

"Everything but... lighter, everything but ... more than."

Moishe, is that star portal something you personally earned or is that something you carry with you (as a transporter)? And how does it relate to Tony? Is that what he's working towards?

It's a funny feeling, it's like um... many people in the world, but not of this world. It's like they're on loan from somewhere else.

What do you mean?

Never thought it before, but it feels like I don't belong here.

(Note: While transcribing this, I realize that Tony may have meant either "I don't belong here in this chamber speaking to my guides in such a casual manner that reveals some of the mysteries of the universe.")

Tony doesn't belong here? Let's examine that for a moment. Here we are in this chamber... what does the room look like?

A cave.

A nicely designed cave? What are the walls like? Smooth?

Rough.

Is this a cave from his consciousness?

A safe space.

Here we are in this council chamber with 8 different people. In terms of his evolvement, it seems like Tony may be a guide at some point for other people, or a council member for other people... is that correct? (Meaning eventually, he'll be on someone's council as a guide.)

"Yes."

(Note: Michael Newton reported some council members wear some kind of symbol that represents the person's spiritual evolvement.) [16]

In a way, you're giving him an example of what he's going to be. Is that correct?

"Yes."

How many people are in Tony's soul group, the folks he normally incarnates with?

37 comes to mind.

Is our friend Will is one of the members of this group?

Yes.

---

[16] Michael Newton discovered this when researching his second book "Destiny of Souls" and offers some diagrams of the various symbols his clients observed during their trips to the council. I've never heard of two symbols being exactly the same – as if each symbol is tailored to the person's accomplishments.

Let's take a look at Will. What does he look like now?

He's... tall, dark. Handsome.

Do you recognize him as anyone in Tony's current life?

No.

How old does he look?

About 30.

Let's go over and take a hold of Will's hands. What does that feel like?

Like a brother.

So, Will, have you incarnated? Put it in Tony's mind. What country are you in?

Spain. He's a male. His name is Luis.

Are you going to meet up with Tony in this lifetime?

(Nods.) Mm-hmm.

When you do run into him, would you remind him of this conversation we're having here on this Paramount lot?

(He nods.)

Is there anyone else in his group he needs to take a look at?

No. It's a very strange feeling... it's a strange feeling, it's exhausting trying to hold (this focus).

Ok, let's wrap this up by thanking everyone who showed up in our adventure today. What did you learn in that difficult lifetime Will? Tom learned kindness. What did you learn?

"To be loved."

To be loved. Thank you, Will. See you on the flipside.

… … … … … … …

As the transcript shows, I had no idea if this avenue would bear any fruit, and when we examined the last day of "Will Collins' life" and tried to go further along this path, we didn't get past the ball of light that Will was able to see, and a tremendous sadness engulfed him.

I was thrilled at the very end of our conversation he could see his brother Will again. By asking him about his "soul group" (Michael Newton's research showed that soul groups typically have between 3 and 25 people, but larger groups are common as well) and asking if Will was a member of his group, Tony saw Will had "moved on" from that point where he was frozen earlier on.

Further, Tony was made aware that will meet his brother "in the future in Spain." But how could Will be incarnated in Spain and "back home" as a member of Tony's soul group? It's because we only bring a portion of our conscious energy to each lifetime.

Thanks to Tony Stockwell for introducing me to some of his spiritual family. This discussion serves to prove that we do have access to this information. It just requires an effort to focus on it.

******

CHAPTER FOUR :

"THE GOLD REPRESENTS WISDOM"

Kimberly Babcock. (Photo courtesy Kimberly-Ray.com)

INTERVIEW WITH MEDIUM/INTUITIVE KIMBERLY BABCOCK

One day, I got a call from Dr. Elisa Medhus asking if I'd meet a medium that was about to work with her son on the flipside (Erik, "ChannelingErik.com") In the half dozen or so mediums I've met through Dr. Medhus I've yet to meet anyone who wasn't "called to the work." Some event in their life changed and shaped who they are – and they offer this gift to people who are suffering.

I have close friend, a well known screenwriter who did a session with Kimberly after I had filmed this interview with her. He shared the recorded interview with me, and insists everything she told him was absolutely accurate about his life and parents no longer on the planet. I mention it because I've come to know that Kimberly is an excellent medium, and has a unique talent to speak to people no longer on the planet.

My first question was about how she came to realize she had access to spirit, and she spoke of her guardian whom she calls "Gabriel." She described some events as a child, and then the second question was *"What happened when she first worked with Erik?"*

She began to tell me that she someone had called in to Dr. Medhus' program, was asking to access details about her mother, with the assistance of Erik and Kimberly. I asked if she had traveled ethereally to help observe what had happened?

Kimberly: There was no traveling, (to access him); I was there simultaneously... My experience was being out in the hallway (of an operating room) and there was a lady on the bench outside that I saw. And then I was with Erik (Medhus) and he was showing me this woman being operated on, the doctors literally working on her open chest.

When he looked over at the woman being operated on, that's when he changed his perspective so I could see what *he could see*. They were clamping vessels to reroute the blood flow; I saw four hands holding the heart... Erik looked at me and said "She's cold" and I was telling my client everything and then all of a sudden there was

a feeling of "Let's go" and we were looking down and watching (the operation.)

I could see all of the guides who were guiding the doctors – they were all peach colored lights. I watched this great thing come out of her chest.. and Erik's kind of like "It's okay, just look at this." They'd stopped her heart. I didn't know they had stopped her heart... and the client texted me later to say that's what happened.

But I think because I was so unaware of what was happening, I was blocking Erik from telling me what was happening... I felt physically ill from the experience.

Rich: Let's go back a bit, to when you were first able to access your guide Gabriel. If I could ask you to shift your consciousness to Gabriel, how does Kim look like to him?

Kim: She looks like a light. And um... the way that I would describe her, she looks very vertical; like straight up and down.

Is the light solid, vibrating or a color?

I went right into it before you said the word "color..." – this is wild - there is color on the outside, lavender and purple, and when you look inside... I'm wondering what the inside is... it's like yellow.

So it's purple on the outside and yellow on the inside? What do those colors represent?

It's more like gold, or like a yellow gold... the gold represents wisdom or the time of evolution of the soul – the purple represents... this is all coming from Gabriel; the purple represents the ability to move from one realm to the next.

To move in different realms and planes?

"Yes. The yellow is like the inner part... is what you've learned or evolved as a soul; the purple represents the capacity to continue."

Gabriel can we skip down a bit, and can you show Kim her council?

Kim laughs. He says "Why sure, she's never asked."

(Note: I didn't tell Kim that we were going to visit her council, and at this point, I'd only done this a few times in public, seeing how far we could get with asking someone to visit their council.)

Describe the journey.

We're inside. There's a big long table, there's two people here that I recognize, there are 8 altogether.

Going from left to right, describe them, or if they have names?

"I told you; she prefers males."

(Note: It is noted later that she saw mostly males in her "soul group" so this is a comment that her guide appears to make in a way that is teasing about who surrounds Kimberly on the flipside. Not often to hear jokes from guides.)

So are the council members all male?

Quite a few are male.

From left to right, what's the first fellow's name?

There's Gabriel, and then next to him is a man who is telling me his name is Arus...

What quality does he represent in your spiritual evolvement?

(Note: Each council member represents a quality, some "essential lesson" the person ("soul," or "conscious energy") has learned during a lifetime.)

It has to do with "protection." It seems my connection with him is to understand and share that there's no need for protection. (Kim listens) So there's no need for protection; to avoid fear.

Rich: So his quality is showing you how to have a lack of fear?

Kim: That there's no need (for people) to protect themselves.

Let's go to the next one. Asur; what's his role in your life?

I see this spelling, A S U R; but he doesn't go by that; he prefers "Zeus."

Should we call you Asur or Zeus?

He goes by Zeus.

(Note: Guides say "My name is not important" or "You don't need to know my name, my telling it to you diminishes who I am." I've also had guides say simple names "Mike," "Pete" as well as "Jedidiah" and "Kajeera." The name is only a *place holder* for the conversation, to differentiate who is communicating. In this instance, I could have asked "Zeus" if he was related to the Greek myths – as I have in the past with other named "deities." What I hear often is that they "vibrate at that same frequency" and that is how their myth came into being. A topic for another tome altogether.)

Zeus, are you the lead member of this council?

There is a person that is but it's not him ... He says "There is a lead person but I'm the one she talks to all the time. One council member represents protection , one is safety, one is a continual support – the need to feel comfort or comforted," he says. They're showing me (my spiritual evolvement) like an incarnation from an infant to adult. Almost like going from an infant to who I am now... and there's a big gap in between. I am remembering who I am; (the quality is) like "Remembrance" is the quality I'm getting from him.

Thank you.

In order for me to trust myself who I truly am, I have to trust this (process).

Who's next on your council?

There are the two guides that I see all the time (in my work). This one man I've asked for his name many times; and he just wants to use the word "Chief." I see him as a Native American; full head dress on.

May I ask what tribe that represents?

He's saying "Little Foot" or "Black Foot."

(Note: "Blackfoot, also called Blackfeet, North American Indian tribe composed of three closely related bands." *Britannica.* There is an interview with a Native Black Foot later in this book.)

Okay, I know someone who is Black Foot. Let me ask you Chief – did Kim have a lifetime as a Native American?

(She holds up two fingers)

Two. What tribe was she with, can you show or tell her?

Sounds like – Powell.... (Kim looks into the distance) Wow.

(Note: The Navajo settled in and around lake Powell which is in upstate Arizona, Eastern California and Southern Utah. As a sidebar, this is the 12th person I've interviewed who recalled a previous lifetime as a native American (including myself as reported in "Flipside.")

Rich: Why did you say "wow?"

Kim: That's interesting, um I've had visions of this life, but didn't know what it was, a long time ago. I had issues with physical abuse... and I had a quick flash of being a past life Native American female who slept with everyone but my mate, who found out, and because of that I was burned alive. I was tied up that's when they burned me.

(Note: Some tribes were famous for burning their victims for transgressions. The Iroquois were famous for torching those who they had felt transgressed the tribe.)

Where in the U.S. was this tribe?

Feel like it's from a map I go way over actually to state of California, upper right hand corner.

Well, from a flipside perspective, you chose a lifetime as this wild native American woman, apparently, which in the context of choosing lifetimes, sounds like fun actually; except the end part.

Crazy.

Unfortunately, you had to suffer physically, but you didn't suffer spiritually?

I have to process that. My guide said to tell you that he represents this memory. By the way, he never speaks, I've never heard him speak, but he wants to tell you this.

Thank you for telling us that and showing it to her. May I ask, who is next to you...

It's my guide "Kristen." This is the guardian I met years ago, while I was on a flight to Sedona. I was reading this book on the plane, and just before I closed my book, I read "Her name is Kristin." So I opened the book back up, looked for this sentence - which is nowhere in the book, and then I asked for a sign... and they literally showed me one "Apple orchard this way." Then when I got to Sedona, we were driving around, and I kid you not, in Sedona, there's that exact sign of an apple orchard and I was like – "Oh my god! Stop!" And these people were like "Do we need to go back and get apples?"

So what quality does Kristen represent on your council?

"Communication."

Well, she's good at that, to put a sentence in a book that didn't exist in order to communicate with you. Very good. Who else is here? To your left?

(A long pause. Kim smiles. Shrugs.) It's Mother Mary.

(Note: Fans of my books will recognize that Mary has shown up in some of the deep hypnosis sessions referenced in "Hacking the Afterlife." In particular, I know two people who gave me the same story, relatively, about seeing her. Again, we've learned from these councils that guides (whoever they are) can serve on a number of councils. Further, we try to not be caught up in the physicality of "seeing someone." In essence, we're seeing or experiencing a frequency, or vibration. So the idea that two other friends (one is shaman, one is a medium) might have the same Mary as a guide isn't surprising.)

Okay, let's thank her for coming. How does she appear to you?

When she stands, each time we address her, she stands. I can see she is shorter – she is wearing blue. She has on something casual, like a casual dress that's blue. She has dark eyes and her hair is brown... but not dark brown. She said "go a little bit lighter with (the description of) the hair. Not dark brown."

Can I ask you a direct question Mary?

"Ask me a direct question."

Can you show Kim why it is that you have brown eyes and your son is often reported having blue eyes. Is that because his father was a Roman or Greek soldier as some have reported? Or are people just seeing him as they need to see him and it's not accurate one way or the other?

This is her response; she looks up (at me). First thing she said, - and I'll just offer everything as it comes to me - first thing she said was "He is not like me – but it's not about his features; he is not like me. And the idea of his father being a Greek soldier; that resonated with her deeply.

(Note: I pursued this line of questioning in "Hacking the Afterlife" with multiple sources. Whether or not having people report the same story that is contrary to the common story of someone isn't proof that it is accurate, but it does offer an alternate story line. It was hard to hear at this moment in the restaurant, and it seemed like she said "resonated.")

What I mean to say, is that from what I understand, in your lifetime as mother of Jesus, people have claimed you were a servant for a Roman soldier, a common practice during that era. His name was reportedly Pantera... and he was the actual father of this child that you had who was so unusual, and explains why his features have been reported as they have been in my research. Is this accurate?

(Note: I wasn't trying to get into a philosophical religious discussion, but I did report in "Hacking the Afterlife" that the Roman historian Josephus, a known historian reporting on Jesus, called him Yeshua ben Pantera" (son of Pantera). Pantera was reportedly half Greek/Roman soldier, and I'm tossing this "genetic question" into Mary's lap for a number of reasons – so we don't have to focus on *that Mary*, as well as we might hear something contrary to what I've heard before.)

Kim: All I can say is that when something is inaccurate, the energy stops flowing. But as you are speaking, her energy – her energy

goes right through me... it just keeps flowing. But she's doing something, can I ask you this? (Asking me, Richard) Why is she sprinkling rose petals in front of you as you speak?

A sign of respect or sense of humor, perhaps? No idea. We've met before – is this accurate that you serve on other councils?

She says, "Yes." (A pause) She says the rose petals are for safety.

You mean so I don't slip and fall? Or so that I do slip and fall?

No, "for safety."

(Note: Neither of us know what this means, and it shows we can learn new information from someone on the flipside. Also, in editing this book, I realize I've chatted with a whole host of people who remember being in the life of Jesus.)

I have asked Mary this question before, it popped into my head during an interview. And that was why when she appeared to people on the planet, she'd say simply "Love your neighbor" kinds of things. I was told she said what people need to hear; that love is universal, and god is love and love is all there is.

I turned and looked at her and asked her to tell me about my journey, what I'm doing (as a medium) and she said, "You see everybody that you see as your children."

That's a lovely sentiment. Love those you meet as your children.

(Note: I've heard this before, and it's hard to define; *unconditional love*.)

Mary, can you introduce us to the last person on Kim's council?

Kimberly looks into the distance. She pauses. "That's interesting. He's like this gruff guy... – Arrgh.. Edward."

Is he young or old?

He's feels like a young 50ish; but he's gruff, he's a "toughen up" "charge ahead" kind of guy.

Does he keep you going? Charging ahead? What's he represent?

"Striving, passion..." he's so passionate and he's – not proud, but grounded. That's a really good word to know yourself. He's so...

Edward what's your experience hanging out with Mary? Do you all hang out together here or do you appear when called?

It's more of a response, it's more like this... if you have a traffic light, the light turns green to go, so when Kim's colors shift this way or that way it's like a magnet, we move when there color is moving – it's not like a conscious effort – it's more like I resonate or emanate different colors.

(Note: It's a way to describe frequency. At this point, I hadn't visited with enough councils to know that they serve on other people's councils, and they "appear" when the frequency is "called." Like a "Bat-signal" from the Batman films.)

Kim, we had a question from your mom – have they had lifetimes together prior to this one?

"Yes. Her mom is a teacher, a facilitator."

And she's giving you a space to become Kim the healer in this life?

That's a difficult job, it's not easy.

It's almost like being a stage manager – the person who behind the scenes helps facilitate the production?

Like a stage manager who gets the productions together.

Have she and Kim had other lifetimes before, can you show her one?

Edward says yes, and he showed me being her father (in a previous lifetime.) Kim tends to choose masculine roles.

Kim was playing the role of her mom's father. Let's tune into that guy for a second. What was his name? What era was this?

I keep hearing it sounds like Julius...

What country are we in?

I see like Greece.

What era is this? What date comes to mind?

This is like 1300's. But I keep hearing "older... ancient."

Maybe 1300 BC?

Like "ancient."

Is it a city in Greece? Athens? Piraeus?

When you said Piraeus, I got a nod.

Piraeus is the port of Athens. I remembered a lifetime in Piraeus. Let me ask this; did I know Kim in a previous lifetime?

"Yes."

Can you show her what that was?

It was aboard a ship – and it's really hot aboard this ship. Things are going wrong, we're on a boat and it's not good.

Hmm. I don't like boats, that's probably why. Were we both men at that time?

We fought a lot. Like brothers. I can't see the year because I'm so in this experience of everything malfunctioning and I'm freaking out.

Let's go to a happier time with these two brothers...

It feels like Greece.

So we were fishermen in Greece? Was this near Piraeus? Poros? Hydra?

They're nodding... like you're correct.

I think it's interesting. I've been there; what was my role in that lifetime?

You were a teacher. When you asked younger or older; we were kind of even, but you were the teacher.

Why did we choose this lifetime together, what were we trying to learn or teach?

It's like you were sharing what you knew with me; like you were a master of fishing and you were trying to teach me. You knew it all and I was trying to learn.

When you see me now do you have a feeling of brotherliness to towards me?

I feel attracted to your work like a brother.

Very good my little sister/brother. (To Kimberly's mom: Did we answer your question?) I want to bring us back a bit. Can we speak to your guides?

Kim laughs. There's four females but one is funny. She keeps pointing at you. She keeps pointing at you, your higher self, they're bringing you forward; she's just being playful.

Very nice I'm honored to meet you.

She brings this guide forward, this feminine energy, her name sounds like Eleanor.

Nice to meet you Eleanor. Can we ask you some questions?

She's very willing – for what it's worth, when I connect to her the energy feels very high, don't know how else to explain it...

Can you show Kim her soul group – the people she normally incarnates with?

She's showing me like... it's funny she calls it a classroom – a room full of different souls.

(Note: I've been filming people under deep hypnosis for over a decade, and they often talk about how their soul group, the people they normally incarnate with are like a "class." The same way in medical school one group of people work together on a particular discipline – osteopathy, biochemistry, microbiology etc, the people in our soul group may all work on the same topic; "courage" "compassion" "addiction" etc.)

How many are here?

Over 20. As we plug into them, I can see them but what Eleanor is saying is that Kim prefers to associate with masculine energy because apparently I carry more of it myself.

If there was a theme for your class or group to work on over many lifetimes is there a theme to what you're doing?

This is so interesting, as she does things, she... as I see Eleanor shift her awareness; it's like I'm looking through her (point of view). She went like this... (lifts her hand) "Stand up everyone, introduce yourselves," and I hear Gabriel – this is the archangel, the angel known as Gabriel. And to answer your questions (about names) the names aren't important, it's important why you're plugging into these vibrations because of how it changes your essence, your soul, like your vibration, has nothing to do with our physical self; when you plug into these – Eleanor is saying you're not one consciousness you're threads of a compilation, and this is who you belong to... the threads you belong to this classroom; they're contributing to the essence of who you are.

(Note: That's a lot to unpack, and I won't try to explain what Gabriel is saying. I will offer that I've met a few "angels" in the past during these sessions, and I ask questions about why they are seen with wings (*"The wings are etheric, they're a metaphor for how we can travel at the speed of thought."*) I've met some "angels" and "archangels" in talking about councils. All I can say is that people have repeated the names Michael, Gabriel and others. I'm not sure why they share the same names, or if they are the same frequency, but Gabriel addresses this issue here.)

Can I ask Gabriel to come forward? Come as close as you can... can you reach out and touch him, what does that feel like?

As he comes forward I feel like he's standing at my right, and I feel what's the word? Invincible. It's like I am very tall, like invincible... like nothing can touch or harm me, like a strength not of this world... it's him. He's claiming that.

Are you the same Gabriel that people refer to in history or is the identification a way of explaining frequency?

He responds; "I am Gabriel." That's how he responds to you – he takes my breath away. It's so strong.

I guess my question to you, is are you the same Gabriel that visited Abraham, Mary, or the prophet Mohammed in a cave? Or was that another Gabriel or the same frequency?

Before I can answer, he wants to point out that got a massive rope around his chest and he keeps saying for me to look at it... And he says... "It represents strength." It feels really dry, he's showing me all the threads now, and how they're intertwined. They're close together... and (thus) it is really strong – "You see where it's frayed; it's really weak, that's what you're supposed to teach, tell people to come together because together we're stronger (when together), and when we aren't we're weak." It's taking my breath away.

(Note: It's an unusual concept – that we are all like strands of a rope, and that when we work together, we are stronger, and when we don't we are like the frayed ends of a rope. Not something I've ever heard of or contemplated.)

Is this this rope something you've earned?

"No, it's just a metaphor to help her understand what I need to say."

Okay. Thank you for that. Interesting point, and well said. Kim, is there anyone else in this group we need to speak with?

He says yes (to you) about the story about the cave; he says "Go back to that question."

The question about whether you're the same Gabriel who runs into these people over various time periods.

He keeps saying "Resurrection." I asked him if that's what he meant about (referring to) the cave. He keeps saying "Resurrection." Wow.

Resurrection?

"Yes sir," he says. He keeps giving this over and over; "Resurrection."

(Note: The term is often used regarding Jesus "coming back to life" or "the rising of the dead at the Last Judgment." But as a noun, it means

"The action or fact of resurrecting or being resurrected." Synonyms are "Raising from the dead, restoration to life." I can argue that this research is resurrecting the dead in one sense – once we come to realize they aren't gone, they're just transformed into another frequency, the way butterflies have changed to caterpillars, we are in essence "raising the dead" by demonstrating they still exist; just not "here." By showing people can connect with their loved ones no longer on the planet, or to anyone who has ever been on the planet, we are demonstrating a kind of resurrection of spirit. I don't know what Gabriel means by this – whether he's suggesting a topic we need to address, or suggesting that's what we are addressing. Or he may be prompting us to get into a discussion about Jesus, who is coming up later.)

Before we go, can you show Kim a place of healing where she can go after this lifetime where they took her to heal? Is there a place for her to heal?

(Tears fall from Kim's eyes). He's showing me. He just shows this room... like we walked down this hall, and it's all white, but the whiteness feels tangible. He's on my left and this is Gabriel leading me, and he's sort of there at this opening and he goes like this (points with her hand) and there is this room... it's like gold inside. There's nothing here, but the walls are gold the walls are the vibration of Kim; not the earthly Kim, but the higher (version of) Kim.

He's talking about... he's talking about the way that you heal others or help others, those words don't really... they don't grasp the depth of what he's saying... (the ways you heal others) are what makes the walls so strong here – that's what is healing for you.

Gabriel is talking about how something might have a stamp of time on it, but it's really not defined by that stamp of time. It's always occurring, it's always in existence, so therefore, that's what upholds this vibrating place, this room that continues to grow.

(Note: Healing centers are reported in Michael Newton's "between lives" deep hypnosis sessions. A person may "return home" to the afterlife, and their guides may take them to a "place" of healing. People describe them differently, sometimes it's outside, a field of grass with trees, sometimes its inside in a crystal room made of energy, or perhaps a room that is filled with energetic light. In this case, he shows her a room that is composed of the energy of healing – the healing that Kim has done in this lifetime and perhaps many lifetimes, and the structure is made of the energy of those healings. I sense that Gabriel is saying the same thing to Kim about her healing center.)

Is this a room that Kim created?

"Yes."

From her experiences healing people? Is this a construction of things she achieved in her work?

He says "Yes." He says "She'll go and she'll see by running my hands (over the walls), merging with that energy, she'll see both sides of it... so if healing were to occur from someone else, if I did something to make someone else heal, I would experience not just the Kim perspective, but their perspective too and that's why it's so strong – but this is for everybody.

Let me ask, can you give her a sensation of remembering this room now?

She reacts. "Oh." She sighs, begins to cry softly. "He... um. He brought Christ forward."

Oh, our pal Jesus. Can we talk to him a little bit?

(She laughs.) Jesus is like, "Well do we have time to talk to Jesus?"

I'm familiar with talking to him.

(Note: Kim has not read my book "Hacking the Afterlife" where I did a number of interviews with people claiming to have known him, or are seeing him directly during their sessions.)

He (Gabriel) brought him (Jesus) forward and (Jesus) said "This is her home; she knows her home in me."

Describe what he looks like to you.

Depends basically what I ask for, either emotionally or vibrationally what I'm seeing.

Let's ask for a visual, a physical feature. What's he look like?

He's taller than me, not a whole lot. His hair is like dark brown... his eyes are like a blue green. He's wearing like really plain... (begins to cry) He had me feel the hair on his face.

Jesus, can you step back a few feet? We can't have a conversation if you're going to freak our friend out here. I need to change your clothes to something more casual...

He's wearing a jeans and a tee shirt now! He just did that as you were speaking!

(Note: In the conversations I've had when Jesus appears, he has the same effect on people. Tears, cheeks turn red and they can't breathe. So I began to ask him to "step back a bit" and to "change his clothing" into something more casual so that the visual of him isn't intimidating.

Let her see your tennis shoes please. Let her see that you're a regular person.

He's just so compassionate... "but I'm also just like you," he said. (Points at me.)

You mean like Kim or like me? I know he has a sense of humor.

"Both of you," he said.

I have a question for you that Kim doesn't know the answer to, but you do. Has anyone complained about me writing about you in my book "Hacking the Afterlife" where I have a number of people who remember lifetimes with you?

He says "It brings a level of truth and awareness that is important right now. It is needed."

Okay, thank you for that. I know that Kim doesn't know what I'm referring to.

(Note: I'm not trying to get a review of my book out of *Jesus*, but after it was written, I asked the medium Jennifer Shaffer if she could "access" some of the people mentioned in the book (I.e., Edgar Cayce, Robin Williams, Prince) for something that I could "put on the cover." The "blurb from Jesus" was "More people will be changed by your words than the ones who can't hear what you're saying. It is a *challenge frequency* that always hurts initially.")

At this point in the interview, I shifted gears and began to ask Kimberly about my friend, the actor Bill Paxton who had just passed away. That portion of the interview is in another chapter in this book. But I came away from this interview thrilled with Kimberly's ability to open herself up to whatever she gets from the other side and have sent friends to her since this interview.

They've shared their amazement at being able to speak so clearly to their loved ones on the flipside. At the moment, Kimberly is working in her home state of Ohio, and can be found online. Highly recommended from yours truly.

CHAPTER FIVE:

"WHAT'S A COUNCIL?"

Ancient Roman council; Virgil. Vatican Library

FLIPSIDE INTERVIEW WITH DR. DREW

I was invited by Jennifer Shaffer to appear on Susan Pinsky's blogspot radio podcast. Susan has a number of mediums who appear regularly on her show, and this time, she had Jennifer and another medium appear. In this case, the panel was Susan Pinsky, Jennifer Shaffer, Rebecca Fearing and Susan's husband, Dr. Drew Pinsky on "Calling Out with Susan Pinsky."

I had met Dr. Drew at a party, and I told him about my research. He politely smiled and said "I'm a skeptic about the afterlife, actually." So prior to this show, he greeted me, and I said "Maybe you might want to try to explore the flipside during the show," and he said "that would be great."

So during the last 15 minutes, I did a demonstration of "walking" Dr. Drew into the Flipside - using an event that happened in his youth as a gateway to introduce him to his "spirit guide" and his "council." As he put it "This is very strange, but I'm seeing the people you are asking me about."

Indeed. I'll add that this experience has not changed Dr. Drew's opinion of the afterlife; he remains a skeptic. He thought that somehow I had "hypnotized him" as he had no idea why he could "see" people during this interview. But as I pointed out to him (and as you'll see) what he says during this interview, coincides with what "everyone says" about their council, even if they've never heard of "their council."

Rich: Dr. Drew, if it's okay, I wanted to ask you a few questions. (to his wife Susan) How long do we have?

Susan: We have dinner reservations in about 25 minutes.

Okay, let's see how far we get. Drew, let me ask you a few questions...

Dr. Drew: Do you do hypnosis yourself?

No, but I've learned the process... or how to do it by filming so many sessions.

You were helping me nap (earlier as I was speaking on the show); you've got that vocal quality.

I have taken a class in hypnotherapy and I've filmed enough so I understand the process... but here's the premise of what I'm going to ask you. Anyone can do this, there's no science involved – let's just call it a version of a parlor game since we're both fully conscious. You mentioned earlier you had a disconcerting memory in your youth?

Yeah, when I was under 2 or 3 had this horrible dream, and had some flashes later in life, which led me to believe this (dream) was actually a memory.

Was there a person involved?

Yes.

Can you picture this person?

A male, about 40 (years old), glasses, moustache, dark hair and dark eyes.

What was his clothing like?

1950s.

And you were born in..?

1958.

What's this guy's name?

I'm associating it was a friend of my father... Jerry. He had a terrifying feature (in the dream). He had red crosses instead of irises.

In life or in this memory?

Memory.

But red crosses don't mean anything dark or evil, do they?

Well, I put it all together when I was in Boston and I saw a cross on the side of an ambulance...

A Maltese cross? (It's the image that came to mind, no idea why, but I said it).

Equal lengths on the cross.

Emergency crew crosses (Photo: Boston.com) Dr. Drew

Okay, let's do something interesting. Let's put this "Jerry" in front of us. Think of him as a photograph of hologram. Are these crosses still a reflection in his eyes?

I've lost the cross thing because the crosses aren't there when I access it after therapy.

Let's stand in front of Jerry. What's he wearing?

Button down khaki; non-descript.

Take hold of his hand in your mind's eye, shaking his hand. Is he a mean, or happy person? What's the feeling associated with him?

Warmth. Familiar.

As in "someone you know?"

Yes.

Let me ask Jerry a direct question. Do you know this boy? Jerry gives you a feeling of familiarity with you Drew – Jerry, would you show him in his mind's eye of some place, a journey that he can relate to? A place where he has a memory of you? Drew, take hold of both of Jerry's hands in your mind's eye. Sometimes that helps.

This is not the same Jerry that I was talking about... he's morphing. Now he's like a Burgermeister with hairy arms.

What year is this?

Turn of the century.

Let's look at his clothing. I asked him to show you an image and he did – he showed you a "Burgermeister." [17]

In ... what's that called? Lederhosen.

I'm talking fast... my apologies, but where are we?

I'm free associating here. I want to say "Neuschwanstein" the castle (In Southern Germany)

Are you on the ground on dirt?

Dirt.

Take a look at you – are you a boy or a girl in this memory?

I'm me.

I mean from the Burgermeister point of view. He's looking at you. What do you look like?

---

[17] The German word Burgermeister means master of the town, borough, fortress, or citizens. A Burgermeister is chairman of the executive council (or cabinet) in many towns and cities in Germany. The title is usually translated into English as Mayor, but the position of mayor is not quite the same as the Burgermeister. (Wiki)

I can't quite do it.

Ok. No worries. So far we're on dirt... near a castle.

I'm me the whole time...

I'm asking from Jerry's point of view. How does he see you?

As a boy. About 12. Dark hair, dark eyes.

Is he looking at you?

Yes.

Jerry; what's his relationship to you?

Great grandfather?

Okay, thanks. Are we in Austria or Germany?

My conscious mind is interfering – we don't have German relatives.

Try not to judge (whatever comes in). Where are we?

Northern Germany. Near Berlin... but there are more important cities... not Berlin.

Mr. Burgermeister – what year is this?

Mainz? Not the port city...

Burgermeister, show him the house that he was living in..

Okay, free associating here. It's greenish with ports, I don't like it.

Is anyone in this house?

It's empty.

Is this the Burgermeister home?

Yes.

Put into his mind your last name?

Schmidt.[18]

(Note: Karl Schmitz was the Burgermeister Mainz, Germany from 1861-1864.)

Thank you so much – because we're skipping around, Mr. Schmidt. I want you to invite Drew's spirit guide here if you can. I know this is counter-intuitive (to Drew) but I'm skipping ahead. Whoever is Drew's spirit guide, could you please join this little crowd? I want you to look around... do you see anything?

Nothing. Nothing. Uh... I can discern a light.

A light. Okay. Can I ask this light to come forward? What's the light look like?

It looks like a sunset but brighter, almost like a fantasy sunset. It turns into a candle.

Is it two dimensional?

Like a sunset on the ocean.

Is there an energy to it?

Yeah.

(Note: In the many sessions I've filmed or investigated, a person's spirit guide doesn't always show up in "human form" at least to begin with. They often appear as a light or some form of energy.)

Focus on this energy, put your imaginary hand inside this energy; what does that feel like?

Goo. Warm.

Is there any emotion associated with that feeling?

Peace.

Okay, I'm going to ask if this light could transform into an entity for the purpose of this conversation, could you morph into a person? (I don't know for certain that this will happen – people are certainly free to say "no," or "I can't imagine that" or even "it's not possible.")

Okay.

[18] Karl Schmitz was Burgermeister in Mainz, Germany from 1861-1864.

And can you give us a name for this entity?

My father's name... Mort. This is getting weird by the way. I had another weird important dream as a kid, in my own psychological development – not about my actual father...

Ok. I understand it because this in this research – some part of your higher consciousness is always back there "back home." Can we ask him (your guide) direct questions?

I'd like to stay with the candle. (That he is viewing in his mind's eye.)

Okay, can we hold this candle?

Yeah.

Mort, what do you think about what we're doing here? (Having this unusual conversation with Drew)

Weird.

Is it ok to ask you questions?

Sure.

Would you show Drew what he looks like to you? (I'm asking Drew's guide "Mort" what he sees when he looks at Drew.)

He sees me as a baby.

Is there an emotional association with that baby? A feeling?

Warmth.

I want you to take Drew by the hand and walk him into his council.

Council?

Mort knows what I'm talking about. Mort can you lead Drew to them? Are we in a room or outside?

(After a pause) **In a room.**

About how many people are here?

Twelve.

(Note: The average is from six to twelve people. People who have twelve on their council, generally, are those who've been around longer, as each new member of the council represents some aspect they've earned during a lifetime.)

Take a look at how they are aligned.

Against the wall. (sighs) This is hard. I'm having trouble seeing individuals.

That's okay. Just let them come to mind as they appear to you.

(Laughs, as if confused) **I feel like Native Americans are here.**

(Note: Drew was chuckling as he said this – because when someone "sees" a person "in costume" in the afterlife, the question would be "well, why are they wearing a costume? What's that about?")

Let's go to the first person on the far left. What's that person look like?

(Laughs) **Like a female Pilgrim.**

Describe her. What's her name?

She's the only woman in here. She's wearing dark with an apron and wearing this bonnet. *Marie.*

Thanks Marie; can we ask you some questions? Can you put in Drew's mind how you earned your position on his council? What's the that you represent in his journey?

She brings "history."

Ah. Hence the Pilgrim's outfit I'd guess – very clever. Can you take her hand? Describe how she looks. Eyes, hair color?

She has blue eyes, light hair.

What's the emotion you get from holding her hand?

Kindness.

What kind of kindness are we talking about?

Gentle, wise, deliberative.

Marie, how do you feel about what we're doing?

"Everyone thinks this is weird."

Susan Pinsky: I don't think it's weird.

Drew: **He means the council.**

(Note: I'd consider this "new information." Here is a person inside a council chamber, seeing 12 people that he does not recognize consciously but apparently, they all know him. Further, when asked how these people feel about what we're doing, he replies "they all think it's weird" which is not the emotion someone would offer if they were "making it up." They might say "This is normal." "This is how it's done." But Dr. Drew answers what he feels they are expressing. Weird indeed.)

Marie, can you give drew a sentence that we need to share with our audience?

"Wisdom is wealth."

Thanks. Drew, have you ever heard that suggestion before?

No.

Well, it's pretty cool.

(Note: Another example of new information or something that is not "cryptomnesia" or a product or an imagination; it was not a concept he's heard before. In fact, it's a proverb in Swahili; "Wisdom is Wealth." Wikipedia)

Let's go to the next person (on the council).

This feels weird, because he's a Native American.

How is he dressed? Does he have a headdress with feathers?

Yes.

How many feathers in his headdress?

A lot. 90 all the way down his back. Up and then down.

(Note: A headdress worn in this fashion represents someone who has "earned" each feather for an act of bravery or courage. Depending upon the tradition of that particular tribe, each feather may represent a victory in a life's journey.)

Look carefully at his face. What's the emotion you get looking at him?

I'm having trouble staying with it... "depth?"

Let's take a hold of his hands, sometimes that helps.

No. He doesn't want me to.

Look at the front of his dress, is he wearing any symbols or emblems or jewelry?

Beads.

What's his name?

This one is like... he's making me emotional, that's why I'm having trouble looking at his eyes...

Just try to focus on his beads... can he give us a name or the tribe that he represents?

"Humanity." Is there a tribe by that name?

The Sioux considered everyone in the tribe to be humanity. Everybody who was not in the Sioux was not humanity. Let me ask; can I characterize you as Sioux?

"You could characterize me a Sioux."

Are you Lakota, Dakota or Nakota?[19]

"Nakota."

(Note: Yes. When I saw myself in a past life memory of being a Lakota Sioux, I did some research and learned the Sioux consider themselves "the people" and the other groups outside their tribe as "not people.")

Okay, thank you; "Ne ho eh, na ha." You've been watching over him for so many lifetimes, do you feel as if Drew is doing a good job?

---

[19] "The Sioux are groups of Native American tribes and First Nations peoples in North America. The term can refer to any ethnic group within the Great Sioux Nation or to any of the nation's many language dialects. The Sioux comprise three major divisions based on language divisions: the Dakota, Lakota, and Nakota. (Wiki)

(Note: Not quite sure why I thought I could speak to him in his native dialect, but I tend to speak first and think about it later. I said something that may make sense; "ne ho ey" means "father" and "na ha" means "he's wild." "Hey a hey" is an interjection to call to spirit beings (according to "Black Elk Speaks.")

"He will."

Can you show Drew why he's doing the kind of work he's doing, saving lives (in his practice as a doctor)?

He's waving a spear over me.

What kind of spear? The kind someone carries into battle? A warrior?

(No, it's) ceremonial.

Like a peace pipe?

It feels like he's doing a blessing. Like some power is being transmitted (to me.)

What does that feel like?

It's all very...

(Note: Later, Drew said that during this event, he could viscerally feel an energetic feeling coming over his body, perhaps some form of healing energy.)

Is it (this power) focused on you?

Yes.

What is that feeling? With your counselor's great knowledge of humanity... – What's he imparting to you?

(To have) patience and (there's) work to be done.

(Note: He's answering the earlier question I ask about demonstrating or giving Drew a visual of why he's chosen a lifetime for doing the kind of work he's doing in his lifetime. His answer was "he's learning to have patience" and "there's more work to be done.")

Interesting. In your council, we have the first person who gave you "patience," and this counselor is imparting "kindness and patience?"

She said "Wisdom is wealth."

Drew, if you can, focus on the person in this council who is the chief counselor who represents everyone else.

I feel like I'm the head of the council. There's a reluctant person...

Can you come forward please?

"Okay. "

Is this person a male, female or something in between?

Male.

What's his name, or something we can call him?

Bill. He's very non-descript. Clean cut.

Can you put in Drew's mind the reason why we're doing this?

"For patience."

To learn patience? (or for patients? Interesting twist of phrase) Patience seems to be a common theme for Drew. I wish we had more time; before we go, Bill, could put a feeling somewhere in Drew's body so he knows when he experiences that feeling?

Okay.

Whenever you have that feeling – know you're connected to your guides. Is there anything else Bill wants to impart to us?

"Scram, get out of here."

Okay, thanks Bill. All right, well, (to Dr. Drew) that's what I do – and we did that in only 15 minutes.

I feel like you had me under hypnosis.

But I was drinking coffee and your eyes were open. How could I be putting you under hypnosis by having a conversation?

It felt as if we were creating these images together.

*Well, everyone says relatively the same things about their council;
between six and twelve individuals, they're here for you.*

Fascinating.

I appreciate Drew's ability to allow himself to answer these questions
live on the air without prejudice or blocking them. He indeed was the
person doing the seeing, hearing or sensing, all I supplied were the
questions. It was thrilling to behold.

CHAPTER SIX:

"LIGHT BETWEEN LIVES"

Pleiades; "The Seven Sisters"

INTERVIEW WITH SCOTT DE TAMBLE

Scott De Tamble[20] and I crossed paths when I first began my documentary "Flipside." I was in Chicago filming Michael Newton's conference, and I learned later that Scott was in the audience when I filmed the first session for the film and book.

I reached out to The Newton Institute, and inquired if they knew of any hypnotherapists in the Los Angeles area that I might be able to work with. They recommended Scott, and since then we've become close friends. He's conducted 4 of my deep hypnosis sessions that I've filmed of myself, and has allowed me to film dozens of sessions with clients that I've brought to him to see if they could travel to the same places everyone else does.

Scott has done a number of personal hypnosis sessions (as client) with other hypnotherapists, and in those sessions he's had some unusual past life memories and journeys into other realms. At this moment, Scott and I are having dinner in a restaurant, where I start to ask him some casual questions to "see if we can go anywhere" without hypnosis.

---

[20] Scott can be found at Lightbetweenlives.com

My comments are in italics. Scott's are in bold font. Prior to hitting *record*, Scott wondered what it would be like to contact his council directly without hypnosis. I said "Wanna try?"

He laughed. Scott is a virtuoso at hypnotherapy. I said, "Let's just go there; be there now. How many council members are there?" He paused, looked over my shoulder and said, "There are nine to 11, but at the moment I can see seven." I ask to speak to the first person on the far left as I turn on my recorder.

Richard: Just give us a name for this guy on your council... the person to the far left. What's his name?

Scott De Tamble: The names are going to slow us down.

Okay, but it will help me. Any name will do.

"Al."

Okay, we're talking to Scott's council member Al. What's up? Why are you steering him in the wrong direction?

He's laughing.

Have you heard of me or my work?

"We know you."

Is this an appropriate method, shortening the process?

"You're doing what you do."

Annoying people on the flipside?

He's just laughing.

What's so danged funny?

He's just laughing at our struggles.

I'm glad we amuse you.

They just enjoy watching the antics of us.

Yes, like the flea circus. We get that ... but can you grab Al's hand? What does that feel like?

He doesn't really have hands... but okay. I don't mean to be difficult but the hands thing is not that important.

Can you connect with him in some way?

Feels like connecting with a very wise and large intelligence.

Can I ask you some questions? I promise they'll be both pertinent and impertinent.

"That's what we expect."

How many councils do you serve on?

"Thousands."

What would you like to tell Scott, aside from what you tell him every day?

"Have more faith in us and connect with us, even as we're doing now in a flippant way — follow your heart, follow your dreams. Standard stuff."

So can we call this the flippant-side?

"Brilliant."

Along those lines, allowing people to have a normal conversation with you not based or steeped in all the things they normally have to go through to get to you – it's a way for them to realize that they can speak to you in any venue, correct?

"Agreed."

I learned this from Scott... is there any sensation you can impart to Scott that tells him you're there tapping on his shoulder?

"Sure." The feeling is when the wind is in my hair and face...

Look around the Council a bit. How many are there here?

We'll call it nine women and men.

Some are in attendance and some are out?

Yes. There could be seven, eight, ten, eleven; depends.

Those that are not here; are they working?

Not needed.

To the left or right - anyone else want to weigh in on Scott?

There's a woman who looks like Deanna Troi from Star Trek; she's about 50…

A name we can call her?

Call her V. (Scott laughs.) She's wearing a dark jewel-tone dress.

What do you represent for him?

"Passion."

You wanted to speak earlier, what did you want to say?

"He is a very passionate person... he holds it back for whatever reason, but we would like him to explore and express his passions to a greater degree."

Passions toward work? Talent? People?

"Just to feel that passion – doesn't really matter how."

What does it feel like?

Like a lot of energy… happy, kind of bouncy.

So V, have you incarnated before with Scott?

"Yes, but in very ancient times before this civilization; in other worlds, or other dimensions."

Where you with Scott when he was a Commander of ships and people many lives ago?

(Note: This is a reference to a memory Scott shared with me, of a lifetime a long time ago, where he saw himself as leading a war.)

"Not with him, but knew of him."

I know Scott had a memory of leading them into battle; he felt bad because people were lost, but I've spoken to someone else [that he doesn't know in this life] who knew him in that era. And they said that he saved millions of lives. Is that correct?

"Yes, he has gone to war many times. But long ago."

So how come is he not leading people into battle? Or is this another version of that in this life?

"That phase is over; this phase is more about shining light."

You wanted him to be more passionate, or enjoy more passion?

"He already is more passionate, but he needs to allow his passions to be expressed."

What color are V's eyes?

Violet.

How long is her hair?

Dark. Long... to mid-back.

V, have you incarnated in the past? When was the last time you incarnated?

"A million years ago."

What do you miss about being here if anything?

First she says "nothing," but then says "Well, there are pleasures... physical pleasures."

Like... what?

"Like touching... and eating..."

What would be something you'd remember eating that was tasty?

"Fruits, like grapes... and drinks, somewhat like wine."

Let me ask you a question that might seem esoteric... about Greek mythology – when they talk about the ancients and Mt. Olympus. Are they talking about their Guides and Councils? Just translating that into words?

"It's a mishmash."

How many other Councils do you serve on, V?

"Hundreds of thousands."

Is this odd for you to have a conversation like this in a café in Santa Monica?

"It's fine. He doesn't always need the long form of ritual."

If you were going to give Scott an image of something that happened in a lifetime that you were the most responsible for, what image what would that be?

She showed me a star and a rocket ship. I've always had a, well, a passion, to explore other dimensions and other places.

Does Scott still travel around deep space even though he's not aware of it?

"Even in this moment."

So some part of his higher consciousness is out there?

"More than one."

Let's pick one that's traveling around.

"He knows of the one that's monitoring in a space station; there is another one that is in a long journey on a ship."

Can we zip over there to visit the one on the spaceship?

"Yes."

How many on this ship?

"One."

It's his ship?

"It's part of the Service that he belongs to."

Tell me about this Service that he belongs to... is it something new?

"Ancient. It's for a federation that still exists."

Is there a name for this federation?

She says "It comes across as being timeless, but it also was to do with time itself. It's exploring space but also exploring time... not just space travel, but traveling through time."

How much of percentage (of soul energy) does this fellow have of Scott?

"It's really.. (an) elementary way to think about it."

But that's where I live; elementary land.

"We have so many levels, there's so much to us... it's hard to put a...."

I mean based on the roughly 30% of our conscious energy being here, this commander, does he have the same amount?

"Perhaps six percent.. he has a lot of things going on."

Are you saving people or just exploring?

"He is both exploring and ambassadorial... meeting new people and connecting them to something like a federation." Also, I get a feeling of a time-travel mission... there are some things to fix in time, to change or correct it.

Wow. So your mission is partially to… meet people… on an etheric or physical level?

I think he can shift between both.

If you appear on a physical level to them, does that alter someone's path?

"You have to be careful... it's really hard to explain, but there's an awareness of the whole culture through time; and at a certain point you might pop up to give a course correction."

Are you showing up on Earth eventually?

"It's a different part, and a different thing."

If we were going to characterize where you are currently, is it in this universe, or in another realm?

"It's variable. You can travel in this physical medium, you can also... well, there are universes stacked within universes, there are dimensions that we can leap."

Zip around in. Are black holes portals of a sort?

I get the feeling we don't understand... "He doesn't understand what black holes are or what they do."

Very good. I've had conversations with people who claim they've been through them... "portal" not being the correct word.

I get the feeling that they aren't predictable – you may go through it and wind up somewhere else. (Some other part of a universe or realm.)

Is anyone in charge of those laws and physics?

"No."

We create them?

"No, they were created before.."

Can you tell me who created them?

"We don't know."

Who does?

"No one that I know."

Is it possible for us to find the answer to that?

"I think that's one of the things we're searching for, all of us."

Sorry, what name do you go by over there... Commander Scott?

"You could just... the star Antares comes in as a nickname."

Can I call you Commander Antares?

"I'd prefer it if you didn't! Let us clarify. I work as an explorer and ambassador. The part of him monitoring and sending people on various missions, that is where the 'Commander' comes in. The part that was a monarch who was forced into a defensive war, that was a past lifetime of long, long ago."

So as the monarch, he felt the responsibility.

"A great responsibility. His people – they inhabited seven worlds."

Was he the son of a king?

"Hereditary. Yes."

Antares, I've heard the definition that we're all from the Creator, but Creator isn't the right term. There's no person, no him, or it, but a connection of all people... and if you open your heart you can experience the Creator – does that ring true to you?

"Yes, there is more to it, more that we... it's unfathomable. Like when the scientists say 'More of the universe is dark matter, than not...' It's like that."

Beyond comprehension?

"There's a greater portion of God or energy than is detectable."

Do you come and visit Scott often, Antares?

"We are linked."

When he wants to link with you how can he do it?

"He already is; he can travel."

I'm curious about the people you've met in your role as ambassador.

"I've met many."

In terms of how you solved issues or problems, from the past – is it like introducing matches or fire... is that correct? Same thing that happened on earth? Like the introduction of fire and the harnessing of it? Is that something someone did on Earth?

"Yes."

It would be fun to hear those stories.

"This person has played that role on Earth."

So Scott's the guy who brought humans matches?

"No, he's aware of this – in ancient Mexico, he brought a strain of agricultural seeds and introduced it to the planet. This was part of a larger program so that different parts of the world would be able to help people feed themselves and to help themselves. We can carry seeds with us."

Is that something Scott learned to do in a classroom? To alter seeds... how was he taught that?

"He doesn't do the lab work; he's more of the Johnny Appleseed."

I'll call him that.

"He'll love that."

There was another Scott you mentioned, the guy not traveling, let's go back to him for a sec.

"The one who monitors."

Yes, the hall monitor... what can we call you by?

(Listens) "Um... where is that? Boy that's hard to say... (to me) "It's in space." Cosmos. Silly nickname."

Cozmo. Antares and Cozmo – what do they look like?

Not Cozmo... that's Kramer from Seinfeld! 'Cosmos.'

Sorry. What does Antares look like?

Medium height, long hair, dashing, a little taller than me... like blue or green eyes.

How about Cosmos?

He feels... let's see... somehow a little darker... Caucasian... but darker eyes, dark hair.

Cosmos, in terms of where you're observing — are you in a physical spot?

"In like a bubble, but it's technological... it's like a space station."

Somewhere in our galaxy or a distant one?

"Distant."

Can you travel around?

"I'm stationed here for now – and this is more like a Commander."

Commander Cosmos – cool. Are you in our universe?

"For a time."

Outside of Earth?

"Not just outside, but in this quadrant."

In terms of you moving around, is it etheric movement or do you actually appear in places?

"I have different methods of propulsion – physical or magnetic."

You're a physical presence?

"Can be."

Do you normally incarnate on some planet?

"I've been incarnated in this personage for a long, long time."

I know you're appearing to Scott as Cosmos; how do you appear to your family and friends the same or different?

"The same; I don't sense family and friends. More like colleagues, people that I send on missions."

Any of those people working on Earth today?

(He names a friend.) "She's one of ours."

Anyone else. Someone I might know?

Do you know (another friend)? I get a sense of him.

Is he aware of that?

No. But he feels a kinship.

Is there any value in me telling people these things? If so, what's the value?

"No, this is private. Don't tell anyone anything."

What are you going to do if I do?

"There are ways for you to be silenced."

(Note: Scott is smiling as he says this. I wasn't sure if he was quoting a Guide or saying something offhand. He told me later it was a Council member, referring to the privacy of some of the people we had mentioned, and we have maintained that privacy in this interview.

Needless to say; whenever my computer breaks down or shuts off suddenly, I assume someone on the Flipside wasn't happy with what I was writing, or not writing. Nothing quite like getting a warning from someone outside this realm.)

Everyone chill out up there, I'm kidding. What's the value of Scott knowing about this?

"Just to open his awareness and not be so focused on his 'Scott' life and whatever little problems may be there."

Ok. So your mission, if I'm correct, are you helping in your Cosmos gig... to help the consciousness of wherever it is you're working?

"That mission is to expand our knowledge of the universe, and to expand our range of touch and influence; and to gather new information, and to gather people in different ways of thinking."

In a benevolent or compassionate way?

"Absolutely. There's always something to learn from everyone. Values from different people."

In terms of the tech you're using – who created it?

"A consortium."

From outside of planets or on them?

"It's a collaboration between physical and non-physical."

Have you encountered anyone on our planet Earth that someone has seen you?

"No, not here on the Earth."

I get there's no point in appearing here because you're already here... as Scott. Let me ask, so Scott's higher self is all these people, Scott on the planet, Scott in space?

"All that and more.... as are most of us (humans); all of us."

How many personas does Scott have working simultaneously?

"It's hard to divide into numbers."

I just mean as an average...

"We'll say 16 in an earthly way... let's don't limit it to that. Put it this way, around 15 or 16, sort of embodiments, but there are other portions of him that are not embodied which probably constitute the greater part of him."

Okay, that would be "his higher self" for a lack of a better term. The reason I ask is that there are some people who say they can incarnate in more than one person at a time. But I've never met anyone who was aware of it.

"It would be more common; if you ask, you'll find it."

Very good – any questions I should be asking? Shortcuts to get to you?

Something like "the best thing you could do is to somehow... have people just connect with us – and let that 'greater awareness' come to you; or whatever you want to call that."

Al, can you bring a friend of Scott's into this conversation – someone who taught him, someone who shows up now and then – we call him Morton. How's he look?

"Showing much like he was on earth; a little younger and a little happier. There's a lot of emotional and mental interference in this setting (the restaurant). "'I'll be happy to chat the best I can.'"

The reason I ask to speak to Morton is to help set that emotion aside, let's put it into a suitcase...

"Flippant-side is right! You can call me Michael."

You show up often in my communications with Jennifer, is that correct?

"An aspect of me."

I went through asking you questions that (someone) provided, and he said it wasn't you.

"I'm not really interested in proving anything to anyone else at this point. I've done my work, I'm happy with it, it evolves there on earth... and I have other things to do."

You've also been helping people over to learn how to communicate to people over here.

"I have many jobs and interests."

What do you want to tell Scott?

"We are... we were delighted to have him in the Newton Institute. I know and appreciate his contributions... now I understand them much better."

You mentioned to Jennifer that you were keeping an eye on Scott. What did that mean?

"I've looked in."

Would you show Scott one time when you looked in?

I'm not really getting a specific client, but I can feel my office. And he never went to my office when he was alive.

Well now he has.

"There are lots of others who look in on these sessions — spiritual beings, and we really like that Scott invokes that. We wish everybody would. To be asked is to be given more latitude to help."

Anything else you want to impart to Scott?

"Write your books and stand on the work; that would be a good thing. If he wants."

Does he want me to help him do that?

"Sure."

How's your wife doing?

He's in contact with her.

Is she aware of it?

"She is, maybe not in a fully conscious way like seeing a ghost, but she senses my presence."

Any sensation you can give Scott that you can put in his body that would feel his presence?

"Let's say it's a feeling right now, an itch in his eye."

So he'll know when he's doing a session that if he gets an itchy face, that's you.

"You're a real cutup."

Look where we are... in ten minutes we got Al, Miss V...

"It's an honorable group."

Let's look around anyone else we need to talk with?

Someone's saying Jennifer and you are doing good work.

(Note: He's referring to Jennifer Shaffer, our friend the psychic medium (JenniferShaffer.com) We have two books on the interviews we've done with people on the Flipside, "Backstage Pass to the Afterlife" and she appears in "Hacking the Afterlife" as well. I'm aware that Scott isn't trying to give a compliment here – I know him well enough to know he's "hearing" from someone on the Flipside who likes the work. It's nice to hear either way.)

Let's say hello and goodbye to everyone – we bypassed Scott's guide, and walked into his council – Miss V I'd like to know more about you.

Get in line. My guide says, "We're all cool with this, we know you."

Michael, thanks for coming by, we appreciate that.

"Pleasure."

Many are curious about your path and journey; they ask if you are available on the Flipside.

He doesn't really care about that; he's got his own travels. I see him as an explorer or traveler too.

I remember his telling me that had visited like 23 different spirit realms... how many have you visited since being there?

Seems like 8 more.. but he's taking his time. It's not quantity, but really exploring a world or a dimension, spending time there and learning what he can learn.

Can we thank everyone for this unusual journey and demonstrating how easy it was to do in public? Thank you!

Scott has facilitated literally hundreds of deep hypnosis sessions, and as demonstrated here, there's nothing deep or hypnotic about any of my questions. The only caveat is for a person to "open themselves up to an answer."

This was a rapid fire interview; he'd answer and I'd have the next question pop into my head. Scott's answers were detailed. He has done sessions in the past, deep hypnosis sessions where he's accessed some of these answers about his journey, but for fans of his work or my work in this arena, this is about as improvised a question and answer session might be.

If you're looking for a good hypnotherapist, I can't recommend anyone higher. He also does distance sessions on Skype, so you can be anywhere in the world and connect with your higher consciousness. Thank you Scott! (He can be found at lightbetweenlives.com)

CHAPTER SEVEN:
"YOU GOT THIS"

Bramanta Staircase; The Vatican (Wikipemedia)

TERESA ANN SESSION

This friend of a friend is not a medium or a hypnotherapist. In fact she's about as far removed from the "*woo woo*" world as can be, with a career in law enforcement.

We met through a mutual friend and asked if I would take the time to chat with her about an issue that she was having with regard to a boyfriend.

This is one of those sessions that must remain anonymous because of "Teresa's" career (not her real name) and the idea that she would be chatting about a past life with anyone might be detrimental to her career. I can't tell you what agency she works for, but I can tell you that you'd know it if I said it.

In my first chat with her, prior to turning on my tape recorder, she was able to recall a lifetime in Calabria, southern Italy. Her name in that lifetime was Anastasia and she recalled a date of 1432. She remembered the life death of this woman, and when she died, she recalled "returning home" to her friends on the flipside. She was met by her guide – her current grandmother Josephina (who has been with all of her lifetimes.)

I asked Josephina if we could go in to visit with Teresa's council. Teresa said that once inside the council chamber, it reminded her of a scene in "Indiana Jones" when he was below, and all of those judging him were above. (I don't recall that scene, but made a note of that memory.)

As she entered her council she said she saw 5 individuals and when she said "the first individual looked like an alien" I took out my cellphone and begin recording. Again – she's not under hypnosis, I'm not trying to guide her into hypnosis – we are just chatting over lunch and she is "connected" by looking over my shoulder into the distance.

Richard: Okay, I'm recording now to help me transcribe this – (at this point) We are in our friend Teresa's council now and her guide Josephina is still here.

Teresa: She's next to me.

What does your guide look like, how old is she?

She's 26. She has blue eyes, brown hair.

Does she look like you?

Yeah.

What is she wearing?

She's dressed like Dorothy from "The Wizard of Oz." Wearing like a dress that has straps and comes across. It's blue.

How is your guide dressed?

I see her wearing black. Mauve paints and a beige sweater.

Let's go back to our first council member – can you give us your name?

"Lilly."

Can you take hold of her hand? What's that feel like?

Her hands are smooth.

Is there an emotion associated with holding her hand?

It kind of scared me - the look of her hand.

When you're holding her hand does she seem familiar, does she feel distant, what's the emotion?

It feels secure.

Secure. Lilly are you familiar with what I'm doing here in your council chambers?

She said "Yes."

I hope I'm not being intrusive.

"No."

So Lilly describe the quality that you represent on Teresa's council? What's a word that represents the reason you're on her council?

"Faith. Faithfulness."

What does that mean? Being true to someone else? Your beliefs?

I'm getting both - I'm getting faithful to people that I love and also having faith in the universe...

Faith in how things work? You mean how the universe works?

Having faith in yourself.

That's more specific, thank you. Lilly, can I ask a personal question?

"Yeah."

What planet do you normally incarnate on, or have in the past, is it in our universe?

(It's) "In another."

Can you tell us what the environment was like? Did you ever have a lifetime with Teresa on your planet?

I'm getting "No."

Thanks for answering that. It's unusual to meet someone like yourself and I appreciate talking to you. When you describe Lilly, is her face round, angular?

It's oval, and huge, and flat... like she has no wrinkles almost like shark skin.

Her eyes?

They're big like alien eyes. Big... they're her big feature.

Does she have an Iris? Is it all one color?

They're black but I feel like the lid is like a lizard's and comes in from the side.

(Note: This law enforcement agent is not a fan of science fiction, but is a fan of digging for facts. So my asking for specific questions is not something she wouldn't apply to her own work – but at the same time, it's unusual. There's no hypnosis involved; we are sitting in a noisy pizza restaurant in Manhattan Beach.)

Try to take both of Lilly hands in yours. Lilly tell us, how is our friend Teresa doing?

She says "Fine."

Can you give her advice about her path and journey?

"Keep going."

To have faith?

Keep going.

(Note: At this point Teresa listen, then makes a face - shakes her head. Tears come into her eyes.)

What's happening Lilly?

(Teresa aside) It's like I don't want to hear it.

Say it aloud and we can judge it later – just say it aloud. Let Lilly play her role. What does she say?

"Everything's going to work out."

(Note: I'm aware that "Teresa Ann" has had some relationship trouble, so I'm guessing that she's asking Lilly this private question on behalf of what she wants to know.)

Lilly I so appreciate this – is there any advice you can give the planet how to save our planet?

"Love."

That's pretty specific. Now, can you introduce us to the person next to you on the council?

It's a man.

By the way, what is Lilly wearing?

She's wearing cloth, like a robe kind of like a greyish purplish color. With a belt. It's nothing fancy.

So the person next to her a man, how old is he?

He's wrinkled. Old... like 80; his name is Joe.

Joe, is this odd for you to have one of your charges interview you?

He says "a little."

So I take it you don't know me or have heard about me talking to councils.

He says "No."

(Note: For those keeping score, sometimes council members say they "know me" even though the person I'm interviewing does not. Sometimes council members say "we've heard of you" from someone else who has mentioned the work to them (around the council water cooler, I guess?) but it's just as interesting to hear someone say "I don't know you" to demonstrate that the subject is not supplying "friendly answers" to the person asking them.)

I appreciate you talking to us. What's a word that signifies your role here for Teresa?

"Power."

What does that mean?

"Personal power."

Power of conviction? Doing the right thing?

"Recognizing her own power."

Are you available to help her recognize her own power, are you the person who rejuvenates her when she needs it? Do you help rejuvenate her?

He's like "That's what I'm here for..." – but I don't think the rejuvenation is mutual.

How many other councils do you work on Joe?

"I got three."

Lilly?

"Seven."

Joe. Here's a chance to tell our friend Teresa something that can help with her path and journey. What can you say?

"Stay the course."

It's a complex thought, but simple. Should we talk to other council members? Who's in charge?

The one in the middle.

Male? Female, neither or both?

(Laughs) A female who looks like Whoopi Goldberg.

What's a name we can call you?

"Susan."

Describe her.

She's 50. Hair is black, has long dreads... she's wearing purple, a magenta purple outfit.

The fabric?

Feels like the stuff that curtains are made out of.

Okay, is she wearing jewelry?

She has a hat on but I feel like I'm interposing this from when Whoopi was on star trek.

Susan, this image you're presenting of you on Star Trek – is this so she can be amused by seeing you?

"Yes."

(Note: People see council members differently – some seem familiar, relatives and the like – some look like other people, some look completely different, like Lilly (who appears to her as an alien.)

Would you consider yourself a spokesperson for the council?

"Yeah."

What quality do you represent in Teresa's spiritual evolvement?

"I guess laughter. Comedy."

And what's the quality of the person next to you represent?

"Strength again..."

A different strength? Physical?

"Yes."

What about the fifth person at the end – what quality of yours do they represent?

"Quiet calmness."

Okay, let's ask Susan, how is our friend Teresa doing? Anything you want to tell her?

She's laughing at me, like, "This is what you signed up for... she's laughing that I'm here using you..." (to access her) not in a menial way, but she thinks it's comical that I need help.

Let me clarify – you're chuckling because our friend Teresa is using me to address you?

"Yes."

Is this unusual to access you?

"Most people can, they just don't try."

How is it that you're able to do this?

"Through me."

Through you Susan or through Teresa?

"Through *me.*"

Why are people able to do this now and why couldn't they before?

"Consciousness."

How has consciousness altered or changed?

"More aware."

Because they're thinking or talking about it?

"Yeah."

Teresa Ann has seen a number of mediums, is that so she can see her own gifts in this area?

"So that I learned to trust."

Trust what?

"Trust herself."

Are you aware of the previous conversation Teresa and I had about analysis with emotion was I saying the right thing?

"How to separate the emotion from the analysis? Yeah."

What would you like to add?

"That I can do them both but not take it so personally."

Okay. I have a question about consciousness being altered – who's doing the altering?

"We're doing it on our own, but the fact that more and more people are talking about it makes it easier, more people talking about it, the veil is becoming thinner. I feel like they're closing in."

I've heard that often – an unusual thing to say, because we don't use veils (in public) anymore. Wedding veils are getting thinner... or disappearing. We have screens. But rarely veils, and yet I hear it often "the veil is thinning." What can you tell us about helping our planet?

"That consciousness will assist.. keep doing what we're doing and eventually it's going to get there."

Okay, and specifically for Teresa, she has relationship issues – without disrupting her path, can you tell her if everything is going to be okay and work out?

(Shakes her head). I just don't get anything.

Let me ask council member Susan why she isn't getting anything.

"She doesn't want to know."

And the reason for that is?

"She wants to have hope that it will work out."

Okay, that makes sense - but the reason she won't access it is because she won't learn the lessons if she sees the answer in advance – is that correct?

I'm resonating "Yes."

Can you put a sensation in her body so she knows it's you?

It kind of felt like a ... someone squeezed me from both sides like a vibration.

Okay, is that your "bat signal" Susan?

"Yes."

When she gets your signal what should she do?

"Calm the f*ck down."

May I ask, how many councils do you serve on?

"Two."

Have you heard about me talking to councils?

She says "Yes. That you do this often."

Who did you hear that from? How did you become aware of it?

I got a picture of her chatting away with others at lunch time – like lunch gossip with to others.

So I'm the cooler conversation – thanks for telling me, I like to ask. What would you like to tell humans about their journey?

"Calm the f*ck down."

Okay, but what do you mean by that?

"Relax and enjoy."

Because you chose to be on it?

She said, "Yes, but that we're not going to hear it."

Except when I write it in my next book – and I say we talked to your guide who said "Calm the fuck down.... some people will appreciate that.

She doesn't really believe you.

You're probably right. Any specific message to our friend Teresa? Can you show her a previous lifetime? Is that allowed?

I feel like she said "No"... and they are not showing me anything.

I appreciate you guys speaking up with us – any last words you want to give Teresa?

"You got this."

Thank you for stopping to chat with us today.

They said "Oh of course, anytime." They are blowing a kiss en masse, like the panel in The Newlywed Game.

The reason I'm having this session with this law enforcement person (agent, defense dept employee, detective – I'm disguising this person's identity for obvious reasons) is we've had a couple of chats about her personal life, relationship issues, and so I offered to see if "we could get anywhere" over a slice of pizza.

I had no idea where we would go, or if we would get anywhere. She had no conscious idea that she had a council – had never met them before, but as we will see in many of these sessions, they're just people who have more experience at more lifetimes than we do, and have advice for us.

So let me put it this way; in the architecture of the afterlife, we all have councils, we all have guides, we all have people who watch over all of our lives. We are never, ever alone, we always have them at our disposal, no matter what the crisis might be. They may not be able to answer our questions directly ("father why hast thou forsaken me?") but they may generate a "signal" of some sort for us – a feeling in the back of the neck, a buzzing sensation, or something physical to let us know that they are with us.

I know how odd this all sounds if you're new to this material – but if you're not, welcome to *The Martini Zone.*

In the lobby of the CIA. (Not the employer of the interviewee in this chapter, but could have been as I know a few employees after working on the film "Salt.") On one wall, a statue of Bill Donovan (my grandfather's pal and fellow campaign manager for Frank Knox) behind him is carved the slogan "The truth shall set you free."

CHAPTER EIGHT:

"PIECES OF EIGHT"

Piece of 8: A friend's collected artifact from a long time ago.

OFF WORLD MEMORIES WITH JAMES

James is an old friend who I met while working on my second feature film "Limit Up." He's African American, a talented music producer and photographer. We've been friends off and on for three decades occasionally chatting online, sometimes over the phone – he's a bit like a touch stone in that way.

He knew me when I was "a famous film director!" as he used to tease me – and when I didn't turn into a famous film director in those three decades, he teases me to say "I was there when you didn't turn into a famous film director!" Funny guy.

Over the years, we've chatted about this research casually – a close friend of his died suddenly, and he told me cryptically that he had a visitation from him – so I offered to see if we could "connect to him" over lunch. At no point in this following conversation is he under hypnosis – he may have closed his eyes to "look more carefully at something" but for the most part, we're just having lunch and interrupted by coffee or tiramisu.

I'm keeping this anonymous, as James too has a career that he may not want people to know he's been "chatting with the departed" but his session is pretty much like the others – except in this case, when I met someone from "another galaxy" I took the opportunity to get a tour of that planet.

James and I are having lunch at a local Italian eatery. We are chatting about a range of things, and something prompted me to "turn on the cell phone recorder."

Hello world. I just asked James if he ever had a UFO experience, and before he could answer, I turned the recorder on.

James looks at me, like "really? You're recording this?"

You gotta trust that whatever you say I'll show it to you before it goes into print. And I likely will mask your identity Superman. So back to your UFO story. Do you remember where you were when that happened?

Yes. I was sitting at our house in Venice – we had a deck I would go up and look at the stars. One night I looked up and there was 6 maybe 8 orange triangles pretty high up – kind of slowed down a bit, then went up a little faster.

Okay, was there any element of missing time?

No.

(Note: "Missing time" for those fans of UFO stories, is when someone has an experience of "being abducted" or being "spirited out of their body." Often they become "conscious" hours after the event, and can't remember anything that happened before coming back to consciousness.)

(I'm not a UFO researcher – but am aware of Whitley Striber's book on the topic, and have spoken to a number of individuals who claim to have seen UFO's. I'll note that there have always been logic problems with the stories I've heard – those kinds of "I flew through the air" or "through a locked house" kinds of things. But in the past I became familiar with those accounts, read Harvard Professor John Mack's work on the topic – where he examined artifacts that people felt were planted in their bodies, etc.)

(But until doing this kind of deep hypnosis research, I had ignored this issue. Until a year or so ago, when meeting a stranger who said he had read "Flipside" and wanted to chat with me about his UFO encounter. I asked him some questions about it – the same way I do here, fully consciously – and when I asked him detailed questions, I realized that these "aliens" in the "UFO" were not alien at all. In fact, when asking him "Are these people inside the craft strangers? Are they just driving by, or do you know them?" He recalled a lifetime on their planet. In the chapter "Over the Rainbow" in the book "Flipside" I interviewed a fellow who recalled normally incarnating on another planet, but had come to earth with a specific mission.)

Rich: In your mind's eye it's pretty clear when you see six orange lights?

James: Yes.

Freeze that – turn that into a hologram that you can move around.

You mean like 3D?

Right – About how far away are the 6 objects? I know it's a rough guess. But whatever comes to mind.

I would say about 50 miles.

Single one out – lead one, middle one....

Okay, the one that is in the rear end left.

So it's now frozen in time and space – zoom up to it, like a close up - get up close to it within a few feet – and describe it to me. Is it triangle shaped?

The bottom is triangle shaped the rest is not triangle, not an octagon.

You mean above?

Yes; below its three points – above it's like scaffolding.

Can you put your hand on this triangle? Where it's light?

Yeah the whole thing was lit up. It feels warm.

Is it smooth, metal, plastic, corrugated?

It feels ... smooth. I can feel it but I can't feel it.

I'm just trying to get a clearer picture in your mind that you can see that I can't. About how far apart are the points of the vessel?

Pretty big – like a couple hundred feet.

Okay, couple hundred feet – now I'm going to ask an odd question but you know the answer to this. Is there anyone aboard this ship?

No. Not that I can see. No one this one... maybe the lead.

Let's go over to that lead ship. How many are aboard this ship?

One.

Try not to judge it. I'm going to ask you about this person, this pilot. Your higher self knows the answer – is this pilot a male, female, neither or both?

Are neither and both the same? Neither.

So – let's take a look at the pilot. In your mind's eye – whatever comes to mind – How tall is this pilot?

He's sitting down.

Is he wearing anything?

How people describe the grays... this person is gray.

(Note: For those familiar with UFO stories, many have described the classic look – "large eyes, gray skin, slender" etc. I have no idea how much research James has done on the topic, but ultimately, he can't have done any research on what he's about to say.)

Don't judge it. Is it a male or she? Let's ask him directly. Are you male or female?

I'm getting neither.

Does he/she have arms and legs?

Long skinny arms and legs.

What color is that skin?

Grey. looks like no animal on earth – looks like cement.

If you could put your hand on it what's it feel like?

Smooth. It has a look of a heavy... cement.

Take a look at his face...

I can't see that.

Okay, can I ask him/her questions and put the answers in your mind. Is that okay?

(Note: If someone was making this story up for my benefit, we'd think they'd be able to access this detail.)

"Yes."

Why are you not letting James see your face... does he have big or small eyes?

He's saying I already know. What I'm seeing is what I've seen before.

Tell me about his skin.

You know how people with bad skin have pockmarks? Kind of like that.

Can we address him as something? A letter is fine.

"Q."

Mr. Q. Are you leading this group of ships are you here because you're driving by, like a tourist? Or are you here for some other reason, scientific in nature?

(James aside) I don't know.

Let me ask him; do you know our friend James?

"Yes."

Would you show James where you know him from?

(Shocked) Woah. That's really weird.

Are we inside or outside?

Inside. Wow. I got chills from that. My old house we lived in in Kansas, and okay.. I was a kid... and I had this recurring dream for years and years and years of being in bed, going into the kitchen, sitting in a chair and all of sudden I could see – and coming through the back door, these skeletons... and they would come over to me.

So Q was that actually you? Masking the part of his brain that could see you and translating that into skeletons? (pause) What does he say?

I'm hearing "Yes." But part of my brain is judging it.

I understand – your conscious mind is going to fight this memory. But what's unusual about it is that you're not saying anything different than what I've heard before – in your mind's eye they were allowing themselves to be seen as skeletons – memory will transpose things out of fear.

I couldn't move; I was frozen.

That's what they call the hypnogogic experience of being frozen in place. But these reports (talking "to aliens) show that when people have an "alien" experience – they realize they aren't "aliens" at all. Am I being accurate Q?

"Yes."

Are you a friend or colleague of James?

He says "I'm a friend."

Q, without causing stress to James, show him the planet that you and him have incarnated on before, when you were friends. Are we inside or outside?

"Outside."

Look at the ground. What's it appear to be?

"Dusty."

Look on the horizon – is it day or night?

"It's dusk."

Look at yourself if you can – look at your hands – are they like the hands you saw earlier or different?

(They are) No different, about the same.

So he's not a "brother from another planet?" That was a joke.

(James aside: Smartass.)

So you're seeing that visual...

But some reason I don't think this is right – I should look different. He looks the same as I described to you...

And that's a bit different than anyone else' report; the pockmarked skin doesn't exist in the canon of UFO reports but it exists in your mind's eye. Where is this planet located?

It's not in our universe, it's totally in another universe, outside of what we see as the border line of our universe; it's way beyond that.

To move from one place to the next, how to you transport?

You just kind of go.

What's your occupation on this planet?

I don't... nothing. (Either I'm getting nothing, or "no occupation.")

Let's go to the place where you reside. Are you in a home, a structure – some place you would consider home?

We're still outside.

People around?

I haven't seen any at all.

How about Q? Can you show James yourself on this planet, what do you look like there?

I just saw the typical alien.

Are you guys walking around?

Yeah.

Let's go somewhere – let's go where others are hanging out – maybe your scientists are located.

There's like nothing around, not buildings... but it's not on the ground... it's hovering.

How many of your entities are on this planet, what's the population number that comes to mind?

Thousands.

Are you part of a greater planet system are you part of an outpost?

Yes. (Outpost).

Are you working for someone? Q put in James' mind the name of this planet, just the first letter of the place.

A...

Like alpha?

I can't pronounce it...

How many letters does the name have?

15.

So like Alpha Centauri is close?

Close.

Q put in James' mind's eye – what does he look like over there – is he taller or shorter?

Just like him – right now there's a covering... (over his skin) like armor.

Q, are you part of a science mission?

"Yes."

Are you trying to help or harm us?

"Help."

How are you helping?

"There's cures for all diseases we have but you don't do it."

So if you're here to help us take care of the planet, what's a way to change the paradigm?

Oh shit. It seemed like something that's really intense... very detailed... but something I can't access.

Can we examine it?

I'd rather examine my skin.

Give me a "1, 2, 3" for what we can do to help our planet?

"Get rid of religion."

Okay, what else Q?

We have a government where everyone is a natural leader.

Everyone is equal? Q have you had any lifetimes on earth?

"Yes, several. Back in the 1940's. A man."

What city did you live in?

Actually in Hawaii.

What did you learn from that lifetime; was it happy?

Very happy, everyone helped each other. (James aside: First time I went to Hawaii... I felt like I was home and I cried when I left.

Q are you talking about James' lifetime in Hawaii or yours?

Both.

Q; are you James?

Yeah. I think so. That's weird when you asked that.

Let me clarify. Q, I don't mean in terms of triples quadruples – the energy you share is with James, correct?

"Yes."

So you share that frequency?

"Yes."

You're here to technically help the planet, to help people to communicate with you? Is that part of your mission?

"It is with everyone."

What were the 6 ships doing here? Does each go out and capture intelligence and process it?

I don't know. It was just something I was always hoping to see... (seeing the UFOs).

People like Q travel here to gather information, not intelligence per se, that somehow James can impart to him – is that what you're doing?

"Yes."

Q, were you here to gather info on your trip here or to download information?

"To pass it along. Communicating but not physically."

I've heard that before, that people here do their "work" while asleep. Also that people get "scanned" for information from their friends from their other planet back home. James you were saying you felt you were being scanned? How big was the scanner?

It felt like it was big enough for two people, it was invisible going up my front and all the way back down and I wasn't dreaming. I was so freaked out I called my friend who is a big UFO fan, a ufo-ologist. He said he'd heard of this before.

Do you know what the scanner does?

"I do."

Q; what does the scanner do? Download or upload information?

"Upload."

Q what's the upload? All the information and intelligence that allows you guys to help this planet?

"Yeah."

Is there any sort of a download?

"Not right now."

And so what are you scanning? You're uploading intelligence so Q and friends... are getting intelligence. Every event you've had – the sum of human knowledge, what they fear, that's why they haven't shown up here – because we haven't gotten to a point in our consciousness where we can't not kill them – but it's worth trying to save this planet. It's a lovely place.

But sometimes you wonder.

Sometimes you wonder. Let's skip forward Q, I want to meet James' spiritual guide. We're going to ask for his guide to come forward. Is it a male, female, neither or both?

I see a woman. My grandmother Elizabeth Pearl.

Who was there to greet you when you crossed over Elizabeth?

My grandfather.

Can I ask you some questions about James?

"Yes."

Tell me what she looks like.

She's in her 70's... late 60's. Brown eyes, hair... grey.

When you hold her hands, what's that feel like?

So soft. But has this energy to it... I feel safety – love.

Pearl are you his guide?

"Yes."

Pearl, let's walk James in to visit his council. Can you do that?

"Yeah."

Are we inside or outside – where are we?

Outside.

How many people are here?

About 20.

How many are members of your council?

13.

How are they arrayed?

Just standing. I'm sitting.

Let's go to the first person on the farthest left.

Female in her 80's. It's my grandma Betty. She's wearing a dress with small little flowers, a flowered reddish orange dress. She still has her tattoos... she was in the Holocaust.

Let me ask you, Betty. How is James doing?

She laughs. "All right."

What is the quality that you represent on James' council?

I'm hearing "happiness and love."

Who's next to her?

My grandfather that I never met – he's wearing a long braid. (Blackfoot). His name is Henry.

Hello Henry. Are you familiar with what I'm doing?

"Very much so."

How can that be?

"I heard about you from my dad." (James aside: that was a weird thing to say.)

(Note: It's an odd question I've started to interject into these interviews. ("Are you familiar with me asking councils questions?") Sometimes members of a council will say they "know of me" or have "heard about me speaking to councils" and sometimes members of the same council say "no." That tells us that councils don't "go over the minutes of previous sessions" or "plan in advance" what is going to be done. Apparently when it's time, the councils appear. It seems to indicate some level of spontaneity and improvisation. I've also visited councils that have empty chairs, and sometimes mid-interview more "council members" arrive.)

Not so weird - thanks for talking with us – James take a hold of Henry's hand. What's that feel like?

Rough. He's a hard working kind of... he's in his 70's.

What's he wearing?

Brown pants, brown shoes, a tan colored shirt.

What word represents your role on his council?

"Protection."

On how many councils do you serve Henry?

"4."

How about Betty?

"1."

(Note: The amount of other councils the council member is part of is not uniform. Some say "thousands," others have said "millions." Some have said a handful, like these. I have no idea if that represents something about the council member or indicates something about the spiritual evolvement of person appearing before them. But I try to ask the same general questions with councils to observe the variations.)

Henry – how do you feel James is doing?

"Better than he thinks."

Pearl are you familiar with his life on another planet?

"Yeah."

How does that relate to this lifetime? Why did you allow James to come here today to see this?

"To get some truth."

Who said that?

Pearl.

What is that, Pearl? You mean as in "The nature of reality?"

"Yes."

How is this new information going to help him with his work and career?

Something's going to happen – I don't know what it is – but it's good. (James aside: I used to have these feelings about something about to happen.)

Somethings going to happen to him or the planet?

"To him."

What do we have of Pearl's? Do you have anything besides her genetic code?

I have the chills... and this. (From around his neck, James pulls a Spanish coin from the 17th century.)

Where did this come from?

Pearl found it buried in our yard... in Kansas.

Whose coin was this?

I don't think she knew, but she found it buried in the backyard, we used to play "Combat" and found it back there.

So Pearl you know what I'm looking at – did you give this to him so he could think of you, stay connected to you?

"Yes."

Who did this belong to? Put it in James' mind.

"Old male. Black hair, native... A native who got it from the Spaniards..."

What tribe was he?

Cherokee. (James aside: But my grandmother was Blackfoot...)

(Note: Blackfoot is a tribe in Kansas.)

What year did this fellow deliver it? Before the house was built?

1670s... 1600's... before 1650.

(Note: Looking up its origin, it appeared to be a coin known as "Pieces of Eight," commonly given to sailors. One coin was worth 8 Reals, or Spanish money. From the markings on this it appears to be from a Portuguese sailor. https://cannonbeachtreasure.com/blogs/news/how-to-read-a-spanish-piece-of-8-pillars-waves-edition)

Okay, let's thank everybody for coming forward...

(James aside;) Jesus, that was amazing.

Speaking of Jesus... before we finish up here – has anyone in this room met him?

(James surprised) Yes, everyone.

(Note: I have no idea why I suddenly asked this question, but for some reason suspected the James had some connection to him. I never assume I'm going to get a "yes" or "no" answer to any particular question, but am not surprised if and when he does "show up." In "Hacking the Afterlife," there are a number of interviews with people who claim to have known him.)

Can he come into the room?

He already did. He's sitting next to me.

Describe him.

Olive skin – dark brown hair... wavy... shoulder length... brown eyes.

(Note: I always ask this question as well – when Paul Aurand, the former President of the Newton Institute told me he had a number of people who claimed to have remembered lifetimes with him, I asked "what he looked like?" The reason I ask is that if everyone said "red hair, freckles" we'd have something to discuss. I also ask for them to "put him in normal clothes in their mind's eye" so they aren't intimidated by the memory of him. Oddly, as you'll see when he does "show up" he often complies with the request.)

Take his hand. Is there any sensation holding his hand?

Massive energy.

What's he wearing?

I don't see any of that...

Let's ask him to put on jeans and a tee shirt.

Okay, now he looks typical. Barefoot. He has dirty feet.

Any holes in them?

James laughs.

He knows I love teasing him. Have you interacted with James before?

"Yeah." A few months ago.

Does James know you from a previous lifetime?

"Yes."

The life you had when you were here doing the cross routine?

"Yes."

Put in James's mind what he looked like back then.

"Same."

What was his role?

"Close friend."

Someone who hung out and traveled with you?

"Yeah."

What was his name back then?

"James."

Is he referenced in... any of the books? There are a number of James.

"Yes."

I assume not your brother James – but put in his mind's eyes what he looked like.

"Lighter... hair... too much hair."

(Note: I'm aware that names are problematic – Jesus was referred to as Issa (or Essie) by his friends "back then" (according to these reports) – so for him to say "his name was James" could either mean he's using the colloquial version of the translated word – or something else entirely.)

Color of his eyes?

Brown.

So James, you're accessing a lifetime you're not consciously aware of; so this is new information. But let's explore it – go back to the first time that you met this fellow, Jesus; what happened?

I felt his energy.

The first time you met him?

His energy – it was overwhelming. The closer you got to him, the more...

(Note: In the film and book Flipside, "Molly" recalls a lifetime where she knew him in Jerusalem. She spontaneously went into this memory on camera, and when she spoke of being near him, she burst into tears and described this "overwhelming feeling of love" when near him. In my filming encounters (reported in "Hacking the Afterlife" I had three different mediums (Jamie Butler, Jennifer Shaffer, and Kimberly Babcock) described seeing him in the same fashion; all three lost their ability to breathe, tears fell from their eyes, and their faces turned bright red.

It's not something that can physically be faked, or created consciously – and when I asked a direct question "Why do you have this effect on people, making them feel awful and look sick?" he said "Because I brought more of source energy to this lifetime, so when a person is near me, they feel that source energy of love." I was surprised he didn't use any religious terms to describe this – and it is in line with what people claim about incarnation. We each bring a "portion" of our conscious energy to a lifetime, so his saying he'd brought "more" made sense, at least to me. In this case, James is not aware of these reports, but is reporting what he's hearing verbatim – not under hypnosis, but sitting in an Italian restaurant.)

How old were you when you first met him?

About 13.

Did you live near him?

The same block.

I've met someone else who lived on his block. Did you travel with him when you were 13?

No.

(Note: This same account is covered in "Hacking the Afterlife" and I know that James has not read it; a woman reached out to me from back East, she'd had recurring dreams about that lifetime. I interviewed her, and she spontaneously recalled living in Jerusalem with him at an early age, described his frequent trips along the silk road, and his profound effect on people who knew him, etc. She claimed that from 12-30 he traveled (taught, learned) back and forth to Kashmir.)

Were you aware that he would go and come back?

"Yeah."

When were you aware things were going bad for him?

"It just became apparent slowly."

(Note: This is reported as well in "Hacking the Afterlife." Dr. Brian Weiss recalls a previous lifetime (in his 3rd book) where he claims he knew Jesus, and had invited him to his home for dinner. Weiss recalled that lifetime while under hypnosis but had not shared it with his audience until he was doing a session with someone, and that fellow recalled seeing Jesus "carrying the cross" up the Via Dolorosa. The client said "And I see you were there too Doctor Weiss" and he described the same unusual "toga with orange piping" that Weiss had identified in his own past life regression. The point being that "things slowly went badly for Jesus" in this account as well.)

Were you there when he was arrested?

"Yeah."

Put it in James' memory – Where were you?

"I was hiding behind a bush."

Did you witness him going up on the cross?

"Yeah."

Did you witness him carrying it?

"No."

How far were you away from him when he was put on the cross?

"About 40 or fifty feet. Just me by myself."

You're looking at your friend being put on this thing; were his hands tied up?

"Yes. Around the wrist. Around the waist."

(Note: In "Hacking the Afterlife" two others reported similar visuals – seeing "his arms tied with leather straps" instead of the traditional "nailing of hands and feet" scenario. I don't know how common it was for people to have their arms tied with straps in this Roman tradition, but it's the third mention of it.)

In your mind's eye – freeze it – zoom up to him and get up there close up – to where he's on the cross. Can you do that?

"Yeah."

Look at your friend. What's your emotion?

"Everyone is around him is crying."

Describe him – what's he wearing?

"He's naked."

His arms are tied?

"Yeah. There are no nails. His feet are tied up."

Does he have that INRI thing above his head?

"No. None of that; he's just up there."

(Note: Again, I'm asking to compare his account with the other two that I've heard from eyewitnesses. What are the odds that I would run into two other people in my lifetime who claimed to have witnesses this event? It's possible that somehow consciousness allows us to "shift" into the consciousness of an event in the past, but in this case, we went back to the age of 13 and have moved forward.)

Go forward, what happened?

"I left because I couldn't take it."

Did you ever run into him again?

"No."

You don't know what happened to him after that?

"No."

Let's ask him – let's go back to where he's sitting down in jeans and tee shirt – this is someone you know, correct?

"Yeah."

Let's ask him – so were you married when you went up there on the cross?

He says "Yeah."

Did you survive the crucifixion?

He says "Yes."

Did you leave with your family and then go off to India eventually?

It wasn't India (at first).

Where did you go? Who were you with?

"Family and some friends."

Did you initially hide out in the caves?

"Yes."

How long did it take you to recover from your wounds?

"A month."

And then you traveled along the silk road?

"Right."

Where you lived out your days?

"Right."

(Note: I could have asked these questions differently – instead of asking for a positive response. But I've done this so often, had at least a dozen people claim to know the same events, that I am "skipping down" in the narrative. I know from these same reports that he was married to Magdalene, had a child, that she was spirited away to France by people who were in on the plot to save his life – including Roman soldiers – that he was moved from the "death cave" up into caves above Jerusalem to recover.

That eventually he met up with his Apostles before "leaving them" to return to Kashmir, where he lived out his days in Srinigar with his family. I'm not digging for those answers, which are laid out in "Hacking the Afterlife." Apologies if it seems as if I'm leading the witness, or making it easy for him to say "yes" or "no" – since I've already heard this story before. I'm just focusing on James' learning this information for the first time.)

I bring this up because you're not gone, you're still here – on the flipside - witnessing without calling attention to it – I asked if Jesus knew your council, James, to see what they might say. So let's ask Jesus a question. So how do you think James is doing?

"Good. Couldn't be better." (James aside: Oh God.) He says "The biggest thing would be to take care of his health so he can do those things."

That he signed up to do?

That I signed up to do. Yeah.

James isn't aware that I've spoken to Jesus a bunch of different occasions, with the help of different people. Mediums, people who've seen him in past lives... and he tells the same story; he's a rebel – but let's be clear this story of you being a god is not accurate, but you brought more source with you like other avatars. Is that correct?

"Yes."

Who do you hang out with over there?

"Pretty much everyone."

Please correct me if I'm wrong, but how much of your conscious energy did you bring to the life of Jesus?

"100 percent."

How about those moments when you were preaching about the future?

"It's not religious what he was saying; just what people claim it is."

*****

As the reader can see – I ask questions and then whatever pops into my mind I pursue. This friend of mine is not overtly religious or overtly alien for that matter. A very talented photographer and musician – and all I can say is "thanks" for allowing me to dig through his journey.

It was a mind bending for me to hear as it was for him to hear himself saying it.

As we'll see – he's not the only one who has memories of alien lifetimes, or knowing Jesus, or even seeing him on the cross. I know how controversial that statement is – but I see my job not to hamper or deny the research – it's to share it. (Again if this bothers the reader, or the listener, please, get a refund, return this book! Do not turn the page!)

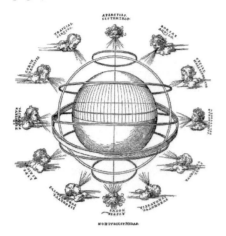

A map of the heavens.

CHAPTER NINE:

"DEVOTEE AND DOCTOR"

Hindu deity

HINDU AND OFF-WORLD MEMORIES WITH "OLIVIA"

This is another really unusual session, entirely unplanned. A film industry executive, who has had a hand in making some of the most successful films of all time, was meeting with his friend, and something she said to him made him think of me. He called me up and said "I have this friend here in my office you should meet."

Olivia (Olivia isn't her name; I've changed details to make her and the film producer anonymous) and I are meeting in the prolific film producer's office on Valentine's Day of all days. The film producer has been involved with blockbusters in the past, and produced one of my feature films.

I asked about a vivid memory or dream that Olivia might have had in her life, of someone, or something.

She mentioned "meeting Shiva" during a trip to India. She saw him as a tall fellow, described him in terms of light and energy, said he was her "guide" (or one of her guides.) She described the typical artistic vision of "Shiva" - hair up in a bun, jewelry around his neck and the trident by his side.

I asked we could speak directly to him and he said we could. I asked him if he was a guide to her alone and he said he was a guide "many." (I think I asked "how many," he may have replied hundreds of thousands, but I didn't have my recorder running) I asked if she could stand behind him and observe herself looking at him, to see what she looked like - she described herself as she is now, but with longer hair... she saw herself as having elaborate makeup on her face like a devotee of Shiva.

I asked Shiva if he could show her a previous lifetime that she had... she described herself in a field in India; a young girl working in the field, who had elaborate paint on her face. I asked about what her life was like back then.... and this is where I remembered I could record this conversation:

Olivia: She's having her family business, (she's) taken care of, I think they have like a farm... she lives in a small city.

Rich: Tell me the name of the city. If you don't mind.

Like Riksha.

(Note: Riksha is actually the name of a village in Rajasthan that is flat and has no mountains.)

Olivia: It's like flat on the field, and I'm seeing that there are cows around me... in the field.

Rich: Are you seeing the makeup we saw earlier with Shiva? Can you describe it?

Olivia: There are some colors, yes, blue and yellow – paintings here... (Olivia has her eyes closed, runs her fingers over her eyelids, under her eyes, and then makes a gesture, like a "curled up" layer) layers and then a yellow layer first, then of blue, red up to my eyes and here as well (swooped up at the eyebrows)

Devotee of Shiva. Photo: Wikimedia

Rich: Is this makeup an indication of your devotion to Shiva?

Olivia: Yes, my mom told me how to do this and I have all this jewelry, this nose ring, flowers in my hair.

What's this young girl's name? Or a name that we can call her by?

Eline...

(Note: She pronounced it Alene – Elina (pronounced Alena) means "shining light" in Hindi)

What year are we in? What year comes to mind?

(Quickly) 1432.

Where in India?

In Riksha...

Let's go to a happy time in this home of Eline – does she have brothers and sisters? Where is she in this memory, does she have a family?

I see her wedding a few years later, there's like a whole.. the whole village or city turns into a festival, I see her on this, like you know – she's going with her fiancé on the streets, everyone is celebrating.

What is she wearing?

She's wearing something like an orange dress.

Like a sari?

Yes.

What is this festival celebrating?

They're celebrating our wedding; everyone is cheering for us.

(Note: Not sure how much Olivia is familiar with Indian Wedding attire, but the Orange Sari is a typical wedding dress)

Rich: Take a look at your fiancée.. does he look familiar in this lifetime of Olivia?

Olivia: "Not yet."

Not yet? But you may?

I may, yes.

What does he look like? Moustache? Facial hair?

He has short hair, he's tall and he has like these dark brown eyes, and then he's wearing also this kind of yellow white dress, these funny shoes on his feet.

(Some common wedding outfits in Rajasthan including "funny shoes" they always wear. Wikipedia)

Rich: What's his last name?

Olivia: Bir... bir..a...

(Note: Bir : Indian (Panjab): Hindu (Khatri) and Sikh name meaning 'brother' or 'hero' (from Sanskrit 'brave', 'heroic'). Bir is also the name of a city in India, connected to Rishikesh or Riksha by road, bus or train.)

Rich: Is he from a poor or wealthy family?

Olivia: He's from a wealthy family.

(Note: If he's from Riksha in Rajasthan, had money in 1430, he's be dressed in the same traditional garb they are today. The town of Riksha is north east of Jaipur, during 1432, the fellow below was the ruler of the region.)

The Rana of Mewar (Rajasthan) circa 1500. Wikimedia.

Rich: Do you have any children?

Olivia: Not yet.

Okay, but let's go into the future of that life. Do you have children together?

Yeah, we have three children – two boys and one girl.

About how old are they when you're seeing them now?

They are 2 or 3 years old – the sons are twins; the daughter is older. So the daughter came first...

Without pain or stress, or fear, let's go to the last day of Eline's life – are we inside or outside?

Hmm. It's night and the I'm in a house... mmm.

Is this your home?

No, it's kind of like a hospital or something they put me in here. I'm not that old, I'm only 35. I had something... my whole family is there; my kids are around me.

Your husband?

Mm-hmm... (yes); he's very sad.

Let's go to the moment after you've expired, do you stay around or head off? What does that feel like?

I want to stay with my family so after I left this dimension I stay around... –

Do they see you?

They feel my presence. The children feel my presence.

Let's move on to the next destination...

Morocco...

Before we come back to the planet... Shiva, I need your help here, where does she go, does she meet with her guides?

(Quickly) Yeah, I'm going up to this meeting.. to have a meeting with the.. 12, like a group of 12 and everyone is there they're asking me, "What did you learn...?"

Rich: Are we inside or outside?

Olivia: We're inside, it's like a room.

Describe the room; what do the floors look like?

Very white.

Very white. Are they slate... marble?

Marble.

Are there seats, pillars, chairs? What's the interior look like?

There are big pillars and long chairs.

You said there were 12. How is this group arrayed? Are they waiting for you? Are they in a line, standing sitting, in a semi-circle?

There's a long table and they're sitting along the table spread out – one of them is standing.

Which one?

The older one.

Is he in the middle?

No, he's on the left end.

Can we speak to these guys? How are you, folks? I hope you don't mind us interrupting you, can we talk to you?

Mm-hmm. (yes)

Let's go to the guy standing, describe him to me.

He's old, and wise; a wise man.

About how old?

About 65.

Does he have any facial hair?

He has long white beard. He's wearing a long white robe to the floor.

Do me a favor, if you don't mind, go as close as you can, what color are his eyes?

Blue.

May I ask a direct question?

Yes.

What's your name, for the purpose of our conversation, a name we can use?

Michael.

Can you look from Michael's point of view at Eline or Olivia, about how old is she or how does she look?

(Describes Eline) She's uh.. about 35. The same person... I see (from the hospital) Same as before, long dark hair – she came (directly) for this final meeting, she's wearing the same clothes, white, kind of bluish that she had in the hospital.

A sari?

Yes.

Can you hold Michael's hands? If so, what's that feel like?

Hard... harder. Dry skin.

You mean he needs some lotion?

(Smiles). He's older. He's old; sometimes they...

I know Olivia doesn't know the answer to this – but Michael, you do – what quality do you represent in her journey? In a word that describes how you earned you this position on her council?

"Learning."

Rich: Learning? What do you mean by that? Book learning?

"Experience."

How do you think she's doing?

"I'm here to help to guide her through life lessons and difficulty she's facing and I'm here to remind her what she's supposed to learn in this life, so she doesn't have to learn them in the next life."

How is she doing?

(Referring to Eline) "She's doing well, in this life she was a little stuck with her parent's pressure, living the life her parents wanted her to live, so she didn't get to learn about (much) and then she married this guy and was living the life he wanted her to live."

You mean in her life as Eline in the 1400's?

"Yeah, it was a lot of pressure on her."

Michael, shift your perspective to Olivia in this lifetime; how do you think she is doing now?

"She's doing good; she's learning a lot of lessons, also, she's went through a lot of difficult tests in her life, examinations."

Correct me if I'm wrong, Michael; Olivia chose this (particular) lifetime.

"Yeah, she wants to finish it. (The journey she started as Eline? or to get back to Elle whom we meet later?) She wanted to finish the journey she started out. She wants to return to life and finish off and come back to live with them... A kind of existence. "

Rich: She wants to "finish her life?" You mean this one or the previous one as Eline?

"She wants to finish her lessons."

So you represent learning. By the way, is he wearing any jewelry on him, necklace on his robe?

I saw a cross.

Let's ask for a second, what's the cross doing around your chest, what does that represent?

"Wisdom."

In terms of what... Is it a decorative cross, Coptic cross, a Jesus cross?

It's a "Jesus cross" but for Michael it's like... health... (could have been "help") **like a talisman.**

You mean it's not a religious icon – not a catholic one, or that it represents religion?

No.

Rich: So Michael I'm going to ask you a couple of questions; are you on any other councils?

"Five."

Are you familiar with the fellow we know as Jesus?

"Yes."

Do you represent anyone (who is also) on his councils?

"Yes, I represent him."

Can he come forward now, can you bring Jesus into this room?

"Yes."

So let's have a little applause for our pal Jesus... tell me what he looks like? How far away is he from you?

From Michael? He's about 3 meters away.

How is he dressed?

All white, long sleeves, (robe) really loose, his hair is brunette, red kind of, with curls... tight curls. And facial hair.

Jesus can you change out of those clothes for the purpose of our conversation?

"Yes."

How's he look? What did he change into?

White shirt. Black pants.

Shoes?

No shoes, barefoot.

The only reason I ask this is it helps to see you not as an icon, but as a person. How do you think our friend Olivia is doing?

"She's doing great, doing a good job."

Did you know her from a previous lifetime?

"Yes, I've known her several lifetimes."

Do mean knowing her in between lives, (where you are now) or past lives?

"Both."

Did she know you in the life as the dude on the cross?

"Yes."

Rich: What was her role in that lifetime?

"She was a man."

Do you want to show her who that man was?

"I was one of his helpers, like a prophet..."

An apostle?

"Yes."

Which one, what name is associated with this one? It's okay if you don't remember the name.

"It's Paul. I see myself in a cave walking with my stick and there an animal behind me and I'm going to find him because I know that he's been in hiding somewhere."

Rich: Where was Jesus hiding?

"He was in a cave for a few days."

Did you find him?

"After a week I found him."

How did he look? Disheveled or healed?

"He was looking very weak."

Rich: Where was he hiding out?

"Up in a hill in a cave, far away."

Who was taking care of him?

"Two people; one man one woman were taking care of him... he wanted to be alone and away from everyone."

Who was the woman?

"His mother."

That makes sense. That must have been pretty startling and shocking that he had to go on a cross.

"He looked very weak, he survived; but he was very weak."

Did you stay friends with him after that? Or did you go off and teach?

"No, we stayed in touch."

Did you go visit him?

"Yes, five years from this point."

Paul, I heard this yesterday; that Jesus' family was hidden for 5 years, and after 5 years they went to see him in Kashmir; was that accurate?

"Yes."

Rich: Did you know his family?

"Yes."

How many children did he have when he left?

"3. 3 or 4."

(Note: Again, consistent with other accounts in this book. He is reportedly to have had at least 3 when he made the journey back to Kashmir. Two boys and a girl. Oddly enough, I had heard this repeated a day earlier and occurs later in this book.)

Rich: That's pretty fascinating to hear. How many girls and boys?

"Two boys and one girl." (Audio is unclear; she may have said two girls and a boy)

So you went to visit him where was he living ...?

"He went to .. first he wandered throughout India... like as a road tripping... he went to all these places and ended up in Kashmir in the mountains."

Rich: So I've heard that he was there before in India and Kashmir. Is that correct?

"He had been in Kashmir before, in his past life or something. He went back to that place."

When you saw him in Kashmir, that must have been wonderful for you.

"Yes, he looked really good, longer beard, looked healthy and strong."

What did you call him in that lifetime if you can remember?

"I knew him from past life; we had a really strong connection. We made a promise to help each other in the next life; that's how we stayed connected."

Jesus, are you helping Olivia in this lifetime?

"Yes, I'm giving her guidance."

What about lottery numbers?

"No, it's not about that. Winning the lottery wouldn't help her."

I'm just kidding. I did ask Jesus for lottery numbers once, via a medium, and she gave them to me. I bought a lottery ticket and won – a dollar. When I won, I heard a voice in my head say "Not very specific, were you?" So Jesus you know we'd love to talk to you all day and night...anyone else on this council want to speak up? I assume because he's standing, is Michael the lead counselor?

"Yes."

Can you put a feeling into her body so she knows this is you reaching out to her?

"Mm-hmmm. Yes."

And you can amplify it? So it's almost like a doorbell ringing, for her?

"Yes."

*Any message you have for our friend **The Producer**? Who happens to be here in the room? Are you familiar with him as well? What would you like to pass to him?*

"Hmm. Keep creating, keep doing what he does."

Is he going to work with you, is he going to work with Olivia?

"Yes. They met for a special reason, so they're going to create something together."

Is this normal Michael, for you to have a conversation with someone you're keeping an eye on? How often do you have these conversations?

"Yes, whenever they need me."

So you serve on other councils?

"Five."

(Note, it's always interesting to ask a question later that was asked before, sometimes to see if the story has changed. It has not.)

Have you ever heard of me?

"Yes. Of course we see everything you guys do down there."

Well, I talk to councils, I'm like the "council guy..."

"What would you like to know?"

*The other day someone said it's **like water cooler conversation**. I'm not asking for my benefit.*

(Note: This **water cooler** reference will return later in another council meeting.)

So Michael, going to your left, going down the row, the word that represents what you're doing on the council. How'd they earn their seat? The person next to you?

"Unity."

Okay, the next?

"Love."

The next?

"Hmm. He's the guy in charge of the others."

Let's go to him for a second.

"This person makes sure that – sometimes, because they are very different people, it gets hectic (in here) so this guy is the one who takes care of everyone."

What's his name? What can we call him?

"Julian."

How's he look?

"Younger. About 30 years old. Blue eyes, short hair. Tall."

Julian, are you sort of the "key person" in this council who herds all the cats to come in here?

"Yes, he's the kind of person who if he sees something is going on that's difficult, he helps. If too much is going on..."

He helps? So what's your quality that you represent in Olivia's life?

"Her higher self."

Okay. The kind of the person who connects her to... to spirituality?

"Uh huh." (yes)

How do you do that? How do you connect her to spirituality?

"Um... through many sources really, signs... and books like – a lot of different sources, he always makes sure she's connected, sometimes she gets disconnected."

Let me ask a mechanical question. Is it easier to talk to her when she's asleep?

"Yes. I send messages to her by night."

But she doesn't remember them when she wakes up, but her higher self does.

"Yes."

Do you have to lower your frequency in order to send those messages?

"No."

Rich: So why did you bring Olivia to this office today to talk about this stuff? For The Producer's benefit or hers?

"No, for all of us. And its uh.. we need to make something happen. It's really powerful and we need to create something... we need like a messenger path for this, also for messages (that come) from up there. They want to help humanity; they want us to do something... like a project or something.

Let me ask you about that... Michael, council, you can all weigh in – in terms of "adjusting the consciousness of the planet?" Why do we need to do that?

"Because we need to raise the vibration of consciousness, otherwise the earth will be destroyed."

Will it be destroyed by others or by humans?

"By humans. We are creating new species or some kind of robots or viral things that will attack us in the future; we are destroying our humanity we are doing something very stupid, so we need to change that."

Is this a likely outcome if we continue down this path?

"Yes."

Has it happened before on other planets?

"Yes. That's why we want to warn them – some other planets like earth were fucked up because we didn't warn them."

Rich: So guys, why don't you just make a dramatic appearance and show up and tell us?

"Because people need to take the actions.

Does Olivia had any conscious memories of living on other planets?

"She's started to remember about six months ago."

I'm going to ask you about that journey. Who wants to help?

Julian.

Julian, I'm going to ask some questions to you about our friend's journey, I understand she has incarnated on another planet, does she often incarnate on that planet or have there been many?

"She had a conflict on this other planet, so they sent her to earth. She needs to go back."

Can we ask about this planet? Is this in our universe?

"It's in our universe a different planet."

"Is Olivia aware of the name of this place?

"Pleiades."

(Note: Here's the wiki entry on the Pleiades, also known as "the Seven Sisters." It's been something that a number of people have claimed (along with other places) where they have come to Earth from a lifetime back on the Pleiades to help with the shift in consciousness.)

Rich: Okay, I've met some folks from there, has Olivia?

"Yeah."

Someone who was introduced to you, or by accident?

"It was like three or four of us were together and we somehow just started chatting."

Let's explore this – can you show her a lifetime on the seven sisters planets? And put her on her planet and tell us, are we inside or outside?

"Outside."

Look around; what's it look like?

"Very dark, it's kind of grayish. It's night... but then I see there is path, like a beautiful bright light... there's a huge building (in the distance)... funny looking."

Why is it funny looking?

"It's not square; it's like bubbles. It's "spacey" looking."

Are you on dirt, ground, or a manufactured surface?

"It's the ground."

Look at your clothes.

"I'm wearing like a jumpsuit and I have really high forehead and big eyes and I've very tall, I'm very big..."

Taller than Olivia?

"Yes."

Take a look at your hand.

"It's bluish. Light blue."

What's the skin feel like?

"It's soft."

Are you male or female or both?

"Female."

Do people procreate in the same way they do here?

"No. I have a white belt and it attaches to machines, so they charge me up or something."

Is it like a healing mechanism?

"Yes; every week we hook up and they put all the information into this port, so you kind of load (it in), like a newspaper but it's our version."

What's this woman's name or something we can call her?

"I just see an L."

Let's call her Elle. Nice to meet you, Elle, and thanks for sharing your evening with us, can you take us to your home?

"Mm-hmm; I have this little flying car, and they go fast."

What's your house look like?

"It's big, it's nice, has two floors, you can ... (pauses) I have a guy - a husband or someone."

Take a look at him. Is he someone you've met on earth or is he only there?

"He's only there."

What's his name?

"Also like my name, I saw a letter. It's the letter Zed."

He's the Zee man and you're Elle? Do you have kids?

"Two boys."

And when you look at them are they smaller version of you?

"They're still younger, so they're smaller."

What's the day like? Is it dark or light?

"It's light, everything lights up daytime."

How many suns?

"One."

During the day, what do you do?.

"We don't call it anything (in particular); we live in communities; this is the community we live in. We encounter each other, we help each other, create new projects together, we have like a working space (together), have these studios, like developing a huge place where we all.. not "work" but we go there, and we are developing new technologies..."

What are some of the new technologies?

"There's a car, like a flying car."

Are there any problems or social issues on the planet?

"No."

What was this conflict you were talking about earlier? What happened with Elle?

"She ... (long pause)"

You said it she did something wrong, got in trouble?

"She just wanted..."

To experience life on Earth?

"She wanted to help humans, they were debating if they should do something or send someone and she..."

She volunteered?

"No, they chose her. She wanted to be here (on her planet) with her family, and they chose her and sent her. She felt betrayed. From their side, they thought she was ..."

How did she come here? Did she have to die in order to incarnate in human form?

"She had to go through like a portal."

Like a black hole?

"She changed her body and everything and she was reborn to this earth."

Rich: You had a life, Elle, on this planet, but to clarify, are we talking about a physical life?

"Yes."

In the Pleiades – What was the name of your planet? Was it the actual Pleiades, or is that a place holder for some other star system?

"No, it's a different than earth. We are in the Pleiades, on a different planet."

What's the name of your planet there?

(Pause – trying to pronounce it) "Kro. Something *Kro*. K, R, O; something like that. They have different letters, you know, in the Pleiades..."

So what do the letters look like?

"It's like signs."

Can you draw the word "Kro" with your hand?

"The k is like this twisted, and this one... (second letter)"

(Observing how she draws the first letter, like the Sanskrit "O" in "Om") It's almost Tibetan.

"Yeah."

Please, draw it again.

"First letter is like that... the L is like this twisted, (circles back on itself) the second letter is like an E without the middle part, *chro*...? and the third letter is like a half moon."

And that means "Kro"?

"Yeah. (There are) like a thousand to two thousand people live in this city."

(Note: Interesting answer, as I didn't ask the question. Almost like she's supplying the answers to questions I should have asked.)

Rich: How many people live on the planet?

"About one million, I think; we're very spread out."

Do you have any conflicts on your planet?

"So, we are debating; I was part of this judging or in charge of whatever this is; I am in charge of whether to help or not to help people in other galaxies. We know that there are people who live in different galaxies and (there are) different planets and life, and we're debating whether to stay on our planet or help out on other planets. Or do some charity work."

And hang out on their planet. Could you breathe on earth? Could the people from Kro exist here?

"No; we have very clear air there, and water. Different kind of oxygen, (it's) a mixture. So, when they come here they have a difficult problem breathing."

So, this lifetime as Elle – was this previous to this lifetime as Olivia or was this a while ago?

"She incarnated as human, she had several lifetimes here, it was not her previous one, she incarnated as a human (before), so she's been here many times."

So, she likes it here?

"She cannot go back because she's completing her mission."

She can go back now (mentally).

"She can't go back and live her lifetime. She wants to go back full time."

Has anybody from Kro visited her in this lifetime?

"Yeah."

Is she consciously aware of that or did it happen while asleep?

"Some asleep, some awake."

So, was she awake (when) seeing a spaceship?

"One time, yes. It was night. She was outside. The craft came really fast, she was standing in a parking lot and the spaceship was coming to her and her ... I had this feeling coming over me that felt like (I was receiving) a message..."

Hold on, let's examine the message. Olivia, when the ship was getting close, freeze the footage. How far away is it in your mind's eye?

"It's 20 miles away."

So, freeze the frame, and now in the frozen frame, move closer up to the ship and put your hand on the side of the ship. Is it hot or cold?

"Cold."

What's the texture of the skin of the ship?

"It's cold but it's smooth."

And how many people are aboard this craft?

"Three."

Rich: I want you to go inside the craft and look at these three people. Do they look like your friends on Kro?

"Yes."

Can we ask the pilot questions? Is the pilot male or female or both?

"Yes, kind of both. More male than female. "

May I ask a direct question?

"Yes."

Hello Pilot. Have you come here for a reason or are you like a tourist just zipping by?

"No, we came to see how she's doing and pass a message."

And to get information from her?

"Yes."

What was the contents of the message?

"We downloaded all the information from her body, which (or what) state of consciousness she's been in, what's happening with her on the planet and we sent some information down as well; but it's (located) in the back of her head." (touches the back of her hair)

Rich: Can we access this information? What can we call you?

"Dee."

Dee, can we access this information you downloaded to her? What is it?

"It's like – codes and numbers."

What are the codes and numbers referring to? Is it information for future use or is it something we can access now?

"It's something that is... um... I got two messages, first one I didn't (know, but) got a month prior to this. I've gotten some other messages, but this time, they just sent it out there because they didn't want me to see anything (consciously), but they wanted to give me a message that will slowly unfold."

What are the messages about? Are they scientific in nature? Are they about consciousness? People she should hang out with or contact?

"These are more like codes (coordinates) – to navigate her to some people in her life. It's like to help her to meet people in her life that will click with some information ... (and then) to pass along secrets."

So, it's like waze for the folks on Kro. Dee, do you direct those codes or does she?

"Whenever she's ready, she gets to one place, and then another place and another person, whenever she completes one task then the next one opens up... like a (video) game, you know?"

I do. Thanks Dee, I appreciate it; I hope we can pass this information to the planet, let us know here that this is an ongoing operation, and let everyone know that this is an operation to heal the planet, to save the planet. I've also heard people say it's to open up or repair the etheric grid around the planet... to protect it... How would you describe Olivia's main job here on the planet?

"She's like a light... a light... worker."

Okay, I've heard that as well. So why did she choose Olivia?

What do you mean?

Why did Elle specifically choose the body of Olivia for this role she was tasked to accomplish

"It was meant to be for her."

So, in your case, you actually volunteered to come here?

"No, they chose me. They volunteered me."

But you're saving the planet. Our planet.

"But I didn't want to."

Well, on behalf of our planet, thank you. All right thanks Olivia!

PRODUCER: You recorded that?

I would never have remembered what she said; I can tell you, people who do this kind of investigation don't remember anything either. So, I've learned my lesson; always turn on a recorder, just in case, and you can transcribe it all later, and see what makes sense. In this case... wow.

I typed up a transcript and sent it to the both of them, the producer called me later and said "So now you're telling me that people remember little green men on Mars? What's all this got to do with the afterlife?" I tried to explain it as best as I could – but suffice to say, it only makes sense in light of the other reports.

Again, I'd never met this person before, she has not read or has any awareness of my books or research, the Producer has a casual awareness of it, but I don't think he's read any of the books either, perhaps watched "Flipside." He heard her talking about some of these concepts and invited me in to explore it further.

Olivia is an actor, but I've never met her prior to this interview, and have not met her since. I'm fairly certain she doesn't remember anything she said during it, but she was not under hypnosis at any moment in time, we were drinking coffee while I asked these questions.

If it was by itself, one could argue that it was fanciful thinking, but as demonstrated, it falls in line with the other sessions that I've included in this book, including off world experiences.

But it is fascinating to hear someone confirm what everyone else says, even in this casual improvised way. I follow this person on their Instagram account, and it's funny because I'm aware that she had no conscious memory of this interview (as noted, she wasn't under hypnosis, people who do these sessions often "forget entirely" what they said during it.)

If I run into her in the future it will include me asking "so how much do you recall of what we spoke about?" But the point is – she's not "making any claims" about these memories at all. She's just answering my questions – just met her for the very first time, and within a few seconds of me asking if she can access a memory or dream, we are off and running, talking to her guide and council members, friends on other planets.

I wouldn't have believed it myself if I didn't have the foresight to pull my cellphone out of my pocket and hit the "record" button and keep a record of everything said. Since this interview I haven't run across "Olivia" but when I see her on social media (a successful model) I can't help but marvel at her session.

Please allow me to say it one more time; this interview only makes sense in light of all the other interviews in this book.

CHAPTER TEN:

"TIBET; THE LAND OF SNOWS AND NEAR-DEATH ADVENTURES"

Josh at the foot of Mt. Kailash

My friend Josh lives in New Zealand. He was a film student at NYU, helped edit the documentary "Journey into Tibet with Robert Thurman" and this conversation came out of my hearing that he "had a near death event" while we were on Mt. Kailash in Western Tibet together. I was on this trip but was not aware this event had happened, and when he told me about it, I asked if he wanted to "explore it" on skype.

He's not a medium, we've never chatted about the flipside before in detail anyway, and although we shared an incredible journey into Tibet and a kora of the sacred mountain, this is the first I've heard of any kind of "flipside" experience with regard to my friend.

Rich: So, let's have some fun – you can access any memory. Let's go to back to our trip to Kailash. Where were you when you had a near death experience?

Josh: We were at the highest point up on the Drolma pass – it was daytime, what happened was we got broken up – (our guide) Sanjay Saxena was not around, group kind of separated, I don't know who you were with on the pass,

I was walking with that girl who walked Kilimanjaro – she taught me "the alpine mountain step." Honestly think she saved my life; I had no problem walking at altitude with what she taught me. I was fine. You know "move your hips, not your legs."

You're not overloading your spine.

People passed me who were gasping for oxygen, but I was with her and I was fine.

She's a Facebook friend of mine – probably yours too… she was walking with that Korean doctor on the trip – he and my sister saved my life that day. At the time, I wasn't walking with my sister, Emily, but I was keeping an eye on her. All I remember is getting to the Drolma pass and seeing the prayer flags... There was a German mountaineer up there – he looked at me and we were giggling. Prior to that, the entire day I had a headache that was literally a jackhammer – trying to turn inside out in my brain.

The higher you got the worse it got?

If you want the definition of ignorance is bliss – I had no idea was cerebral edema was – I just didn't think about it. It was super-duper intensive headache. Seeing that guy was the first time I laughed – I was criticizing myself, "How could I not enjoy this moment?" I was chewing Tylenol like M & M's – he was super-duper high and I said, "What's so funny?" He said, "It's so funny to see someone from another fascist country up here."

That is the last thing I remember hearing – that's why it really sticks out in my head. After that – I don't remember hitting the ground, but I was on the ground.

What was your next moment of consciousness? You don't know how long you were out for?

I don't think it was long.

So, let's talk about this outside of time moment – this is the part we can explore. What's the first conscious thing you're aware of?

I'm above my body – but I don't know I'm above my body – a point of view that is slightly higher than my body – maybe ten feet.

Can you see it now?

Yeah.

Go to that moment and take a freeze frame – a hologram, a screen shot – make it a hologram, so you can move around it. Look down. Are you looking at yourself?

Yes. I'm wearing a north face jacket; silver metallic black.

How's your body arrayed?

Like in a fetal position. The thought process was... it wasn't a white out or black out - it was a straight cut – "Cut to." From talking to this person, to being about ten feet up from my body and the thing that I most remember is my voice this voice, same voice no different.

What are you hearing yourself say?

I was getting my bearings... "What's going on, what's happening? Where did we go? What just happened?"

Freeze that if you can. Put yourself above your body – look up and look around you. Is there any other thing or person around you or nearby?

Yes, there's white light. I call it "The glitter milk."

Okay. How far away is that?

It's in the sky. I didn't pay attention to it at the time until I turned my consciousness up – while I was above my body – what I realized was here's my consciousness – "Where am I what's going on?" ... hearing that voice. So first it was the landscape, which was amazing, looking out from the mountain, then looked down and saw my body – and I remember thinking... well seeing your dead body and going into the habituated thought – "Jesus that's bad" - but another part of me said "It's not bad. It's not anything. That's your body."

Then I thought "I'm still me, I don't have my body but what else do have? I don't have guilt or shame or pain or history... all of these things that I really owned as a physical body were gone. Gone." And it was the best laugh.

The feeling of what?

Lightness... of just being. Of a million different people in your life and your own untrained mind – I had never been free of that. That was a radical dip into that universe – it was amazing, and I loved it. I literally looked at my body and went "Okay, that was fun ... it was good to cruise around in a convertible on Sunset Blvd, but I'm done."

And my consciousness turned around – facing upwards. The sky instead of blue it was like two giant vats are being poured into the sky – a kind of like glitter glue – from two different vats.

Mixing together? Look at the one on the left.

It's like a "pouring" of this light. Like a milk/sky type thing. It's hard to describe. It's an all-encompassing light that you can enter.

Did you enter it?

I wanted to.

That's why I'm asking. You're facing that light. Take a hologram of that. Now go up to the light – not in it. Just closer to it. Try to put your hand inside of it... what's that feeling?

Like... "you're home."

Okay.

You're really home.

Okay, they aren't the first person who's said something like this to me – but let me ask; what does "home" mean to you?

You are absent of all the of the... You're like a leaf of lettuce returned to be the lettuce... imagine a salad... and you return to the head of lettuce. And there's no salad dressing. Raw lettuce.

Are there any feelings associated with that?

Yes, but it was more the absence of the things – like an absence of guilt.

So here we are at the edge of this – glitter milk. You put your finger in and you have this exponential feeling of home, right? Now put your foot in there. Step halfway in. Can you do that?

Yeah, sure.

What's your body feel like?

Just … totally… love. And um... yeah. Love.

Okay get your ass in there. Now what?

It's OM. Just *om*. Not home.

You mean Home without the H. Okay, let's got to the next event. Especially if people are around. I'm going to ask your guide to show up – male female or neither or both. What comes to mind?

Robert Thurman comes to mind.

Because he'll confuse our narrative – let's for the sake of our conversation – ask your guide to appear as someone other than Robert. First, let's ask him – are you Robert? Or someone like him? Are you showing up as Robert because it's easier for us to access this visual?

I'm asking him.

He's going to put the answer in your mind. What does he say?

He said "No, I'm Stephen Spielberg."

That's funny. What's that joke mean?

I think it means "I'm someone that Josh holds in high regard, but on a temporal basis."

Okay, I understand. He's a guide, he appears as Thurman, but it could be anyone he can appear as. For the purpose of our conversation, it's mundane to appear as someone we know– as Bob the Cable Guy – but for the sake of the conversation, can you choose an avatar? Perhaps choose somebody that's familiar to Josh or yourself. What do you appear as?

I see my father.

Is your dad still on the planet?

Yes.

Let's look at this guide carefully. How tall is he? What name does he want us to call him?

He's about 5'8 and he says, "His name is Bob."

Okay, Bob, can I ask you direct questions?

He says "Yes."

Are you Josh's father? Yes or no.

"No."

Give us a hint as to whom you are – put an avatar that Josh doesn't know in his mind. Describe him.

Okay, he's got on a vest, a button-down white shirt corduroy pants, professorial. Mid 40's brown hair, hazel eyes.

His name?

I get an A... then R... then T.

Can we call you Art?

"No."

Arthur?

"Yes."

(Note: I asked "Can we call you "Art?" The answer was "No," which indicates that Josh is not trying to "help with the narrative" and that people on the flipside can be very specific about what they want to be called, for whatever reason. "Not Art. Arthur.")

Okay, very good. Thank you – I'll refer to you as Arthur for the purpose of our conversation. How long have you been with Josh?

80 years.

Have you been with Josh in any of his other lifetimes?

"Yes."

So that's a joke; "80 years?"

"Yes."

I get it – if I have to, I can translate his jokes to you.

Josh aside: I've never done this.

It was a trick question – I know that he's been with you for all your lives or at least many of them. So, I figured I'd ask. If I may Arthur, have you ever incarnated with Josh?

(Note: People on the flipside are not in any state of "Gee! I'm talking to the people on Earth!" - the way we sometimes feel about "channeling" someone not on the planet. And in those cases, we can miss the "jokes" or their ways of teasing us with an answer. In one case, (in "It's a Wonderful Afterlife") a guide was seen wearing a monk's cloak, and when the hypnotherapist asked him directly, "Why are you wearing that outfit?" the women started to laugh uncontrollably and then said "He said "His clown outfit is at the cleaners.")

"Yes."

Can you put that in his mind's eye? Where are we?

Outside. I can feel sand. I'm wearing a toga... it looks like I'm an extra from the film "The Ten Commandments."

Let's find out. Where are we on the planet?

We're in Egypt.

What's a date that comes to mind?

I'm in Egypt. It's desert – biblical times. We're talking B.C. Probably about 2000 years B.C.

What city are we near?

Near Alexandria.

The lighthouse of Alexandria from antiquity.

Step outside of this guy – look at him.

He is early 20s, has brownish brown hair - good tan, good complexion.

What's his name?

S or an M. I... M... like "Sim." (Selim?)

Let's call him Selim for now… so what occupation does he have?

He's a slave. He's moving brick... or stone…schlepping.

Go to the moment when Selim is having a hard time moving this stone… Is he building a pyramid?

Some construction that is not his own.

In Alexandria?

Outside in the desert. We are in the desert building this thing.

Go to a happy time when Selim was a kid – sit down look around who's there?

I see my mother; I don't see a father; he's got two little sisters.

Look carefully – they look familiar to you in any way?

Not really.

So eventually he becomes a slave worker – who is in charge?

He certainly doesn't know – it seems like a pharaoh – it's not a pyramid thing… at the point at which I'm seeing right now I can't tell you.

Is it a tomb, house or temple?

It's like a temple.

Let's go to the last day of Selim's life.

We're outside. He's beaten to death.

Who did that? His master does that?

Looks like it; looks like he didn't finish the job.

What happens after he dies? Does he hang around or go somewhere?

He goes… he's released as well.

You're back in that light, the glitter milk, aren't you?

Yeah.

Who greets him on the other side?

His father.

Where does Arthur take him? Should we go and visit his council?

He says "Yes, let's do it."

Arthur, thank you for doing this. Let's visit his council.

We're inside; it's like a courtroom but built out of white pearl.

So, you can see the walls?

Yeah, the floor is white pearl as well. There are columns; it's a circular room with columns around.

How many counselors are here?

Six; in a semicircle.

First person on the left – male or female, neither or both?

It's neither… kind of a… more male.

Is it okay to ask you some questions?

Yeah.

What's your name?

"Sith."

Thanks, Sith. Describe this person to me –

He's sitting down. But if he was standing, he'd be about 6 feet tall. No hair... back eyes.

Sith, can Josh take your hand in his? What's that like?

(Feels) Kind of dread.

He doesn't like to be talked to I'll guess. What do his hands feel like?

He kind of seems alien. He's got three sort of fingers – it's like almost like a claw; but very benign looking.

Soft or hard claw?

Soft, kind of mushy.

How are his eyes?

Normal sized eyes – all pupil; all black.

What's he wearing?

Doesn't look like clothes – looks like the same skin on his hand, like a putty... but it's like a sheeny putty.

Cream colored?

Grey.

Sith – can I ask some direct questions?

"Sure."

Are you familiar with me or the work I'm doing with councils?

"No."

What's one word that represents your quality on Josh's council?

He said "Discipline."

Where are you from Sith? Are you from a planet in our universe?

"Another universe."

Let me ask you this; has Josh had a lifetime on your planet?

"Yeah."

If it's all right put that lifetime in his mind. Where are we?

Inside. (I'm) In a building, seems like a very mechanical, almost like a fertility clinic.

Have you been in building like this one in this lifetime?

No!

Is this a fertility clinic? Is this where he works? What does Josh look like? Male or female?

Neither – he kind of looks like Sith.

What is Josh's role in this lifetime? Scientist? Doctor?

Yes. Doctor. It has to do with fertility.

I assume that's why he put fertility clinic in your mind. Are you guys having difficulty with fertility on your planet?

No.

Is there a problem related to it?

No.

Do people from your planet come here to Earth?

Yes.

What can we call your planet?

Organ.

Oregon? I've been there. (Keeping this light)

(Josh laughs)

I only ask because if I run into someone else from this place, I will know – is there a role that Josh has on our planet related to this lifetime? Is he a kind of doctor helping the people on this planet?

You mean Earth? Yeah.

Put that in his mind. What role does Josh play in terms of helping the Earth – is he visited by people from our planet for information?

"Yes. While he's sleeping."

So, he's not consciously aware of having an event or talking to aliens?

"No."

But you're showing it to him now (that he has).

"Yes."

How does the information or intelligence get passed?

"We experience it while he sleeps."

What's the value of that information back home on your planet?

"To make better people."

To make better people on your planet?

"No. Making better people on Earth."

"It's a cookbook!" Just kidding. So, you're helping alter the consciousness of this planet; is that correct Sith?

"Yeah."

Is it a physical thing? This altering the consciousness of the planet?

"No, it's changing thought patters and habituation – I... yeah..."

(Note: The idea of "making humans better" isn't a reference to physical alteration (DNA etc) but often to a "spiritual adjustment" which may be understanding how thoughts turn to language, how visuals turn to information in the brain, and how humans emotionally react to different situations. I've heard consistently in all these reports people are not allowed to "interfere" with the progress of another planet (sounds very

Star Trekkian) but they can help humans to "sense" or pick up on information they previously may have missed.)

Thank you Sith. Let's head back to his council. Sith represents "discipline" – let's speak to the person on the council next to him. Who is that?

It's a woman, she looks about 65. She's blonde, in good shape. She has blue eyes.

What's her name?

"Sonam."

Thank you Sonam. What is she wearing?

Like a white – not a toga – if you saw "Defending Your Life" the film – like that.

(Note: Odd yet cogent reference. Michael Newton described the film in "Flipside" as being accurate, and I reached out to Albert Brooks via his assistant, mentioned these references to see if he was aware of the similarity between his film and deep hypnosis reports. He replied that he was not aware of any connection between his film and these reports, but here's yet another one.)

"Defending Your Life" Meryl and Writer/Director Albert Brooks. Wikipedia.

I did. Yes, a plain toga. Is she wearing any jewelry?

Her smile is incandescent.

If I may ask; what quality do you represent on his council?

"Beauty."

The appreciation of it?

The "beauty presence" in all things.

Sonam, has Josh had a lifetime in Tibet before?

(Note: I ask because Sonam is a typical Tibetan name.)

"Yes."

Could you show that to him – where is he?

"He's on a mountain."

What's he do for a living?

(Josh aside) It looks like I'm always schlepping, Rich. It looks like he's a Sherpa.

I would have thought monk – but in retrospect, Josh is a guy who has chosen lifetimes where he helps people from one place to the next by moving and assisting, is that correct Sonam?

"Yes; he likes to help."

Why did he choose that life?

"He likes to help; he also has trouble standing still."

Sonam and Sith – for both of you; how is Josh doing in this lifetime?

"Pretty good."

Any adjustments he needs to make?

"He needs to stand still."

By standing still do you mean stay calm. Meditate? What's a good way for him to practice that?

"Stand still." It's quite profound what they're saying… I've been moving a lot.

Sonam, Sith, give him a visual of how to do that; stay still.

"He can do that where he is."

Let's talk to your lead counsellor.

He's a bald male...kind of boring in my judgement.

(Laughing) Well, I wouldn't say that about my council leader.

He kind of looks like an attorney. His name is M...o...n...t... y.

Okay Mr. Monty, thank you. Would people on this council consider you the lead guy?

"Yeah."

How many councils do you sit on?

"6000."

How about you Sith?

"4800."

Sonam?

"26,342."

Jesus you guys are busy – I appreciate the answer – either that or y'all have a great sense of humor. How about you Monty? Are you familiar with my asking these questions?

"Yes. They think you're on the right path."

It is a little unusual – usually when people meet their council - they've just died, and they have to go through those emotions. In these sessions, we're visiting briefly, not planning to stay.

"You're like the court reporter."

It does help center people and it does help them with some kind of encouragement. What's a word or emotion that would describe what do you represent in Josh's spiritual journey?

"Equanimity."

Thank you. Other than "slow down" - what does he need to do?

"Find the laughs."

That's pretty valuable. Anyone on this council represent laughter?

"Yes. He's kind of Robin Williams/leprechaun kind of guy."

Let's talk to him for a minute.

He looks like a wild-eyed half leprechaun, half satyr.

Cool. Like a gargoyle?

Like a leprechaun torso and head with a horse/pony like legs and attachments.

What's his name?

"Skizmack."

Can I call you Skiz for short?

"Skizmack."

(Note: Again, I tried to shorten the name, he insists I repeat it precisely as we'll hear in other council sessions. Like, "If I'm going to tell you my name, the least you can do is respect it and say it.")

A leprechaun from "Role Amongst the Fae" W.B. Yeats's book

You represent laughter in Josh's life?

"The lighter side of things."

Can we visit the planet you're from? Has Josh had ever had a lifetime on your planet?

"No."

Can you take us there? Is it here in this universe?

"Somewhere else. In another universe."

Okay. Let's look at your family Skizmack; how many are in it?

"About 8 children including himself, a mother and father."

Do they all look like him?

"Kind of."

Skizmack – I'm going to ask you some questions if you don't mind - is your planet the source of our myths about leprechauns?

"No."

But people on your planet have appeared to folks on Earth, correct?

"Yeah."

I'm not saying <u>you</u> in particular are the source of those myths – but someone from your planet showing up on Earth – maybe a whole crew of them having fun?

"Maybe."

Put that in Josh's mind – you guys sound like you might be the source of those stories; am I wrong?

"You're right." It's blurry though. You can't get a direct answer from the guy.

It's not exactly a normal conversation.

(Josh laughs.)

I've talked to folks who've had a lifetime as a fairy… a medium who when she was a little girl, remembered meeting a gargoyle – I interviewed the gargoyle – he said "It's not my fault I scared her as a little girl, most people don't see me…" So Skizmak, I'm just pointing out you're a Leprechaun – so where the heck is the Lucky Charms? Have you heard that one before?

"No." He doesn't know what you're referring to.

Okay, sorry. Let me ask; does your planet look like Ireland?

A little bit – it's very green, but it's quite dark.

What I'm suggesting is, perhaps an Irishman had a near death event and saw these leprechauns on this planet...

"Yeah, whatever."

I'm observing that most mythological creatures in our history are not from our planet, but they met or saw them in their actual existence.

All I'm getting from him is him saying "Interdimensional travel is very real."

(Note: If Josh were trying to convince me of some kind of mythical reality – even with a Joseph Campbell reference – he likely would have said "yes, *we are the source* of your fairy tales." But instead it's **"interdimensional travel is very real."** I can't imagine any reason for Josh to create that thought. We have to wonder why most of us are not aware of it – perhaps the filters and limiters on our brains not allowing us to see or access these other folks.)

Would the other two council members come forward?

One looks like the father in the TV show "The Brady Bunch." His name is Ennit.

What word or quality do you represent on Josh's council Mr. Ennit?

"Peace."

Thank you. Did he earn that from a difficult life or were you bringing peace to him?

"He earned it."

Does he want to see that?

"He can examine it. We're inside a cockpit of a plane."

Is this World War I or II?

"Two."

Take a look at him.

He's American. His name is Major Deluca or Deluise -something Italian.

(Note: This is the crew that flew "Lady Belle." Pilot   HANLON, JACK T., 2LT, 0672084 CoPilot   HATTLE, JAMES S., 2LT, 0692786 FE   MCCARTY, WILLIAM L., CPL, 37196353, RG   **DE LUCA, EUGENE E., SGT,** 33586632 From a military website which lists all WWII flight crews.)

Major – what squadron are you in?

"I'm in Mayfair – he's in the Air Force. I'm hearing Mayfair."

Did you die in Europe or Asia?

"In European theater."

Were you shot down?

"Yeah."

Over what country?

"England."

Over Mayfair?

"Yes."

Thank you- what kind of plane were you in?

"A bomber."

Other guys went down with you... Name of your bomber?

"Lady belle."

Was that the Memphis Belle you're referring to? The one in the film?

"It's a different plane."

Any reason for Josh to look up your lifetime?

"Not really."

(Note: How accurate are these memories? I'm casually asking a friend over skype to recall something and he suddenly remembers dying in

World War II in a bomber. So, I took the time to track down Major Deluca (He was a Sergeant when he arrived in England aboard the "Lady Belle.")

The bomber Lady Belle that Josh has neve seen but is remembering.

What did you learn from that lifetime?

"Not to die in fear."

That's an unusual choice for Josh; mostly he's been schlepping – why did you choose a life to fight?

"I thought it was right."

It was an adventure – did you have any kids; a family?

"No."

You had an adventure… if you're going to be on stage 100 times might as well be in a bomber at least once.

"It's similar to other lives – he wanted to help."

Let's go back to Arthur for a second. How much of your conscious energy did you bring to this lifetime? How much of your conscious energy did you bring to Josh's life – to the guy who nearly died on Mt. Kailash?

"26%"

Why did you allow him to have that event on Kailash?

"To change direction."

We met a monk at Lake Mansarovar – Bikash Giri; he said the mountain changes people who make a trip around it. Is that accurate in terms of Josh's journey?

"Yeah.... I... (unintelligible)

You were saying something?

I was talking to Arthur. About the change that occurred in Josh. "He's got to figure a way to get the best out of himself. And make the things that are very complex and frightening in their complexity make them... simple."

What's a 1, 2, 3? Is there a particular meditation he should try?

"Teach himself or get himself to a place where he can – teach others to go inside and experience the lightness he and the others have."

****

As noted above, I took the time to track down this World War Two lifetime to see how accurate it might be. I did forensic research to find that the manifest of the Bomber he mentioned included a fellow that he mentioned. It's not an opinion, theory or belief that Joshua remembers being on that plane; he remembered the name of his fellow airman. I know that Josh has no awareness of this previous lifetime. I would be remiss if I didn't pause here for a moment to thank Sgt. Deluca – who is now my pal Josh, who is living large in New Zealand.

Thank you for your service, sir!

CHAPTER ELEVEN:

"WE WERE BLESSED TOGETHER"

Staircase of the Peabody Library in Baltimore. Architect E. G. Lind

I was doing a radio interview with a blog radio host in Australia, when she told me that one of the members of her "inner circle" wanted to try to see if we could "get anywhere" with this *"no hypnosis technique* I'd told her about." I don't actually know the woman's full name – but for purposes of the interview, let's call her "Rosie." She's not a medium, psychic or friend – just someone with an interest in the flipside.

After asking Rosie if she had any odd dreams or events in her life, looking for a "gateway" for this technique, the following occurred:

Rosie, tell me a dream or visitation you've had, something visual. Your mom passed when you were 12 did, she come to visit you?

Yes.

What's her name?

Lydia.

What's the first event that happened?

Seeing her in the kitchen in a light blue nightie.

Okay you were awake. I want you to go into this time packet; picture her standing in front of you – can you remember that moment?

Yes.

Freeze it – tell me about her nightgown.

It's floor length.

Is it one she used to have?

She could have owned it don't remember.

Okay, in this frozen photo – take her hands in yours. What's that feel like?

Soft. And cool compared to mine.

Let's warm them up; Lydia can you warm up your hands for her?

Yes, they're actually lighting up.

About what age is she?

20's late 20's... she passed at 47.

What color is her hair?

Blonde, strawberry blond, my eyes, blue. Shorter hair. Shorter than mine, curly.

In your mind's eye shift behind her; how does she see you?

"As love."

At the age you are now or then?

It's like "Dr. Who" – you know, like morphing all at once?

I think so... don't judge it – multiple images but the first thought is love. Lydia are you familiar with what I'm doing?

"Yes."

Lydia – who was the first person to greet you?

"Her mother."

Was that a shock or expected?

"It was a given."

How do you think your daughter Rosie is doing?

"Better than she thinks."

Thanks – important to hear – "better than she thinks." Let me ask you some questions – is Rosie on the path she chose?

"Yes." She's showing me little diversions… Woops!

Show her sometime recently when you were there to help her.

She's showing me playing music… I sing, I dance.

When she's outside of herself singing and dancing; you're connected?

She's saying "It's more than that."

Stay with us, would you ask for Rosie's guide to come forward? Who comes forward? Light, a male female, neither or nothing?

The first I can see is a friend of mine that's passed – her name is Rana.

Rana can you come forward? Take her hand in yours.

It's very light. She says, "very light."

Are you Rosie's guide?

"At this point in time." She says I have multiple, but she's been working with me recently.

Are you familiar with what I'm doing?

She's familiar with it, but not with you.

How do you think Rosie's doing?

"Step by step," she's saying.

A little tougher or a critic than her mom. How do you manifest in her life? Dreams or … how do you guide her?

She's my guide in meditations.

Rana, can you walk Rosie in to visit with her council?

"Yes," she says.

Describe what you see going in.

What I'm seeing is the room is quite dark, a bit of a light sort of table... with light. There are a few empty chairs, there's about four or five (people.) Sitting, but one has an empty chair next to them. There's space around the side.

The reason I ask is because we can ask why there's an empty chair. Who's the first person to the left?

Male... has the appearance of younger, but his wisdom is much older. He's about 30, sandy hair, salt and pepper. He's wearing a robe. He stood up – the robe is paneled not really a color, just getting dark and light (colors), a feeling of a gold in there.

Let me ask him – what's your name?

"Martin." I got that before you asked the question.

(Note: It's one of the things I like to point out. "When you hear an answer before there is a question," it means you're connected.)

Nice to meet you Martin. Do you get a lot of people asking questions?

He said "He's done this before. Not with you, someone else."

You've had an interview where you spoke to someone from earth who's come to talk to you?

"He's spoken to an intermediary," but... I'm getting the impression they weren't on Earth.

How many councils to you work with?

"Many."

So, this happened on another council?

"More than one," he says.

Have you ever incarnated on earth?

"Yes," was the answer.

Have you ever incarnated with Rosie?

"Yes."

Do you want to put that in her mind?

Oh... he's saying, "Sorry -- the empty chair was mine."

I was going to ask – what was your relationship to Rosie in that previous lifetime?

He said, "We were blessed together."

Where was this lifetime?

"In America." I'm getting it was in the 60's... but I was born in the 1960's.

Near what city was this life?

I'm hearing Begona... Pegona?

(Note: There is a "Patagonia" in Arizona and a "Begonia Bend" in Texas.)

You're showing her a lifetime in the 1960's?

"Yes. 1960's."

Let's not judge it. Martin what was your role in that lifetime?

"Mentor."

What was Rosie's role?

"Student. Lover."

I understand what you're saying but Rosie does not. This lifetime she had in the 60's was this one of her lifetimes, she had some of her conscious energy in that lifetime?

He's saying, "Yes."

What did she learn from that lifetime?

"Freedom."

Is this person still alive?

"Yes," was the answer.

We only bring about a third of our conscious energy to a lifetime, it's not often, it's rare, you're the first person I've met who is aware of it. But by having a lifetime now as Rosie, you can also have a lifetime as someone else – we don't want to get into it too far because the revelation would disrupt Rosie's current life, correct Martin?

"Yes."

You could tell us who she is, where she is, etc… that's unusual. By the way – Martin is wearing a toga, does he have any jewelry or medallions? Wearing anything?

When you said that he held something up, but it wasn't there before. It's almost like a mandala.

Martin show it to her.

It's very geometrical… it's like sacred geometry but very, very intricate.

Is this something Tibetan from the earth or off the earth?

Off the earth.

Tibetan Sand Mandala; it represents a blueprint for a 3-D building one meditates into existence.

Martin, what's a word that signifies your role in her life – your journey? What's a word that represents your role on her council?

"Producer" is what comes to mind – doesn't make sense to me.

It makes sense to me – Is that associated with this mandala?

(Note: In my interviews, each member of the council has some role that they represent for a person. In this case "Producer" likely means "someone who orchestrates things.")

"Yes," was the answer.

Symbolic of the production of creative things or of people or what?

Creative (things) came to mind first, then I was shown light coming out of the center of it.

(Note: Interesting visual. In terms of other councils I've never heard of something like this, but I have heard of ornaments or one who saw a "star that was literally a light that could be used as a portal." So, while it's not something we might understand, it represents symbolically the quality that it represents in Rosie's spiritual evolvement.)

Has Rosie ever seen this mandala other than here?

Yes, he's showing me like a thing elsewhere – up above – (Rosie's hand is in the air) multidimensional...

So, she has seen it before in her sleep or subconscious but not here?

"Yes."

(Note: I ask this because there are many mandalas that represent something else; since she's never seen it while being conscious, it's interesting to hear that she's seen it before, just not when she was awake.)

Give us a glimpse of what Rosie looks like to you Martin, from your perspective?

Okay, what I'm getting is the picture I got from the other lifetime – the tall thin... like...

Say that again?

Tall, thin, but similar features... but slightly different.

Do you recognize this person as you?

No, not initially no.

But this is you – this is her, correct, Martin? You're showing Rosie what she looks like between lives?

He's saying, "other aspects."

(Note: It's an unusual perspective, seeing ourselves from their point of view between lives. I pointed out that when I was able to see myself during my second session, looking as I did in my 20's but hadn't seen that visual since then. It also had "other aspects" of who I am/was.)

Martin, could you introduce her to the person on the other side of the empty chair?

It's a female. I'm getting "No words for now."

May I ask why doesn't she want to talk to us?

She's saying, "the time is up."

(Note: Later Rosie noted that she felt she meant "the time of the zoom session we were doing was over.")

Before we go – who is the spokesperson for this council?

"Besides Martin? No one."

Martin is fine – let me ask this question – so how do you think Rosie is doing? You'll be the third person we've asked. How is she doing in terms of her spiritual evolvement?

"She's doing well."

Can you put a sensation in her body that is like your "Bat-signal" for her so she knows you're trying to reach her?

"Yes."

You don't have to tell me what it is… this is her way of knowing you're always connected, always tethered, is that correct?

"Yes."

Anything else we can share with people?

"Allowing. Allowing is the most important thing. In order to make things happen you have to allow them to happen."

Let's return to Lydia for a moment, if I may ask, why did you have to check out so early? Does your daughter know the reason?

"No."

Do you want to tell her?

"It's not the time."

Do you want me to tell her?

"If you want, yeah."

I can only tell her that based on the research, each journey is for a reason, each ending as well. But as we've heard; Lydia, you are never apart from your daughter.

"Yeah. What she's saying to me is... that "It wasn't for me to say it, but for her to realize it.""

May I ask Lydia, have you incarnated somewhere else?

"Yes."

How much of your energy is currently in that lifetime?

She said, "a quarter." (25%) It's what I got before when you talked about that.

(Note: People report that they bring "about a third of their conscious energy to any particular lifetime" so this fits.)

Does her daughter need to find her? What's she doing?

She's doing humanitarian work. In India. In the south.

Are you in Kerala? (the southernmost Indian state)

"Yes. Kerala."

Are you male or female?

"Male."

But you're helping people what? Eat, construct, produce?

"Eat and drink..."

And how old are you in this lifetime?

I'm seeing a tall, thin male - the body looks young, but the face looks older, it's shifting from smooth to older.

Kerala is a very interesting place in India; it's where Thomas the apostle landed. I've been there…

My mother's maiden name was Thomas.

Is that going to be disconcerting to your daughter, knowing her mom is already back on the planet?

"No."

Moderator: "Okay everyone, we've run out of time…."

*****

Prior to an interview, I have no idea if these sessions will work or not work. I have no idea if they've read my books or have any familiarity with what I'm about to ask them. I'm as surprised as they are that we get anywhere. But just another of example of how far one can go in a short amount of time without any hypnosis required.

CHAPTER TWELVE:

"SING AND DANCE MORE"

Actress Scottie

I was chatting with my friend Scottie about the flipside. We met through a mutual pal, the film director Phillip Noyce, and she was reading something I had written about the flipside and reached out to me to see if I could learn anything about her recently crossed over relative. I told her I'd give it a shot. What I know about Scottie is that she's a Harvard graduate and a successful actress. We met up at Hugo's restaurant in the valley. My questions in *italics*, her answers in **bold.**

Richard: So, put yourself in a space where your guide would be, where do you normally go when you meditate?

Scottie: A light place. I feel like it's got some green.

Describe that to me.

It's warm, it's like a yellowy green.

Any trees or water?

No, just color.

So where in this space?

It's kind of soup-like.

Let's ask Scottie's guide to talk to us – is your guide a male or female?

I think it's a male.

You feel like he's a male, about what age – young or old?

Old.

About how old? Over 50?

Millennia.

Let's ask his name.

"Oscar."

Have you met him before?

My psychic friend says we did. But I haven't really met him before.

What's he look like?

He has blue eyes, brown hair, he's a little bit taller.

Oscar, can Scottie take hold of your hand?

Woah. (Reacts) An electric shock of goodness. Just really warmth, familiarity and comfort. Wisdom. Purple light.

While holding his hands, imagine yourself looking over his shoulder at you. How does he see you?

Just like a big light... a purple gold aura. Kind of lit from within.

Oscar if you can help her manifest a physical form of Scottie instead of this light; what's she look like?

Kind of like wearing a Greek goddess like thing. I'm about my age now, maybe a little older. Rich, brown hair.

Like Hera? More Hera than anything else?

Yeah. A bit of Venus too.

Goes without saying. (laughter) Is she wearing any jewelry?

"It's like a sparkling white gold outfit, the whole dress is like sparkling."

What does this costume represent if anything?

"Royalty."

Show us the lifetime where she was royalty. Where are we? Inside or outside?

Outside. I see green. Grass. I'm barefoot. We're like outside in rolling hills. Feels like England.

if I was going to ask a date for this, what's the first one that comes to mind?

1520. I'm in north London. Like further north.

Why are you in this outfit?

I'm kind of escaping my duties.

What's your name in this lifetime?

Sophie.

So, who's family are you related to? Queen or king?

Queen Anne. She's like a cousin, sort of.

Go to your home, inside having dinner at a younger age, who's at the table? Do you recognize anyone from your current lifetime?

My older brother.

What's your mother's name?

Maria; she's French.

What's your dad's name?

Drake. Last name... Rem. Something Rem.

What's his occupation?

He's wealthy. Landowner perhaps.

From Drake's point of view; about old is Sophie?

15. She's smart.

Let's go forward in her life – does she marry, have kids, get married?

No, she's not married. She preferred not to be owned.

Okay, let's go to the last day of her life. Where are we?

Inside. Some sort of stomach illness. She's 80.

What did she learn in this life?

"Feistiness."

Where does she go after she dies?

"She goes up."

Is that familiar?

Like a pull... like a powerful pulling; it feels really good.

Who's there to greet you?

Oscar.

How does he feel Sophie did in that lifetime?

"Pretty good. She kind of skirted some responsibilities."

How do you think Scottie is doing in this lifetime?

"Pretty good. She's actually trying too hard. She feels as if she's skirted..." (laughs)

First where do they go after coming to this place?

"(To) A place with lots of feminine energy... sort of like a spa... like a witch's circle. Like a "good witch" circle."

Is this a place for her to recover?

"Yeah."

So, look around this coven.

"Yeah, there are 8."

Is this her soul group or council?

"Feels like a council."

(Note: If someone mentions a crowd of folks in a room or outside, they're often either a "soul group" or a council. I'm skipping ahead because "Oscar" knows where I'm aiming.)

So, he's taken us to visit the council – are we inside or outside?

Council anyone? This from Virgil, courtesy Vatican library

Feels like inside, but because of thick tree overgrowth.

How are they arrayed?

In a circle. Some are sitting; some are standing.

How about you?

I'm lying down. It feels like (I'm) healing.

Let's pick some council members to talk to – who wants to go first?

Isabelle. She's elegant, gentle, about 50, wearing a flowing blue dress. Big blue rings around her neck.

What does that represent?

An expression or emotion.

Take her hands in yours, how do they feel?

Soft.

Any emotion?

Relief.

Can I ask Isabella a direct question? Is that okay?

"Yeah."

Are you familiar with what I'm doing?

"Yeah."

What am I doing?

"Guiding."

As well as asking councilors questions. Is that annoying?

"It's okay."

How many councils are you on?

"Nine."

Does Scottie know any of the other people you serve with on?

"All of them."

What quality do you represent that you earned this spot on her council?

"Truth."

Is that something Scottie learned during a lifetime?

"She's learning it now."

And next to you?

"Elizabeth." She's golden. She's like 25 (years old).

If you hold her hand, what do you feel?

Radiance.

What's the quality you represent in Scottie's journey?

"Radiance."

(Note: Funny. Answered my question before I could ask it.)

How many councils do you sit on?

"Three."

Is that because of your age – does someone older have more councils?

"Not really no, I just like to keep it light."

How is Scottie doing?

"She's been through it – she's starting to connect to me, to build up radiance."

Is there anyone on this council that is the spokesperson for your council who wants to come forward?

I feel like a man is here.

What's his name?

Edwin. Looks like Gandalf. Blue eyes. Beard. About 80.

Let me ask is this familiar what I'm doing?

"Yeah." He says, "Amusing."

Why do you find it amusing?

"Because it's just... it's important work."

How is Scottie doing?

"She's... funny. She's doing well."

Anything you want to tell her?

"Lighten up."

She needs to lighten up. Is she on the right path?

"Yes."

Anyone else want to come forward and speak to us?

Teresa. She's kind of like punk.

Teresa what do you want to tell her?

"Dance more. Dance around with life more and dance physically."

How many councils are you on Teresa?

"Five."

Edwin?

"Twelve."

So, Edwin, you are aware of what I'm doing?

"Yes. She's been waiting a long time to do this."

Is there a sensation you can put in Scotties' body head to toe?

"We want to give her a good feeling... there's a tingle in her hand and pain in the back."

Oscar, I want to walk her into her soul group. Observe the people who've been helping her through all of her lifetimes if you can. Are we inside or outside?

We're outside. There are 12 people, five boys and seven girls.

One of you come forward to talk to us, you know who she is, give her a high five – not every day she gets to come and visit you guys.

It's my big brother.

There he is again – in your life and with Sophie in that life.

He's solid.

Can I ask him a question about this boyfriend she broke up with recently? Give her a thumb reply. Up or down?

(frowns) He's giving a thumbs down.

Let's go to the lifetime, Oscar, are we inside or outside?

It's the same one I was talking about... where he was shooting me.

(Note: When going into a discussion about her current boyfriend, she mentioned a dream where he was shooting her with a bow and arrow.)

What year is this?

It's during the Inquisition.

What country are we in?

In Spain. He's a soldier...

Is he wearing armor?

No. Like a rebel outfit.

So, he's fighting against you?

No; *for me.* He shoots me – because I'm on the pyre and he's trying to make my pain shorter.

Burning a witch at the stake was popular in Europe during the Inquisition.

Are you a man or woman?

I'm a woman.

Who put you up there?

A priest.

Are you a heretic?

I'm a witch.

(Note: There was a vast witch hunt that went on in Spain during the Inquisition which outpaced the Salem Witch trials. Nearly 7000 were rounded up and dozens burned to death. The burnings "auto-da-fe" were scheduled for Church holidays so the townsfolk could watch them burn on a holy day. (Wikipedia "Basque Witch Trials"))

So out of love for you, this fellow ended that lifetime? Where did he shoot you?

In the throat.

Got to give him that. Tough shot to make.

He's a very good shot.

Let's go back to a happier time in that life, before the witchiness happened, describe it.

I'm with my girlfriend... and he's a young soldier. We're like in a village. It's outside of Barcelona.

Let's talk to someone in the town... you recognize someone?

A girl. She's my friend (in this life). She's tall and ethnic... brown eyes. We're good pals.

Why were you accused of being a witch?

Predicting the future.

So why did Sophie choose this lifetime which included torture and being shot?

Because I tortured people in a previous lifetime. I was being very judgmental.

(Note: This is a common refrain; people often report an alternate experience to the one they've just experienced in a previous lifetime, to learn "both sides of the coin.")

What did you learn from that lifetime?

I learned "fear of expression."

Not that you should be afraid of expression, correct?

Yeah.

By examining that life and this life and what they have in common. Who represents that life on your council?

"Isabelle." She represents Truth. I'm also getting a "Jasmine" is here.

Let's talk to her. Take her hand – what's she represent?

I'm getting "singing... and harmony."

Oh, we said that earlier – describe her.

She's very exotic. Black hair, long; all the way down. (I'm seeing) This is somewhere in South Africa maybe...

Jasmine, do you represent dance in our friend's journey?

"Song and dance."

What do you want to tell Scottie?

"To sing and dance more. She knows that."

What's she wearing?

A thick necklace and beads.

How many councils are you on?

"Five."

What's the beadwork represent?

"Africa."

Anyone else on the council want to come forward? How about Jessie. (Scottie's grandmother) Jessie do you mind?

"Sure."

How old does she look?

Like 70.

Can I ask you some questions? Was that me and Jennifer talking to you last week?

"Yeah."

(Note: During a session with Jennifer Shaffer, I asked questions on behalf of Scottie to her grandmother who had passed away.)

You told Scottie to do something more? What was it?

"Sing."

What kind of stuff should be singing?

It's... a noise. No, it's like mantras.

You mean like Buddhist chanting?

"Yeah."

(Note: That's the first time this kind of advice has shown up. We've heard "people should meditate" that meditation helps people to adjust to the planet, as well as to help them access loved ones no longer on it.)

Tibetan monks in prayer.

(Note: I've filmed various Tibetan chants which are said to promote long life, heal people in general, or to express some metaphor of enlightenment. I've witnessed the Nechung Monks chanting while the Oracle of Tibet goes into a deep trance, as if their chanting helps him to access the frequency required to make a connection. See "Sacred Chants of Tibet" for a music CD that I made with the Nechung monks.)

Anything you want to tell Scottie or your son her dad?

"That he's done a good job."

Oscar, kudos to you to allow us to have this journey – thanks to all of you including the boyfriend.

"It feels like there's going to be more with him."

At least now you have context about those dreams; you can't save him, and he can't save you, but you can enjoy each other's company – that's important to discover.

"Right."

....

By just asking simple questions, one can access their council, their guides, their loved ones on the flipside. They may feel that they are "making up the answers" but when the answers are compared with the other cases, the same details are offered.

Dance and sing more indeed.

Author with the State Oracle of Tibet; Nechung Oracle Kutenla

CHAPTER THIRTEEN:

"A LIGHTER POINT OF VIEW"

Wrigley Field; hope springs eternal.

I've known "Mitch" since my early days in Los Angeles. He is originally from my hometown and actually worked in Wrigley Field selling hot dogs. He went on to create series like "Doogie Howser" and others with his writing partner (and pal) Nat Bernstein (who appears anonymously in another book).

Mitch told me a story that is included in "Flipside" about how one day his mom told him the story of seeing her late husband walk into the room dressed in pajamas, go the edge of the bed and get in it, just as he'd always done while alive. He looked at his wife, said "You were wondering where I was, I'm right here" and disappeared.

We met in my local cafe; Cafe Luxxe. My questions are *in italics*, replies are **in bold.** I turn on my cellphone recorder:

To recap, I asked Mitchell if he had a guide, and you saw a woman?

She's willowy, hippie-ish, moderately thin, green eyes, blonde gray, straight hair.

I'm going to ask her some questions – is that okay?

"Yes."

Did you bring Mitch here today?

She's like that's why we're here.

What's her name? First initial?

She said "Brook." First thing she said.

Sometimes people do get a visual, this is not someone you know or someone I know. She's going by Brook. Is that a metaphor?

No, she's saying it's straight up her name.

Brook, how many lifetimes have you been keeping an eye on him?

"I've always been," was her first response.

Okay, that was a trick question. If she's your guide, then it would be all of them. Let me ask you some questions. How's he doing?

She's happy. He needs to chill. "Sit by the brook and chill."

(Aha, she is a metaphor!)

You were there when he planned this journey; you and Mitch worked out what he was going to do, kids, etc. Is he on the right path?

"Yes." She's saying yeah, she's feeling like for the most part, he's on the right path, following the path.

You want to show him where the path veers?

The metaphor I get is rocks in the river, I've gone around them, I've had rough waters, I've handled them for the most part.

Are these rocks lessons or jewels for Mitch?

She's saying "They're more like an obstacle course – like a river with rapids, you have to maneuver around them, sometimes you tumble and go over them in the water. And sometimes you come up spitting water, I've worked through those stresses."

Is there any time you've been with him Brook, during his lifetime – some incident where you interceded?

She went to ... she's showing my daughter's adoption – she was taken from me and she came back.

(Note: Mitch and his wife adopted a baby girl, and the mother changed her mind at the last moment. And then after a few months, changed her mind again and they adopted her.)

Did you intercede emotionally? Structurally?

She helped the birth mom be okay with that.

Brook let's walk Mitchell in to visit with his council. What comes to mind?

We're outside. It's not really a place, it's like clouds, like in a clouded place...

Outdoors but like in deep space?

Just a floaty cloudy place.

Look around this structure – is there a floor? Or clouds?

We're above the clouds, when you look down you see down to the earth, there's like this classic like council place with five people.

Are they sitting in a row?

Semi-circle.

Go to the first person on your far left.

It's a male. About 70. Sitting. He has a kind face, grayish beard.

If you were going to cast him?

He looks like the actor who played "The most interesting man alive."

What's this counselor's name?

Begins with J. Like Jedidiah or something.

Jedidiah. Is that right? What can we call you?

"Jed's good."

Walk up to him, take hold of his hand; what's that feel like?

Very welcoming, firm but also soft. He does a two hander. The emotion makes me feel like I'm "Okay." That idea of that I'm met with calm. It's also encouraging, supportive, also kind of... to not forget to be on, to stay on the path. It's almost like a proud father.

Let me ask Jed some questions. I'm just curious. How many councils do you sit on?

"Many. More than a 100... countless."

Does Mitchell know any of the people whose councils you sit on?

He's saying "no" –... now he's thinking.

He's got to go through them all! Let me ask what quality you represent that got you a place on his council – your role in his life and journey.

He's saying, "I'm just one of the pillars of support."

You're a guy of support – but correct me if I'm wrong, please. You earned this place or represent something Mitchell learned from one or all of his lifetimes. Is it being a pillar of support? Being a standup guy?

"I'm here because he has something to share, has always had something to share and I'm here to help him support him in that sharing."

Am I familiar to you what I'm doing (talking to councils)?

He says, "In an indirect way, people have attempted to communicate with him (before) but never as directly."

So why is this becoming more prevalent now? Something that used to be sacred or sacrilegious... here we are in a coffee shop just yakking with you. Has there been a shift in consciousness? What's happening?

He's saying it's specific to the recipient, the openness where I'm at. Everyone has a specific reason (why they might access this information).

What's Jed wearing?

Just like casual linen pants and a white linen shirt, open; chest hair.

Let's go to the person next to Jed – is that a male or female?

That person... he's showing me a woman, she's similar to Brook but different. She's in her 70's. Her name is... I'm coming up with Mia.

That's fine. May I call you Mia?

"Sure."

Take her hands – what's that feel like?

It's exciting. I feel like... thrilling. She's communicating a feeling of thrilling.

Is that what you represent? Being thrilled? (She says later "life force.")

"Yeah."

How many councils do you sit on?

"Not as many."

So, Jed was bragging?

(Mitchell laughs) Her response was "not as many as Jeeed."

I like to stir it up with councils I meet. So, Mia how many?

"100's."

That's a lot.

She says, "But compared to Jeeeed...."

Ha. Okay, what do you represent in Mitchell's journey - the thrill or excitement of being alive?

"It's all of it, mindfulness of the moment."

What's she wearing?

She's got some necklace with some amulet... I don't know what it is.

She knows what it is. Describe this amulet – is a creature? A thing?

She's saying, "It's a living stone."

Okay.

"It's a life force."

(Note: In the many councils I've met, I've heard of many unusual pieces of jewelry that represent some kind of insight, teaching or symbolic metaphor. The "star" Tony Stockwell saw was described as "a portal to other dimensions.")

Stone amulet

What she's showing me is when she and me experience those moments of excitement; this thing literally pulsates.

Who created that?

It was passed on to her by her ... she's saying, "It was given to her by a counselor."

Cool. Mitch, have you ever heard of such a thing?

"No."

I just wanted to clarify. You're seeing something that is new for you to observe, not part of your consciousness. I've never heard of such a thing, it's new information.

She told me she has a little version of it. (?) By the way the person sitting next to her is an older man; he's telling me "Everyone here is getting their sense of humor from me."

Mia can you put a sensation in Mitch's body? A feeling of this life force stone.

She just did.

Okay, let's talk to the guy next to her.

His name is Henry. He looks like... what would be a Borscht-belt comic in his 50's... loose tie, Rodney Dangerfield kind of a guy...

Henry, how many councils do you sit on?

Rodney Dangerfield. I played his "hands" in "Meet Wally Sparks" where a friend had me dress in his clothes and play the piano.

"Just a few. Between 10 and 20." He's very specific that he's saying he's offered (to sit on councils of) people but he makes discerning choices.

(Note: First time I've heard that a council position is part of their choice as to whose lives they'll actually put up with.)

Who makes the offer?

It's not a higher council, it's almost energetic; that's how councils come together.

Henry have you ever had a lifetime on earth?

"Yes, a long time ago." I think he's saying somewhere 3 or 400 years ago.

Were you a funny guy then?

"Yeah."

Funny with your friends? Or for money?

He says "It was both survival, the conditions, but seeing that era that was like.... medieval... It was in the middle east, there was a lot of stone and markets."

Would you call yourself a standup back then?

"I had a light point of view."

Let me ask, how do you think Mitchell doing?

"He was a good choice – he's saying he was a good choice to take on."

What do you represent in terms of Mitchell's spiritual evolvement?

"Humor."

Are you the spokesperson for this council?

"We all speak but that's Jed. (He's the spokesperson) When they need to communicate he's there."

Henry, who's on your left?

It feels like a young girl. She's like 12 years old. Her name is A... Aly.

Nice to meet you Aly; how many councils do you work on?

"Just a few – ten." She's wearing like a sun dress and she has her bike. I feel like she doesn't want to be hanging out – she'd rather be riding her bike.

What's the quality you represent in Mitch's life?

She's saying that (the quality is) "there's more to come."

You represent the future?

"Yeah."

Take hold of her hands.

When I take her hand, I feel like I'm on my own bike and riding.

So, this is the embodiment of that kind of emotional thing?

"Yeah."

I appreciate you coming by to say hello, never met anyone quite like you. Okay, who's next?

Oh... that's my dad.

Is it your dad or someone who looks like him?

It's him. He says, "call me Frank."

What's he wearing?

Casual windbreaker; dressed casually.

Frank this must be a little weird for you – is it?

"No, it's nice." He's saying he talks to me all the time.

Funny, it's one thing to talk to our relatives, but another thing to hear them reply!

This is what I was going to tell you, but we veered off to the talk to the council. He did reach out to me.

Let me ask you Frank; how is Mitch doing?

"He's doing well."

How many councils are you on?

He hasn't been around that long; he likes to be close to my family – a few.

Have you had any other lifetimes with Mitch previous to this one?

Two or three.

You want to show him one?

Yeah, he's showing me. We're in an old ballpark and he's in the stands watching me play.

You're playing. How are you dressed?

I'm in an old uniform.

The year we're in?

"1942."

City?

"Polo grounds."

That would be the Giants, I think.

"Yeah."

Give me the name of this player. Who was he? First name?

"John.... "

Second name?

"Williams."

Any relation to Ted?

"No, unfortunately. "

(Note: There are websites for everyone who played baseball, stats of all players who were on the Giants, but then, it could have been a team they played, or even could have been minor league as the polo grounds had three fields. I've found "Woody" Williams who played for the Dodgers in 1940's, but in 1942 was on the Reds... but he could have been "playing at the polo grounds" against Brooklyn.)

The Polo Grounds, 1940's

Who said that?

He did.

So, John Williams, your dad has introduced us.

Now he's saying I got it wrong; my dad was the player and he was in the stands.

So Frank, were you John Williams? Or is this your son playing or someone you know that's playing?

He's saying the dates may be wrong – but this is *him* playing on the field.

Okay. I'm told we only bring about a third of our consciousness energy – you can be here, the higher Frank somewhere else... is that what happened Frank?

"Yeah."

(Note: I reported in a previous book how Mitch told me his mother reported one night after Frank's passing, he showed up at her bedside wearing his pajamas, got into bed with her. She was shocked as she watched him walk in, sit down and get into their bed and then disappear.)

Frank, what did you say to your wife when you went to visit her in Florida. You walked in wearing your PJ's... right?

"Yep."

Why'd you scare your wife in this way?

"To reassure her everything was going to be okay. And as I communicated to her, I wanted her to know I was okay."

So, you picked a scenario that was calm?

He says, "There was no good time would have not freaked her out..."

Why are we being allowed to talk to you today? What's the reason behind it for Mitch?

They know I'm struggling.

What's up with Mitch waking up in a panic, worrying about stuff? Is this from a previous life?

His response is "I thought I took care of it!" I didn't tell you, we got sidetracked, but he came to visit me. I was fretting about this, half awake, and I felt a hand on the back of my head. I knew that

was my dad and he was saying "It's okay." And now he's saying, "I've been over this (with him)."

So tell us; what are the lottery numbers Frank?

He's saying, "It's not about being given, it's about the work."

Yeah for your son Mitch, that's true – but for me, I need the frickin' numbers! (Laughter)

"I'll come to you privately."

Okay! Let's hear some applause for Mitch for what he's doing. Frank when Mitch chose this lifetime and pitched this idea "I'm going to do comedy and write;" who's idea was that?

What they're saying is, that "It was a combination of all of them being ready for this life, for me to follow what they planned, but they allowed me to (ultimately) make the choice."

Say that again?

"They came together as a council, formed the opportunity for me to choose that path."

(Note: They all came together to make sure this lifetime worked.)

Did he turn down any other choices?

Yes. My dad is saying he was a businessman and "Mitch could have chosen a safer path" and the council is agreeing.

Instead you decided to take a detour and go into comedy?

To go to Hollywood and do something creative. That's where the council came in and allowed me to feel secure to take the risk.

Brook – anything you want to show us? Applause for all of you. High fives.

She's saying... she's showing me in my backyard with my dogs, new dogs and new wife and being okay. She's saying ... "Whatever happens is okay, everything is in its place."

What's a way to help him when his mind is accessing the fear, the part where he freaks out. What image can you put in his mind to combat that?

I think there are two – "The reassurance we are here, and (then) striving to have the life force (creative spark); that combination is going to sustain you."

Mitch, do you have any questions for them or anyone? You can't ask questions about your future – you can ask about the past.

My instinct is to say "Put the word out to my daughter's council to reassure her (everything will be okay.)"

Well, I'm going to type this up for him, and maybe he can show it to his daughter – you said "reassurance..." Can we reassure his daughter?

They're saying "absolutely."

In terms of her journey... what was behind that choice of coming to Mitch in the first place?

"We did this."

Who's we?

My council.

So, Mitch is not responsible for screwing anything up at all?! Let's just say that. They could have said something different like "Mitch is responsible..." but they didn't. They said, "We did this." Cool.

They're kind of saying that... Brook is the one saying this, "It's up to her to access her council more."

Brook correct me if I'm wrong, but people who adopt children sometimes see the process in their dreams. My agent adopted a girl in China, and then through deep hypnosis, saw that he knew her from a previous lifetime.

Interesting apropos of my wife, for whatever reason, I always remember this recurring vision of finding this California blonde that I eventually found.

Let's ask your guide Brook if that's accurate?

Brook is saying it's "spot on." It made so much sense to me when I met my wife.

Is there anything else he needs to explore or examine?

Her first response is to say "As much as I want things, work, to be on my schedule; it's not on my schedule. It's on their schedule." On the other hand, my dad is saying "She's right and it's okay and you gotta trust in the process."

Thanks everyone.

"Come again bro."

Any lottery numbers? C'mon...

He says, "While I appreciate you helping Mitch, I've got a lot of grandkids."

Hilarious. Thank you!

I've known Mitch a long time – I know that he's a writer and a professional storyteller. But as demonstrated, his experience, trip to his council was pretty much the same as everyone I've interviewed without hypnosis as well.

All Star program from 1942

CHAPTER FOURTEEN:

"YOU DON'T WANT TO BELIEVE WHAT I'M TELLING YOU"

Bestselling author of "37 Seconds" and film/TV producer Steph Arnold

Some years ago I sold a screenplay to Paramount. It was a comedy about spies, called "Spy School" and I wrote it with an actual Mossad agent. The studio ultimately passed, but I met the head of film production at the time, David Kirkpatrick. Out of the blue (there are no coincidences) I got a note on social media from David, who had heard one of my audible books about "Hacking the Afterlife." He suggested I have a chat with his pal Steph Arnold.

Stephanie is a best-selling author who had a near death event that was so dramatic, she's been on Oprah, Dr. Phil and others talking about it. I suggested we might try an online Skype session to see "where we might go" by me asking her about her experience. We chatted a bit about her background in science, her education and background in the television industry, and various other topics before we began.

Rich: Did you have any experiences before your near-death experience that were other worldly?

Stephanie: I would see things like in high school that others did not know. For example, I knew that a school mate was being sexually molested, and she hadn't told anyone.

Where'd you go to school?

Palm beach. Ultimately, I felt like was willing stuff to happen because I was thinking about it – like when my uncle died after I knew it would happen. So, I shut it down. I spoke to my Rabbi about it. My grandfather grew up in Cuba, and I knew my grandmother had this ability (to see or sense things), but his family didn't believe in it. But when my grandmother had a heart attack on New Year's Eve, I just knew it. And it was the exact moment (it happened.)

I think that's the definition of quantum entanglement.

It's too hard for me to understand the intricacies around it – "Quantum Physics for Dummies" is my guide.

Tell me about your near-death event.

Three months before my NDE, I saw what was going to happen. I was about to have our baby by C section, but I had a premonition of what was going to go wrong. I went to the head of gynecology at the hospital, I told my doctors and anyone who would listen that there was going to be a problem – they did many tests, and all were negative. They thought it was related to my being pregnant with a boy, perhaps something to do with his testosterone. They were dealing with data.

Then I delivered a happy baby boy which I always saw in my premonition; and then I was dead. The only reason I'm alive now is because of an anesthesiologist saved my life. She heard me talk about my feeling something bad was going to happen, she flagged my file and just in case, brought a crash cart to the operating room. As she has put it, "there was no reason for her to be in O.R.;" There already was an attending anesthesiologist and there was no medical reason for her to be there.

She said she "just had a bad feeling" and about 20 minutes after I delivered my baby, it happened. Kidney failure, medically induced coma for 7 days. Exactly what I had told them.

Afterwards, they're in a teaching hospital in Evanston and they wanted to know how I knew, "How did you know?" I was like "You tell me!" As my recovery happened, I was able to talk again, breathe, but I had PTSD, and I was afraid to live. I had seen everything so clearly in advance and had no idea why.

It was like I imagined a car crash that was going to happen, and it happened exactly as I pictured it. So, I went to a traditional therapist – they'd ask "How can we help you?" And I'd say "Tell me why I knew beforehand what would happen?" They couldn't. A friend of mine suggested regression therapy – I was willing to try everything, as I couldn't function – my husband was like "Why do you want to go down this path when you're healthy?" But I was beside myself.

So, I sought out an associate who worked with Dr. Brian Weiss ("Many Lives, Many Masters") in Florida. We did video conferencing. She got licensed in Illinois in order to treat me. That worked because there was a calm familiar aura about her; I was in my own home. I've never been hypnotized; I don't know if I can be because I'm type A.

I taped my sessions because my memory was awful; I spoke fluent Spanish prior to the flatline event, and promptly forgot. I had thirty sessions with her.

Was she doing one-hour sessions?

Yes.

Well, that's one thing about the hypnosis I've filmed – they do four to six-hour sessions, and people just are able to deeper in one or two days.

She asked if I wanted to know about my past life – I said no, I'm interested in the 37 seconds when I was dead and what happened prior - and what happened during my NDE? She took me back into the operating room; you go in as an observer, you're unlocking the film strips in your brain.

There I was, as Steph, watching me on the operating table – then my pov shifted so I could get the different moments clearly. I was having a C section, there was a curtain, my eyes were taped shut. I was able to see who hit the Code emergency button, what was happening down the hall, I saw the nurse who jumped on me, I saw my husband who wasn't with me as he was on a plane – and a number of other things. In the footage from the event, you can see me on camera violently reacting.

With the doctor's hypnosis, I was able to feel the release of that – I was relaxed, and you can hear her say on that audio "It was powerful." She said sometimes the patient feels better under hypnosis – and that's all you need. (Without explaining what happened.)

I said that's not good enough for me, I have witnesses. I explained to her that I saw spirits, hundreds of spirits, there were things I saw, and I've read enough about it to realize I was someplace else.

Well, you're speaking to the choir. In my research I try to focus on new information – information that occurs during a near death event that you couldn't know or did not know – later on you are able to verify what happened.

The hypnosis represented a sense of peace; my therapist said, "You get validation and you'll feel better." I had tapes of me under hypnosis describing exactly what happened, but I had never heard from anyone in the hospital what happened. For example, I said our doctor didn't deliver the baby – the resident delivered him – which was not in our file; my husband thought I was batshit crazy. My husband was like she's not even in the file – and I was saying "No, this other person delivered the baby, not our doctor."

So, I gave the tapes (of the hypnosis sessions) to the Doctors. The anesthesiologist saw the tape and said, "What you've said under hypnosis is accurate, it's identical." A nurse came down the hall while I was there, and I said to her "You're the one that broke my ribs!" She began crying and ran back to her office. My husband was like "What just happened?" I told him I saw it in my therapy. And I confirmed that our doctor did not deliver the baby, and the doctor told me "I was down by your feet, but you shouldn't have known that." I told her she was saying "This shouldn't be happening; this shouldn't be happening" over and over. I said to my OBGYN – "Did you say that?" She said "I did. But in my head. Not aloud."

That's great.

And then I interrupted her. "So, you didn't deliver the baby?" She said, "I didn't." I said I would like to know if the gynecologist resident delivered the baby. She looked at me and said, "How did you know that?" She said "Ten minutes before we delivered, we asked the resident if they wanted to substitute in, so I asked her to come in and do it. It turns out when I called the gynecologist – the tests showed there was an emergency; they're operating, taking out my uterus, and I die. The gynecologist tells the resident to go tell the father the grave news, and my Ob-gyn said when she turned the corner and saw her face – her stomach dropped. Because he was in the consultation and had described what happened.

So, what was the first incident in your life when you felt you had connected to the flipside?

It's when I was ten – I felt a sharp pain, I said to my dad have you talked to Grandma?

What happened physically?

There's a tell – it all goes into laser focus and I see a male or female figure, and I already know that relationship.

Okay, let's focus on your grandmother for a moment; can you see her now?

Yes.

What's she wearing?

White.

How far away is she?

Four feet. She has black hair, glasses, her skin looks good; not transparent but glowing.

In your mind's eye, go up and take her hands in yours, describe that.

Um... my hands are throbbing. I feel warm, caring...

Any emotions?

Yeah... love.

What does that mean?

Like feeling protected.

Shift your consciousness around to her point of view – looking at you. What do you look like?

(Makes a face) An angel!

Describe this angel. Are there any colors associated with this visual?

A golden beam of light and its surrounded by white.

Is it a solid color? Describe it.

I'd say it's got a glow and radiant and when I smile there are sparkles in the eyes. I see more from waist up – I see a dress… all white.

Any jewelry?

Simple gold bracelet. Looks like an ID bracelet.

What's that bracelet say?

It says my name on it. It says Steph.

Part of your name – isn't it? It's in gold?

Yes.

Do you own this gold bracelet?

No.

Let me ask her name.

Ida.

Ida, thanks for showing up, can I ask you a direct question?

"Yes."

How is our friend doing?

Steph wipes a tear. "Struggling."

Are you there to help her?

"Yes."

Is this conversation we're having meant to help her?

"Yes."

Ida can you bring Steph's guide here – it might be you. Is it a male female neither or both?

A male. It's not her.

Let's look at him.

Tall but ... in between a dad and a grandfather; a large presence. 50's. blondish gray hair. Blue eyes.

I'm going to ask your guide a direct question; he understands what I'm doing. Can I ask for a name to refer to you?

"Sam."

Sam and Ida. Nice to meet you both. Can I ask you some questions Sam?

"Yes."

Take hold of Sam's hands and tell me what that feels like if anything?

Feels like I'm being cradled, solid rock foundation.

How many lifetimes have you been keeping an eye on her?

"Six."

(Note: I asked because I thought he would say "all of them," but by saying "six," that would mean that she may have had another guide, or guides, prior to his involvement. I don't hear that often, but I didn't ask what he was doing prior to working with Steph, or if that's the full number of lifetimes she's had on the planet.)

Can we walk her into her council?

"Yes."

Are we inside or outside, describe the journey?

We're standing outside walking on the path, there's a door in the distance, it's a sidewalk path; like an arch...

Is there a building in the distance?

The door is attached to a building. It's white but a little gray. There are no markings on it …One way in, one way out.

What's it look like inside?

Um; it feels like the room is wide open… It feels spacious like if you were looking at a regular classroom – there's like ten feet between each chair. This is bigger.

How about the walls?

A warm white.

How many people are here?

Like 30. Anywhere between 18 and 30. They're kind of stacked.

Let's go to the first row. How many in the first row?

Six. In a line.

Let's go to the first person to your left.

It's a female with black hair and glasses in her late 20's. Like hazel eyes. Wearing like a white tee shirt. Simple tee shirt and a long skirt – like off white.

If you are allowed, reach over and take her hands and describe that.

It's like a friend, an old friend, somebody who's warm and very smart and kind eyes.

What name can we use to speak with you? May we speak to you?

"Yes." Priscilla came to mind.

Thanks. How do you think Steph is doing?

"She's going to be fine."

That's a little different than what Ida said; "struggling."

(Nods) Mm-hmm.

She's doing pretty good?

"Yes. She is."

Have you heard of me?

"Yes."

How so and put that in Steph's mind.

"Through a dog."

Okay, that's unusual, which dog?

I see like a German shepherd mix.

(Pause. Stunned). Wait. Is this dog part German shepherd and part miniature collie?

"Yes."

Is it... are you saying you know of me via my dog, Sam? How do you know Sam?

I don't know.

Well, Priscilla does.

(Steph laughs) I just am seeing her playing fetch with him.

Just trying to clarify, if you will. Is this my dog Sam or some other German shepherd?

"That's how we know each other; through the dog."

*Is it **my** dog?*

"I believe it is." She's smiling. She's saying, "You don't want to believe what I'm telling you." She's talking to me... that I don't believe it.

Okay, this is a bit odd, but I talked to my dog Sam a month ago with the help of a medium. And Priscilla just described him.

(Note: This is one of those mind freezing moments that sometimes happens during a session. A month earlier, I spoke to my dog, Sam, because I invited him to a session with Jennifer Shaffer, my medium friend who works with law enforcement ("Backstage Pass to the Flipside: Talking to the Afterlife with Jennifer Shaffer.") Sam told

Jennifer the details of his passing which included him seeing my brother just prior to dying. These were details I didn't know as I was out of the country at the time. But they occurred 40 years ago. My brother confirmed what Sam told me about his seeing him just before he died. And now – speaking with Steph, whom I had not met prior to this skype session, her council member is telling me that she knows of my work "speaking to councils" through my dog Sam. Who died 40 years ago? Can I just say "Wow!" Mind officially blown.)

Author with his dog Sam circa 1969.

Priscilla, Steph sees you as a friend. Does she know you outside this council?

"No."

How many councils do you sit on?

"About 40."

Any of your charges that Steph might know? That you oversee that Stephanie might know?

Who's alive or who's passed?

Either. If something comes to mind.

No, nothing.

What quality do you represent that allows you to sit on Steph's council?

"Compassion."

Can you introduce us to the person to your left?

It's a male, stiff as a board. He's tall, his torso is very long. He's wearing a vest and a tie. And a white, white shirt, but he's got on a brown tweed vest.

I forgot to ask if Priscilla is wearing jewelry?

A ring with a pearl on it.

What does that pearl represent?

Her mother.

How about this vest guy fellow; what's his name?

"Fred."

Is it okay to ask you questions?

"Yes."

(Note: She seems to take on his persona of aloofness.)

Can you take his hands?

They're rough and they're cold.

What do you represent in her spiritual evolvement?

"Logic."

Have you had any lifetimes with Steph?

"Twice."

Does she want to explore one of them?

"Not right now."

Okay, so is there a person in charge of this council, the spokesperson? Who's that?

There's a woman, almost looks like a character from "Little House on the Prairie." A teacher at the school, old fashioned with buttons up to the neck and a long straight skirt – her name is Mildred.

May I ask how many councils you work with?

"A lot. I've lost count."

Sorry, Fred, how many do you work on?

"Four."

Mildred you have the benefit of all of these lives and lifetimes, this vast knowledge of observing and guiding and it's amazing job you have, and I want to thank you for allowing us to chitchat – have you heard about what I'm doing?

"Yes. They said there's somebody always knocking at the door."

What's the value of what I'm doing?

"Tethering - connecting from one side to the other and showing that there is a line."

That's a beautiful way to put it; we're always tethered to our guides?

"Yes. But it's more like if you imagine Jack in the Beanstalk... the tethering comes from the boundless infinite; there's always a hook into that world that will always be grounded in this world."

What one word would you use to represent her?

"The producer."

Have you been helping her with that?

"Yes."

Thank you. Let's ask everyone, what's the purpose of allowing Steph to see things that would happen in advance? To make her life miserable?

"No, she has the ability to connect."

Is Steph tapping into the matrix? Into consciousness?

"It will soon become clear and it will launch this really high-speed highway."

Stephanie and others are helping people to work on this highway?

"Yes, everyone has this piece (of it.)"

What's the time frame for this highway (connecting us to the flipside) to come into existence? In our lifetime?

"Yes, you're going to see the start of the roller coaster in the next ten years."

So, Mildred – do you have some lottery numbers for me?

(Steph laughs) "It's the intention behind it that counts."

Is Steph doing what she's supposed to be doing?

"Yes.*"*

And if you could put a sensation in her body somewhere for her so she knows when you're reaching out to her. Can you feel that?

Steph nods.

How was that Steph? Fifteen minutes.

(Steph aside:) How do I know that I didn't make this up?

Because you just said the identical things others say – you'll see it when I include it in a chapter in my next book. You say basically the same things everyone else has said about this journey. If you're not familiar with my books, or with Michael Newton's reports, how could you possibly imagine this place or these people or even the concept that you are tethered to them?

Wait; I know what the gold ID bracelet is! I remember it now; I don't have it anymore. It was a gift my father gave me – and it did said Steph on it... from my dad.

Can you tell Steph where the missing bracelet is? Is it inside or outside somewhere?

Inside.

In a house you live in or someone else's?

It was in a safe. I'll check this jewelry box I have I haven't opened in a while.

Cool. How was that?

Amazing.

******

I was flabbergasted when her guide said that she was aware of my work through a dog and proceeded to describe my dog from 40 years ago. I was startled as I had done an "interview" with Sam just weeks earlier, something I wasn't aware I could do until I did an "interview" with the dog of my old boss Robert Towne, the Oscar award winning screenwriter.

While doing a session on Skype with Robert and Jennifer Shaffer, we were speaking directly to a mutual friend Edward Taylor who had crossed over, and he was describing to us through Jennifer a recent trip we took in Marina Del Rey harbor to scatter his ashes. And I asked Jennifer if it was possible to speak with "Hira" as well.

Jennifer asked "Why am I seeing a giant white shag rug?" (Hira was a Komondor, his fur was like a giant white shag rug.) We asked Hira questions over a number of sessions, and he said basically the same things everyone says; animals are like humans in that they choose to reincarnate. He also "told us" details of events that only Robert was aware of.

In that vein I conducted an interview with my dog "Sam" who had passed away 40 years ago. I wasn't aware of the exact circumstances of his passing, and asked him for details. He gave me new information about seeing my brother prior to passing (a detail I confirmed with my brother after the session) and other things about my life only he would know. I'm just reporting. Our pets apparently know who we are, communicate on a level we don't comprehend, and have been with us in other lifetimes.

So for Steph's guide or council member to comment that she knows of my work through a dog – and then describes my dog Sam – and then I ask "Are you talking about my dog Sam?" it was a mind bending moment. I could have taken the time to draw out the response in a more detective like fashion – but what's the point? I've been confirming these things for over a decade now. Sometimes you just want to shout out the answer when it presents itself in front of you.

CHAPTER FIFTEEN:

INTERVIEW WITH "MR. BIG"

Andrew Mellon - "Mr. Big" - is his great nephew. *(Wikimedia)*

I got an email from an old pal who was distraught over the recent passing of her friend. My pal never mentioned the fellow's name, but wondered if we could communicate with him about his sudden passing. It wasn't too difficult for this former journalist (Variety, Premiere, Inc.com) to figure out who this person was based on what he said from the flipside.

Based solely on what he said from the flipside, I realized it was likely I had been speaking with someone who may or may not have been (let's call him) "Mr. Big" Mellon who died in rehab at the age of 54. Allow me to state unequivocally – *I have no proof it was him*. The person I was speaking with **never** said it was him, I never asked if it **was him.** Later in this interview, medium Jennifer Shaffer takes up the conversation, but even then, she had no idea who he is either.

I was not aware of him; his fame, or his journey until this session. Normally I would keep his identity out of the account but there's no way to ask his family for permission to include him, or for me to argue on his behalf that people should believe or *not believe* it's him. All I can say is that when I started to edit this chapter, I got the impression he was saying "*Tell my story. I want you to.*"

I'm not referring to my friend's name who wanted to speak to him, but for the sake of this story, let's call my friend "Sean." (Name is not Sean, we may be friends, we may be strangers. This story isn't about Sean who might live in the U.S. or Europe, may or may not work in the film industry. Sean could be anyone.)

I don't do this kind of research to upset anyone or their family and friends; I do it to demonstrate our loved ones are never far away. By making the person I'm interviewing anonymous, I eliminate claims of trying to trade off "fame." One could argue by including his name, I am "trading off his fame" but he wasn't famous to me. Never heard of the fellow. *And no one who considers him famous will ever read this book.* So there's that.

This "Mr. Big" died suddenly and was haunting my friend's dreams, and reached out to me for help. I recorded the session, and my friend did their best to not reveal his identity. The following was recorded on Skype in a filmed interview. Sean is **in bold,** my comments *in italics.*

"Sean": Rich, I've read some of your posts about how you do things and I thought it was really interesting.

Rich: Well... in a nutshell, I mention in my books how a friend passed 20 years ago and started to visit me – (Luana Anders). Like anything (at first) you think it's a dream...

Sean: Was it in your dreams or in real life?

Rich: Well, I could hear her voice, and it was her voice but at an age I didn't know her. You know how some dreams feel more like life? The Inuit people have many words for snow, Bushmen of South Africa have many words for water; we only have one word for dreams.

Sean: What would happen in the dreams?

Rich: I won't go into all the details, (they're in "Flipside") but she was saying things like "Isn't this fucking amazing?" My thing was like "How can you be here?" And if you're here, how do I visit you?

Sean: You mean like direct communication? Was the dream in black and white – or in color?

Rich: In color – at first, I could hear her voice, and had a sense of a younger woman... then I went to see her directly. Because of that experience, it pushed me into this rabbit hole. Did I see you my film "Flipside?"

Sean: Yes, Yes... I spoke to my friend (on the other side) through a psychic ... who helped me talk to my friend – and she has helped many people access this kind of information. She told me about people being cured with psychosomatic illnesses (while under hypnosis).

(General discussion of Dr. Brian Weiss, Michael Newton and Dr. Helen Wambach, a psychologist in New Jersey had 2000 cases she reported.)

Rich: I like to ask, "So who was it who died that convinced you to reach out to me?"

Sean: Well... I spent the last year recovering from the death of this close friend. I think he wants to tell me something; I don't know what.

Okay, let's ask him. Did he come to visit you after he crossed over?

Yes, four times. I went to the psychic – he came and spoke to me and told me a lot of things. He's appeared three times in my dream and I dreamt three days before he died. The psychic was very nice, but my dreams have not been very nice.

Well, that's why I'm here. What was a dream you had?

I had this dream; I think it was in Malibu. We were at this dinner table and (he was with another woman, his ex girlfriend) and I was like "Oh I was right all along!" I was upset (he was with her).

Before you got upset – did you have a thought "There he is, but he doesn't exist?" Was your first thought happy?

Yes.

Let's examine that. Where is he sitting?

Opposite me. Across a dinner table at like a restaurant.

How many people in this dream?

Just three. We're outside over a balcony overlooking Malibu.

Have you been to this place before?

No.

Freeze the frame for a second. What's he wearing?

Casual (clothes) like going for a stroll.. a white... maybe white – beach shirt... He's sitting normally.

Is your friend the same age as he died?

He looks quite healthy. Probably a year younger (than when he passed).

What are you wearing?

I'm wearing like a sarong with a bikini or something.

Take hold of his hands. What feeling or emotion is associated with this?

I feel his pain – he's in so much pain. But I'm angry with him..

Ah ah..... let's set your emotions off the table. You're feeling pain not from you but from him, correct?

Yes.

Generate a feeling of healing towards him, put it in your hands and into his. Does it lessen?

Yes, he needs a lot of that.

Well do that – what do his hands feel like?

They're cold.

Let's ask him to warm them up – can you do that?

"Yes." They are warmer now.

Are we allowed to ask you questions? Have you orchestrated this so we can have this conversation?

"Yes."

Show our friend here what she looks like to you at this point. She's wearing a sarong, correct, or how does she look to you?

She laughs... "He said, "She's beautiful.""

(Note: That's a pretty unusual answer. It wasn't "He says I'm beautiful" – but replied as a quote "She's beautiful.")

That's not what I asked, but okay. Let's (try to) shift your consciousness over his shoulder – what's behind you?

The ocean.

And you are wearing a sarong?

Yes. It's multicolored.

Do you know this sarong?

No.

So let's ask him; did you create this or did she?

He did.

So, you don't own it – he does. Let me get this straight, this dream she had... you helped orchestrate the dream?

"Yes."

(Note: That's why I'm asking "how this sarong came into being" as my friend doesn't own it, has never seen it before.)

So, he created this outfit which you don't own and this dream. Can I ask you some questions about your journey?

"Yes."

Who was there to greet you when you crossed over?

"A boat man. Like a boat man. He's got a pole in the water."

Is this the proverbial boatman on the River Styx?

"Yes."

Gustave Dore' "Divine Comedy" Charon on the River Styx

(Note: I'm familiar enough with this history of what people report about the flipside to recognize an homage to the River Styx boatman. "In Greek mythology, Charon is the ferryman of Hades who carries souls of the newly deceased across the rivers Styx and Acheron that divided the world of the living from the world of the dead. A coin to pay Charon for passage, usually an *obolus* or *danake*, was sometimes placed in or on the mouth of a dead person. Some authors say that those who could not pay the fee, or those whose bodies were left unburied, had to wander the shores for one hundred years." Wikipedia)

(Chuckles) Ok, so were you a scholar of Greek literature? Where'd you find this dude? Or are you saying that was the first thing that you saw?

"Yes."

Can we access this guy, the boatman?

(To me) Is this my imagination or his?

I'm asking him. How old is this boatman?

"Old; he's got a white beard. A 100 maybe. "

He's got a big stick?

"Yes. He's got a raft."

(Note: This is the first time I've heard anything like this – he may be joking for my benefit, as in "This fellow is asking me questions, I'll give him a fun reference." But it also may be accurate, as our mutual friend is "seeing" this; he's the one putting it in her mind. It's not a normal reference for her.)

Okay, let's go across that river; take us across. Are you feeling better on the other side? Is all of the pain from this lifetime dissipating?

(She nods).

And who was there to greet you on the other side?

It looks like a lot of clouds. White. Also pink and yellow.

Describe them – are they flat colors, or are they (vibrating) energy?

"Yes."

Who was the first person to greet you on the other side, did someone come out of those clouds?

It's not clear but there's a godlike figure; at the top.

Did you talk to the "Big Man?

He says "Yes."

What was that like?

He says "Fine, great."

Describe it.

"It was like a journey through the clouds."

What's the answer to "Who was there to greet you?" on the other side?

"His mom."

I'm sure she must have been happy to see you; where you startled to see her?

"Yes."

Let me ask you some questions about your journey – have you and our friend here had a journey together before?

"Yes. We were married before."

Let's examine it; where are we (in this memory)?

It's a wedding in a garden. I'm dressed in a 1920's wedding dress. (I have) Shorter hair, like dark hair, brown eyes. It's 1929.

What country are we in?

It's tropical. Mexico sort of but not Mexico – I don't know where this is. It's very green almost jungle. There's a stone balcony. It's a white beach house. Costa Rica maybe. Nineteen years earlier. I see wicker chairs... and my father...

What's he look like?

Quite formal. He's Latin American.

What's his name?

Lomaz or Lomez.

(Note: A name with roots in Costa Rica: https://www.ancestry.com/1940-census/usa/California/Manuel-Lomez_2mjymh)

Let's go to the last day of Natasha's life – where is she?

A vehicle accident. I think she's a passenger. She died, he survived.

Let's go to that moment just after the accident – what happens next?

She's looking down. From about five feet up.

Is there anyone you want to see or say goodbye to?

I want to say goodbye to him.

Where do we go next?

I'm floating.

Okay, I'm interested in talking to your guide. Can you bring your guide forward? Is that a male, female neither or both?

It's a spirit. It's just like a light. Quite close. It's white – like Tinkerbell. Small (she gestures with one hand).

I'd like your guide to manifest as a human so we can talk to you – what do you see?

My guide says "no."

I'm asking your guide directly to manifest as someone we can chat with.

She's a fairy.

Okay don't judge it. About the size of your hand?

Yes.

What's this guide's name?

"Tara."

Describe her. How many wings does she have?

Four. They're like a fly's wings; quite strong.

What color are they?

Clear – translucent. She's a woman. About 4 inches high, she has brown hair, light blue eyes; she's very sweet. (Wearing) Like a fairy outfit... it's green blue...

Like Tinkerbell?

"Yes."

Tara. Can I ask you direct questions and you'll put the answers in her mind?

"Yes."

Have you ever incarnated on our planet?

"No."

In the place you come from does everyone look like you?

"Yes there's a lot."

Tara, I spoke to someone recently who resembled someone like you. Are you aware of this?

"Yes. I am."

(Note: There's no way that this person would know this detail, as I hadn't told anyone. I'd met a member of a council that was "small" about four inches high, and also looked like a "fairy." I asked her the same questions I'm about to ask Tara. She said roughly the same things.)

Tara are you aware of me?

"Yes."

What's your opinion of what I'm doing?

"Good work."

Next question can you walk our friend in to visit her council?

Into my what?

She knows what I'm talking about.

She says "Yes."

Funny; Tara knows your council but you don't – do you know what I'm talking about Sean?

No, I don't.

I'm just verifying that you don't understand this (idea of a council) but your guide does. Are we inside or outside?

(Note: I can't think of a more clear way to point out that this isn't a conscious memory. I asked her guide if she was familiar with my work and she said "Yes." Then I asked the guide to take Sean in to visit her council and Sean asked "What's a council?" Can't be aware of my work if you don't know what a council is.)

Inside. It's like a white room; everything is very white.

What's it made of? Marble?

Yes. It's clear as a bell white, the ceiling is normal sized; it's very white. It's a very big ceiling – large ceiling; it's flat.

How many people are in here?

There are people walking around; like ten people.

How are they arrayed – in a line, semi-circle?

Walking in front of me. I'm standing at the back.

Let's move forward – ... what do you look like to Tara?

I'm still dressed in the sarong actually.

Let's see if we can talk to your council. How are they arrayed?

Everyone is still walking in front of me...

Tara, let's go to the first councilmember on your left.

It's a man. Dressed in Greek clothing – in a white toga. He has a wreath on his head, like a gold wreath. He's 40 maybe. Dark hair, brown hair, brown eyes.

What's a name we can use to call you?

"Simon."

Have you known Simon before or only here?

He seems familiar even though I don't know him.

May I ask; do you know me?

"Yes."

Any comment about this work I'm doing?

"Good work."

Let me ask you Simon – how is our friend doing?

"She's fine."

How many councils do you work on?

"A few. About 20."

What's the one word that represents your role in our friend's journey?

"Good."

What do you mean by that? Doing good, acting good, being good?

"Like (having a) solid foundation."

So the word represents someone who does good is that correct?

"Yes."

Just for context – did she earn that in one lifetime or in many lifetimes?

"Many lifetimes."

Simon, let me ask, in this memory of a lifetime when our friend was married, what (theme) did she need to examine?

"Love."

Why did she choose this current lifetime? What's the connection between this and that one?

"To help him."

And... who else?

"She can help a lot of people."

How so?

"She can get messages. By listening carefully."

Put in her mind's eye how she can help people in the future (in terms of her creativity and work.)

"She just has to listen carefully. Just follow and listen." (Sean aside) I don't know what you're asking.

Simon. Can you introduce her to another person on her council?

He says, "No." (A pause) They're all walking away.

Who's the spokesperson for this council?

There's a woman. Yes, she's quite powerful.

Can you give us a name to converse with you?

"Nora."

Thank you – Nora, am I correct in asking this? You represent the council for our friend here?

"Yes."

Is there something about the questions I'm asking that aren't appropriate?

"Yes." She says they want to kick us out.

Before we go – are you aware of what I'm doing?

"Yes; she doesn't agree with it."

Okay, let me clarify – you don't agree with it because you don't want to alter Sean's path by showing her what's going to happen next?

"Yes."

I don't want to do that – If I may ask you, what quality do you represent in her spiritual evolvement?

She says "We have to leave. We shouldn't be here. Enough questions."

Okay, before we go, is it true that our friend is always connected to you at all times? Can access you through her heart at all times?

"Yes."

By the way how many councils are you on?

"Hundreds." (Sean aside) They want us to go.

(Note: This is the only time this has ever occurred. Fortunately I was able to ask "Are you worried about disrupting her path by letting her access this information?" to understand why we were being "86'd." I don't want to disrupt anyone's path. But if your guides want you to read on; then read on.)

Thank you council for allowing us to come and chat with you – Tara can you walk her in to visit with her soul group?

"Yes." I'm in the wedding garden.

Tara, please take us to her soul group.

We're outside – like ten people. My friend is there. He looks the same, about the age we saw him earlier.

Anyone else you recognize?

My sister.

How many boys and girls here?

Ten. More men than women.

How does your sister look? She's still on the planet, right?

Yes. She's not really all there.

Tara, correct me if I'm wrong, the reason she's not all there is because only part of her energy is back home, correct?

"Yes."

But when you compare your sister to your friend; she's etheric but he's all there correct?

"Yes."

How many lifetimes have you had with your friend?

"Ten."

Tara, correct me if anything I'm saying is inaccurate; we choose lifetimes with a significant other because we trust them... we have unconditional love for them.

"Yes."

Can you show our friend her life planning session for this current one? Are we inside or outside?

Outside.

Are we with a small or large group?

Smaller group.

(Note: In "Journey of Souls" Michael Newton mentioned people having a "life planning session" where they work out the plot points of their lifetime with their friends, family and associates. I rarely ask this question to people not under deep hypnosis, because it's foreign to them – but in this case, we did get an answer.)

Are there any of the people we saw at the council?

"No."

These are the folks helping you plan this (lifetime's) journey – at what point did you say that you would sign up for a lifetime with your friend knowing that he wouldn't stay here long?

"Yes." I somehow say "Yes, I'm happy to do that again."

Can I ask you a simple question?

"Yes."

Why did you ask her to participate in your life? What was the story line you wanted to learn from?

"It's not about money."

(Note: I have no idea what he means by this comment, but I later I discovered that this friend "Mr. Big" was a wealthy person.)

Does she know what that means?

"Yes."

Tara, everyone in this lifetime is just another incarnating soul, and we are all connected, is that correct?

"Yes." (Sean aside) It's funny I keep getting that message over and over again.

What's the purpose of holding onto anger?

"Let it go."

Let me ask your friend this question; "Are you dead?"

"No."

So not only is he still alive, he's trying to say "let it go." Is that correct?

"Yes. I had nothing to do with it."

Did you ask everyone in your life to participate in your journey?

"They agreed."

So Tara; why did you allow Sean to access this information?

"Because she has to let go."

Tara is there a sensation you can give our friend to remind her she's always connected to you?

"Yes." It's like a light. Like a little light.

Tara, is this your way of letting her know you're close by?

"Yes."

Also your way of reminding her to let go. Is that correct?

"Yes."

Let me ask your pal, why did you let her reach out to me?

He felt sorry for me that I had these things running around in my head.

How did you find me?

He lived in LA; he knows people you know.

By the way Tara, can I ask you about the planet you're from?

"It's in another universe."

Has anyone come to visit your planet you're aware of? In their sleep?

"Yes. Yes."

So the idea of fairies comes from your planet?

"Yes."

Fairy isn't the right word. What would you call yourself?

"A being."

A light worker?

"Yes."

Okay, thanks everyone!

It's so interesting!

I'd like to point out; none of the visuals you had come from me.

What are they like compared to other people's visuals?

The same. Identical. You've never heard of your council, but everyone has one – at least that's what the research shows. Your council was the first to ever boot me out of the room, but there's a reason for that. So... I will make sure this session is anonymous and no one can bother you about it unless you want them to.

Wow.

Love to all your guides – and Tara "Boom-dee-ay" – thanks for the information!

So, as I often do, I followed this session up with a session with medium Jennifer Shaffer, to see if I could get more information.

Rich: Luana, anybody else? Who else wants to chat? Oh, I know, (I mention Mr. Big's name.) Should we talk to him?

Jennifer: She says "He's here. Yeah."

Well, "Mr. Big" what do you want to tell us?

"It was painful," he said.

What? Crossing over or living your lifetime?

He says "Living. It was easy to cross over."

What do you want me to tell our friend?

"That he loves her hair."

So when I talked the to her the other day via Skype; were you aware of this conversation?

(Note: She answered the next two questions before I could say them.)

"Yes."

Did you hear us talking to her council?

"Yes." He showed me the initials... J.P. Like J.P. Morgan.

Like the banker; yes his family is (from a wealthy banking family.). Very wealthy. So why did you check out at such a young age?

He shows me it was like a losing buzzer... that he was "winning, winning and then got the losing buzzer."

You were married....

"Three times," he said.

(Note: This is accurate according to Mr. Big Mellon's bio.)

I think that's accurate. One of them started an empire.

He rolled his eyes, but I (Jennifer) own (that product. Ding! She was correct about the product.)

People tell us they want to be billionaires, but not everyone gets to be one. What did you learn in this lifetime as Mr. Big?

"That money helps. It helps to make everything okay, but then it creates more problems. He showed me like a fungus that is growing out of control."

A fungus? That doesn't sound okay.

"It creates other problems."

So what will you be the next time around?

He's showing me, he'll be a beggar, showed me like a little flip – a coin into a cup. He says "He was that before, in a previous life" and they're showing me it happening right now...

Which life was more fun?

He says "the billionaire for sure." He says he gave a lot away - he said "He gave a lot of it away."

That's good to hear - I'm sure you had some foundation.

Hold on – he's showing me the book – something like "How to Be Rich" I know it's not the title – but he's showing me this book.

(Note: "How to be Rich" is a book by author Andy Stanley. The subtitle is: "It's not what you have, it's what you do with what you have.")

People should buy or ignore this book? It's about being rich?

"Rich has nothing to do with it, obvious puns about your name aside. It's energy."

It's an accumulation of energy?

"It's about your strength as a person. If you're weak and a billionaire it doesn't matter." He showed me Bill Gates. "If you're a billionaire and you give it away you gain points for that."

So find a way to give your money away?

"Yes."

Who was there to greet you when you crossed over?

He's showing me like a pet cat.

(Note: Sometimes it's when a pet shows up that we realize we are in the afterlife. It's like we're disoriented, then we recognize our pet – and the frequency changes.)

And what do you miss about being on the planet?

Feels like that mansion (that's) in North Carolina, like Asheville. It's a big mansion kind of house where he grew up.

(Note: Again Jennifer has no clue as to who I'm referring to. Mr. Big lived much of his life in London.)

Who are you hanging out with on the flipside?

He showed me John Lennon. He says "The Brits." He says "he used to collect music or guitars or paraphernalia."

What was that like to meet John on the flipside?

He said, "How do you think that be like? It was amazing."
(Listens) But "He felt he knew him when he crossed over, so seeing him was like seeing an old friend."

Do you guys play music together?

"Yes, it's Rastafarian music feels like. It "feels like the pulse of the planet."

Any message for our friend "Sean" who is missing you?

He says, "Tell her she was too good for me."

You want me to pass along this as your message to her?

"She still won't hear it – maybe later."

Maybe in the next book?

"Yes."

Thank you Luana, Mr. Big – we'll see you on the flipside.

"Yes, bye."

For the record; "Matthew Mellon of the Mellon and Drexel banking families, was an entrepreneur who spent decades working in fashion and earned a fortune in cryptocurrencies. He died April 16, 2018 (AP) Mellon, (who spoke) of his addiction to OxyContin, died at a drug rehabilitation facility in Mexico." (*Family statement*).

It's always good to know that our loved ones haven't gone anywhere, and that each lifetime is done by choice; whether a pauper or king, whether *rich or poor*.... Or just plain old *Richard.*

Mr. Big and his family of Mellons

CHAPTER SIXTEEN:

"JUST FEEL WORTHY"

Bucking bull belt buckle (Ebay)

Some years ago, a young German filmmaker was making a film about her adventures in Hollywood ("I Am A Creative Soul") She was trying to track down the artist Jason Mraz, and while she was doing so, was making a film about her adventures in Los Angeles. Jessica Hahner may have attended a book talk, I forget, but Jessica is good friends with the subject of this chapter; Jennie.

In her documentary, I told some stories about my journey to this flipside research, including the story of how my son had revealed to us that he remembered his lifetime as a monk in Nepal. (As reported in "Flipside: A Tourist's Guide on How to Navigate the Afterlife.") Some unusual things happened when I met Jessica the filmmaker; I encouraged her to film an interview with Jennifer Shaffer, my medium friend (JenniferShaffer.com) who I had just met that week she was filming.

While we were filming, I got a text message from a close friend back in Chicago reporting that our mutual friend Billy Meyer had passed away. I got the text, swore aloud, and Jennifer Shaffer asked what the issue was – and I told her. Jessica Hahner filmed our conversation – where Jennifer spoke directly to my friend on the flipside, who had come to our location on Santa Monica beach to say goodbye (or hello, depending how aware of this research you might be.)

So that was a bit unusual.

Then some five years later, Jessica Hahner was showing her documentary about her journey up at in screening room in Topanga Canyon, and invited me to see it for the first time. It's always a bit startling to see oneself on screen – bigger than life – but Jessica had an excellent camera man who made me seem like I actually knew what I was talking about.

Sitting next to me was a woman from Topanga Canyon – someone I've never met before. Let's call her Jennie for the sake of this conversation, but we chatted a bit after the film, and she invited me to meet up for coffee to tell her a little about my research. At some point, I told her how I had been "interviewing" people about their path and journey – and curious as to what the connection might be for her, asked if she was interested in "exploring" this avenue.

We are in Caffe Luxxe in Malibu, in the back yard, having one of their excellent cappuccinos when I decide to turn on my cellphone recorder. My questions in Italics, Jennie's answers in BOLD. She said she wanted to "speak to her dad."

Rich: So, here we are at Caffe Luxxe, and I was asking Jennifer who in her life wants to talk to her, we settled on her dad, John. What I do, generally, is to try to walk you into a memory – a place something happened to you where John was... perhaps in a dream?

Jennie: Yep. This was... in a dream. It felt... like we flew together.

Here's what I want you to do – try to remember a moment where you recognized him. Did you see him or sense him?

Sensed him.

Who was holding onto whom in this dream?

This was many years ago...

Just open yourself up to the memory; think of this as a game, like a mental word game and we'll see where we get. I'm not a medium, so I won't say let's "invite John" – but in my research if you're here that means he's already here.

I've read Michael Newton's "Life Between Lives" when he published it. (That was Michael Newton's third book, written for hypnotherapists.)

I recommend doing a session with a Newton Institute trained hypnotherapist, but I've found we can kind of "skip down" with this method. It's not for everyone, but some people find it a way to be introduced to the topic.

I already operate in that way.

In this memory with your dad, John, is there a particular moment you can recall?

Yes, I remember what it's like to connect with him.

Where are you? Are you in the sky, outer space in this dream?

Whenever I fly – whenever I go, I kind of connect...

Let's just picture him – without flying. Give me visual.

I'm not very visual in this life.

How old is he in this image of flying with him?

He seems ageless. He appears with gray hair.

Just allow this is an imaginary portrait.

I just want to feel my answers are truthful.

(Note: As do I. However, our conscious mind is constantly battling with our subconscious, like a bouncer preventing entry to other realms. We can always "review the transcript later" to see what felt "made up" or what felt "real.")

Okay, what age is he in this imaginary visual you have of him?

Like 62.

What's he wearing?

Jean shirt. He has short hair, hazel eyes. He's presenting himself as a healthy version of himself. I can energetically see him now.

Okay. What kind of pants is he wearing?

Jeans and a cowboy belt.

Does he have a buckle?

It's gold and silver.

Look carefully at it.

It's a cowboy and a horse.

Is this a buckle he owned?

I don't think so.

If you don't know it, then that means it's a buckle he's creating. Is that correct John? Look at him and let him say to you a reply – either "Yes, no or I don't know."

(She nods – then begins to cry, realizing he must be creating the image.)

Hang on. We can't talk to John if you're sobbing. (Trying to keep it light) John were you a bull rider or horse rider?

"Horses."

John, who was there to greet you when you crossed over?

Mary, his mother.

Was he surprised to see her?

He wasn't surprised – between the talks we had leading up to his departure; he would have accepted it.

Let's ask him. What does he say when I ask that question?

"No, he was not."

Take hold of his hands if you can.

Ok. They're hard. He had working hands. Warm.

I want you to do something unusual – step around behind him, shift your consciousness to his pov – how do you look to him?

He keeps showing me Debra winger in "Urban Cowboy" and laughing... he's got a really good sense of humor. It's me, he wants me to understand...

About what age in this visual?

Mid 20's. (Jennie, wiping away tears:) I'm sorry I'm crying.

It's okay. John, I know you're here for a reason, the only reason you hooked us up is to have a conversation for her with you.

"Yes, yes, yes!" he says.

How is she doing?

"Great." (Jennie begins to cry.)

Are you lying John? She doesn't sound like she's doing great.

"She's crying with happiness."

Put in her mind a moment that you remember about her that she does not. Something you did that was funny. Can you do that?

The first thing that came was me as a young girl with pigtails and something about scraping my knee – but I don't remember it.

That's very specific – I asked for a memory he has that you don't. Put that little girl in her mind's eye. Is that the same kid? Is this the same daughter? This picture of a person?

"Yes yes, yes, yes, yes!" he says.

John why did you put her in my path?

She laughs.

What do you want to impart? That you're still here?

"Also that she understand that she's not alone moving forward."

She needs others to talk to – bring her guide forward please.

My guy?

Guide. Is it a male, female, a light?

A female. Beatrice. She's got brown wavy hair, and um, she's about 50...

You've met her before?

No, I think she's my great grandmother. I feel like she's related.

John, is this her great grandmother?

"Yes. The one that sent me the roses."

Take Beatrice's hands in yours.

Okay. They're soft, very soft and little – she's got little hands.

Is there an emotion associated with that?

There's a lot of love there.

What does that mean?

Good question. Okay, well, what it means in this case is "guidance."

Beatrice – how's she...

"Well. Really well."

You answered it before I could ask my question! Well, every good. How is Beatrice dressed?

She has on a long robe, off white, more silvery, something there on her head.

What color are her eyes?

**More black than brown... because I'm looking through them.
Her hair is brown wavy long with tiny curls. She's Italian.**

So you were her great grandma? Where did you live in your lifetime?

"Naples," she says.

What year was that? Put a year in her mind.

"1794." I don't know if this makes sense.

Try not to judge it. Were you keeping an eye on her in Naples?

"Yes."

Who was she?

"Female." She has long braids. "A young girl, 7 or 8."

What's her name?

(shrugs) I keep getting Heidi.

Last name?

Begins with P ... Predone? Perdone? Heidi can't be right.

(Note: *Pra* is a last name in Sicily – it means "family of." Donne is "women" in Italian. "The surname Pra was first found in at Lecce, the historic city in southern Italy on the southern tip of the Italian peninsula." House of Names com)

Let's call her Heidi for now. Where does Heidi live?

"In the city."

Show her her family.

"She doesn't have one. I was a member of the community looking out for her, she was an orphan..."

Last day of Heidi's life?

I think she was burned.

Were you burned in a fire or was it deliberate?

"Deliberate." They didn't get me.

Who did that? Religious clergy?

"Yes."

So you were a "strega?" ("witch" in Italian) Let me ask Beatrice why she chose that life? What did she want to learn from that?

"Strength."

Related to the choice of this lifetime?

"Yes, yes, yes. Same thing."

Can we go and visit her council?

"Yes."

Describe it please.

We're inside, it's like a ... okay, looks like the war room in "Game of Thrones." Where Kaleesi would sit around the map table. That room.

How many are here?

Eight. Like I'm in front and they're around – semi circle.

Let's go to the 1st on your left – male or female?

Male.... I recognize him... my friend Duncan. Same age as when he died - no sorry, younger than when he died. Sorry Duncan. Early 70's.

What is your role on her council; what word represents her journey?

"No doubt."

She's been provided that for many lifetimes?

"Yes."

Are you the spokesperson?

"No, just one of the members."

Are you familiar with what I'm doing?

"Yes. "

Who told it to you?

He said he was very... okay... he's saying "he was really closed in this lifetime, so this is...." he's really excited, (to be here) because he was kind of mean around... I mean... he didn't get...

Duncan, you've known her for many lifetimes?

"Yes."

How many councils do you serve on?

He said "ten." He was saying to me this was his first time as a council member on *her* council.

But you're on other councils?

"Yes."

Beatrice, let me ask you what's that thing around your neck (she mentioned earlier)?

It's like diamonds... That's like – a metaphor – it's um... what's coming... The future – and some rubies and emeralds."

The future (for Jennie) is diamonds and gems?

Duncan wanted me to know that the cameras are the connection between us; he gave me a camera and he's showing me that... is our connection.

Is he responding to my question "How do you know me?"

How he got on my council. He felt the connection with me – the connection of the two of us... he's saying he realized when I visited him in the nursing home and he gave me the camera, that was when he realized there was a connection. So when he got to the afterlife, that's how he got onto my council.

Okay, thanks for clarifying that. Duncan, giving her the camera was that a selfless act on your part?

"Yes, ironically one of the first."

So in his life it was hard for him to be selfless but by giving something to you he showed other councils members that he deserved a place on your council?

"Yes."

Duncan who's to your left? Male or female?

Male. It's my grandfather... Frederick.

What is the quality you represent on this council?

"Peace of mind" he says.

Is that something she's working on? "Peace?"

"Yes."

Let me ask are you Frederick, are you familiar with what I'm doing?

"Yes yes yes."

How so?

He said "cooler talk." (Jennie aside: What's that mean?)

What? (I laugh.) *I understand it. I often say it during a session – that they know from "hanging around the council water cooler and talking about it."*

(Note: Doesn't get much weirder than having a council member refer to a joke you've only made to other council members – and having the person in front of you say "I don't get it.")

I'm just curious Frederick; can you put it in her minds' eye who told you about this?

He says "Jack."'

He thinks I'll know who Jack is? Is it Jack Nicholson?

(Jennie aside) He's still alive right?

He is.

He says, "You would know."

Let me ask; what's the first letter of his last name?

N. He laughed – first thing he said was "Nicholson" and then said to me "Tell him Nelson!" But he actually said "Nicholson" first.

Well that's funny – I am aware of what he means. Let's ask him again – see if he says something different. Who made you aware of my work?

He keeps saying "Jack."

"...in the box?

Does that mean he's dead?

No it's the fast food restaurant.

(Jennie laughs) He just says "Yeah."

How did he present it to you Frederick? Did jack present it as an image or a memory or a conversation?

A conversation... as a concept. (To me; do you understand this?)

I do.

(Note: More than Jennie could know. She doesn't know that Luana Anders was/is one of Jack's oldest friends. When Luana was cremated, I arranged for him to have some of her ashes. She introduced me to him, and after her passing she's had me pass along personal private messages to him (doesn't mean he believes me, I just deliver them) and I've chatted with him about a number of things including death, consciousness and LSD, (our chats are few and far between, but always memorable).

Luana photo of Jack in her acting class with Jeff Corey

But beyond the idea that Jennie has no idea that I know Jack Nicholson personally, the idea that a member of her council would be the one to point that out is beyond the possibility of coincidence.

The more important point – everyone we come in contact with has the ability to share information about us on the flipside. He's saying "He knows of my work through Jack" even though Jack is NOT AWARE OF MY WORK, other than being aware of it *on the flipside through his friend Luana.* I've never mentioned any of this research to him – other than that sometimes my medium friend has a message from Luana to him.)

In terms of Jennie's spiritual evolvement, you represent "Peace" – can you put a sensation in her body somewhere that represents peace? It's like a "Bat-Signal" for what peace means; correct me if I'm wrong "Fred."

He said "Frederick." (Correcting me because I was wrong.)

You did correct me. Jennie is always tethered to you, correct?

"Yes."

That's the whole point of this exercise, isn't it? We are talking to people you don't consciously know...

Yes, I didn't know him.

But he's connected to you in a profound way. Let's talk to the spokesperson of your council.

Frederick is claiming that role.

Okay, thanks. What do you want her to realize about anyone else on this council?

He says "Not at this time."

You've met a couple and I think that's the most important part of this exercise; to meet a couple. So Frederick how is she doing in terms of her path?

Yeah... he wanted to pick the right word.

Your dad said "great" Beatrice said "well" and Frederic says "meh?"

That's why I want to wait – he's choosing the right word.

(After a pause). So Frederick, how is she doing?

"She's right where she needs to be, right on the cusp," he said.

Thank you sir. That on the cusp comment relates to the future, to Jennie's future, correct?

"Yes."

Those diamonds around Beatrice's neck. So Beatrice - you stuck her in front of me (sat her next to me at a screening) to do what?

(Jennie aside) I know.

What do you know?

"She needs guidance and to understand her power in this life to actually bring forth the manifestation of the prosperity associated with this energetic power."

Correct me if I'm wrong Frederick; prosperity doesn't mean money, does it?

"No; the ability to prosper in this lifetime."

We use it as a term related to money... but it's the energy or prospering?

"Yes, it's very different. I understand that the energetic part of my lesson, he's saying was... the whole point (is) what I'm on the cusp of is.... that going from believing – being not worthy versus worthy."

Thank you Frederick. What's one sentence you want to tell her in terms of her relationship to her mom?

"Just feel worthy."

Thanks everybody... applause and high fives, Beatrice anything else you want to show her. John?

They're saying... they're just saying... no... they're saying...

John let's go back to that belt buckle for a second...did you earn that belt buckle?

He says "Yes."

What lifetime did you earn that? In this life or previous one?

"Previous" he says.

Does she know what a cowboy belt buckle means?

No.

I do... I'll tell her afterwards.

(Note: I worked on a film called "Cowboy Up." Cowboys earn belt buckles for winning events – races, buck riding, etc. They're victory emblems. It represents "winning a tough ride.")

"Yes."

It was a gift to him for a difficult lifetime he went through where he (literally) "rode the bronco."

"Right."

A metaphor or literally riding?

"A metaphor," he says.

Let's get a high five from everyone, you know how to reach her at any time.

*****

A belt buckle earned for riding a bull for 8 seconds. An oft heard metaphor for accolades earned from a difficult lifetime. Person gets "dusted" by a bull ride, they get up, dust their boots, pick up the golden buckle, and return for another "go round" for another wild ride on the bucking bull.

CHAPTER SEVENTEEN:

OFF WORLD MEMORIES WITH "IRIS"

Raphael's version of "Home" on a Vatican wall.

I've known "Iris" since high school. She's funny, witty and has become a wildly successful person since then. She appears in "It's a Wonderful Afterlife" (under a pseudonym) where she shared some mind bending memories of the afterlife. She decided to attend a workshop given by Scott De Tamble (LightBetweenLives.com) where students practice deep hypnosis techniques. I conducted this session, as they were short a partner. Iris demonstrated her abilities and after my session where Iris walked me into a previous lifetime, we switched places:

Rich: Iris, what do you want to explore?

Iris: I want to explore a past life and see if I can get in touch with a guide or my council. And maybe visit that planet I once dreamed about.

Okay, close your eyes; we're going to start a staircase... imagine where that would be.

In some big estate.

Let's picture that a beautiful estate that's got a staircase with 63 steps...what are the steps made of?

Marble.

(after a while) Bring your guides forward to help us examine when you chose these contracts with your parents. Where, when these agreements were made. Are we inside or outside?

I feel like I'm in electric light – white electric light.

Is it in the distance?

I'm in it, almost like it's lighting but it's not hurting me, gentle but sparking everywhere. I'm .. my skin looks brown or tan.

Take a look at this person. Male or female?

A female... She looks 22, or 23... I don't think this is her age, because she's really old but looks young. Her hair is black grey she's about 5' 7 or 8. She's dark skinned but she has almond eyes.

Take hold of her hands. Is there any sensation doing so?

Yes, I feel happiness and light. Her eyes are glowing green like emeralds; they're glowing.

First I want to thank her for being here – is it okay for me to ask you direct questions?

"Yeah."

Could you give us a name or a letter to address you with?

I'm getting an S.. like Starlo... I can't quite get it.

I'll call you Miss S. Can you show Iris what she looks like to you while holding you hand?

She looks like Iris. Same age.

Can I ask, are you one of Iris's guides?

"No, she's me."

Are you Iris in between lives or from a previous life?

She's saying "She is me."

If I was going to characterize you as her higher self would that be accurate?

"No, she's me from a different planet."

Okay. That's why the emerald green eyes - thank you for anticipating this journey. Would it be all right for you take us to the planet you normally incarnate on?

"Yes."

Are we inside or outside?

It's all black... dark. Hard to see. It's like... I'm seeing black ice, or black stone... like midnight black stone that's jagged.

If you can help bring up the light in this memory, so she can observe things; let's go to a place on this planet.

Okay. Now we're on top of like, it's almost like jagged black mountains looking down. It's quite beautiful; it's not ice but it's black stone. Looks like a marble or granite.

Like black marble?

Yes, but jagged and very sharp. She's standing above it. She's wearing a black or burgundy dark robe. She has like a gold medallion, it's kind of ... this shape (gestures a star) but it's this shape inside.

What's this medallion represent?

It helps her (to) feel what everyone is feeling.

Like a communication device?

(Nods) It heightens empath abilities.

Miss S, you're showing Iris herself in this lifetime, is that correct?

"Yeah."

Let's go to a home, a place you normally reside. Are we inside or outside?

"We're outside. We live outside; we need to be inside."

Is this a manufactured environment or just the natural environment of this planet?

"It's natural."

Is it in our universe?

No, it's far away.

Has Iris consciously been here in a dream she's aware of?

No, but she comes here all the time.

And we're here now consciously aren't we?

"Yeah."

What kind of work do you do Miss S?

"I am ... I heal."

You're a healer? A doctor of sorts?

"No, it's energy."

Energy healing... let's call it that as a way to examine this lifetime. How long do people live on your planet?

"We don't die."

How does incarnation occur or does it? Is there birth or death?

"We've always been here – we go to other solar systems."

So you're helping others ... is there a name you refer to this planet as a place or name?

I get ... "Kenar."

I ask that because if I meet someone else, I can ask them if it's the same planet. Are there many people from Kenar on Earth helping people?

"Yes. But on other planets as well, we go to help and heal."

In terms of earth, roughly how many people from Kenar are here?

"There are hundreds of us."

(Note: I've had similar answers from people who refer to those from their "home planet" who are currently incarnated on earth and doing the same kind of work. See chapter "Over the Rainbow" in "Flipside.".)

Let me ask you about the empathetic device. How does that function? Is it a frequency device?

"It has energy through to heart."

An amplification device of heart energy?

"Yes, you heal heart to heart."

In your experience Miss S, you have no beginning, nobody dies on your planet, perhaps that's beyond my capacity to understand. But you're saying people from your planet are around the universe helping and healing. Are you going to manifest on our planet to help us what's going on?

"No. This is a service."

I'm aware that Iris is very familiar with astrology and uses that knowledge to help people?

"I don't understand the question."

Iris is conversant with the charting of stars; is that related to your healing work?

"Astrology is something that is not on our planet; it's something that Iris learned somewhere else."

Okay. I was asking if your empathetic healing is related.

"It's something she picked up to help her heal people."

Do people from your planet travel here to earth physically or etherically?

"It's energy. "

Miss S, are you aware of the kind of work I'm doing?

"We're very aware."

Is that a good thing or a bad thing?

"It's a very good thing Rich. You're opening people up to the realm of possibilities so that they can live fuller lives. And let go of their bondage."

I appreciate that. I think Iris has been doing this work for many lifetimes. But you're saying the core of who she is, is who you are, is that correct?

"She's me."

Has Iris had a glimpse of you before?

"Not consciously."

Do me favor, show me her your arm, your skin.

She's looking at it. "It's mahogany brown and very soft, there's no hair... It's very soft and beautiful."

Do you have... this is an energetic construct but do you have toes and fingers?

"I have human form."

Is that for our benefit so we can have a conversation?

"Yes."

May I ask how you appear to other people from Kenar?

"I have light... I am a ray of light with an emerald center."

So the emerald center is reflected in your eyes?

"My essence is emerald."

What does that color represent in terms of energetic construct?

"Life. Higher life. Serenity and higher life."

What do you want to tell Iris, why did you allow her to come and experience this?

"She's supposed to be healing people."

Will she start practicing hypnotherapy and helping people?

"There are many paths she can take. That's one."

But the important part is for her to realize she needs to be healing people?

"Emotionally healing people. Not as a therapist."

Does she do that while she's a sleep or awake?

"That's a good question, but she does much of it while she's asleep."

Can you walk Iris in to visit her council?

"It's another place."

That's okay, let's go. Are we inside or outside?

(A pause) We aren't there yet.

Okay. I'll wait for you to make that journey.

"We traveled at the speed of light. We're outside."

Thank you for allowing me to ask you to do that; what's that experience to travel at the speed of light?

"It's quick."

Like the speed of thought?

"You've gone from a place in deep space to another place. We're in the clouds.

When you're in the clouds can you see down below?

"I can see down below, but up above is blue sky."

How many people are in this council when you look around?

"Like ten."

How are they arrayed?

"In a semicircle."

First I want to thank Miss S for escorting us, and staying with us, if you don't mind. Council may we speak to you?

"Yes."

How far away from you are they?

"A couple of feet. They're over here (gestures) – and I'm sort of over here."

So go to the person on the far left, is that a male, female, neither or both?

"It's a ball of light."

Get as close as you can to it. How large is it?

"Like a volleyball... When you're close it feels good and energetic and warm. It's soothing."

So this ball of light, can I speak to you directly?

"Yes."

Would you do me a favor and manifest as a human so we can converse?

He keeps trying but it goes back into the ball.

What's a name or letter we can address you by?

L. Lila... sounds female, but is not.

Can Iris put her hands around you?

Yes. It feels soothing, feels good, feels like I'm at peace. makes me feel like I'm at peace.

Lila, what quality do you represent in Iris' spiritual evolvement that earned you this place on her council?

"Peace."

Did she earn that in this life or a previous lifetime?

"Previous."

How is Iris doing?

"She needs to pause more."

Is she doing what she set out to do?

"She's getting there."

How many councils do you sit on ?

"12."

And the person next to you? Male or female?

Neither. A light again. Navy blue. Lila was white with a gold center.. a white center, looked gold because of the light.

Can we ask you questions? Can you manifest as a person?

Okay – again it's hard, it's flashes in and out. Neither male nor female, has no gender.

What's a name we can address you with?

"Pamash."

Thank you Pamash. When Iris puts her hands around your light what does she feel?

"Compassion."

Is that the quality you possess that earned you a place on her council?

"Yes."

How many do you work on?

"22."

Are you aware of this work?

"Yes I am, Rich."

Is it a good or bad idea?

"It's a good idea, but public awareness is difficult."

I'm not fishing for a compliment, just like to hear different points of view.

"You're a pioneer. It's good. There's no glory in being a pioneer."

Most pioneers wind up on crosses. I always ask for lottery numbers but they never give them. Are you going to be different Pamash?

"It's fate."

Okay, so you're on 22 councils, compassion is your main focus. Who's the comedy guy on your council?

"Well... one is laughter."

Let's have that person stand up.

"Another light. This one is purple – it's Amethyst."

How many councils do you serve on?

"81."

A name to address you ?

"Liam."

How do you think Iris doing?

"She laughs a lot."

Let me ask; you represent laughter, on her council, correct?

"Yes."

Laughter makes people heal; is that what her ability is?

"Yes. A lot of healing through humor – a lot of laughter through healing humor."

Who is the lead council member?

"It's Kolabra."

Let me guess. A light?

"Yes."

What color are you?

"I have every color. Not a rainbow, but every color. I reflect all light."

So you're mostly white?

"No, I'm every color, I'm a ball of every color light I'm a prism... I'm reflecting all light."

How many councils do you serve on?

"Thousands."

Is there a word associated with your service on her council? A quality she's earned?

"I'm all qualities."

I understand... all variations of light. When she looks at you what does she see?

"A prism of colors, they're vibrant, they're mesmerizing."

Is there a feeling or emotion associated with them?

"I would say it's every emotion, every feeling; it's everything. I am everything."

So Kolabra, how do you think Iris is going?

"She's here doing what she's supposed to be doing."

Is she fulfilling that?

"Sometimes yes, but not everything yet."

Can you but a sensation in her body so she knows when you are trying to reach her?

"Yes."

It's important for Iris to know she's always tethered to you and everyone at the council. Anyone else want to speak up?

"Yes. It's I don't know their name but this light is like a burgundy color and represents "pain.""

What's your role in her journey?

"You need pain to grow. You need pain to grow. You need pain to grow."

Did she earn your place on her council from previous lifetime?

"Yes, previous ones. We all grow, but she grows through pain. We all grow through pain but she really grows through pain."

How many councils do you sit on?

"Four."

On all of them do you represent pain? I would think they'd be disconcerted when you show up.

"Yes. All emotions are good, there's not good or bad – we're light. Light leads the way. Light leads the way; there's no good, bad, male, female. We exist for growth. All emotions lead to growth. All emotions lead to growth. You grow through emotions. Emotions are energy."

So when you work with Iris in terms of pain, how does that work? I understand how laughter works, compassion, courage –how does pain help them grow?

"Through the pain experience they develop memories – these base memories compounded help them see the light. I'm seeing a flash of almost like blood vessels, they're like blood vessels from lifetime to lifetime that like a tree, grow."

So they're always connected like roots.

"Like roots going up but not down. They're growing. In the light."

I want to thank you all for allowing us to speak to you – you have a reason for her to experience this. Does someone want to speak to her about why they allowed her to do this today?

"They have a message for you Rich; I'm trying to get it... I'm getting "keep on the path, that you're going to your council is lighting the way, and you need to listen more – they want you to listen."

Story of my life, my wife says it every day.

"You need to listen. To stop and listen."

What do you want Iris to do?

"We want her to connect with more people. Iris meets a lot of people and this is a way to introduce this work."

Here's a question for you – this technique where I have people access councils, is this something Iris should do?

"No, it's only 25% of the time that you are getting the councils. 24.3% of the time you're getting to the *real council*. You will know when you know. People hesitate; they're not giving you everything. Not everyone understands."

When we first met Iris in the flipside she was teaching a class in energy transformation. (In "It's a Wonderful Afterlife.")

"She is still teaching. She's teaching people to move energy."

How many in her class now?

"It changes, and right now it looks like about 18. They're always different."

Can we talk to one of your students?

"Sure. Female. Blond. About 55. Larissa is her name."

Have you ever incarnated on earth?

"I'm here now."

What's Iris like as a teacher?

"She's very, very enlightened."

Describe what her teaching method is.

"She teaches me to connect your mind body and soul to the movement of energy."

The energy you're talking about, is it etheric, or are you in another realm moving things?

"We are (physically) moving things."

In our universe or another one?

"It has many layers. We are moving energy on earth and we're moving energy in other solar systems."

Scott, the hypnotherapist and Iris had a feeling of energy pass between them earlier.

"It was a match striking, it was both. It was a combustion."

Related to what we're talking about now?

"Related to classes they've done together. They've been in many many many classes together."

Could Iris' main guide come forward?

He looks like Balzac in a black robe. I don't really see his face, he's not male or female. He's big, towering over me.

Can you take his hands?

I don't see hands.

Hold on to him – what does that feel like?

Energetic; kind of interesting, happiness and concern. It's confusing.

Are you concerned about her?

"That's my nature."

It's what a good guide does. Be concerned and happy, correct?

"Yeah."

How is she doing?

"She's doing good; she's difficult. She's stubborn."

How did you meet – did she choose you?

"It's always been."

For all of her lifetimes?

"Yes."

Take her back to the moment when you became part of your care or charge – like a life planning session of who you are as a soul. what did you discuss?

"There was no discussion; we came together because it was written."

In terms of her journey, did you help her decide or was it already decided?

"Already decided."

So you're a guide following a map?

"It's all been decided."

But it's like a blueprint, you're like an architect helping follow the blueprints, otherwise she wouldn't need you.

"Yeah."

She must come to you for advice.

"I don't know if she knows it."

Consciously she doesn't but does she show up sometime?

"When things don't go her way."

Do you guide anyone else?

"No. She's a lot of work."

Does she like your sense of humor or is just me?

"She gets me."

What do you think about this work we're doing here?

"Very exciting."

Is this new or old information?

It was taught in Atlantis.

Is Iris aware of Atlantis?

Oh yes, she was there.

Is it on earth or in another realm?

It was a replica of another planet. Part of a city. Atlantis was a planet.

Was it in our universe? Was it destroyed by science or nature?

The planet is still around.

The replica on earth?

Destroyed by water. The earth opened.

Was Iris there?

Yes. Iris was a priestess and she got hit by a falling temple.

Can you put in her mind's eye what she looked like?

Blonde, tall, green eyes.

Why did she choose that lifetime, what did she want to learn from that lifetime in Atlantis?

Spirituality. On another level.

Why did she choose Iris and what do those two have in common?

Iris chose Iris to break barriers; she was breaking barriers as Lil in the spiritual community, she was showing people there are many ways, and science and spirituality can work hand in hand. In this lifetime, a lot of science is not spiritual. they need to walk hand in hand.

They aren't but they need to?

"Yes; to save the earth."

Can I ask everyone, your guides, how do we save the earth?

"It's science and spirituality; they have to marry."

And how do we help that occur?

"You have to stop eating flesh."

What else?

"You have to realize that the earth is a being. And treat it with respect. Also to not slow down science, but there are ways of making more natural things. you need to get away from synthetics."

To paraphrase, stop eating flesh, treat the earth as a being, and to create more natural things instead of synthetic.

Yes. But also, know ... (to her guide she says "Slow down.") I want to say the water – there's so much water – I don't know what that means... "Slow down the water." I don't know what that means.

Do you mean a method to create energy from water? Or slow down pollution of water?

I'm getting "Hydroelectric needs to take over, and nuclear energy has to go away."

There was a Wall Street Journal article months ago on this topic, and that we heard the same thing from a scientist no longer on the planet; using water as fuel, that the water itself contains energy - that sea water has naturally occurring uranium which can be used and recycled.

"Iris is not aware of that; she's very surprised but I'm not. I'm aware of it."

We got a similar concept from Nikola Tesla. May I ask, have you met Tesla? Einstein? Hawking?

"I have met them. Their knowledge was downloaded from us."

I've been asking that question to see if you can help us save the earth. Is this something Iris can do when she's back home?.

"She doesn't have the patience."

Does she know anyone who can do this?

"No, I am supposed to tell you. That was your message.

Thank you Katar. Dr. K.

"We don't spell over here. But it's K dash Tarrr – three rrrs."

K-tarrr.. maybe an h in there?

"No h."

The reason I ask these questions is to help me access you – perhaps via a medium.

Who's the medium?

Jennifer Shaffer.

Let me see if I can find her. I'm sending her my frequency. I don't know her, but I'm sending her my frequency.

I didn't know you could do that, but thank you.

Hold on. She should be able to ... she just acknowledged me.

I'll talk to her about that.

She's a good person. She really helps you Rich. She is doing good work.

Iris, I had a question for a friend of yours (Penny) that you accessed previously, who is a teacher. Can she answer some questions?

"Yes."

What are you teaching on the flipside?

"Psychology."

How many in your class?

"They're big I have many classes. I lecture to probably a thousand."

What form of psychology to you teach? Human behavior or behavior of beings on the flipside?

"It's how to function on other planets, the psychology of functioning on other planets. There is not just earth, there are many other planets, many solar systems and each has different customs and ways, and psychologically we need to learn to maneuver within those cultures."

Are there any sacrosanct rules, like "no interference?" What would be one?

"You cannot interfere. And if someone's not getting the message you've got to let go."

Do you mean a culture or individual?

"All. Someone is not getting the message... an example is that war is bad, and clearly they didn't get the message. War destroyed Mars. Not the atmosphere, but war – they blew up the atmosphere by war."

(Note: I transcribe these sessions and sometimes realize to my own shock that I had just heard about a war on Mars. Not from Iris, but from a few other people who claim to have lived there, and this actual battle for Mars was reported during Heather Wade's interview.)

What kinds of beings were on Mars, then?

"They weren't lizards but lizard-like; they had many many toes and many feet but they were small lizard like..."

(Note: In Heather's description, they were lizard like as well. Also these "lizard like" fellows show up in a later chapter.)

Battled with each other or other creatures?

"They battled with each other."

Ultimately what snuffed out their planet?

"They snuffed out their atmosphere 100's of millions of years ago."

Did some of those souls wind up on earth?

"Some of those beings are also in our classes, they're here, they're everywhere."

We heard this from Stephen Hawking, "Stop using the word alien and you'll understand consciousness better because we all choose to incarnate." Is that correct?

"Very true."

What other planets has Penny been on or aware of?

"I was on Mars, I was a peacekeeper on Mars, but it didn't really work. I feel like the Earth as well, and I was also in Atlantis.

Did you know Iris from then?

"Yes. She was a priestess then."

(Note: As mentioned earlier. It's not that Iris is quoting Iris – Iris has no recollection of being a priestess anywhere – other than maybe being a "princess" when she was in high school when I first met her. But her guide told us she was a priestess on Atlantis, and now her friend is saying the same thing. I know this is Iris talking, but just pointing out she's shifting perspective and saying the same things.)

Are you a member of Iris' soul group? How many are in her group?

"Yes. There are 100's."

In terms of a core group?

"Fifty two. It's quite large."

Does she recognize people in her group? Family members?

"Oh yeah."

In a previous session, she explained that her core group was working with addiction – is that still accurate, or is that just part of one class?

"That is part of her "energy class;" How To Heal Addiction. It is energetic."

Are all 52 of the class healers?

Yes, and peacekeepers. Peacekeepers are healers.

What activities do you participate in aside from teaching?

I study and play games. Mind games. An earth example would playing chess by linking our lives with the board.

A chess game played in multiple dimensions?

"Yes."

What other games besides chess?

"We don't have time for many games; we listen to a lot of music."

Where's it generated from?

"It's ethereal."

Are there musicians that help you create that music?

"Not really but there's a group, I've never met them; but they are in charge of music."

K-tarrr, I need your help, let's take Iris to meet them these music creators. Are we inside or outside.

Okay it's inside; there are 100's here, it's an auditorium.

Can someone come forward to answer my questions?

It's a male. He looks like Bob Dylan in his 20's. He has a guitar, no hat. The guitar is slung behind his back.

If I may ask you some questions; are you someone appearing as Bob for Iris to communicate with you, or are you actually Bob Dylan's higher self?

"Higher self, yes. (Robert Zimmerman aka Bob)"

(Note: I've been doing this for long enough to know that it's an either/or question. Either someone is creating the image to go along with the energy they're communicating with, or the "higher conscious energy" of this person shows up to converse. I'm aware his energy has had other lifetimes, prior to the one he might have appeared in Hibbing, Minnesota, but again, I'm not here to prove or disprove anything; I'm just asking questions about the architecture.)

So if I can call you Bob; I've met your daughter and granddaughter in life, I've spoken to a number of musicians on the flipside, many you know. My question is, when people manifest music either here or on the flipside, is it math, are you generating it, or is it a combination of both?

"Music is math but it's also emotion. It's emotion tied to math. And we all generate it, we send it down people to download it. But they download with their lives; anyone can ask us, if they are aware."

(Note: I think "downloaded with their lives" means "by choosing their lifetime, they are equipped with a certain frequency that allows them to appreciate certain types of music.")

Do you create songs or just a method to create songs?

"We create the feeling of the song; they can hear it in their head and they translate it."

Who do you hang out with over there? Anyone that we might know here?

"Well, John Lennon. Eric Clapton is here too."

(Note: As noted prior we bring "about a third of our conscious energy" to a lifetime and "two thirds is always back home." Eric's son and John were interviewed in "Backstage Pass to the Flipside" but Iris hasn't read it. Our "higher self" can see and communicate with others, while our "planet self" may not be aware of these conversations at all.)

Should we speak to John?

"Sure."

John, please put in Iris' mind what you've told me about your son Julian. Something you told Julian before you passed – if you were going to communicate with him...

"White."

Show Iris what that is.

"A white feather."

Thank you.

(Note: Some years after his father's death, while touring Australia, a local tribal chief asked for Julian's help in getting fresh water for his people. As a gift he brought him a large white feather and Julian named his foundation after the gift "The White Feather Foundation.")

What do you want to say to Julian, in case I can pass it along?

"Tell him he gives me a lot of joy watching him."

He's become an incredible photographer; are you helping him?

"Um, no; that's all him."

About what age is John appearing in front of you?

40 with glasses.

John you didn't like wearing glasses in life – yet you manifest with them; why is that?

"I need them. It makes things clearer."

Your glasses function as a mechanism to help you focus?

"It helps me to see things clearly – without them (over here) I was tortured by seeing things *too* clearly."

I'm curious your impression of my friend Luana, whom you've met via Jennifer Shaffer. What does Luana look like?

"She's floating. It's not like she has wings, but she floats around almost as if she does; she moves and navigates as if she has wings... she has blue eyes, blonde hair, shoulder length."

(Note: I've had a lot of conversations with Luana since 1996, but this is the first time someone has described her in this manner.)

Let's ask Luana how she thinks I'm doing.

"She's very proud of you, Rich."

It's all about me *isn't it? Does Iris have question for John Lennon?*

(Iris aside) I met him once. (to John) "Do you remember meeting me?" He says he does. I met Yoko at La Guardia airport; we were going to Camp Stanley; we were at the airport and first I noticed Yoko because she had like 8" platform shoes and hot pants cut down to her navel – and my mouth dropped because she was so hot. And then next to her was John and then Eric Clapton was with them and they sat next to me.

(Note: Camp Stanley was a camp in the Catskills where Iris went during high school. My first trip to NYC, four pals from high school drove out to visit her on her way to our first trip to the Big Apple.)

How old were you?

I was 16. I was with my sisters and they sat at the table next to us and said "Hi." My sister said "Hi, we're big fans" and we talked to them and John gave us his signature with a little drawing... my sister has it.

Wow, John what a treat to see you here – you can always help Iris.

"Her singing isn't that great."

That's funny! I want to thank everyone who has participated in our journey today, I appreciate everyone's input and their help - you've all be incredible. I'd like to leave behind a backstage pass to come back at a future date. Let's say goodbye to Iris guides, thanks for the amazing journey.

I want to thank them.. and Rich... they all have really good feelings about you. You have a very good healing soul.

Let's thank everyone for the journey and for Iris allowing us to go deep to this place we've been.

Well. How about that for a ride and a half?

I've known Iris since we were in high school. Needless to say, we have a shorthand with each other that comes from years of friendship, and this points to lifetimes of friendship. She's done two other sessions of deep hypnosis, both I was able to forensically look up details of her previous lives.

There's so much to unpack in this session, that I'll just leave it at this; those who are supposed to understand what she was talking about the flipside will comprehend it, and those who feel like this is a lot of imaginary magical thinking shouldn't have been reading this far.

Either way, thanks for the ride, Iris!

CHAPTER EIGHTEEN:

GURU RINPOCHE

Guru Rinpoche in the Jokhang Temple in Lhasa, Tibet. From my documentary "Journey into Tibet with Robert Thurman." Also called Padmasambhava, or "Lotus Born."

My old friend Chuck Tebbetts sent me a link to this young filmmaker's film "Guru Rinpoche" – a documentary he made about the famous Indian Pandit and Tibetan Saint "Padmasambhava" or "Guru Rinpoche" (Precious Jewel Teacher).

I was fascinated by the documentary because it covers a number of topics that are near and dear to my heart. It travels to some of the same places I went to in Tibet with Robert Thurman (Samye Monastery, Lhasa and footage of Tibetan faces.) Plus, this filmmaker was inspired by a "visitation" he had from the flipside, where he captures on camera, someone "telling him to make this film."

Guru Rinpoche is credited with bringing Buddhism to Tibet. He arrived at the behest of the Tibetan King who asked him to build Samye monastery and bring Buddhism to his people. He was not a monk, but traveled with four different women known as his "consorts." He was practiced in esoteric tantra and yoga, and is considered to be a Buddha by the Tibetan people.

He was famous for his battles of wit with local Bon priests who represented the original Tibetan belief system. Reportedly, he had one such debate outside of Samye with these practitioners of ancient Bon practices – his victory over them so complete, they packed up and moved East. Some claim those Bon people wound up in the Western United states. (The Apache people share identical DNA to Mongolian peoples, and some of the native American religious practices, including the swastika as a symbol of eternity are in the Apache religious practices. When the Dalai Lama first met an Apache chief, he exclaimed "I'm looking in a mirror!")

Guru Rinpoche was an important person in the history of Tibet; many things are ascribed to him, including being a master of the "rainbow body" which during a deep and profound meditation, a monk can reportedly shape shift, or turn into pure light, or a rainbow of light. In the documentary, the filmmaker Hideto Edward Uno shows some amazing footage taken of various monks who had reportedly attained these "rainbows body abilities" and there are modern accounts as well with accompanying mind bending footage of physical and light anomalies.

But the fact that "Uno" was "channeling" a higher power to make this film, the idea that he films himself accessing these visions, as well as the fact that he went into some of the same caves, and saw the same phenomena I did – where Guru Rinpoche had "burned" his handprint or footprint into solid stone in various places across Tibet – caught my attention.

I called him to compliment his filmmaking, which I was startled to hear was his first effort. I wasn't planning on us taking the following adventure, but as you'll see, it also hits a number of bases from the architecture of the afterlife canon.

My questions *in Italics*, Uno's replies **in bold**.

Rich: Taishe Delek Hideto Edward Uno. So what can I call you?

Uno: People call me "Uno."

As in "Uno, Due?"

(Uno chuckles) Yeah.

I loved your film "Guru Rinpoche" and I just wanted to say hello. Our mutual friend Chuck Tebbetts introduced us on Facebook. We do share some things in common – we've both been to Lhasa, Tibet, I made a film about it, and I will send you a link to "Journey into Tibet with Robert Thurman."

I just came back from India filming there too.

That's great! I've been fortunate to film in India from Kashmir to Kerala. I even got to make a Bollywood film ("My Bollywood Bride") so that was fun... tell me about your journey.

Most of it is in the film in terms of channeling and Buddhism. The film documents the beginning of it for me. I was fascinated by Guru Rinpoche and I heard certain things, from an esoteric point of view. As was in the film, that thing (hearing a directive that he should pursue Rinpoche's path) happened where I channeled, and heard that I should go Tibet. So I went.

Were you raised Buddhist?

No, no. I was Christian, raised in California. When I was really young, I loved Jesus – and I have heard of that film about Jesus being in India. And I realized later that Jesus is like a Buddha – what he had to say was really like a yogi.

(Note: It's important to note that in his film, Uno has an experience when he sees a poster of Guru Rinpoche having a rainbow body experience. After that, while meditating a voice comes to him that he channels on camera. The voice tells him to travel to Tibet, Bhutan to visit the places that Guru Rinpoche taught. As mentioned in "Flipside" I know someone who was a monk in a previous lifetime who had a "rainbow body death."

Also, fans of "Hacking the Afterlife" have already come in contact with the research that claims Jesus lived in Kashmir and returned with his family after the crucifixion, but let's not get ahead of ourselves. At this moment, I suggest that maybe we can go on an adventure together in a session without hypnosis.)

Rich: Well, Uno, do you want to explore this?

Uno: Yeah, sure!

When you talk about Jesus, does he seem familiar to you?

When I was a little kid reading the bible I used to think "I already know this." (Uno laughs.)

Well, in my book "Hacking the Afterlife" I talk to people who remember knowing him. But let's set that aside, because I know you had a visual during one of your sessions of seeing a gold faced Buddha.

In Bhutan? Yes, I saw Shakyamuni.

So let's see what we can access of that memory. (Uno closes his eyes) You don't have to close your eyes. Let's see where we can go. Let's pick a visual of someone you've seen during your meditations.

Shakyamuni is fine.

Great, as you've already seen him. But it's not like wearing a name tag, right?

Right.

Something in your inner voice says "This is Buddha." But to clarify; we're talking about Siddhartha correct?

Yes, or the "Archetypical energy" that is growing with every human experience, etc.

I've learned we can access a slice of time by asking simple questions. Let's examine what you're seeing; is he sitting or standing?

He's usually like in a meditation pose. Left hand up – right hand down.

Is that the same visual you saw in Bhutan?

No. He had the sun disk behind him.

Just to make it easier, let's ask this person to manifest to you in normal attire.

Modern attire?

Yeah. If that's okay. What's he wearing?

(Uno smiles). He's wearing kind of like what I'm wearing. I definitely saw like a hoodie coat, jacket, jeans.

How far away is he from you?

A few feet; like four or five.

Try to hologram this visual; freeze it so you can move around it. Move closer to him.

I should go closer?

Yeah, or let him come to you.

That's easier.

Take hold of his hand and tell me – does he have rough or soft hands?

Hmm. My instinct is that they are rough actually.

Is there any emotion with holding onto both his hands?

Warmth in my heart.

Any familiarity – do you know this fellow?

Yeah, but I work with him in meditation often.

Let's ask if it's okay to ask him some questions.

Sure.... But I always ask him questions. So let me ask him. (Uno closes his eyes and is silently moving his lips.) He says "Yes of course."

Thank you sir. We've frozen this image, move behind him. How does he see you?

Hmm. (smiles, shrugs). Kind of lizardy. I've already been told (by someone) that supposedly my soul is half reptilian and half Pleiadian.

That's fine – try not to judge it, if that's how he sees you. What's your skin like?

It's greenish; brownish. My eyes are like a snake's eyes. The pupil is black. White around it.

Do your eyes close up and down or from the side?

(Note: Uno is struggling with my suggestion he keep his eyes open)

Am I allowed to close my eyes?

Sure, I mean do the lids close from the side?

Yeah, from the side.

Let's ask him... is Shakyamuni the right term for our friend here?

"Yeah." He says "You could say Buddha."

How is our friend Uno doing?

(Uno aside) Do you want me to just talk?

Yeah whatever comes to mind.

It will be easier if I just talk directly... "How is he doing? Uno is doing very well."

Could I ask a personal question? Are you familiar with the work I'm doing?

Buddha says "Yes of course."

Do you recall our conversation before with my friend Jennifer?

"Yes, you were talking about... something to do with your work."

(Note: As egotistical as this question sounds, it's for reference. I have conducted an "interview" with Siddhartha (Shakyamuni Buddha) when he showed up in a conversation in the book "Backstage Pass to the Flipside: Talking to the Afterlife with Jennifer Shaffer." "No" would tell me what questions I might continue to ask. "Yes" doesn't mean "I remember talking to you" but includes "Yeah, well I am the Buddha, so pretty much am aware of everything, including you.")

(The statue of Shakyamuni Buddha in the Jokhang Temple in Lhasa, Tibet. (ibid) It's reported this statue was crafted during Buddha's lifetime, was part of the dowry of one of King Songtsen Gampo's (569 CE) wives. One of his successors Trisong Detsen invited Guru Rinpoche to Tibet (763 CE).)

Yes, that's correct. I asked you some questions about your passing, your "Paranirvana" and how your nephew Ananda apologized for serving you your last meal?

"Yes."

Ananda served you tainted meat, you got sick from it. Before you died, Ananda is quoted as saying "Oh no, I will go down in history as the man who served the buddha a poisoned dinner!"

(Uno laughs.) "Yes, I said, "That's okay because that is also a blessing."

(Laughter) That's reportedly what you said; like "the bad news is you served this meal, the good news is, you will be famous."

"Yes, but that's just the ego, that's fine, that's how it goes, as you know."

(Note: I heard this story from Robert Thurman in his class at Columbia University, and I recalled the notion of "Oh no! I've killed the Buddha!" and his reply, "But you'll go down in history as the one who served his last meal." It could be made up – but he could have disputed the story (and sometimes people do.) In this case, I'm allowing the odd construct that I'm actually speaking to the Buddha, because I've done so with Jennifer Shaffer in the past. Not trying to be disrespectful, but instead of focusing on "trying to prove it actually is him," I focus on whatever question pops into my mind.)

In terms of reincarnation, we discussed the Bodhisattva vow, and in terms of reincarnating, you said something along the lines of "your energy has reincarnated partially or emanated in various forms" – like portions of your conscious energy. Is that accurate?

(Uno asking) "Emanations?"

I mean reincarnations without limiting the concept. That some portion of your conscious energy may be on the planet at any given time?

"Yes. That is possible, because it is not a thing but can be broken up into many things."

(Note: Like how a hologram retains all of the information even when broken into pieces; even the smallest piece retains the same data. So if a portion of an individual incarnates, it still would retain all the elements of that individual.)

I was wondering if our friend Jesus can come forward to speak to Uno?

"Yes. "

Let's bring Jesus into the room – what do you see?

The vary stereotypical kind of Jesus. Not the blue eyed one, but with the brown hair with light colored robes.

Look carefully at his eyes; what color are they?

Kind of brown – but more hazel or green.

Do you see bits of yellow in them?

Yes. They are kind of in-between green and brown.

(Note: I know this is a leading question, "Do you see yellow in them?" but people familiar with my reports will recognize he often shows up in these sessions with brown eyes and "flecks of yellow" or "gold" in them. Here I supplied the image; Uno supplied the hazel color.)

How long is his hair?

At first I thought shoulder length; it might be a little longer.

Jesus, can you also shift into some clothing that's less regal or iconic so we can have a normal conversation?

(Uno smiles) Mm-hm. He's wearing a flannel shirt and jacket, jeans. His flannel shirt is red.

Flannel? Is it cold up there? Just kidding. I want to thank him for coming forward. Tell us how you think our friend Uno is doing?

Should I get behind him and see me through him?

Sure. What does Uno look like to Jesus?

Hmm. Kind of the same – like the lizard thing... Kind of a big vague shape; like a dark shape of a human.

While we have you two guys here. Uno had a connection to the Bible when he was a little kid. Can you show or tell him why that is?

Uh... He's going to just tell me. Jesus says "He was a friend of mine."

So let's let Uno go and see that lifetime – we'll come back to you Jesus and Buddha in a moment, but let's flow flow into that lifetime when you were a friend of Jesus. Where you male or female?

(After a moment) I was a female.

How did you look?

Long brown hair. Kind of tall.

Are you someone that is in his inner circle, supported him or just a friend?

"I was in his inner circle."

What would be a name that comes to mind when I ask that?

(Uno laughs.) I'm holding back, but I think it's "Mary."

Don't judge it. Everyone was named Mary in those days – Maryum, Mary, etc.

"There's lots of Marys. Yes."

When you look at this Mary person, what was her relationship to Jesus? A close friend, disciple or family?

I'm getting "Mary Magdalene."

(Note: Fans of my books will know that I've spoken to a dozen people who've recalled lifetimes where they knew Jesus. So what are the odds that this panoply of people who recalled knowing him would find me? I'm fully prepared to dismiss any account as fantasy or wishful thinking, but I continue to ask questions to see if we can get to some other form of truth or understanding.)

Let's just allow that to be the case. Go to the point when our friend is on the cross. What do you see, looking at him on the cross.

"I see him on the cross. It is very distressing... but I also know that this isn't necessarily real."

Take a look at the people around you – who are you standing next to?

"I'm standing next to a Roman; named Pilate."

Is he a friend of yours?

"Definitely was not; but he was next to me."

(Note: After this session, I did a follow up session with Jennifer Shaffer, my pal the medium. As we accessed the same scene, I asked her to identify who our friend was seeing in this "memory" and she said "I think he was a Roman. A Roman soldier standing near Mary, but was accessing her during this memory." No way to prove it one way or the other, but I did follow up on it. And no one else reports seeing Pilate anywhere near the Crucifixion, but it was a common name.)

Crucifixion scene by Fra' Angelico.

What was Magdalene's relationship to Jesus?

"She was going to say lovers, but do you mean before that?"

Lovers is okay.

"I thought you meant when they were younger."

Well, before he was on the cross. Did you guys have children?

"Yes."

How many?

"They had three children. A boy, girl and then a boy."

Let me ask you what the girl's name was?

"Her name was S..."

Sarah?

"No, Stella."

Okay, let's go back to your position looking at him on the cross. Describe what's holding him up on this wood?

"A rope. There is something in his hands, like a stake in his palm."

Take a look at his feet. Any nails or rope there?

"Just rope."

So let's go somewhere Uno is not aware of. Go to after the crucifixion, after Jesus is reportedly dead. What's the next time you see him?

"Did I see him... where? Or when?"

Where or when is fine; the next time you see him.

"I saw him... a few days later."

A few days later. Is he alive or dead?

"He was alive. And not in the rainbow body sense but in a physical sense."

He's alive. Okay. Just to note, we know that everyone that is talking to us is still alive, because nobody dies, but in this case, you're saying that he's in his physical body?

"Yes; he's alive in the normal sense."

(Note: Have heard this details before and reported it in "Hacking the Afterlife" so I don't spend time examining the details, skipping down to the reported event.)

Skipping ahead; if you and him leave the area, where do you go?

"They go to France."

After France you go somewhere else?

"They went to the Middle East."

And ultimately you settle in a town which is.. not too far from where Uno was recently. Do you want to show him where that was?

"It was in Kashmir."

(Note: Leading questions but based on previous conversations with different people. The report is consistent; that his closest friends were aware of what was going to happen; he insisted on staying and going through it. He used his esoteric yoga training to shift his awareness away from pain, survived the crucifixion (with the help of some Romans and closest friends), taken to a cave where Nicodemus tended to his wounds (the gospel reports he brought 75 pounds of myrrh and aloe – both used as restoratives).

Jewish burial tradition hasn't changed. Bodies are not, never have been anointed. Jesus was moved to another cave, reportedly (the light emanated from his rainbow body yoga left a reverse image on the cloth) his friends played their role in the ruse and later he went to visit the Apostles after they believed he was no more.

In this scenario, he does "rise from the dead" the same way people have a near death experience. According to these consistent reports, Mary had her own following – she and their family went to France with followers. When it was safe to do so, Jesus reportedly met up with them and the family returned to the silk road to live out their days in Kashmir under the alias "Yuz Asaf" which I'm told means "Boddhisattva."

Again – none of this is coming from my imagination, or any work of fiction I'm aware of. The fact that different people who've never met have told me the same story defies logic or reason, the idea that people claim to see Jesus and he thanks me for reporting this alternate story also defies any form of logic I'm aware of.)

Very good; thank you. Are you familiar with my work?

"Yes, of course."

I just wanted to clarify; I'm asking to verify things I've already heard or written about his journey. Let's go back to our friend Jesus for a second. The fact that he feels connected to Mary Magdalene – lovers and parents implies you were married, correct?

"Yes."

Was that a happy life?

"Yes... but also difficult."

Have you incarnated since then?

"Yes.. many times."

And why are you allowing Uno to access this information?

"Because we all need to understand that there isn't any life or death in the normal sense and that we need to realize the oneness of consciousness."

I have a question; do I know one of your children?

"Yes, actually yes."

Put that image in Uno's mind? What does this person look like?

She is a very beautiful person. She has... black hair.

Okay, thank you. Let's go back to Jesus and Buddha who are patiently standing by; can we do that?

"Yes."

One of the three of you; Mary, Jesus or Buddha – who wants to come forward and escort us into Uno's council? Or Uno's guide?

Um. Now it's.. my guide. "I am his intuition since we haven't talked yet."

So how do you manifest in Uno's mind – male, female or both?

"I am neither; I am more of a light. A higher self."

But for purposes of our conversation, if you could manifest as a person, so we can have this conversation I think it would be helpful.

"I am an extraterrestrial actually."

Are you manifesting as Uno? Like a Pleiadian or reptilian?

"Yes. A *"Pleiadilian."* (Laughs.)

What can I call you?

"Just say "Uno."

Well we have one Uno – so I'll call you Due. How's that?

"That's funny, why not?"

Are you familiar with the work I'm doing Mr. Due?

"Yes, both through Uno and from being in the realms."

You mean from the water cooler, where the council sits around and talks about what's going on? Can we go in to visit Uno's council?

"Yes."

Describe this to me – are we inside or outside? In Space or elsewhere?

"Outside. We are in nature on Earth."

Okay, look around; where are we?

"I see more plains and bushes."

How many individuals are here to speak to us?

"You... and I see about three. Standing."

Allow me to thank them for appearing – can we ask some simple respectful questions?

"Yes, of course."

Let's speak to the person on the far left, what do you see? Male, female? What do they look like?

"Yes, I saw this one the strongest, he's a reptilian. He's about 6 feet tall. His eyes are brownish, blackish. His skin is kind of gray, brown, green mixture."

What would be a name to use to address you sir?

"Something you can't really say with the human tongue, but we could just say ... K A M L I N."

(Note: Kamlin is a Hindu name for cupid or love (Kama is the Hindu God of love.)

Let me ask; Kamlin, how is our friend Uno doing?

"Definitely, he's had some trouble dealing with the "reptilians" in his family line, so to speak, but he has overcome this aspect very well."

Have you ever incarnated on Earth?

"No, I have never."

So have you and Uno ever incarnated on the same planet together?

"Yes we did many many many thousands and thousands of years ago."

Where is your planet? Is it in our solar system, universe or another one?

"It's not in this solar system, but near Orion."

Is there a name for your planet?

"You could call it B A S T R A N."

(Note: Bastran is a word that means "to clothe oneself" in Nepalese.)

Nice name for a planet. Can you show Uno what the place is like on Bastran? What's the environment like?

"It's kind of harsh in the human sense... lots of rocks and hot temperatures and we live "under the surface.""

If you could show Uno a place he lived and his family or people he lived with or his friends – what does that look like?

"It is in many caverns that we have. There is technology of course, but it's built within cavern structures."

What's the purpose of Uno leaving your planet where all his friends are and incarnating on Earth? What was the purpose of that choice?

"There are other factors in his sojourn, as people would say, but as far as leaving our planet. It's more... just him coming to earth to try to help."

To help in terms of climate change or in terms of consciousness awareness?

"Yes, more of consciousness awareness, and he the fact that he was reptilian and there's a need for a reptilian energy to come to earth because they know about the reptilians who are influencing others in a negative way."

So there's a plan afoot. How many councils do you sit on?

"I sit on five councils."

What quality do you represent on his council? Like in terms of spiritual evolvement why he is on your council.

"I am his strength and power."

Is he wearing any jewelry by the way?

"I wear some jewelry and some clothes."

Take a look at that jewelry what is it?

He has a ring; like it goes across his fingers.

Does that represent something?

"It represents something to Uno. It represents his strength as it is... like brass knuckles." (Uno laughs.)

A tough cookie. Please introduce us to the person next to you.

There is a female Pleiadian.

What's her name?

"I am a Pleiadian female we are speaking of... my name is (spells) T R A B A S."

(Note: Trabas means "shackles" in Spanish. To help keep track, the Pleiadian council members look humanoid, and the one from Bastran looks reptilian.)

Thank you Trabas. How does she look to you?

"She looks human with long, dirty blonde hair."

What do you represent on his council?

"His compassion, warmth and sweetness."

Has Uno ever incarnated on the planet earth near Tibet?

"Yes he has – a few times even."

What would be one of those lifetimes be close to where he visited Tibet?

"Yes, he was close to Samye."

(Note: Samye is outside of Lhasa, and is where the Tibetan King invited Guru Rinpoche to build a Buddhist monastery (the first) in Tibet in the 8th century. Both Uno and I have been there.)

Trabas, are you familiar with the work I'm doing talking to councils?

"Yes, you have been talking to many people about councils and trying to help humanity at the same time."

Is this a valid thing to be doing? Is there value to it?

"Yes, of course because these are the kind of things people disbelieve but need to hear the most."

Since you're familiar with his lifetimes in Tibet, what is Uno's connection to Guru Rinpoche?

"He was a devotee but not necessarily in person at the same time as Guru Rinpoche."

How many years after Guru Rinpoche was in Tibet was he a devotee?

"Maybe three or four hundred years after Guru Rinpoche was around."

(Note: It's worth noting that since this filmmaker made a film about Guru Rinpoche and traveled across Asia to search for his artifacts, it would make logical sense for him to remember a lifetime where he knew the fellow. He does not say that, however; he remembers being a devotee who lived 3 or 4 hundred years later. The next question I ask is to identify what Buddhist sect this monk might have been in.)

Can you put in Uno's mind what color robes did he wear in that lifetime?

"In this life he wasn't a monk."

I see; a devotee but not a monk? I know this is an unusual way to communicate with you Trabas, what do you want to tell people of our planet that we can pass it along?

"The most important message for humanity right now... is for them to remember what they really are; that is -- a piece of consciousness, that is -- a piece of what you would say is God, or source or what have you; that's the just most important thing for people to know. They are caught up with being a "self" and being "a body.""

One thing I want to ask Kamlin as well. Are you always tethered to Uno?

"Yes, we are always connected to him in the relative sense."

Can you help him in times of need?

"Yes, he should use us more often."

Trabas, how many councils do you sit on?

"I sit on six."

Can you introduce us to the person next to you?

"There is another to my left. It's a male." He looks like a human as well, actually.

Is there a name we can use for him?

"I am (spells) R A N F A D."

How old does Ranfad look? How does he appear visually?

"I look about 35. My eyes are blue, my hair is blond."

Have you had a lifetime on earth?

"No, but, I am a humanoid."

(Note: I don't know how much Uno knows about the new age theories of "aliens among us" but a casual search of "blonde Pleiadeans" yields a number of fantastical drawings and odd suggestions. I don't think it's fair to claim anyone is an "incarnated Pleiadian," if they don't claim to be – after all the process, as described consistently in the research is not that "They come here" as people but that "part of their conscious energy" incarnates as a human. (So we wouldn't see any "E.T's walking around.") However, in the visual of a "tall blonde" who claims to normally incarnate in the Pleiades has been repeated enough to generate websites on the topic.)

What quality do you represent on Uno's council?

"I am his intelligence, wisdom and know-how in life."

How many councils do you sit on?

"I sit on six."

Are you familiar with my work and if so how?

"Yes, because you are known to be working and word gets around."

So there's no magazine up there where people flip around the magazine and read articles about councils?

"There is no need for magazines when we get them in our minds."

A magazine of the mind - love that. How is our friend Uno doing? On the right path?

"Yes; he is doing much better, focusing on more spiritual things and trying to develop himself as a human being in the relative sense as well."

In terms of people on earth who may be listening to this, what do you want to tell people on the planet?

"Humanity is in a crisis because they do not know who they are and there is so much that is changing at the moment. And so people really need to get on track as far as... hm - spiritual things I guess you would say, they just need to get off of the material worries and that sort of thing; the same old story really."

You said you are humanoid – yet you haven't incarnated on Earth; where have you incarnated?

"I have not incarnated on earth, but I am incarnated in an area, close to the Pleiades."

Are you choosing to manifest as a blond haired blue eye guy to make it easier to communicate with you?

"No, some Pleiadeans can look somewhat like me. There's different bloods... going around, you know?"

Were your parents or genetic information from earth at some point?

"No. It's more like the other way around for humanity."

So human DNA came from the Pleiades instead of the other way around. Has Uno ever been visited by people from other planets?

"Many times when he was a child."

Was he aware of this?

"It's been blocked (from his mind) but he knows it's true."

Can you put it in his mind what happened?

"He saw gray aliens at his bed – and they took him away. "

"Due" help us with this memory. These grey people were they friends or strangers?

"Sure, someone he knew but it wasn't for positive reasons necessarily at that moment."

But in terms of his overall lifetimes – these friends of his had shown up to get information from him, correct?

"You could say that."

Almost like Columbus sending people to a distant shore and later his friends show up to say what have you learned?

"Yes, but there are different instances both good and bad."

Well, who can help us with this one? This concept of good and bad. From what I've learned in this research is that concept doesn't exist where you people are, but it exists on the planet because it's polarized.

"Yes, but it's more complicated."

But I want to uncomplicated it a bit – evil doesn't exist as a thing, but here on the planet we find people who act out of self interest- the people who normally incarnate off planet may be having a difficult time navigating the human body so their behavior comes out as hostile?

"Yes.. but it's more complicated."

Okay, just pointing out that humans have latched onto this good versus evil, god and Satan concept; it's not in the research. Or am I missing something?

"Yes, evil in that sense does not exist – but there are extra terrestrials that have their own agendas as well. Of course, Satan doesn't exist and evil could be considered self interest. It does exist in some form with extra terrestrials but the higher you go the less there will be."

Correct me if I'm wrong, but once you're human you're not aware of your lifetime on another planet.

"Yes."

So even if someone normally incarnates on another planet - they might be more aggressive but that is something they can change or contain?

"You can choose."

What do you want to tell Uno?

"Uno needs to stay on the same path he's doing with his practices, try to relax and not get too aggressive in his energies as he likes boxing."

I've talked to people who box on the flipside...

"Sure, nothing wrong with it, but Uno doesn't need it right now."

So before we leave this extraterrestrial world – let's ask your guide, who appears to be your higher self, take Uno to a place of healing.

Okay. We're inside. There's a bathtub; kind of like an Egyptian chamber looking place. Bricks and a brick bathtub kind of thing. The bricks are gold.

I post this example not because it's what he's seeing, but because it's impossible to find an image that matches what he's seeing.

Is there water in this tub?

"Yes."

Can you put yourself into it?

"Yes."

What impressions come to mind?

"Lots of light; like the water is full of light."

So what is that light composed of?

"Source energy."

Is the water associated with an entity or being?

"Yes, but not in a normal sense – it's pretty close to source."

Since it's a yes, I want to ask this entity some questions.

"Yes, but you might not get normal answers."

Let's ask this light which is close to source; do you represent consciousness?

"I represent all things."

Do we have to do something to experience source?

"Yes, but how could you not, because it's everywhere."

I'm just saying humans need to be reminded; if you want to experience source you start by opening you heart?

"Yes, that's true."

What's a way people can help save the planet from climate change?

"I would tell them just to open their hearts and become more who they are... and I'm not answering your question."

Yes, you did. I heard this during an interview with a vision of water the other day – someone else was in a place of healing and stepped into the water and I asked the same question and they said effectively "You need to love water, love yourself and then love the earth."

"Yes because then you reconnect with who you really are so to speak."

So... Uno – soak up this energy while lying in this golden tub and feel that head to toe. Memorize this feeling so it's accessible to you at any time, driving in a car, riding in a plane – know that it's always there; it can always rebuild what needs rebuilding.

"Thank you for offering this visualization to Uno as it will help him."

Oh, we forgot to ask. Let's go back to Buddha; does he mind?

"No, it's fine."

Can we ask your devotee Guru Rinpoche to appear without traditional garb? Something comfortable or however he wants to appear.

Right now it's really extravagant looking. It's almost like light is coming off of him... (Uno laughs). He has robes .. they are golden, like with lights and stuff.

Is he wearing a hat?

Yes, the lotus hat. He says, "He could wear normal clothes too."

Guru Rinpoche in a "lotus hat."

Would you mind?

Okay, now he's wearing a brown fleece – and some shorts. (Uno laughs.) Dark blue shorts.

Wow does he appear?

He's about 6 feet. He's got a beard – moustache.

Thank you for showing up – are you familiar with my work?

"Yes, I am."

What were you doing when we interrupted you?

"I was just meditating, contemplating."

How many consorts did you have in life?

"I had four."

Are you still hanging out with them?

"And yes I do in some capacity, definitely."

You were famous for creating... for bringing Buddhism for Tibet, and also given the credit for tantric sex, what's your opinion about that?

"And they screwed it all up."

(Laughs) Okay, I want to ask you questions both Uno and I have been to the places where you were in Tibet. What was that like for you?

"It was a wild place, because the people were much less civilized than they are now."

(Note: In my interview with him in "Backstage Pass to the Flipside" he said the same thing about the wildness of the people and terrain.)

In terms of you taming local deities, how'd you do that?

"I would use my magic so to speak to tame the local spirits and major spirits."

When you say magic are you talking about the kind of esoteric yogas of consciousness, like "The Six yogas of Naropa?"

A depiction of the various esoteric yogas of Naropa.

"Yes and much more than that."

Where did you learn them?

"I learned it in India, and also in what would be now more Pakistan."

Are they correct who they say who your teachers were? Did you study at Nalanda?

"Not in the normal sense, not in the physical sense, my teachers were the same. I learned most of this on a spiritual level already."

(Note: There are records kept by Tibetan lamas, who passed what information down from what teacher. The Six Yogas of Naropa where esoteric exercises of the mind, which Guru Rinpoche taught, which were date back to Buddha. They were passed along orally (known as "secret" in early translations) but deal with shifting consciousness to create heat ("tummo") as well as being able to shift consciousness outside of the body.)

So when you were in meditation, you were in a state of open access to information from the other side?

"Yes. I used magic in the sense of alchemy and shamanism, you could say."

How were you able to manipulate stone? What's the process for actually getting your hand or foot to melt rock into its shape?

"It's actually pretty simple; you just have to reach a certain level of awareness and knowledge of emptiness and that's really about it."

How do you try to manipulate the rock or does the rock participate in your manipulation of it? The energy that exists within the stone?

"Yes, that's what I'm saying. It's not really "doing something" as much as it's your state of being and awareness... and then it happens.

Is that related to your ability to create the rainbow body or form?

"Yes, and if you can attain such things that will happen naturally."

You're credited with having a rainbow body death; can you walk us through he process?

"To attain a rainbow body it's about your awareness of emptiness as well as your compassion and love that you have within yourself and have for all others as they are you... and then it will happen."

In Uno's documentary, he reports there are quite a few people who have had rainbow body deaths.

"Yes, well we are (all) light and so the body starts to dissolve in the matter sense and then becomes light and then you physically see it shrinking, if that answers your question."

So... our friend Jesus, I know you're standing by – is the reason your body is a negative photographic imprint on the shroud was because of your ability to do a rainbow emanation?

"Yes."

I had never asked you that before – when they studied the shroud, they claimed a light created could only have come from inside the body of the person in the shroud to create that giant "flash" that caused the negative image to appear. Makes me wonder if there are any monks robes with the same.

"If you had a cloth on your face or on your heart perhaps; it's a matter of how much light shoots out as there are many different levels of rainbow body."

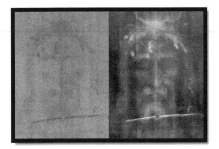

Photo of the shroud.

(Note: There was a "blood spatter" study done in 2018 that claimed the shroud was fake because blood spatter appeared to be "added later." However, the study cited was of a body presumed dead. If the person inside the shroud was alive – as these reports claim – then the blood spatter may represent someone moving, being moved or taken elsewhere. The blood spatter analysis doesn't explain how an image was made on a cloth that could only be created by a light source "from within the body." (From a National Geographic documentary on the shroud.) In this research, when asked "Is the shroud created or real?" I've heard consistently from a number of people "It is real, and so is the face cloth in Spain. The negative image was created by a yoga he learned in his travels on the silk road." I'm fully aware scientists wouldn't believe these accounts, but they are verbatim. "BPA Approach to the Shroud of Turin" July 2018)

Have you incarnated on the planet since then?

"Yes, but not right now."

It's not like we can look you up in the phonebook?

"Hahahaha."

So do you have the same lottery numbers or was she joking?

"She was joking."

Okay, let's thank everyone – high fives all around – let's thank everyone on the council – group hug. But no lizard kisses. Thanks to everyone for assisting us!

Tibetan Sand mandala – a 3D blueprint of a building.

GURU RINPOCHE INTERVIEW (PART TWO)

The following is an interview with a "reincarnated monk" – someone who recalled a lifetime as a monk, and who reportedly died in the process of doing the "rainbow body" yoga (disappeared entirely except for hair, nails, robe, etc). This person has never reported this event, but I knew this person had a memory of being this monk, and I know someone else who claimed they witnessed his departure during a rainbow body yoga event.

Rich: So how does one create a rainbow body?

Former Monk: Be in the rainbow.

How do you project yourself into the rainbow?

You just become the rainbow.

Do you visualize the colors of a rainbow, then focus on the energy of those colors and become those colors?

Yes.

(Note: This "former monk" is not Buddhist, has never meditated nor is remotely connected to Buddhism in any fashion. Even to say "be the rainbow" (which sounds like "be all you can be") is unusual; this friend is not prone to speaking like a monk in daily life.)

Is there anything about shifting consciousness outside your body while doing it?

Maybe. You put yourself in the rainbow.

So focus on the colors of the rainbow or do you focus on the energy of the rainbow and then put yourself into that? How long does that process take?

About two hours.

When you project yourself into the rainbow or become the rainbow, do you try to become light?

Yes.

So, to clarify, two hours of focused meditation, try to become the light and put yourself into a rainbow?

Yes.

When generating this light do you generate heat or warmth?

Cold as well. Both heat and cold.

Does one come before the other or are they at the same time?

Same time.

Simultaneously accessing the duality of light cold, light and dark?

Yes.

Since a rainbow is composed of all the colors or frequencies that make up the visible spectrum of light, while you're imagining becoming this light, at some point do you begin to radiate light yourself?

Correct.

You can generate light?

Yes.

Afterwards - can you recover from this exercise, bring it down to normal? After you are vibrating at a higher degree can you then relax and return to your normal body?

Yes, you can.

In your previous lifetime, how many times were you able to accomplish this? What number comes to mind?

Three.

Was this technique how you exited the planet?

Yes. Sure.

So it was a final meditation for you, were you an old person and knew it was time to go?

Yeah.

Does the body combust? Does it turn to ash? What happens?

I don't know. I'm not aware of it.

That last time you performed this rainbow body meditation, the third time; where did you go after?

Home.

You went home?

Yes.

(Note: For those keeping a scorecard, that's a "ding!" moment when I hear the word "home." This person isn't aware of the many cases I've filmed of people talking about the afterlife, and when they're asked "So after recalling the death from that previous lifetime where did you go?" they always say the same thing; "Home."

The word comes up in near death experiences ("I felt like was "home" – "familiar" "it's a place of nonjudgment, unconditional love") and whenever someone is talking about "the afterlife." If the "afterlife" is "home" then that makes this place – the place where the interviews is being conducted, the place where one is reading or hearing this book - as "not home." When we are on this planet, apparently we are "not home.")

Just prior to going home – were you able to see what your body looked like? What your robes looked like?

I think so. Yes.

When our mutual friend reported this about you, that you experienced a "rainbow death" it was recounted as if they were there when it happened.

Yeah. They were.

From what I understand, the ability to do such a yoga is rare – only a few have been able to master it, including Guru Rinpoche, the fellow who taught this yoga.

Okay.

I'll see if I can ask Guru Rinpoche if that's what happened to him, and to you. Do you want me to report back to you the answer?

Sure.

*****

Inside the Jokhang in Lhasa

This is an excerpt from an interview with Jesus, Guru Rinpoche, Luana Anders and Medium Jennifer Shaffer ("Backstage Pass to the Flipside 3"). My questions are *in italics*, Jennifer's answers are **in bold.**

INTERVIEW WITH GURU RINPOCHE (CONTINUED)

Rich: Jesus, if I may; how did you create the light that's in the shroud of Turin? Was that through meditation, how did you create that?

(Jennifer) The what?

The image that's on the shroud. Science tells us that light on the shroud could only have been made from something or someone with an inner light source. Were you using the inner light meditation yoga, or a rainbow body yoga? Or was it something else?

He showed me two.. as if you need to cut out the "imprint" of the person and make it the negative – I asked "Is that dark matter?" and he said "Yes" and showed me the illumination that comes from that, everything that comes into that space. "By coming into existence, an object creates a barrier; if you're standing there in existence, it's a barrier from what wasn't once there, but if you go inwards and meditate on this, when you're connecting, light years of stars and reflection come in and the dark matter of that space fills it up... and that creates that image."

(Note: This is an explanation of "how the shroud was created" "how rainbow yoga is achieved" and "what is dark energy?" in one answer. We've heard in other sessions "dark matter" is both the "memory of the object that once occupied that space" as well as it's current energy form, whatever that is. We've heard that rainbow body meditation is a yoga that allows one to "become light" and she's saying "that's why the negative image is on the shroud.")

The shroud. Wikipedia.

That energy that created the image is like nuclear fission?

He showed me a transference. You know how Star Wars when they "achieve light speed" all the stars are passing by light melted light? I saw them all coming in.. into the dark matter.

Is there anyone on the planet who can do that kind of yoga?

There's a guy who did – he popped into my mind. His name is.. Yoga... something.

Yogananda?

Yes. Him.

Luana, who do you want to invite to help us with this conversation? Jesus, Guru Rinpoche...

They're all here. They're all radiating in a similar frequency. It's all the spiritual leaders in front of me, out of the 7 dimensions we have complete access to that one now. Wow. Luana is like the medium for all the dimensions. She has a little bit of everything. Yogananda is here.

Well, we chatted with him briefly once before, but I was wondering if we could speak to Guru Rinpoche, known as Padmasambhava, I'd like to ask him some questions.

Luana had to go to Yogananda to get to him. He's here.

Can I ask you some questions?

You did last night apparently.

Yogananda (Wikipedia)

Can you manifest for Jennifer?

He showed me a cricket. (Being corrected) He's saying "A grasshopper!" I'm sorry. I don't know what it means but they're making fun of it.

Like the old Kung Fu tv show? "Yes, grasshopper."

I'm seeing David Carradine; funny I didn't know his name.

We'll speak with him later (we do) Padmasambhava, I was in a cave in western Tibet..

Funny, he showed me you in your car.

Correct, yes, I drove nine days across Tibet to get to your cave. I was in a cave where we found your footprint left in a stone.

Yes; that's all that was left.

How'd you do that?

Lots of movement (she moves her hand back and forth, like vibrations.) He says "Yeah, exactly as I described it before."

What came to mind?

"Forces of dark matter, bringing it through and pushing it out. You're manifesting it, bringing it from elsewhere and manifesting

it. That's the rainbow – extracting energy – to me, its manifesting. Like chanting, pulling it in, chanting pulling it in – focusing that energy like a a mandala. A figure 8 thing of bringing it in."

That's a Tibetan symbol as well, infinity, and pulling energy in and putting into a flow.

"The more you can do that the more you can put it out."

The purpose of that pulling and putting into flow?

"To strengthen."

Let me ask Jesus, so the shroud of Turin is a physical manifestation of a rainbow body yoga?

"Yes."

(Note: He could have said "No." I've heard people say "no" about a lot of things. This "yes" is a confirmation of what others have said. But it's nice to hear it from the source.)

Did you learn tummo?

It came to him.

Did you learn that in Hemis?

I got this visual of the movie Kundun about the reincarnation of Dalai Lama.

Martin Scorsese with His Holiness the Dalai Lama. Wikimedia)

(Note: An apt way to put an image in someone's mind of "esoteric Tibetan trantric yoga" like the kind taught by Padmasambhava that he claimed to have gotten from the Buddha himself.)

In terms of incarnation, correct me if I'm wrong by saying "we come here to play in the mud."

"Some like it more than others."

But it's okay to just come down and play in the mud?

"Absolutely."

So what does Yogananda want to say?

He showed me (Jennifer) meeting one of his grandchildren during a podcast.

In your autobiography, you talked about seeing the physical manifestation of one of your teachers?

"Yes. He is showing me that too."

So who was there to greet you when you crossed over?

"Jesus. It was the same energy; he expected it."

Let's move over to Padmasambhava (Guru Rinpoche). You were never a monk.

Guru Rinpoche's statue in Hemis, Ladakh

Jennifer laughs.

What did you put in her mind that made Jennifer laugh?

I'm getting he was a party animal, he said "I couldn't be a monk." He's showing me Sting as an example.

Ha. That's funny. Tantric sex practitioner. So you had a consort Padma?

He says he had a few.

What was it like when you went to Tibet?

He said "Scary. Wild. Difficult."

They practiced the Bon religion with their scary deities. It's been said that he conquered them with Buddhism.

"They weren't ready to hear it."

People have said you left texts or books behind.

"Yes. Hidden in the Himalayas."

When are we going to find these texts?

I'm getting "2022."

Have you incarnated since then?

He showed me tons of people. He says "It's not about reincarnation." He hit a level he doesn't have to (reincarnate) anymore. He says "It's not about me reincarnating, it's about people drawing on that energy; people being here and using a telephone (so to speak) and drawing on that energy." (Jennifer aside) Like what we're doing in class.

Just to clarify – you don't feel like you... (before I can finish)

He's saying "It's true."

...you've reached a level where you don't need to reincarnate anymore? Are you a teacher? Do you serve on councils?

"Yes; an infinite amount."

Mostly – Asian councils?

(Jennifer laughs) "That's racist!" he says.

(I laugh.) I was testing you. I meant on councils of people who were aware of you in your lifetime?

"There is no color or race over there; he's always been a part of it."

What quality of spiritual evolvement do you represent on councils? Do you represent the same thing on different councils?

Without there being a hierarchy, I got "The same energy as Jesus, same energy as Vishnu." He showed me that blue guy.

Lord Vishnu – that blue guy. (Kamal Kapoor)

Like a deity kind of feeling?

It's almost better to be like that with all the arms versus worshiping someone that was in physical form – it's one and the same.

If there was a quality you represent would it be "sacredness?"

"Yes. Compassion and love. That's what they (all) represent.

Sacredness not so much aspiring to be sacred – but compassion?

Yes. (Jennifer aside) I would love those guys, Luana to tell you directly ... they leave that up to Luana and that crew to express. And how they express where you need to be, or go – like, "You need to go here to eat breakfast with this person - it's like a different microchip. I see all these things like lights that are making coincidences happen.

So they don't physically participate but interact with people that do?

They participate when people are in pain and grieving and show them how to find compassion and love within yourself.

So Jesus – you too? Do you serve on many councils?

He's like the medium for all of them... even though people don't understand it.

You're saying that you have to participate with all of the living who need to access you?

Not really, no, because not everyone believes in it...

(Note: I'm trying to clarify here. Do people who don't believe in you see your, or is it just those who believe in you?)

But if Yogananda saw you when he crossed over...

He knew that he did well, that his life was filled with compassion. So he was not surprised (to see me).

My question is about people who lived prior to you – the manifestation of compassion we know as Jesus has been on the planet for 2000 years, there have been cultures on the planet for at least 60,000 years (in Australia) So who would be someone they ran into prior to knowing who he would be?

He showed me Thor. "Someone like him."

Or Zeus or whatever god or goddess they were praying to?

Yes. It goes back to the blue guy with all the arms.

Vishnu?

(Note: Vishnu is "the preserver" in the Hindu triad that includes Brahma and Shiva – he is one of the five deities, usually depicted as dark blue with four arms. The color blue represents his "infinite force." Krishna is also blue but has two arms.)

Vishnu - Wikipedia

(Jennifer aside) I did not know that.

Vishnu can you step in and introduce yourself to Jennifer?

They're showing me the same energy as Vishnu. Years ago, I had a vision of someone like this – a warrior person. I don't know what Vishnu is known for.

He's not the creator creator, but the warrior creator...

I am seeing the feet of a warrior, the straps of the warrior like Apollo or somebody.

Let's ask him. Who are you?

He's saying that vision was also him. He was showing up in another form for me.

What's your story Vee? What do you represent?

Bravery and confidence. Feeling brave and knowing everything is going to work out.

How much longer have you been in existence than Jesus?

I just saw the "Big Bang." He's showing me "Since the beginning of the combustion... in the minds at least."

In the minds. So people knew you before you were human?

"They charted it, yes."

Once they became human.

I'm getting that he knew you before.

Well, during one of my past life memories, I saw myself as a Brahmin priest living and working in Kerala.

You knew each other then, I'm getting... in Kerala.

So this memory was accurate; was I this Hindu Holy Man?

"Yes," and you transcribed a lot of things I'm being shown. I saw you in a white toga with wings on your head. I saw wings with a forehead band.

Like Mercury or Hermes?

"Yes!"

(Note: I have no idea why these two names popped into my head; "Mercury was the Roman god of messengers, trickery. Hermes was the "messenger of the gods," also the "divine trickster." Described as "moving freely between the mortal and divine, conductor of souls into the afterlife." Welcome to the club. (Wikipedia.)

The message they want to tell you – the message from this conversation is for us to be brave. To be fearless.

*****

Nothing quite like getting messages from the flipside to be brave and fearless. Worth repeating.

Meditating under Mt. Kailash in Western Tibet

CHAPTER NINETEEN:

"WITNESS TO THE CRUCIFIXION"

"Woman at the Tomb" William-Adolphe Bouguereau

I was at a friend's house having dinner. Some of my oldest friends in LA, and one is an actor that I've known since I first came out here. We were in a comedy class together. She got a job working on a television show while we were in class – and she's been on it for over 30 years. So she's done quite well for herself and her career. I joking remember the scenes with did together over our three years in this comedy improv class that boasts alumni like Robin Williams and Bryan Cranston.

This friend, I'll call her Molly, often played my wife in comedy improvs. (Not her real name, if she wanted me to use it, I would have.)

During this casual dinner we were chatting about what I've been up to and I mentioned this method of "accessing a dream or a memory." She said she could clearly recall a creepy dream she had as a child, and I suggested "one of these days" we could access that over coffee. A few weeks later, we met up.

Rich: Hello Molly. I'm going to record this, as I do record these sessions for my books. You will remain anonymous but in case something gets said where we are like whaaaat? I can review the tape.

Molly: I love that.

Okay, we're sitting outside an Italian restaurant; we may go over to to have coffee next door because I'm an addict for coffee.

Me too... I've been making Italian coffee since that guy was talking to me.

(Note: Our conversation began with my pal telling me that during her recent trip to Italy. Staying at a home in Italy, she said she could hear a voice "talking to her in Italian nonstop" – all she could remember from his conversation were the words "Ancora, ancora" – ("again, again").

However, the reason for this chat is because during a previous conversation about seeing a ghost when she was ten, she thought the ghost looked a bit like Jesus – and I suggested we could talk about that at a later date – this was the later date. I had sent her a cryptic text "your pal on the flipside wants to chat with you" so we got together to do so.

Rich: Let's go back to your memory (we discussed months prior). You're in your bedroom as a little girl?

Molly: I was ten. It was in London; I was upstairs in the attic which had been made into a bedroom.

Someone came in who frightened you – we were able to suss out it was a person?

It was a man. (Looks off in the distance) It's hard to see, but I can see what I think I saw. (Aside:) Is that a sentence?

Some parameters before we begin – think of this exploration as a game, there's no right or wrong answers for this game, don't judge whatever comes to you even if weird – that's the game, those are the rules.

That's hard. (Aside) I'm kidding.

People often say "Am I making this up?" The answer is, "Yes, we are, that's why we're here." Okay, this person, you think it was a guy. How far away is this guy?

I'm in bed. The guys over there. (Points.)

Ten feet away. Try to take a photograph of this memory – turn it into a hologram of you in bed, toes under the covers, and ten feet away is this person – can you do that?

Yes.

Lighten the photo up a bit. Is this a man or woman?

A man.

About how old?

30's to 40's.

What's he wearing"

Like a brown cloth, linen, dress thing.

Like a toga?

Yeah.

So I want you to airlift yourself out of the bed to this guy – what color eyes does he have?

Brown.. I saw brown then but I'm seeing brown now – but what's fascinating about this face is how flat and wide he is.. wider than the normal face. As my great aunt Maggie said, "Everyone's a horse or a button" – he's a button.

More of a rounded face. Let's examine it.

Brown eyes with gold inside it. That's what I saw.

(Note: Fans of the book "Flipside" will remember someone else seeing a man with brown eyes with "flecks of gold." (Chapter "Alpha and Omega") Also in the book "Hacking the Afterlife.")

Brown with flecks of gold. Beard? No beard?

I think I originally saw a beard... but at this moment..

No beard. It's okay. It's our construct. 30's 40's?

More 30's.

Jesus sans beard by the painter Raphael

Let's ask him. Does he say yes, no, no shrug? Try to reach over and pull his hand put it in your hand. What's the sensation or vibe?

That they are ... puffier. But normal sized hands. Cold.

I'm going to ask him to warm up his hands so she can get that sensation. Can you do that?

Yes. They are warming up.

I ask this to show he has the ability to respond by warming his hands up. Can I ask you some direct questions? Did you know I was going to ask you questions before we got here today?

No.

I mean him. Did he already know that?

He says "Yes," I say no.

We're not interviewing you! (laughter) So dude. Are you who we think you are?

"Yes."

First of all. Hey, what's up? Would you shift into another outfit for our friend to make it easier to chat with you?

He's (now) in a black shirt. Grey pants. Like a collared long sleeve shirt, still linen.

Sharp dresser.

Sharp dresser... his hair is longer... and now I'm seeing the beard.

Is he big or thin?

Thin.

Okay if we call you "The Jay Man?" "Jay Zeus?"

(Note: Molly and I met in a comedy improv class 40 years ago. Our relationship over the years has always been fun, somewhat silly, and always improvised.)

"Yes."

Was that you who asked me to reach out to Molly? Did you put that thought in my head?

"Yes."

What did you want to tell her?

Just about my grandmother being safe.

(Note: I was asking "What does he want to tell her?" but he's responding as if I'm asking "Why did you show up in her bedroom when she was ten?")

That's interesting. I asked "Why did you show up?" and he answered about your grandmother being safe.

"And to tell her she's on the right path."

You want her to know that she's on the right path, is that correct?

"Yes."

Jay, let's bring in her grandmother.

(Molly aside:) I haven't been able to speak with her.

Let's do so – can he bring her in?

"She's here."

How's she dressed?

It's white, (indicates a robe) wraps around her, her hair is up like *chignon* – not a bun but a twist.

How old does she appear?

About 40.

What's her name?

Her name is Dorothy she went by Toddy.. I knew her as Bubba.

How should we address her?

Bubba. I'm seeing her as the younger Bubba... She was 53 when I was born and passed at 63...

(Note: It's worth noting that seeing her at 40 is not something in Molly's conscious mind, because she didn't know her then.)

Can I ask you a direct question Bubba? Who was there to greet you when you crossed over?

Her father.

And have you been keeping an eye on our friend here?

"Yeah."

How so? Show her a time you showed up she's not aware of.

During my car accident when I was 17... and she says she is with my son – and my father is with (watching over) my other son.

Bubba, tell us, how's Molly doing?

"Finally on the right path."

That's funny, Jay said "she's on the right path." Bubba says "Finally!" – just pointing out the slight difference. They both see you from different perspectives. Bubba, you must know Jay as well. Were you surprised by seeing him?

Well, she was a Protestant... my other grandmother was Jewish.

These conversations have nothing to do with organized religion as we know it – which as he's told me in the past organized religion often screws up his message, even in his name. Is that correct?

Jesus says "Yes."

Let me ask you Molly, what do you want to know about Jesus? Let's ask him something simple; did he die on the cross?

(Surprised) He says "No." (Molly aside) I don't know – that's not right – is it?

Was the fact that you survived that event a miracle, using your ability to go into a trance like state?

He says "Yeah, because it looked like he was dead."

Yet he wasn't; he survived... and eventually you took your family with you? Show her where you went.

I'm seeing a tunnel... like a room within a room... venetian plaster, it's like a yellow wall. arched, very crude.

Are you showing her a monastery?

No it's a room; it's yellow with arched entrance.

Where you went to heal?

I want to say that's where he did die...

Later on?

Yeah.

"Roza Bal" said to be the burial place of "Yuz Asaf, who died in Kashmir. Recently someone told me "Yuz Asaf" doesn't mean "anointed one" but is short for "Bodhisattva." Which if we follow the story of his living in Kashmir (Hemis) in a Buddhist monastery might allow for how he got that moniker. (From "Tomb of Jesus" website)

Reportedly a cast of Yuz Asaf's feet next to his tomb. Note the scars on his instep. (ibid)

Rich: Surrounded by your family and friends.. how old were you in this visual?

Molly: I heard "63" but that's the age when my grandmother died. But I seem him as older.

Let's not judge it.

(Molly aside:) This is odd, am I on the right track here?

This is why I record it – you're saying what other people have said it's outside your conscious mind.

(Molly aside:) I haven't studied any of this.

We can examine a lot about his life using this method – but let's be clear while he's here. Jay Zeus, your journey with Molly; is it based on just this event, helping her with a death in the family?

It was a calling... because my spirituality had been awakened, earlier – I was on this path of spirituality that I lost somehow in my life, (leading) to what I have today.

When you were younger...

I had it before.

The reason we're talking to him now is because....

I got disconnected.

(Note: Her answers are before I can form the questions.)

So is that why he tapped me on the shoulder to talk with you? What does he want you to know?

"That he will never leave me."

Okay, that's a bit more specific. What do you want her to do with this new information she's getting from you?

He's talking about this new show I just got pitched, something I'm going to meet people about soon, something that relates to this.

Okay, whatever it is, , you'll be there to advise her?

He says "He wants me to trust all these feelings, and I've had a lot of confirmation."

So Jay – Who was this Italian guy talking Molly in this villa in Italy?

"The guy who built the house."

He died there?

"Yeah."

What did he want to tell her, or was trying to tell her?

"That I should come back to Italy and not stay away, but to come back."

"Ancora." (same meaning as "encore.") What's this Italian fellow's name?

"Giovanni."

Jay Zeus, I have a question for you; what's your relation to our friend here, does she know you from a previous lifetime?

He says "Yes."

So Molly is not aware of it but he is. So let's put that in her mind's eye. Are we inside or outside?

I'm outside. I'm a woman that he knows well, he knows very well. Back in Jerusalem.

I've heard his name back then was "Issa." That's how people in India and Asia refer to him; someone I interviewed said it was slightly different. Is that true?

He says sometimes people called him "Esaia. "

I'm sorry, did you say Esaiah?

(Spells) E S A I A.

(Note: I've never come across this spelling before, "Isaiah" the prophet of the Bible was originally "Esaia" in Latin, according to the "Latin vulgate references." ("**Scriptum est Esaia profeta**" is "*as it was written in Isiah*" in Latin (Mark 1, 1-3). Not something I've ever come across and am sure Molly has neither. Certainly odd to hear it coming from *him* – "My name was Esaia; look it up.")

In "Hacking the Afterlife" a woman who recalled knowing him said she called him "Essie."

"Essie was a nickname" he said.

Okay. Wow. That just gave me a massive chill. Obviously our mutual friend has a connection to you. Let's put it in her mind's eye – What's she look like to you back then?

Taller and wider (than now); she has chocolate brown long hair.

Is she of the region? Darker skin?

Yes, I'm wearing white... like a toga. Her skin is dark.

Like ebony or lighter?

Medium dark. Like a mix. Dark eyes.

What's her first name?

It's Joanna or something like it; like Johia...

Does she have a last name or house of name?

It's like Johanna.

What house is she associated with?

I'm not seeing that, she's just out with other people. And he sees me and comes to me with other people.

How many people are around you?

Five.

How old is she in this memory?

She's in her 30's.

Who are the five people; male or female?

There's one other woman – and two males.

Are these acolytes, friends, fans?

The feeling... it's a very familial feeling, I think brothers – are there brothers of Jesus?

Yes, at least one, perhaps more.

I'm seeing two brothers of his.

(Note: The Gospel of Mark (6:3) and the Gospel of Matthew (13:55-56) mention James, Joseph/Joses, Judas/Jude and Simon as brothers of Jesus, the son of Mary. The same verses also mention unnamed sisters of Jesus. "Brothers of Jesus" Wikipedia.)

Are you part of his family?

No, I'm not related to him but I'm very close. I've seen this once before (during a meditation). There was a love between us, not intimate or together but inseparable. Like a true love.

Describe what he looks like to you.

(Molly moves her hands to her chest and begins to cry.)

I can feel that here.

What's the feeling?

Love. But more.

"Unconditional love?"

Yeah.

When he gets close or when you see him?

He was at a distance I could feel his heart and love just seeing him. When I got close to him I felt this. Like this.. vroom... literally, physically felt like someone had their hands on my heart... not an emotion from sadness, but a physical experience of love, like totally pure...

(Note: I've filmed this before, when medium Jamie Butler saw him during an interview, when my friend saw him during her interview in "Flipside," when medium Jennifer Shaffer saw him during an interview, when medium Kimberly Babcock saw him during an interview; all had the same reaction; faces turned beet red, shortness of breath and tears. An "overwhelming feeling of love." It's not something someone can "act" or "pretend" – bright red cheeks and tears of joy. It's an odd thing to see, and this is the fourth time I've filmed it.)

Jay Zeus, why did you have that effect on your close friends? You have had that with many... I've spoken to who've run into you and I've asked the same question.

(Molly aside:) People have felt this?

Yes, I've asked him, "Where does that energy come from? What are you generating?"

"It's pure unadulterated love with a purity that we don't have here."

Where did you get that from?

He's saying "(It's) The mother energy."

Like source? He told me once before that he "Brought more of source to this lifetime."

He called it "Mother Energy." He said "Not like *my mother,"* but Mother energy." (Molly aside: I've never heard that before.)

(Note: An example of me asking him a question he disagreed with. He could have said "Yes, like source" since I quoted him saying that with Jennifer Shaffer. But he's clarifying here – "mother energy" is also "source energy" but more specific. He was asked "Why did you have such a profound effect on people?" and he said "I brought more of source energy than others have.")

That's great, just recently during another session for the first time, we discussed what that energy is or means. He offered that "all avatars" brought more of "source energy" or consciousness. And for the record, tears fell on your face as you talked about this.

I did. I felt that incredible pressure.

When I asked him, he said "When people are close to me, that's what they feel - the source energy that I brought to this lifetime.." But you're saying mother energy is a better term?

"Yes."

How does he look to you in this memory? Different than when you saw him in your room?

He has a thinner face.

So he's been eating on the flipside?

It's seems like it... (laughs). If you saw the Albert Brooks film "Defending Your Life" – Meryl Streep was eating endlessly; maybe it's like that.

I've talked to Albert about that!

(Note: I try to keep these conversations light. Michael Newton pointed out that when we return home to visit our councils, it was like Albert Brook's film. And here is yet another reference to it.)

But back to Jay Zeus; this day that he went up on the cross.. was Joanna there when he was put on the cross? Did she witness that?

"Yes."

Okay, try to describe that to me.

Being devastated... standing in the crowd and in the front.

Without connecting to the emotion of that event, try to describe it.

There are others... more over there, (gestures further back) but I'm directly in front of him.

About how many feet away?

Like ten feet.

When you look at him – is he naked?

He has something on his bottom.

Are his hands tied or nailed?

They're tied.

Take a look at what's tying them?

A rope, like very thin rope – ...

How about his feet? The same?

Those are nailed. But they are tied as well.

Rope around the feet?

(Molly aside:) This is so bizarre!

Not for me ... let' skip down; did you stick around or leave?

I stayed to the end.

Did you see him being brought down?

"Yes."

(Note: In "Hacking the Afterlife" I interviewed a number of people who claimed to also be at that event, from different perspectives. I'm not surprised to hear that his arms were tied, that's consistent in this "alternate story" of what happened to him as reported elsewhere in this book. Again – not trying to be a contrarian to religious dogma, just reporting what people say.)

Were you aware of the scenario of what happened to him? To what some people claim really happened?

"No, I was not privy."

Jesus please correct me if I'm wrong about any of this – Joseph of Arimathea went to Pilate and asked for your body after a few hours, when most crucifixions lasted a week. In the original Aramaic he asked for the "living body of Jesus" and Pilate replied "You mean can you take down his corpse?" (Which isn't in the translation). Jay Zeus; is this correct?

He says "Yeah."

Wait a second. (Suddenly having an apotheosis) Was Pilate in on this ruse? Was Pilate a confederate?

(Molly genuinely asking) Who is Pilate?

Let's ask him; was Pilate in on it?

He says "Yes he was."

(Note: Okay. I have to stop here to breathe for a second. First, my friend doesn't know who Pilate is. But I bypass that question to ask directly; "Was Pilate in on it?" There's not much historical record for Pilate – he was the prefect of the city, there's scant documented history of him, outside of coins and a carved name on a building. Also in this book, we hear someone say that he was actually "at the Crucifixion."

But as we've heard the story – he's the fellow who "washes his hands" of the death of Jesus. The historical record shows that Pilate's story has changed over the centuries – at first they painted him as the man who murdered him, then later, he was made to appear as the man who tried to save him.

He was verified by Roman historian Josephus, but Tacitus said that he "had a corrupt administration that took bribes." He was later fired by Emperor Tiberius over some gold plates he put into a Jewish temple, was dispatched to Rome and not heard from again.

If Tacitus is accurate – then perhaps the reason Joseph of Arimathea was involved is that he was the one who paid the bribe to bring Jesus' body down. (Which is the thought that occurred to me. "IT WAS A

BRIBE!") In this scenario, Joseph went to Pilate and said "Can I collect the living body of Jesus?" handed him his money, to which Pilate replied "Yes, you can take down his corpse."

Either way, that bribe concept (if true) would change the historical record (if accurate.) I'm not claiming it is – but that's what came to mind when I asked "was Pilate in on it?")

(Asking again) So Pilate was in on it?

He says "Yes."

(Mind blown) Wow. Jay Zeus, you've just rehabilitated one of the most hated people in history. I'm not going to argue with him about it, and will explain it to you later Molly, who this fellow was.

(Note: I looked up "the women that knew Jesus" in a search engine. The following came up: "The Gospels record that women were among Jesus' earliest followers. Jewish women disciples, including Mary Magdalene, **Joanna**, and Susanna, had accompanied Jesus during his ministry and supported him out of their private means.[Lk. 8:1–3] (Wikipedia: "Paul the Apostle and Women")

"Joanna is a woman mentioned in the gospels who was healed by Jesus and later supported him and his disciples in their travels, one of the women recorded in the Gospel of Luke as accompanying Jesus and the twelve and a witness to Jesus' resurrection. She was the wife of Chuza, who managed the household of Herod Antipas, the ruler of Galilee. Her name means "Yahweh has been gracious", a variation of the name "Anna" which means "grace" or "favor"."

"She is recognized as a saint in the Anglican, Eastern Orthodox, and Roman Catholic traditions." Joanna is shown as the wife of Chuza, steward to Herod Antipas while being listed as one of the women who "had been cured of evil spirits and infirmities" who accompanied Jesus and the Apostles, and "provided for Him from their substance" in Luke 8:2–3."

"Theologian Adrian Hastings suggested that she could have been one of Luke's sources for information regarding the Herodian court. **As the wife of an important court official, she would have had sufficient means needed to travel and contribute to the support of Jesus and the disciples. Joanna is named among the women mentioned in**

Luke 24:10, who, along with Mary Magdalene and Mary, the mother of James, took spices to Jesus' tomb and found the stone rolled away and the tomb empty."

"The accounts in the other synoptic gospels do not mention Joanna as one of the group of women who observe Jesus' burial and testify to his Resurrection. One evident reason for Joanna's prominence was that when the male disciples fled, it was Joanna and Mary who stood by the Lord during His crucifixion, knowing full well that they faced death by crucifixion for showing such solidarity with the victim."

"The importance of Joanna and the other women as witnesses lies in the fact that it was they who had seen Jesus buried, and therefore could vouch for the fact that the empty tomb was in fact the very tomb in which Jesus had been buried. This piece of evidence becomes more crucial the more one reflects upon it."

"An empty tomb was no proof that Jesus of Nazareth had risen - unless there were witnesses there present at that empty tomb who could testify also that it was in that very tomb that Jesus had been laid. And only women, not men, were witnesses of this. The Greek world placed great emphasis upon sight- "Eyes are surer witnesses than ears", Heraclitus said."

"They related to the past visually; for a group of people to be eyewitnesses was considered conclusive. Hence the enormous significance of the way in which the Gospels repeatedly make the women the subjects of verbs of seeing (Mt. 27:55; Mk. 15:40; Lk. 23:49,55). They were the eyewitnesses." (From a study published at Aletheia College: http://www.aletheiacollege.net/bl/19-1Joanna_Character_Study.htm)

Rich: Let's go back to Molly for a moment, because we can. Can you introduce her to her guide on the flipside?

Molly: He's male.

How tall?

Tall. He's like right over your shoulder.

Someone you know or recognize?

He's in his 30's, has brown hair, blue eyes... has a beard.

Can I ask a name?

I heard "Ariel."

Can I ask you some direct questions?

He said "Yes."

Are you familiar with what I'm doing?

"Yes."

How did you become familiar with it?

He says "He's an archangel."

Okay, so cooler talk around the archangel cooler? Do other people know you as an archangel Ariel?

"Yes."

(Note: If I didn't know Molly as long as I have, known her to be a successful actor, that she's famous for her career, I would at this point wonder if she had become a "Jesus freak." But I'm stopping this narrative to point out for those keeping score; "Archangels" I've interviewed include Gabriel, Michael, Ariel and Uriel. That leaves Raphael, Raquel and Remiel (according to the myth of there being "Seven.") What can one say when someone says "I'm an Archangel?" I can only offer that people seem to "radiate" at the same frequency on the flipside. Either there are just a handful of them, or they all reflect the same frequency.)

Have you ever incarnated on the planet?

"No."

When you hang out with the others -for lack of a better term, do you all vibrate at the same frequency?

"Except for one – Michael."

Has Molly ever met Michael?

Yes, I have seen him... I've called them down.

Where did you come up with the idea of calling them down?

I don't know.

The Seven Archangels - Wikipedia

Let's ask Ariel for help. Show her what age she was when she met you.

It was when I moved to the beach and joined a meditation group.

Okay, but I'm going to ask him to do us a favor. Ariel, can you walk her into her council?

"Yes."

Where are we? Inside or outside?

We're inside. It's a big room; they're all in a circle. There are a few; at least ten.

Ariel, I have more questions for you, so if you could hang with us, please. So you are aware ten people? Are you standing or sitting?

I'm standing. And suddenly I'm extremely tired... all of a sudden like weirdly pressured.

Is there a reason for that feeling Ariel?

"No; it's the energy of the room, everyone's energy..." I can feel it.

Let's ask Ariel to lighten this energy – we're not doing something heavy here. We're having a casual conversation. Can you do that?

She nods. "It's lighter, but I'm still tired."

Because we're only here to have this fun conversation. You're standing, they're sitting – there are ten of them. Male or female, other or light?

Male. There's someone here who has got big gold wings – he's standing.

Well, let's go over to him first. What can we call you my friend?

(Listens) Everyone's got these same sort of names. He says "Josiah."

Josiah; are you familiar with what I'm doing?

Yes.

How so?

He has a connection to "Jay-man."

So can we ask you Josiah, how is she doing?

"Doing good!"

What quality do you represent on her council?

"Success."

Ah, hence the gold wings. Take a look at him; what's he wearing?

He's got blonde hair and has these magnificent gold wings, up high, huge, halfway open.

Wow. Talk about an entrance.

He says "You have to go sideways to get anywhere."

Archangel Michael – Medieval painting

That's funny. Josiah, how many councils do you work on?

He's saying "five."

And are you the spokesperson for this council or one of the many?

He says "He's high up but not the spokesperson."

You represent success? Well you've done a hell of a job, with our friend here. What message do you want to tell her at this moment?

"That a lot more is coming. More than I think I can even handle... but that I can do it and not get overwhelmed."

Overwhelmed personally?

Work wise – "Don't get overwhelmed."

Joshia says he's aware of my work via the Jay Zeus. How did you become aware of it? Just curious.

"It was part of somehow... his is with Jay's grouping on the other side."

Like part of his group? Resonates at the same frequency?

"Yeah."

Cool. So success is coming to our friend, what else do you want to tell her that she can pass along to other people?

He said "There has been a clearing. An easier, bigger path."

For the planet or for her?

Sorry; "for her."

He's on your council after all, and I asked him a question that relates to you.

Hang on. He says "But there is a clearing happening on the earth too."

Thank you Josiah. Who else wants to speak up from her council. The spokesperson for her council, perhaps?

The spokesperson is in a long trench coat and hat something from the 30's. It's dark olivey brown, the hat is dark olive. He's male, has a salt and pepper beard – (Molly aside:) Everyone's got a beard.

What color are his eyes?

They're like silver – but not the color silver, like white grey. I've never seen that color before.

(Note: I like to point out when a detail is new information. "Never seen that color before" is a way of verifying to her at least that this is new information, something she could not have imagined or made up.)

Can I ask you some direct questions? What's a name we can use for you?

"Noem."

(Note: That's pretty funny. Not a name or term that Molly or I are familiar with – it's Old Dutch and it means "to mention" or "to give a name to." I ask him "What's your name?" and he answers "My name is "give me a name.")

Like "no em" is in your name? Does that mean every other letter of the alphabet but M is in your name? Sorry, we're having fun – is it weird for you to have someone like our friend here talking to you?

He says "He's been waiting for us."

What quality do you represent in her council?

"Life path." Has anyone said that before?

No, but I've heard quite a few. Makes sense. Like an architect of your lives. How many councils are you on?

Eight. (Molly aside:) My life path number is 8.

Infinity: wikipedia

It's also the symbol of infinity... So are you like a life planning kind of person?

"He is the planner."

How do you think Molly is doing?

"On track."

Why did you guys decide to have this career that she's been so successful at?

"It was decided by the council."

Really? I mean there was a life planning session, they were pitching it, someone pitched it – was that you Josiah? Who pitched that?

"Yeah. Josiah and Ariel pitched it."

Like this is a cool thing for her? To what end?

"To inspire and touch many people not for what we think acting is for. It's all coming now."

I understand – like the millions of people who have seen her perform have captured her frequency on some level – so over there their conscious energy is aware of her?

"Yes, it's now, it's been coming."

That idea that we can become aware we're all connected.

"Mm-hmm."

Who's the comedian on this council?

Noem says "He's hilarious."

So that's you?

He says "Of course; everyone else has beautiful outfits, he's in a trench coat, hat and glasses."

Christopher Reeve in trenchcoat, hat and glasses. ("Superman" Wikipedia)

Has anyone on your council had a lifetime on Earth?

He has, in the 1930's, when my mother was born.

Let's take this moment to reflect on how cool this is, we know you're keeping an eye on our pal here, everything's going to be okay. What's that feel like holding their hands?

"Peace."

And that feeling you got from the Jesus – that bolt of unconditional love – that was a powerful feeling. Have you ever had anything like that?

No, I've never had that feeling that I just felt.

So he can help you experience that at any time. Let's ask – how many people beside Molly does Ariel work with?

Eight thousand.

Okay, that's an interesting answer.

(Note: It's interesting because we were speaking to Ariel who is Molly's guide, who just happens to be an archangel. I know that sounds odd, but I've met other ones, mostly on councils.

They person will see wings, and I ask the same questions – like "What are the wings made of?" Sometimes they talk about a fabric, sometimes they say they're a metaphor for "speed" as in "traveling at the speed of thought." I haven't interviewed enough of them to get a consensus about where they are – since these reports are not religious in nature (I know they sound religious, but if Jesus denies pretty much everything ascribed to him, and claims that there are no religions on the flipside, it's hard to argue with him about it.

But in terms of "angels and archangels" that's almost always associated with "religious accounts." I can only offer that they appear to resonate on a "higher level" – there is no hierarchy on the flipside so it's not a "better level" – just a different one.

They all claim that they have never incarnated on Earth, but some have had lifetimes in other galaxies. We've met two folks with wings for transport in this single session.

It just so happens that what's coming to mind fits into this alternate story of the universe, an alternate history that I've heard from many other people. I mention that having eight thousand people you're watching over might be disconcerting to those involved ("Hey, why isn't my prayer being answered? Is he busy again?) but it's an "outside of time" issue. Each one has his undivided attention – because when time is not a factor he can give it that way.)

May I ask, have I met you before?

He says "Yes." (shrugs) He says, "He watches over you too."

Since when? Since the beginning of my journey?

He said "Recently." Were you meditating and somehow you called to him, or one of my guides?

If I can ask him; where did we meet?

He says "On the flipside, when you were separated from your body – you were in another consciousness."

Doing one of these sessions?

He says "No, by yourself."

I appreciate the answer – something for me to explore. But let's go back to Jay Zeus for a moment, did he want to talk to you?

"Yes."

Let me ask him – our mutual pal, "Pat" (not his real name) and I did one of these non hypnosis sessions; Pat said he saw himself selling you cloth back in the day. Sold him a robe, if I recall. Let's ask him. Did our pal Pat sell you that bolt of cloth?

He's saying "Yes." Wow! Maybe that's how Pat and I are so connected. He said "Yes!"

Okay. That's pretty funny. We all met in this life in a comedy class together. 58 minutes. Not bad!

Wow. That was amazing.

Indeed. I recently received an email from Molly; "one of my guides has been tapping me on my thigh since he was "called in." Our pal!"

I know that reporting this may seem as heresy to some, idiocy to others. But in terms of data, as noted in "Hacking the Afterlife" I've had over a dozen people spontaneously recall knowing or seeing Jesus in a previous lifetime, or knowing him specifically between lives. Most of them are not religious, or not even spiritual. I don't think his "showing up" has anything to do with our current journey, but everything to do with becoming aware that "he's never left."

Perhaps the "second coming" may be about becoming consciously aware that the fellow never left, or that our loved ones who are no longer on the planet never left. That it's we who can't see them, not they who can't see us. We are the ones who have to do the adjustment to become aware of their presence. We are the ones who have to take out the blueprints for the architecture of the afterlife and see where we fit into the overall scheme, and why we are on the path we are on. I include this chapter because I was as startled to hear it as I am to repeat it.

As I'm fond of saying to people who ask me a question about him, "Ask him." He appears to be available to anyone who wants to chat with him. If he tells an alternate story, I'd be happy to hear it.

CHAPTER TWENTY:

"FOCUS ON THE HEART"

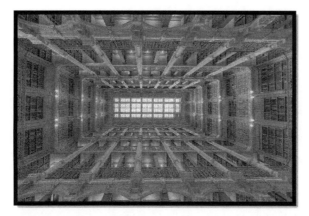

Peabody Library in Baltimore, architect Edmond George Lind.

Interview with Jennifer "Stone"

I got an email from someone about doing a "session" where we would take a shortcut to access her council. In most cases, I tell people about finding a hypnotherapist near them, or about doing the kind of mediumship that would put them directly in touch with a loved one. But in this case, this is someone who is working with clients as a medium, and felt that she wanted to do a direct connection in the way that I have done in the past.

There are many mind bending events in this session, so I'll let the words speak for themselves.

Rich: Hi Jennifer. I just want to state upfront that I consider that we're scientists here.

Jennifer: I've never considered myself that.

So when you were at Harvard, where'd you live?

Cambridge and Somerville... in the Fenway for awhile.

Did you go to those Irish pubs in Somerville?

Oh, yes, I do like a good Guinness.

When I was at Boston University, I was a bouncer at Father's Five; Marlborough and Mass Ave.

I used to go to Father's Two! You know what a dive that was.

I do! But great for college students!

I used to work on pizza night, slinging drinks at Crossroads.

No way! That was our pizza joint when I was at BU. I loved Boston.

So damn cold.

Yes. But enough reminiscing, let's talk about Jennifer's journey – who's Jennifer Stone?

When I was in the *woo woo* closet, I worked for the head of research at a hospital, doing psychic readings on the side, so I made up a fake name.

Did he ever find out?

Yes, and he found it fascinating – so I was worried for nothing.

What I do – I'm kind of like a professional angler, a fisherman; I show people where to drop their line, tie on the right fly, whatever that means, I just made that up that goofy analogy.

It's a good analogy.

What was the first psychic experience you had where you talked to spirit?

That started in the 90's; I started hearing people call my name. I was taking a nap and heard my name "Jennifer" and thought it was my neighbor and went down and checked the door and it was locked – that happened five or six occasions.

It's a bit like another Harvard alum, Gary Schwartz PhD said he heard someone say "put on your seat belt" and moments later his life was saved in a car accident. And you started helping people access that?

Yeah, I had a friend who was a medium, he knew I had done astrology, he said "Come and do readings with me" kind of trial by fire. I was better than I thought. The mediumship began when my sister died and I could hear her clearly – I could feel her hand. I started using a dowsing pendulum – with numbers and letters and started getting people coming through and getting messages.

That's interesting you'd do that – I tell people not to use a Ouija board because it's like going to a pub and standing outside and inviting whoever to "come on over."

I learned that the hard way.

What's your sister's name?

Christina.

Have you seen her?

No.

Who tapped you on the shoulder and said "let's talk to Rich."

It was her.

Okay. I'm going to ask you leading questions; they may lead you to new information you didn't know or you couldn't know, only Christina knows. Have you ever seen her in a dream?

Oh god, yes.

Try to focus on one dream where you saw her. Can you remember that?

Yes.

How far away is she in this memory?

20 feet.

What's she wearing?

Jeans. Sweater. I think she has bare feet.

Freeze that visual like a hologram. Let's go closer to 2 feet. How old does she appear?

45. Brown hair. Green eyes. Sweater is tan.

Take a look at her toes.

Painted red. She always had painted red toenails her whole life.

In your mind's eye, take hold of her hands. What's that feel like?

Very soft – feels very feminine; just like they did when she was alive.

Any temperature?

They feel cool; cooler than normal.

Christina, can you warm up your hands a bit for your sister?

You know what's weird – I feel like they're warmer.

I'm just seeing if we can converse with her. Let's ask – can I ask your sister some direct questions?

She's nodding and smiling.

Sometimes they say no – it's ok. I'm guessing at some point she tapped you on the shoulder. What do you look like to her?

Younger. She sees me in my 20's, even though I'm 53.

Time is relative – right now it's a distant relative. (Ba dum bum) What are you wearing in this visual?

Shorts, navy blue surfer shorts. A bathing suit and sweatshirt over it.

Color of the bathing suit?

Mint green.

Do you own this bathing suit?

No.

Okay, so this is "new information." If you owned this suit, you could create it – but you don't. So in this being able to communicate with people on the flipside, part of it is allowing them to show us what we look like to them.

Wow, this is crazy.

What's the sweatshirt say?

Nothing; it's plain – like I borrowed it from some guy, like I threw it on because I was cold.

When you're holding her hands you sense any emotion?

Peace.

What's that mean?

Like "finally." That's the vibe I get – like "Finally; I have some peace."

Is that for you or for her?

For her.

How do you think your sister Jennifer is doing?

She goes "FABULOUS!" That's how she used to talk too. That's hilarious.

Is that your point of view Christina or others?

Before you even had the question out of your mouth, she said "all of us."

Great. "When you hear the answer before you can ask the question you know you're connected." Not only did she design this swimsuit; she knows what I'm going to ask before I can ask it. Far out. Can we talk to Jennifer's guide?

She's saying there's a lot of them. Not just one.

Let's invite one or two – your principal guide or person to come forward and have a chat with us. Is that a male, female, neither, both, a light or nothing?

I get two – it's more like – I'm sensing one is a light. Like a pastel, pinkish lavender blueish color – and the other one is showing me someone I've talked to before. You probably know him, the big Hawaiian musician "Iz?" He came through to me on my mom's funeral day. I didn't believe it was him, so he went to a medium friend 3000 miles away and gave them the message for me; it was

him! She's showing me him – so I guess he's more of a guide than I thought he was.

Israel Kamakawiwo'ole – YouTube screen grab.

Try not to judge it. I appreciate him showing up. But before we talk to him, I'd like to talk to this light.

(Note: I do this because there's context involved with speaking to a person who used to be on the planet. The mind may wonder how it could possibly be this famous musician responsible for the iconic version of "Over the Rainbow" could possibly be her "guide." Instead of addressing him first, I focus on someone she's never met but may be capable of communication.)

I'm getting "Yes," but I don't know who is saying it.

That's okay. "Yes," doesn't have to be spoken aloud. I'm going to address these to the light. How tall is this light?

Seven feet.

I'm going to ask this light if it can manifest as a human for the purpose of this conversation so we can address this person with more clarity; can you show her a being of some kind?

This happened while you were talking... and I'm kind of shocked, but it looks like a human woman, but she's not – she's not from Earth. She's like big, blonde... and kind of like... I can't describe it. She's not solid like you and I, kind of transparent but more solid than wispy.

Thank you for showing up today, can you give us a name or a letter to use to address you?

I got the name "Trixie" (Jennifer aside:) Which is crazy! Sounds like a hooker name.

Trixie! That's a great name, I love it. Can we call you Trixie?

She's laughing, "Yes."

Are you familiar with me, or what I'm doing?

"Absolutely."

(Note: I ask this question because sometimes they say "No." It helps me gauge what I can ask of them.)

Can you put in Jennifer's mind how you're familiar with me asking questions? Am I a punchline over there or what? Who told you?

This sounds crazy – she says she "knew you before you were born."

Doesn't sound crazy to me. Our friend Jennifer is seeing you as semi-translucent. Is that because you're incarnated somewhere else as we speak?

"No, it's just how I present myself."

(Note: People who have had near death experiences have seen friends "on the flipside" that are kind of etheric, or "wispy." In David Bennett's NDE, he saw a friend who was "see through" who was still alive. Then some years later, when he was under hypnosis recalling the near death event ("Voyage of Purpose") he saw his friend again, but in the interim that friend had passed away and was no longer "etheric" but solid looking.)

Have you lived other lifetimes on other planets or ever a life on Earth?

"Never on Earth."

So I assume lifetimes on other planets or other universes. Is that correct?

(Pause) I don't hear anything.

Sometimes they don't answer because either we're not supposed to hear it, or it's TMI; too much information. But let me ask, have you incarnated somewhere else before?

"Yes."

Has it been in our universe or some other universe?

This is the weirdest answer; she says "You don't understand they're one and the same."

Okay, I think I do; kind of what we're doing – conversing outside of time, but you're saying it's irrelevant to think of it as another universe. Tell me what Trixie looks like to you.

She's Amazonian – like 7 feet tall, big, like a basketball player. Big bones, big hands, look like beautiful face – the hair is weird, bangs that are blunt cut, platinum almost white, it is white, longish, down to her back. I think she has this blue – royal blue headband, bangs are covering it but it has a stone in the middle, stone is like a gold color; she's dressed in white.

"Wounded Amazon" Capitoline Museum, Rome

Okay, take hold of her hand.

I'm trying, but I can't feel anything. It's like she doesn't have any matter; I can't feel anything.

Translucent? Is there any emotion associated with that action?

When I ... I guess I'm holding her hand but I can't feel it... it's almost like touching her I realize she has eons and eons and eons of knowledge.

Like tapping into a library of sorts?

Right.

Trixie – is that a pun? Or a name you've had for a long time?

"Very much a pun."

Ok, "Tricksy." There are tricks here afoot. It's so cool to meet you. I'm going to ask you for a guided tour, but I want to speak to her guide Isreal for a second. What's he wearing?

(Note: Israel Kamakawiwoʻole became world famous for his rendition of "Over the Rainbow/What a Wonderful World." I read that he had a dream about the song, and in the middle of the night, called his friend a recording engineer and got him to meet in the studio. The version we've all heard was "take one." One might suggest he was "channeling the flipside" when he sang that song. "In the summer of 1997, Israel K, by then one of the most beloved singers in the history of Hawaiian music, died of respiratory failure. He was 38 — and just beginning to see the huge success of "Over the Rainbow." Israel's body lay in state at Hawaii's Capitol building, a rare honor. from NPR)

The first thing I notice he's wiggling his bare feet and he's not overweight ... normal weight - same face he had in his last incarnation, he's just thin... *ner.*

What's it feel like when you take his hands?

Super warm. Like a lot of joy – like he's giggly, super happy all the time. Which is why he's wiggling his feet; this is very fun for him to do – he likes it. This interview thing.

How did it come about that you recorded that song everyone got to know you from? If you remember?

Let me see.

There was an incident as it was reported – I thought it would be fun to ask him to put it into your mind.

I feel like he's showing a party – for someone who passed... did he record this for someone else?

Let's ask him. Iz?. Who inspired you to record that song?

He said "For Gabby."

Do you know who Gabby is?

Another musician... named "Poo ha knee."

Are you getting that from Iz or your memory Jennifer?

From him.

(Note: Mind blown. On my first trip to Hawaii, I was given a tour by one of my brother's oldest friends. He took me to a Gabby Pahanui concert – who was considered a famous "slack guitar" player. I had all of his cassettes when I came back. It's a bit odd to know only one famous Hawaiian singer and to have Israel say that he performed that song for *him.)*

Gabby Pahanui (Wikipedia)

*That's correct. There was a famous Hawaiian guitarist named Gabby Pahanui. Wow, let me clarify this – Iz, you're saying that **"Somewhere over the Rainbow"** was performed as an homage to Gabby Pahanui?*

He's laughing. He's saying – "She hu..." he laughed and said "she hu!"

Is that Hawaiian?

Jennifer aside: I don't know. He's saying "She hu, shee hu!"

(Note: Research tells us "Chi Hu" is Hawaiian for "Yippee!" "A phrase commonly shouted by residents born and raised in Hawaii during moments of joyful excitement. Also sometimes spelled as chi hoo, chee hu or chee hoo. (UrbanDictionary.com) (Samoa: "siususu") From "Pidgin English" chee hu (chi who) "alright; woo hoo; yippee" In A Sentence: Chee hu, pau hana! (Alright! I'm finished with work!" (e-hawaii.com) I know Jennifer Stone doesn't speak Hawaiian slang but Iz does.)

Who was there to greet you when you crossed?

"My mother ..." He's showing me her in a uh, in a mu mu – old school mu mu – I don't think people wear these anymore.

Was it a kahuna or your mom?

It wasn't a kahuna... he's saying "Auntie... auntie."

(Note: I wasn't aware of this, but Hawaiians refer to caregivers as "Auntie." "In Hawaiian culture, to call an elder auntie or uncle is to communicate endearment and respect, along with an implied familial bond." *Quora.com*)

Was that a welcome surprise to see her?

He says "He was very happy. He says he was ready to go." (Jennifer aside:) How did he die? I don't even know.

(Note: Israel K suffered from obesity throughout his life, at one point weighing 757 pounds... He endured several hospitalizations because of health problems. Beset with respiratory, heart, and other medical problems, he died at the age of 38, survived by his wife, Marlene and their daughter, Ceslie-Ann "Wehi". *Wikipedia*)

I don't know, but I know he was overweight. Anything you want to tell your family or fans who every time they play that song, cry?

He says "It brings me a lot of joy – it's like..." (Jennifer aside: He showed me a ball bouncing... It bounces back up to him – "Like the love (comes to him) and then he bounces it back down to us – like a ball bouncing back and forth – his music gives us joy and our joy gives him joy; it goes back and forth like a wave. He shows me a kid's bouncing ball."

(Note: I've spoken to a lot of guides, and many council members. This is the first guide I've met that lived on the planet recently. The idea that he is a "second guide," came forward at the same time as her main guide, Trixie, would likely mean that they knew each other in a previous lifetime, which I eventually ask.)

Are you hanging out with Gabby since returning there?

"All the time," he says.

Are you playing ukuleles or other instruments?

He says "They play the ukes, but other stuff too – they can play whatever they want, but they're good at everything."

Are you playing with any other musicians?

He showed me this older African American guy who used to sing with Billy Holiday... It's Louis Armstrong. (Jennifer aside:) Holy crap!

That's wonderful; the singer of "What a Wonderful World." Well, we can talk to Louis as well, but let's hold that thought because I think Trixie wants to show you stuff. We're big fans Iz, I understand you are someone who helps out people like Jennifer; did you know her in a previous lifetime?

"Yes."

Is she aware of that?

"She is now."

You want to show here where that was? On Earth?

He says, "Oh yeah."

What country was that in?

Somewhere mountainy – hold on. He's showing me the Alps – I don't know what country...

We can figure it out. What year was this?

1398?

Okay, was it Switzerland, France, Italy?

No. Austria.

Austria in the 1390s would have been tribes or old Romans who lived up there – what were you guys? Was Jennifer a man or woman?

"A man."

What were you?

"A man. Warriors."

If you could put an image in her mind what kind of costume you'd wear into battle?

Heavy fur - not Roman soldier like, but Viking like garb. Leather and fur and all that, is what it looks like.

What did he look like?

Big, bearded... not short. Big. Like a big guy with a big beard grown hair and grizzled.

Viking Rorik of Dorestad. 687 AD.

Can you show her what she looked like in that lifetime?

Kind of the same – but my hair was lighter. We both looked kind of the same, frizzy hair, wild beards, all that stuff.

What was Jennifer's name?

Begins with a B – sounds like Bjord.

Like Bjorn Bjorg with a D. Were you guys Vikings?

Yes; we didn't come from the Alps; we ended up there somehow.

If you want to put it in her mind's eye where you were born? In Europe?

Way way up; it was cold snowy, snow, snow, snow and more snow – like ew.

How'd you die? What was your last day on the planet?

I didn't die in battle, oddly enough. I was old – like an old guy, happy and old – I don't know how I survived, but I did.

Probably cause Iz was taking care of you. I'm going to assume the last day – who was there to greet you, Trixie?

She says "Yes!" That's so weird.

How many lives have you watched over Jennifer, Trixie?

She says 7.

Were there other lifetimes with other guides before you came long? Or is that the total number she's had?

"She's had more, those were the lifetimes that she needed me."

Thank you, that's interesting. Trixie, can you walk Jennifer in to visit with her council?

We're going – now I'm in this hallway, she's kind of walking ahead of me, and turning around and saying "Hurry up." She's all business.

Describe this hallway.

It's very modest – like a stone... arched... but kind of like 9 or 10 feet tall.

Let's go to where the council is waiting.

That's weird... it looks like we're in a dome shaped room and it's very dimly lit. I can't tell where the lights are coming from the ceiling is navy blue – it's really weird – ceiling is about 30 feet.

How many people are here?

There's a lot. They're sitting around this semicircular table, facing us, back to the wall. It's really dim.. there's got to be at least... they're ten to 15 away. Let me count... there's 16. Sitting around a table like a semicircle.

Trixie can we walk our friend up to the council?

She says, "Sure."

Let's look at the person on the far left. Is that a male female, neither or both?

Kind of neither.... because he doesn't look human, kind of like a creature, kind of green with weird pointy ears that come out the side. Kind of Yoda-like... but scarier looking than Yoda; not very attractive.

Well, let's offer that you may look kind of scary to him as well. Can we go up to him and ask him some questions?

He says, "Yes," but I feel he's hesitant.

Can I ask for a name or letter to address you by?

The name he tells me is "Yerg."

Mr. Yerg. Is he more male or female?

Very male – sorry he reminds me of a troll or animal in some way.

Let's try not to judge that – take his hands in yours. What's the sensation?

Okay. Um... weird. Rough, kind of scaly, kind of cool – fingers are really skinny ... I don't really like touching his hands, can I let go?

Try not to. It's important to make this connection. Look at his eyes. What color are they?

They're kind of yellow with flecks of black, but the irises are reptilian.

(Note: We met someone like this fellow in the interview with Uno, but according to Wiki, they're often referred to in UFO stories. "Reptilian humanoids with the characteristics of reptiles that play a prominent role in fantasy, science fiction, ufology, and conspiracy theories."
Wikipedia)

Mr. Yerg, I appreciate you talking to us, but if I may – are you familiar with what I'm doing?

He says "I know exactly what you're doing."

Okay; my question to you sir has Jennifer every incarnated on your planet?

"Yes."

Can she take a look at that?

He says "She's seen it before."

But if we can examine that; where is this planet? Is it in our universe or is it in another one?

"This one."

If there was a human word associated where the star system is?

He's saying "signet" – signa?

(Note: There is a star constellation called "Cygna." It's referred to as "Alpha Cygni" (which sounds a bit like Cignet.) It's also popular in sci-fi lit: *"The star Deneb, and hypothetical planets orbiting it, have been used many times in literature, film, electronic games, and music. Examples include several episodes of the Star Trek TV series, the Silver Surfer comic book, the Rush albums A Farewell to Kings and Hemispheres..."* Oddly enough, the Chinese name for Deneb is (Tiān Jīn sì) which sounds a bit like "Chitchinu." Wikipedia).

I appreciate that – how many planets are in the Cygna star system? A few or just one?

"Many."

Cygnus star system; Wikipedia

If you could put in Jennifer's mind's eye what her existence was like; was there dirt, trees, water?

He's showing me a dream that I had many years ago I woke up I knew I had traveled somewhere I knew looked beautiful – kind of like Earth except the sky wasn't blue it was pink. The light seemed to come from everywhere in the sky; you could see what looked like moons – he's showing me that's the planet he's from.

How many moons did you see?

Two.

Let me ask, what was the name of this planet?

Its sounds like Chitchinu... Chitsnu.

Were people more intelligent than on Earth?

He says it's not a question of intelligence, it's a question of integrity... the development of their integrity was higher.

That's a wonderful answer, thank you.

He says "It's the truth."

Are there many people on the planet who have lived on Chitsnu?

Not many.

Has Jennifer ever been visited by people from your planet?

He says, "Not from here but from other planets."

What quality do you represent in Jennifer's spiritual evolvement?

He says "scathing self honesty."

The development of integrity. How is she doing in terms of that concept?

Better and better. She's not there yet.

It's a direct question; he answered it "more better than worse and worse."

Jennifer laughs.

What is Yerg wearing?

It's a material I've never seen before, looks shimmery but like Kevlar; if you tried to touch it, it would move it shimmers. It's dark grey with a metallic flecks to it. It's kind of like a robe thing – but I feel like he's armored; he's a badass.

Kind of like a uniform? Is there any animal on our Earth that wears this kind of skin?

He's showing me an armadillo.

So this is armor?

The texture of it – the toughness of it.

Do you serve on any other councils?

"No."

How many of her lifetimes have you been on her council?

Just this one.

So you have earned this position, let's say, earned your participation in this lifetime – is that correct?

"Yes."

Can you introduce her to the person next to you?

A female. She looks interesting, older .. very kind of ... she has this air of royalty or something ...she's nice but not super warm; just kind of regal is the word.

Can we speak to you?

She says, "Yes."

If you could put a name or initial in her mind?

"Kay."

Kay, how many councils do you serve on?

"Six."

Are you aware of what I'm doing, this council questioning?

She says "We're all aware of it."

Am I the only one doing this?

Not many, but you're not the only one.

I'm curious. How did you become aware of it?

She says she can't explain it, they know things that are of importance come to them automatically – not with everything, just with the things they need to know about.

They know things that are important for them to know?

"Yes."

How do you think our friend Jennifer doing?

She says "Marvelous."

Okay – Kay must have been talking to Christina, wasn't she?

"Marvelous darling."

Is she wearing any jewelry at all?

Only this weird giant emerald stone ring on her middle finger – really a weird ring.

Kay, if I may, what do you represent on Jennifer's council. What word or quality of her spiritual development do you represent?

"Discernment."

Let me ask you about that emerald – what does that represent? Is that something Jennifer earned or you earned?

She says I don't want to talk about my ring – there are more important things to talk about.

Let's ask Trixie – can you tell us about your blue headband? What's that represent?

She says "Defending..." She defended someone or many people; she earned it defending people.

You said there's a jewel in the middle – a gold jewel? What's that represent?

She says it's a stone we don't have here on Earth, it represents reaching other beings.

Like a communication device? Does it work like a crystal, amplifying energy?

Nope. It allows her to communicate – I don't know if she means "understand" or for us to understand, it somehow enlarges the communication between her and other beings.

So the jewel itself help you to communicate?

"Yes."

Does it lower the vibration?

She says that's one of the things it does.

(Note: I'm asking questions that relate to "communication." As I've heard in other sessions, they have to "lower their frequency" in order to communicate with us.)

If I may turn back to kay for a moment, I was curious about your ring in that context whether it's function has anything to do with Jennifer's journey?

"No."

Anything you want to tell Jennifer or people in general?

She's saying "She helps me know when I'm getting interference from the other side that I shouldn't be talking to."

"Discernment." Very good. What was your impression when Jennifer was talking to drunken spirits?

She has a funny reaction – she says "Exactly!" and slaps her forehead. It's the first time she's been funny – she's very austere otherwise.

Everyone in this council has helped everyone so this wasn't an issue?

"Yes."

Did you help her with that Kay?

"Yes."

How did you do that? Make her get rid of her homemade Ouija board or close those doors?

Jennifer laughs. She says "Jennifer's still using the (home made) board I keep telling her to use pen and paper. (Jennifer aside:) Someone keeps coming through and saying "pen and paper" – "pen and paper!" She wants me to graduate to pen and paper.

Is that you Kay telling her that?

"Yes."

That's new information for you?

Absolutely.

Should we speak to the lead counselor here?

She just stood up. She ... (Jennifer laughs) I don't want to tell you what she looks like you're going to think this is crazy – She's presenting me as if to say "Imagine me as this; "Glenda the good witch." Oh my God; I just figured something out. She just downloaded the whole reason she's dressed like that; when I was a kid I was scared witless by the Wizard of Oz. Creepy; didn't like Dorothy, flying monkeys – the only part of that movie I liked was "Good Witch Glenda." She just downloaded this to me – this whole woo woo other side thing can be overwhelming and scary but there are beautiful parts to it that you don't have to be afraid of.

Glenda the good witch (From "The Wizard of Oz") Courtesy MGM

Where is she in terms of your council?

She's right in the middle.

Take hold of her hands.

They're squishy like little kids hands; spongy almost.

Any emotion associated with them?

"Love."

What's that mean?

She's a very loving person. She loves helping people; that's her big thing, helping, helping; she loves it.

What does "love" mean?

"Trusting." She says "That's it. That's all there is."

Describe her to me.

She's little – like 5 foot 2, teeny little thing. Blonde, just like Glenda in the movie – wavy blonde hair, that crazy crown on and the pink dress... blues eyes. She's right out of a 40's Hollywood movie.

What kind of shoes?

White satin with diamond butterfly buckles on each one, very very sparkly – she's very sparkly.

Shall I call you Glenda?

(Jennifer aside:) She laughs. "Yeah."

How's our friend Jennifer doing? Is she on the right path?

"Very much so." She's looking at me and saying "You'll be exactly where you're supposed to be in ten years." (Jennifer aside:) I mean I couldn't make this up if I tried – this is like crazy town here!

Glenda, show Jennifer what she looks like to you.

Okay, this is weird. I see... I don't see a person, I see light. It's like swirling kind of, looks like clockwise, like a tornado kind of. It's white, whitish but again with sparkles, opalescent glittery sparkles in it... that's how she sees me. You know opalescent; it's rainbowy but it's not...

What colors?

Pinkish; maybe like a pale blue, barely blue.

This swirly light – a little weird to see yourself that way?

No kidding.

How many councils do you represent Glenda?

She says "Oh so many... Around ten thousand."

What do you think about what I'm doing interviewing councils?

She says "I love what you're doing. It's so important keep doing it, don't stop you don't realize how important your work is. And how many... woah, how many of us are coming to help you – like present tense; still coming."

I appreciate that. I must say in one council session, mid question, they went "I don't like what you're doing and we have to stop" – and got all the members to leave. What was that about?

She kind of goes "Pfff. It's not the first time and not the last time you're going to hear that." She says "You're a threat to some, I know you find that hard to believe – she means like them over there, not Earth people....

Should I worry about starting my car? (Mafia joke)

"No." She says "You have protection around you, trust me you have plenty of protection; don't worry."

Okay, I think I'll need Trixie by my side for sure.

Oh yeah; the defender!

Back to you Glenda... this is fascinating; have you incarnated somewhere else a long time ago before you started this work as a council member?

I know that sounds weird but she says "I don't remember."

But as her councilor, are you able to participate in what she's doing? Like enjoying music or a pint of Guinness?

She says "I have no desire to have a pint of Guinness or anything like that."

This leads to my next question, when a person is choosing a lifetime which include the difficulties they are going to go through – correct me if I'm wrong – what's it like for you? You're connected to them emotionally, but is it like moving chess pieces on a board? Is there an emotional connection to what you're advising them to do?

She shows me a veterinarian, and using the analogy that "You can't have an emotional connection doing what we do or you wouldn't be able to do it." You know how doctors can't operate on their own kids? She showed me that but she's not showing me a doctor but a veterinarian.... (Jennifer aside:) Maybe she sees me as a pet.

(Note: It's an insightful answer. We can't see ourselves as Doctors see us; patients for sure, but also "one of many." This is the kind of insight one can get from these questions, seeing oneself from someone else's conscious perspective.)

The kind of therapy work, the kind of work that Jennifer is doing, it can help save the planet, is that correct?

"Absolutely," she says.

How can Jennifer help encourage people to save the planet in her work?

I'm not getting an answer.

Let me ask why; is the reason you're not giving her the answer because it's better for her to learn by doing... or you don't know the answer?

She says "She needs to learn it by herself."

So Jennifer has 16 active members on her council?

"Yes."

Do they all represent qualities that Jennifer has learned through her lifetimes?

"Yes."

Anyone else on the council you want her to speak to?

There's one guy she's pointing to... she's pointing to her left, my right – the second to last person.

Describe him.

He looks like 60, maybe 65; his name is Herman. He stands up. He's my height. 5'8. Wearing ... something from Renaissance times... kind of leathery, like a leather vest, with little bit of sleeves, I don't know what this is.

Any jewelry, weaponry?

He's got a lot of silver jewelry – rings bracelets. He's kind of channeling the stones guy Ron Wood. Not Keith Richards, more Ron Wood with that hair, brown hair.

Has Jennifer had a lifetime with you before?

"Three."

You want to put one of those lifetimes in her mind's eye? Where are we?

We're outside, it's sandy, desert; looks like Iraq.

What year are we in?

700 BC.

What does Jennifer look like?

Female. He's showing me 30. Very olive skin black hair, skinny, kind of small like 5'4.

What's her name?

Sounds like Saya? Herman is my brother. His name sounds like Schleb? (Jennifer laughs). I'm sorry, sounds like Schlub. I got very

clearly we're in Mesopotamia. He's showing me the southern part. We're Persians but we're not in Persia anymore, somewhere else.

What happened of significance in this lifetime she needs to know about?

He's saying "She was the smart one she saved us..." By having me escape with her, there was something to do with.. one of our parents, I don't know which one. Wanting to harm us.

So your sister Saya saved your life, is that correct?

"Yeah."

Why are you showing it to her?

He says "Because that's what happened."

What quality do you represent on her council?

He says "Looking out for the little guy."

"Saving people." Herman, how do you think she's doing?

He says "She couldn't be doing better."

So she's on the path that she signed up for; is that correct?

"Yes."

What is it you want to impart to her or the world?

He says "Our actions have such ramifications that we have no idea how far into the future and how far they go."

You mean like a stone hitting a pond turning into an avalanche?

I think he took your cue, but he's showing me (something different); a snowball as it goes down the mountain and getting bigger and bigger to have more impact.

Are you talking about her work as a medium?

Not just that - oh God – he's showing me ... so I'm kind of a sucker when it comes to animals, I feed everything. I put out food for the birds, then the crows started eating that, then I put out cat food for

them and the squirrels were bummed; it looks like Mutual of Omaha's "Animal Kingdom" in my backyard.

It's almost a metaphor; you help one person and the next person is helped – he's giving you a visual metaphor of that snowball. Thank you Herman.

He did a little bow like "It's my pleasure and honor."

Anyone else we need to speak with? I was going to see if we could visit with her soul group or somewhere else.

Glenda just waved her crazy sparkly wand; she's holding this wand with a star at the end and she's going "Go! Go have fun!"

So Trixie – where do you want to take her?

We are outside. It looks interesting it's kind of off planet, again, similar to Earth but too pretty to be here – too perfect.

What do you see?

Wow. She has brought me to a place I've seen before in a very vivid dream, I knew this is was an astral travel thing – she's showing me we're back here, showing me a pyramid made of purple amethyst 50 or 60 feet tall.

Pyramid of purple amethyst (ebay)

Can you put your hand on it? How's that feel?

It's cool temperature wise. Very cool and very smooth.

Is this a place of healing?

(Note: In deep hypnosis sessions, guides often take a person to a "place of healing." The one I saw for me was inside, and felt like a transporter room from Star Trek. I sat in a chair and felt my energetic body reforming. Sometimes they're outside in a bucolic setting, sometimes they contain architecture.)

"Yes."

Trixie, is this is a place of healing that exists solely for Jennifer?

"Yes."

Where she comes between lives to regenerate and recoup?

"Yes."

The purple amethyst – how is it created? Is it an etheric energetic thing; objects created by other people or by Jennifer?

"Other people."

Are those "other people"- are they the ones who have loved her or been moved or been changed or lives have been affected by her – this is their gift to her?

She's nodding like, "Oh my god, you get it, you get it!" She's shocked that you know this.

C'mon Trixie! You knew me from before!

She's so happy that you get it!

One of the first sessions I filmed was with a skeptical atheist Hollywood agent. He saw himself in this giant Gothic Cathedral, and he was told "This Cathedral exists because of all the people you've helped over many lifetimes. They created it for you with intent." Have you seen this pyramid before?

I dreamed of it 20 years ago and have never forgotten it.

Has Jennifer ever seen an amethyst pyramid?

"Oh god no."

It's 50 feet high, which means if this is created by intention, you've helped many people. Am I wrong Trixie? Does everyone have a pyramid?

She goes "Hardly." She's walked inside and I followed her – it's lit by candles... There are like... other stones - like crystal or sand objects all over the place. I feel like they're tools not decoration.

Let's take one – can we? Trixie – describe how this crystal came into existence.

She's showing me it looks like a foot long plain old pointed quartz but it's been fashioned into.. a staff... like a wand.

What's the formula for creating this – if you were in a class, and you were telling a person, how would you create this?

She's telling me that you don't know what it's going to look like (at first.) You think about what you need – not what you want, but what you need and it comes together in the form that is necessary for what you need at that time. She's saying "This just isn't for crystals it's for other objects... it's like you don't think "I need a quartz crystal so big..." Because you'll get what you need.

Where do want to take her Trixie?

She wants to go to the library.

Do you have your library card on you Trixie ?

She says "I am the library card."

Cool. Are we inside or outside?

We must have shape shifted or something... because we're inside some structure or building. Like in "Alice in Wonderland," when you get really small.. I can't tell you what this place looks like because it's moving; it's like alive.

It's a building that's alive... are we looking at books? Energetic forms? Monitors?

It looks like kind of small sized blobs of glowing lights in the shape of tennis balls. She says this is how.... and she's pointing at me –

this is how she accesses the information. This is weird – I always pictured the library as beautiful books.

Every library is different – correct me if I'm wrong Trixie, but it has to do with your journey or path... some people see books, scrolls, cups, monitors, or virtual reality. Each is different. Let's take a tennis ball out that has the memory of when Jennifer chose her lifetime, can we do that?

The Vatican Library

"Yes." She is gesturing her arm open like... "pick one." They're floating around – it's kind of... this is like out of a... they're tennis ball sized, they're not really physical; it's like light. The weird thing is the outside looks like hexagonal mesh.

Trixie help with this. Are these the fractals that contain all of our memories that travel with us from life to life?

She's saying "Yes, yes, yes yes!" Like 100 times, she's saying "Yes, yes, yes!"

So you're saying the Akashic library is the fractals that travel with us from life to life?

"Yes!"

You're connecting dots I didn't know could be connected. Fascinating.

(Note: I've heard this often in these deep hypnosis sessions; people seeing "geometric shapes" or "fractals" following them around. I was told they were "energetic constructs that retain all of a person's past life emotions.")

Trixie is that what we're talking about? These balls of light retain the memories of our previous lifetimes?

"Yes."

People do see them as books or as writing; many things. I guess it doesn't matter – you're seeing as it actually is – each one is a traveling geometric fractal or form constant. Let's go back to looking at it from a macro view – is the energy inside of it moving, bouncing around or is it solid?

It's moving. It's like a honeycomb beehive thing. And if you look at it closely, you can see inside one honeycomb thing that can't be more than a couple of millimeters wide, and you see another one.

You see like a fractal... mathematical constants?

Yeah.

Trixie, help her to access a memory from that ball of light.

Okay, she's showing me to actually squeeze the ball, she's showing me that's what you do – I squeeze it to get the download.

Is this an entire lifetime or is this a moment within a lifetime that you've led?

It's a moment. We're on Earth. Oh god, this is more snow.

Is this from Jennifer's current life?

No. We were in the north – like Newfoundland. Not the north pole but way up.

Is this Canada?

You call it that now, but it wasn't then.

Would you show Jennifer who she was?

Female. Showing me as a kid maybe 12, 14. Black hair... eyes look almost black, really dark. she's ... I look like your typical Aleutian or Eskimo kid. Big furry Nanook of the north boots.

What's this young girl's name?

I get the letter K, but it's a long name.

So what about this memory does she need to access now?

I was responsible for a lot of the food gathering; she's showing me my dad was killed or not in the picture, and it was my responsibility to help my mom with the food.

What year is this?

Like ... 12 something... 1250 - 1260 AD.

Important for you to see you could be depended upon my many for their survival. You've been a person who's healed and saved people. Is that correct Trixie?

To show her how resourceful she is and she doesn't use it. She's showing me I had to act like a boy, didn't have time to play with girls because I was too busy with these duties... to grow up faster which was hard but good for me to learn for some reason.

Was she supposed to remember being more resourceful fearless? Have courage?

She's saying "To know she can take care of herself."

No matter what?

"Yeah."

Let's put that memory back into the time frame – anything else she needs to see in this library?

She wants to... she wants us to go over and meet this little little old man who kind of runs the place. She wants us to say hello and to give him a little thanks for taking care of all the ... she calls them books. He's so cute – he's probably just under 5 feet. I don't know his age; his face is timeless. He looks human, really old but really young at the same time – I can't describe it; a million years old.

What's his name?

He says "Huey." (Jennifer laughs.) That is so not what I was expecting.

Nice to meet you Huey – can I ask you some questions?

He says "I'd be delighted."

Are you aware of what I'm doing? I know it sounds like I don't believe it.

He says "In general, yes, but he's too busy to pay much attention to the specifics."

That would make sense. Have we spoken before?

He says "Yes – but not in this manner." I don't know what he means.

Like I was filming someone asking you questions and I happened to be in the room at the same time?

"Yes."

(Note: I just had a flash of a session from my book "It's a Wonderful Afterlife" who was talking to this librarian (him! who else?) who was sarcastic and funny. He's the fellow who was asked; "what is the meaning of a shift in consciousness?" "What or who is God?" He replied "You humans think it's important to name things to get a handle on them. But in terms of a shift, imagine yourself a crab on the ocean floor and you open your eyes and realize you're in an ocean. That's a shift in consciousness.

To the question "What or who is God?" he said "God is beyond the capacity of the human brain to comprehend, it's not physically possible. However you can experience God by opening your heart to everyone and all things." A sentence I've thought a lot about since he said it – and here I am transcribing this session and he popped into my head.

In a subsequent session with medium Jennifer Shaffer, he confirmed to me that indeed, he is "all librarians" and appears to each one in his own fashion, dependent upon their syntax and experience. Wow.)

I'm curious what your opinion is about people talking about a shift in consciousness – what would that mean to you?

The first thing he says "It's been a long time coming; we've been waiting and waiting and waiting."

You mean "we" in terms of humans?

"No, the flipside people." He's saying that he "gets more visits now than he used to and he's excited because he didn't have enough company until recently. He likes it; his thing is the more the merrier."

Did you choose this job? Or was it given to you?

He says "Both."

I was writing about this today – "What or who is God? I'm curious what your answer would be?

He's pointing to all the little balls and saying "This is God." (Jennifer aside:) Probably because he's a librarian. He probably has a lot of time to read.

Has your name always been Huey?

He laughs, says "My name is whatever you want it to be."

What do your friends call you?

He's chuckling; "They call me Maestro." (Maestro is defined as a "conductor of music" or "a great or distinguished figure in any sphere." Funny they would add the word "sphere" in the Oxford dictionary version.)

I understand it's a ridiculous question – speaking to a million year old person – what does it matter what his name is?

Jennifer laughs.

Why does everyone see the library differently?

He says it exists, but not on any kind of plane we can visualize or understand.

You mean it exists etherically, like seeing a rainbow they see it from their rainbow?

He says "Yes and no." You and I, Rich, we're physically unable to conjure what it is so we have to put these constructs around it – we see a tv screen or a scroll or a glowing little ball.

I was curious, since everyone sees it differently; that would mean it isn't a place – but in terms of relative experience to that person experiencing it.

No. he's scratching his head like "How do I explain this to you people?" He says it's almost like um... oh f*%k, he can't explain it to me... He's saying "There are so many dimensions and so weird in other dimensions, there are no words to explain to you how it exists...– the best I can tell you is that what you perceive it to be is as good as what it makes on our side."

Same goes with us having this conversation. But let's say Jennifer and I are on another planet and we're able to access this – it would be different if we are using words or syntax... he's saying "This is beyond words?"

"Yeah: we can't conceptualize it."

Same goes for "God" I suppose. What is it that you want to tell people?

He's saying "Spread the word about my library because you don't remember anything down there." He's referring to us on Earth. He's saying "Reading doesn't make you smarter, reading makes you braver." He's using light balls as an analogy, if we discover what's happened to us (via the library), we'll (come to) understand we have crazy phobias from stuff that happened in the past; we can learn why we're afraid of spiders or windows and it will make us braver.

A version of "The truth sets us free?"

"Yeah; yeah."

What's the best way to access you?

He's saying "You're doing a great job Rich... of learning – he says dream time is particularly easy but you have to set the intention before you go to sleep." He says "That's the easiest way, set the intention you want to come visit and find these books and with practice you can get here very easily." He's saying "For most people," and he's got this cute little old man look – he's making a sad face – he's saying "They'll never find their way here."

In their lifetime?

"Right."

In the future another lifetime?

He says "Possibly."

Were you ever surprised to see someone who stopped by to visit? Someone surprise you?

Okay, this is crazy but he's showing me James Dean with a cigarette hanging out of his mouth.

James Dean: Wikipedia

Let's focus on this for a second – you're talking about the actor?

"Correct."

You had met him before; you knew who he was before?

"Correct."

Okay, I had a conversation with him not to long ago (via medium Jennifer Shaffer). Are you aware of who he has reincarnated as on the planet?

He says, "Yes." He's not telling me who it is. It's like he's smiling, it's a secret perhaps. He doesn't want me to know.

I'm not supposed to tell her?

He says "She really doesn't need to know that."

You mean it's not up to me to turn on the lights in the theater and say "It's only a play?"

"That's right."

It was surprising having a conversation with James Dean. I was asking him my usual questions ("Who was there to greet you, etc) and I asked "Are you getting ready to reincarnate?" and he said he already had." Odd thing was I know this actor he was referring to... and he said "Yeah, I'm that guy."

(Jennifer aside:) Wow; talk about six degrees of separation.

I texted a friend who is best friend's with this actor and asked "Has your friend ever had someone tell him he was the reincarnation of someone?" And he texted back JAMES DEAN. Later, he told me since knowing this actor, that his whole life random people would tell him that.

That must be kind of weird.

Well, he's got his own life and journey. He's a happy guy, has a family and is a successful actor with a great career.

Wow that's such a cool confirmation.

Is this accurate Maestro?

He said, "Oh, indeed your friend is him. It's true..." and um.. he's saying, "I need to get back to work."

(Note: Mind blown yet again. I'm speaking to a person on the flipside through a woman I've never met. This fellow on the flipside is reminding me that we've met before, that the actor that I know that I suspect is the "Reincarnation of James Dean" is actually the reincarnation of James Dean. I could write this scenario if I tried.)

Okay. We'll let you go. But what kind of work do you do? Cleaning, categorizing, fixing up energy?

He says "The books/energy balls are my children and I take care of them like I ..."

Like a mother?

"Like I... would if I had my own child." I get the feeling he doesn't have or never had kids – this was his full time life.

Have you ever incarnated on Earth?

"Never."

That must be disconcerting for you to deal with so many Earthlings.

He's laughing, as if we are the children. He's saying "this isn't just all Earthlings, this is everyone."

Okay, you've got a lot of work then. Thank you.

(Jennifer aside:) That was amazing. I don't know how it all works; I don't know how I got this gift of "talking to dead people..."

Let's ask Trixie that question. What does she say?

"Because you asked for it."

Now you know.

This was awesome, thank you.

Thank you. Wow.

PART TWO:

A CONTINUATION OF THIS CONVERSATION WITH THE LIBRARIAN VIA MEDIUM JENNIFER SHAFFER.

As I often do, when I hear something mind bending during a session with someone not under hypnosis speaking about someone on the flipside, I often ask Jennifer and Luana Anders to take up this conversation where it left off to see what else I can learn. This conversation will also appear in the next "Backstage Pass to the Flipside" book. My comments are in italics, Jennifer Shaffer's replies (*How many Jennifers are in this book by the way?*) are in bold.

Jennifer Shaffer with the author

Rich: Okay, let me ask about a session I did the other day with a woman over skype. In her Akashic library, instead of seeing "books" she saw them as tennis balls sized light; energetic swirling lights.

Jennifer Shaffer: That's how lights attract lights – our whole existence is light.

Her guide was showing her this library, we met the librarian; a million years old with an eternally young face.

I got an image of Yoda.

When we asked for his name, he told us "Huey."

They're saying "like the essence of Yoda." (Jennifer aside) I asked is it how he looked and they said, "No."

Let's ask Luana to bring him forward.

He's here. They have him blocked in. She put him in my head...

Let me ask you a question.

(Jennifer aside) Is this someone you knew ?

No.

He's morphing into various different – he morphs into different looks from what I'm getting. Whatever it is... whoever it is.. (he changed into their perception of him.)

My first question; "What's up dude?"

He showed me stacks of infinite records a mile high... "that's what's up."

Are you the only Akashic librarian or one of many?

Library

"Source." He showed me being him and shooting out thousands of his image in different lights. If I'm getting this right – he said "Source." He says "Our soul is like the ocean," we've talked about that... each wave is a different person.

So you are the source librarian – people see different variations of you in their Akashic libraries?

He's saying it again; "Source." I think he's saying he's God.

Let's clarify that.

He says "You see what you want to see."

Well we've heard God is not a person, per se, but more like a medium or a nexus...

That's what he showed me; like everyone is a light and everyone is connected. Everything that's on earth, all the different layers of the planet.

Have you always been the librarian or did you become the librarian?

Jennifer smiles. He showed me coming from other galaxies, being a part of someone else's world - he became his own librarian... it's funny, you .. it's like he became his own god – the way they talk about it in the Mormon church where they talk about becoming your own God in the afterlife.

Okay, I don't want to pursue that right now. Instead of God or deity, let's use the word librarian - it's easier... you came from another realm originally?

"Yes."

How many years ago?

Tens of millions of years, "square root of pi" kind of answer.

Was that a realm anyone is aware of on our planet?

"Yes."

Not in our universe, but another realm?

(Another realm) That's connected. It's like we (in our Universe) are the power source for the other galaxies.

Okay... your universe is the source of other universes?

"It's complicated," he says.

Just trying to clarify. We've spoken to people from higher realms, give us a level...

"Eleven."

Are you in touch with people from there?

"Yes." He says "He needs a lot of people he needs an army. He's the source for them – (Jennifer aside) I'm asking "Are we the power source for him and his universes and I'm getting "Yes."

(Note: This seems to refer to a previous conversation where we learned that dark matter or dark energy is the source of matter in other universes; discussed in a chapter with scientists.)

But you're the librarian for all Akashic libraries?

"No." He says "There are a lot of libraries."

So the other libraries that you're not in charge of, others are in charge of?

"Yes."

How many libraries are you in charge of?

"It's like you take the population of Tokyo and you multiply that by a billion."

So, everyone in our realm?

"No."

Are you the librarian for everyone on Earth?

"Yes."

And some other places too...

We're connected to all of that – he's in charge of all of that.

In my interview with you, you said the books of our past lives are not about history but were about fear; the times we conquered fear in our past lives.

"Yes. The opposite of fear."

How I overcame fear in a previous lifetime?

"Yes, that's why past life regressions help."

So what is love if not the opposite of fear?

"Love is the heart center." He showed me it's connected to everything; oceans, seas, the earth.

We're connected heart wise to all people and all things? The ocean, an object, a table?

"Yes."

On a quantum level – things don't come into existence until we choose to observe them according to quantum mechanics. Does that apply to everything?

"Yes."

What do you want to tell us Maestro?

"To stop fearing the unknown. The more that you love, the more that opens you up, heart wise, the more knowledge comes to you."

Peabody Library Baltimore. From Library Website.

So why did you choose to show up to this guide during this session. She wanted me to meet you – why?

It should be in your books, the discussions we've had.

It will be.

(Jennifer aside) He's smoking a cigar. A Cuban cigar.

How long have you been smoking Cubans?

He says "100,000 years." (Jennifer aside;) I know they weren't invented yet.

Did they exist prior to being on the planet?

"Everything did."

How is that?

"When we open ourselves up we reveal things that have always existed, we get things. Somebody was really lucky getting the first cigar, someone lucky getting Microsoft.

You're saying those things existed, but our conscious awareness of them does not – until it does? Is there something you want to show us so we can become billionaires?

(Note: My questions may sound flippant, but when I meet someone like this, an intellect that is hard for me to keep up with, I try to throw a few curve balls if I can.)

He showed me your heart center.

So tell me how can people access Akashic libraries?

He showed me lying down – he showed me meditation. If you don't judge anything you can get anything. If you're not fearful of things coming in – it's very challenging to not judge what you see or hear.

Should people focus on you in their meditation to go to the Akashic records of their many lifetimes?

No. They should focus on their hearts.

What's a question for their heart? To say "I'd like to visit my library?"

Another way to say it is "I'd like to visit who I am elsewhere."' Using the word library helps everyone get there.

How about using "heart library" instead of Akashic?

That's what it is but – if you want people to get there, you can't use that word – they might think it's something else.. He says "You should use "Akashic" because it's taken thousands of years to get people to hear the word – even if they're not religious. Akashic means "heart."

I think in Sanskrit it means etheric or "invisible."

But it also means "heart."

Here's my question. I asked you before if the geometric shapes people have seen were books – of those fractals are books; is that correct?

"Yes."

You said calling them "Akashic books" is the right term –

He showed me something being pressurized... "Since there's no time in space, it's a record of time where you are."

Okay; like a packet in time? Who creates them?

"Our higher self does – that's how we get out of this lifetime – we have several outs."

We create the packets?

"Yes."

How many does a person have?

"Thousands. They are not all just one lifetime. Everything makes up one big shape – love, hatred, all these things, loss, that all becomes fractals - eventually they become cohesive and turn into "your books.""

Can I access someone else's Akashic records? Are we allowed to do that?

"Yes; everything is connected; you can see whoever you want – everything that's affected them."

So what's in the books functions like a URL or a link?

"Yes."

I'm aware the brain may not actually store memories in engrams – but function as a "link" to the off-site memory. That theory is that we don't store info in the brain but offsite?

"Yes." He showed me that.

So we have our own personal cloud, and the cloud is our fractals filled with memories from all of our lifetimes?

"Yes."

Wow. Do the engrams in our brains serve as a link a url?

"Yes. It also comes back though – as well - both ways. If we're feeling something on the planet, we get information coming from there, maybe not our past lives but something else."

Is it possible to access other people's past lives?

We're in the bandwidth. It's like me (Jennifer the medium) thinking someone is going to die – it's a frequency I'm translating. I pick up that frequency.

Okay, thank you Mr. Librarian.

(Listens) It's one of his people (is speaking with him) – he's able to talk through people.

What does that mean?

He has a medium up there – he or she or whatever - is talking through someone there right now...

So why did you allow me to ask these questions?

He's showing me you. Because your research is helping people and there's a buzz up there about it.

I asked if you ever met anyone from the planet who impressed you over there, someone in the library, and it was someone from our class.

James Dean.

Yes. Anyways, thanks for answering our questions; I'm sure everyone has a lot of questions, and we're like kindergartners.

He says "Well, sometimes you learn from kindergartners."

****

As I say; mind officially blown.

CHAPTER TWENTY ONE:

BREAKING THE VELVET ROPE

Benedictine Abbey at Avignon

INTERVIEW WITH A BENEDICTINE NUN

I met Marie ten years prior to this conversation one afternoon. I had lunch with her and an old friend, and over the years since then, kept in touch with her via Facebook in two different countries where she was working. Then one day she stopped in Santa Monica, and asked if we could have lunch again. I took the opportunity to see if we could go "anywhere." My questions are in italics, her replies in bold.

Rich: We're in Caffe Luxxe. Your name?

Marie.

Bonjour Marie! (Not her real name) Here's what I do – ask if you've had any dream or memory that was outside of consciousness. I know you're an analytical person but allow me to set some parameters. I'm going to ask questions and ask you to not judge the answer. Whatever comes to mind – you can judge it later. It's literally a game we're playing. Have you had an NDE or a dream of someone no longer on the planet or any consciousness altering event?

Yes, not an NDE, not a past life memory, I connect with death a lot...

Le mort?

Yeah. I (often) feel people on the other side.

What I'm looking for is a gateway or a key. Sometimes people have a dream about a person who died. sometimes it's people you know who died – like your friend Joe who passed away recently. But as we began, you mentioned having a dream or vision that was triggered when you saw your aunt as a nun in a convent?

It's more like I had a strong intuition for some reason.

Let's explore that for a second. You told me you had a memory of being a nun when you saw your aunt the Benedictine nun. So in this memory...

It was in a restrictive convent.

Like your aunt's order?

Yes.

Benedictine as well?

Yes. I'm trying to not let the memory of her interfere with this memory, but yes.

So you have a vision in your mind of what you looked like in that lifetime. Ask that memory to come forward. Are we inside or outside?

(Note. It looks like I'm leading her. I am. I'm aware that every memory we have still exists, and even if we can't access it, the fact that we once did means it's still "there" in its own packet of time. I've found by asking simple direct questions we can access those packets of time.)

It's inside. It's dark abbey. I'm inside in an area where there's a fountain. What do you call it? An area inside the convent where there is some grass and a fountain. Like an inner garden.

(Note: Here's the Benedictine Convent that Marie is recalling. This Benedictine Abbey in Avignon, has been in existence since the 15th century)

Nuns of Avignon   The garden she is describing.

Recent photo of that the abbey. (Map of the convent from 1769. Note the gardens depicted inside the walls of the Fort.)

Are you standing or sitting?

I'm on one of those corners. I'm standing.

Take a close look at her. How is she dressed?

She's not so tall. She's wearing a black robe...

Is the fabric thick or thin?

I don't know if I'm mixing it with (memory of) my aunt's stuff. But it's rather thick.

Tell me about what's on her head?

A veil that's white.

Where are we on the planet? Whatever comes to mind.

It's France.

What year?

I think 1726.

What color eyes does she have?

They seem blue. Very light.

Put your hands into her hands if you can – what does that feel like?

I was expecting she would be upset, but she's super at peace. She's very calm.

What's your first name?

M... A... I hear Marie. Like my name... it's just.. I heard "Madeleine."

Let's ask her directly; is your name Madeleine? She can nod, shrug, shake her head if she wants.

She says "Yes."

What about your last name?

S... E... R... T... I... N....

Sertin?

An e at the end. Sertine. Sister Marie Madeleine.

What's a year during this lifetime? What comes to mind?

1726.

(Note: Dates can be problematic unless a person is very specific. I'm asking for a general answer that will give me a time frame to look up. In this case, it led me to the forensic search; from a French genealogical site: "Sertine, Marie Joseph, Father Albert Claude Marie. Lived between 1725 and 1775 Saint-Claude, Jura, France. (Geneanet.org) It turns out her description of the convent matches the location in Avignon.)

How close are you to Paris?

I am in the south of France. Avignon.

Are you enjoying this lifetime?

I am looking for god or finding god.

Well, we'll help you find him. You mean your life is okay, because you're looking for god?

She was in the right spot to look for him!

Let's go to your home before you became a nun. Having some dinner with your family. Look at your home and look around the table.

Super poor parents, very thick in build, kind of tree trunk kind of people.

How many brothers and sisters?

I see two children and the parents. Four of us. Me and a boy.

What are you guys eating?

Soup.

Potage du jour?

A potato thing.

Any good?

Meh.

What age did you join the convent? Was it planned for you?

Late teens. It feels like a choice.

Was everyone happy with that?

My parents were like "It's one mouth less to feed..."

But I'd guess at the same time they get to participate in church events, elevates them in status in some way.

Yes, correct, so they're happy with the choice.

Let's go to the last day of that lifetime.

I am in bed. In the convent by myself. Wearing my black robe... I have my hands clasped around my rosary, lying in bed.

So you're laid out after your journey. What happens next? Where do you go after this?

I see myself on a horse.

Is that an etheric horse or one back on earth?

I'm a human on earth in another life.

Before we go to another lifetime on earth, let's go back to Madeleine for a second. After she's died. She's risen up out of her body... and where does she go? Who's the first person who greets her?

She pauses. Laughs. "It's Jesus."

Don't judge it. She sees Jesus?

Yeah.

How far away is he from you?

He's right close to me, like two feet; where you are.

Look at him carefully. What's he look like?

There's a huge kind of light... like it radiates... and he's wearing a white beige robe. He has facial hair, he's young, like 20, 30, his hair is beige.. brown. His eyes are .. noisette. Brown but lighter with some yellow in it.

Yellow? You mean like flecks of gold?

Yes. That's it. Flecks of gold.

(Note: There it is again. It was in the book "Flipside" where "Molly" described knowing Jesus, seeing him with brown eyes with "flecks of gold.")

Let's freeze this for a moment. You're seeing someone you have never seen before in this lifetime – or has Marie ever seen him?

No.

I just want to clarify – he's not someone you often see.

No.

And this is the first time Sister Mary Madeleine has seen him?

Yes.

Just allow this moment to be here – He's here for a specific reason. Can you reach out and touch his hands?

Yes.

What's that feel like?

Very loving, very caring, even more at peace than Mary Madeleine felt in the convent.

Can we ask him some direct questions?

He says "Yep."

How are you doing?

(Laughs) He says "I'm perfect."

Would you do me a favor? He knows what I'm going to ask. Would you change into an outfit more conducive for us to chat?

As you said that he changed into another costume. He's wearing a tie and jacket... The tie is kind of navy blue and grey, same color jacket with a white shirt.

Very dapper. Same hair length?

Kind of to the shoulders... long and kind of not so wavy. A little wavy.

And you're looking at this brown eyes with bits of yellow?

He's very kind looking.

I'm going to call you Jay instead of Jesus – just to keep this light. But first, can you give her a hug put your arms around her?

Yes.

What's that feel like?

It feels... familiar.

Any other emotions associated with that?

Kind of feeling an undisturbed... like a known place. Like I'm not experiencing, "Oh wow, I'm hugging Jesus." It's just - this is familiar.

So Madeleine knows him – else how could it be familiar unless she knows him?

Right but... I'm not aware of that.

Yes, but somehow she knows this feeling. Let's go to Jay Zeus and ask him some questions. Dude. Did you have a lifetime with Madeleine before?

"No."

Have you met her before or just on the flipside?

"On the flipside."

When you were alive she was not there?

No, but I followed his teaching back there – when I was on the flipside, I followed him.

I don't know if Marie is Catholic....

I was born a Catholic.

Okay, some Catholic questions – I don't know how familiar you are with my books... "Hacking the Afterlife."

A long time ago.

Let's ask him a question; did you die on the cross?

"He did."

(Note: I report verbatim what people say. She replied as I asked the question.)

But I want you to put it in her mind's eye. What happened to you? They put you on a cross for sure. But what happened after the cross?

"When they brought me down?"

Yes. What happened then?

"I got put in that tomb."

Then what happened? Put it in Marie's mind – what happened after you came off the cross, after the cave, where did you go?

(Makes a puzzled face.) I see .. some people traveling.

Is he traveling with them?

"Yes."

How many are with him?

I see his body... but (it's) his flesh body but not his spirit.

So that's actually him traveling with people?

"Correct."

He's traveling, so he's still in existence? So if this is after the crucifixion, therefore...

"He didn't die."

I'm trying to get him to tell you this. Let's skip down; let's ask him, did your wife Magdalene go to France? Give her a "yes, no, I don't know."

He says, "Yes."

Okay, I've heard that. Did you go later on and pick her up in France? "Yes, no I don't know, eventually."

He says "What matters is that I left the mattress."

(Note: I don't know what he means by "left the mattress." I don't know if he meant his "home" or "the mattress he was recovering on." I'm assuming he means "left where I was living" and am focused on his saying "that's what matters.")

(Laughs) Okay, I won't go into this in depth, I just wanted you to put that in her mind's eye – not only did you survive one of the greatest events in human history...

(Marie aside) It is interesting.

Am I right or wrong about that?

"Totally right."

So why are you letting Marie see this event today? Put that in her mind.

He says "She doesn't know how powerful she is." Marie laughs. "She needs to embrace her power."

So let's go back to the moment you're holding her hands. Where you her guide?

"No. She was looking for me for so long and there I was."

And now is here again. Not so hard to find was he, Sister Madeleine?

He was there, just "beyond the door."

Okay, let's talk to your guide. Can he come forward?

He's a big f*&ker. He's big... like bigger than two meters. He's not so young and he's not so cool – he's tough like a teacher.

What's his name for this conversation?

"Sorus."

(Note: Haven't run across this name. It's Greek definition is: "stack, pile or heap.")

Nice to meet you – welcome to Cafe Luxxe, I'd get you a coffee but... how long have you been her guide?

He says "three or 53..." a number of lifetimes... "Not just that one. A lot."

How is she doing in this one?

"She's learning."

Have you ever incarnated with her?

"No."

But you've been keeping an eye on her?

"I'm in charge of her."

Charge meaning a loving charge? In charge of a child.

"In charge of making sure she gets what she came for."

Is it all right to bring her to her council?

(Marie hesitates:) "He says she's not ready."

Very good. But I am. Why don't we go visit her council for me and she can sit in the back?

(Note: They're fully capable of saying "No," and there is one account in this book where a council didn't like my line of questions, and disbanded in front of us.)

I'm in front of a table with people.

Okay. That was fast; Sorus said she's not ready but allowed it. Thank you.

"As a human she has the free will to do it without permission."

Okay. I don't want to disrupt her path in any way.

"She's strong she can take it."

I'd like you to participate.

"I'm here."

I just want to say that I'm not going to alter her path in a bad way.

"She cannot go in a bad way." (Marie aside:) He's tough!

Are we inside or outside?

Neither inside nor outside. It's a long table like a banquet table.

How many people?

More than ten sitting down. I'm in front of them standing.

Let's start with the person on the far left, male or female, neither or both?

I see only males. Far left is a male, he's older, but younger than the others.. like 25 maybe... dark black hair, he's far away. Has brown eyes.

Let's go closer to him. Look him in the eye. Let me ask; is it okay to talk to you?

He says "I'm not (the one) supposed to talk." He says we are the ones doing the talking.

What's a name to address him with?

He says "no name that you would understand."

How about a letter?

He says "call me Mo."

(Note: I refrained from doing a "Three Stooges" comment. "Hey Mo.")

Nice to meet you.. and thank you for allowing us to have this conversation. Mr. Mo.

(Marie aside:) They don't laugh. They aren't laughing.

I don't always get laughs, but are you familiar with what I'm doing?

"We know you."

I get the feeling you disapprove of me asking questions. Correct?

"Yes; she has her path."

I won't disrupt her path – we're not going to talk about her future. I'm only going to ask about you.

"She needs to open the doors herself."

Here's my question to you; what quality do you represent on her council?

I hear "Justice."

How many councils do you sit on?

"Three."

How is Marie doing?

"She cannot go wrong."

So then there's nothing to worry about here; thank you Mo. Have you ever had a lifetime on earth?

"Never."

Where do you normally incarnate or did you incarnate?

"That's none of your business." (Marie laughs, shrugs)

If you know me Mo, as you say you do, you know I ask questions. Did you have a lifetime there?

"Yes."

Is it in another galaxy?

"Yes."

Something she would know? That she remembered in a dream?

"We've been there together."

Put that in her mind's eye, without fear or judgment, show her this place – Are we inside or outside?

It's a very cool place. it's like outdoors... like very colorful elements... colors are more vivid, more flashy.

How many people exist on this planet?

"Three million."

Is this planet in another galaxy or in another universe?

"Other universe."

I've heard descriptions of a few so this is not unusual for me.

He says "He knows (that)."

Sorry to be so persistent Mo. What do you call this planet in case I run across it again?

"You cannot know the name, it's a different way to name things. It's not comprehensible to you."

Can you show her what you look like on that planet? Present yourself in front of her – or what does she look like? Did she have arms and legs?

"It's more like etheric, not completely *ghosty*... but a different density and dimension."

Kind of like you can see-through a person?

"Exactly – it's like fluid; there is no legs or walking."

(Note: I've heard of these descriptions in Michael Newton's work, as well as some of the deep hypnosis sessions I've filmed – people have various existences on these other planets, might be a water planet, a gaseous place or something like the film "Arrival.")

Is it more of a mental planet?

"Yeah, yeah."

Is there a lifetime on that planet?

"Time doesn't exist there" (as you know it.)

So you exist over there now?

"Yes."

So does she exist over there now?

"Yep."

What percentage of her energy is on the planet?

20.

What percentage of her is on our planet?

"Say that again? Her consciousness is with her everywhere."

I asked how much was over there you said 20...

"Her entire consciousness is with her on earth."

(Note: For me this is an example of how Marie is not aware of my books, as I've reported often that people bring "about a third of their conscious energy" to any particular lifetime. Later, after we discussed this she said "I heard the number 30, but was confused by it." I pointed out that if 30 percent of her is here, and 20 is "over there" then that leaves 50 percent "back home.")

I understand that 100% of who she is, is here; but back home – between lives, some percentage of her consciousness is in front of Mo at this moment - so it can't be 100... But in terms of your journey, do people from your planet come to earth?

"All the time."

To gather or pass along information?

I'm hearing "It's a luxury... it's a luxury to have the opportunity to incarnate here. It's elective."

(Note: Some claim that they've incarnated on Earth to help their friends "back home" in other galaxies to help them understand or adjust consciousness of people on Earth. I asked if people from his planet came here to gather or pass along information, and he's noting that incarnating on Earth is something that people want to do.)

She chose to come here?

It's hard... (to incarnate on Earth) but it's like when you pass this game test, you learn much more on earth than anywhere else, like a condensed form of spirit knowledge.

Mo, can I ask why you've never incarnated on Earth?

"I don't need it. My frequency is a different frequency. I don't need to incarnate."

What's Mo wearing?

All are wearing white, same clothes. Some wear pendants.

Let's go to a person wearing a pendant.

It is a guy in the middle...

Hello. Sorry to interrupt, but we've traveled a long way to talk to you so I hope you don't mind.

Not really...

(Note: I think she's replying "not really traveled a far way – it's just a shift in consciousness" but I'm trying to press on to see how far we can go.)

Let me ask about the pendant. What's it look like?

A planet. Looks like Saturn with a ring.

Saturn: NASA

What does that represent?

I don't know how much my mind is making this up.

(Note: It's important to repeat; the information is coming into the mind in the same fashion imagination does. So it may feel made up – or it may *be* made up.)

Try not to judge it; let me ask him, does it represent travelling to a planet?

"It doesn't have anything to do with the planets; it has to do with what kind of community or section he is from."

What quality do you represent in her spiritual evolution?

He's like a part of ... he represents "education."

We had Justice, Education, Learning.. What's a letter we can use for you?

It's a sound and not a letter. Life Effff...

We'll call you the Eff bomb?

(Note: Marie doesn't laugh. Shrugs that they aren't laughing either.)

I know I'm not getting any laughs. Are you familiar with what I'm doing?

"Yes we know you. You have found a bridge to us."

Where did you hear that I found a bridge?

"You came through people to us many times."

(Note: Reminds one of the film "Coco" by Pixar where the "Day of the Dead" is a bridge to the flipside.)

That's my question – is this a good or a bad thing?

"They cannot judge. They cannot do anything."

Well, normally they only talk to folks who have died. This is a bit different.

It feels like we're interrupting them.

Have you ever incarnated on earth Eff?

"Never."

How many councils are you on?

"Ten."

What's he look like?

He's older, has white hair, white beard... dreads.. like the Celtic guys...

Take his hands.

(Shakes her head) "I'm not allowed."

What's the emotion you're getting while being near him?

He's like "You don't want to fuck with him." (Marie laughs)

Well he is a teacher... it comes in all forms.

"It's not like they "judge your growth," they measure it.. they meet to.. not to judge, but at the end of the day they know how to measure. Not measure progress, but..."

Judgment is associate with sin... I think I understand.

"There's no right or wrong; it's a measurement."

(Note: Interesting point. Clarifying that the word used should be "measurement" – the way people might compare statistics or architectural measurements.)

Do you not want to talk about your planet Eff?

"It's not something you can comprehend."

Like Mo's planet, more etheric?

"More different than that..."

A planet with water or air?

"It's a different more subtle, even more subtle of density..."

Did you like it there, did you have friends there, people you loved?

(Nods) "It's home."

How did you earn this spot on her council?

"Work."

Just part of the job. You were called?

"No she earned it... (my role); consciousness."

She earned your role through a difficult lifetime?

"She knows a lot."

When did you appear?

"It's been a few lifetimes."

If I could speak with the lead council member – could wave us over. (A pause. No reply). Just a couple of questions.

(Marie shrugs, aside:) They're not inclined to help, eh?

Is there a leader of this council?

He's a little bit more kind, has an open face. He's right beside the previous guy.

Next to the pendulum guy. How old does he appear?

Like in his 70's; he is less closed faced.

What's a letter or word we can use to address him?

"Bee."

Thank you Mr. Bee. Are you familiar with what I'm doing?

"Yes."

Is this a good thing what we're doing, talking to her council?

"It depends."

How so?

He showed me... "It's like ... parting the chrysalis and forcing the butterfly out." They're worried or are advising caution about not forcing the being... "Sometimes this work, you need someone to tone up the muscle first before opening up the doors of the chrysalis – some are curious and some are ready to hear it – the curious people should go first to the readiness place."

(Note: Here's a council member arguing this kind of investigation can be harmful. It's hard to argue with him because he certainly would be more aware of the end result than I would.)

Mr. Bee. I know that you know more than I could ever know on this topic, but once a person experiences something it becomes a knowledge based event. So even a person reading this passage may not believe it, but it allows their higher conscious to embrace it.

"They may need more experiences to reach that bridge."

(Note: He may be recommending our dear reader get a refund).

But we are in danger of losing our planet. That's why it's important to share this information so that people will become aware that they choose to come here, and therefore need to leave behind a health planet.

He says "It's all part of the cosmic timing."

So you're agreeing with me?

He's agreeing that "it depends." (Marie aside:) He's nicer than the other guy; more soft, but he's strong.

My point is the people who read this chapter who are in their chrysalis stage won't understand it.

"Sometimes there's a shock and the shock is making them lose time more than helping them. ("Lose time" in terms of their spiritual evolvement) Because it's like almost like a handicap, instead of..."

Instead of learning or absorbing it?

He's saying "Slowly and one little window at a time in accessing this understanding or this knowing."

Well, don't some people need to be pushed out of the next to learn to fly?

"That is against cosmic timing. They want you to be aware that (this information) it's not for everyone."

I say it often; this research isn't for everyone. I put that in the books; If it's disconcerting, return it, get a refund. "Not everyone is supposed to know how the play ends."

They are acknowledging that you are cautious with this information. On paper it could help everyone; but it's not for everyone.

(Note: This is an interesting and cogent point. Paraphrasing "This research is not for everyone. Be cautious who you share it with, because some are not ready to hear it and it will alter their path. If there is to be a cosmic shift in consciousness, be wary of "hurrying that along.")

If I can ask you, how do you think Marie is doing?

I'm hearing "She's perfect."

Can you put a sensation in her body? Like a Bat-signal to let her know you're connected?

(Marie aside:) I just got a chill in the back of my neck.

How do guys do that – give her a chill?

"Because she's plugged in."

And you're able to turn the switch?

"She's on."

Why did you allow her to access this, come into the council today?

"Because she can."

We were told she wasn't ready, but she is?

"She has her free will."

She barged her way in here. Anyone else want to speak up? My I ask why there are no women here? It's a sausage fest?

(Marie aside:) I was looking but I didn't see any.

I've never run across it before – is there a reason for that?

"It's her path."

Not something to worry about – we all know that the source of all energy is the mother energy, you guys are all just slaves to the mother.... that's a Jesus joke.

And they say "Wrong!" But not wrong -- in a way...

I'm playing with their own words.

They're not against female energy... they're just...

Without telling her the future, what's she supposed to focus on?

"She knows."

How often are you connected to her?

"She is always connected to us."

Jesus showing up again! Wow, had a conversation with him via Molly yesterday – can't believe you showed up the next day.

"I like you," he says.

Ha. I'm putting that on the cover of the next book. "Jesus likes me." He's funny. I think he's a complicated cat; not only do you embody the hopes and dreams of everyone, but you're not afraid to take a swing at organized politics or religion when asked.

He says "It was not easy to bring down (to Earth) the principle of love" But now what I hear or feel is "My job was to inject or engrain, inscribe the principle of true, real love."

The kind people consider "unconditional love"?

That's not what he says but it's what he means. "Before, we didn't have the principle of love."

There must be some reason you're allowing me to talk about this without an attachment to organized religion. You said once because "it was time."

"They're ready not to leave their religious beliefs... but is time to unravel... to open the rope..."

The rope of religion?

"It was necessary before, we don't need it anymore, so we can unravel and just retain this principle of love."

Excellent. and how are we gonna do that?

"From within... like listen to the heart kind of thing."

Can we pound people over the head?

"What does that mean?"

I should beat people over the head with that idea of listening to the heart?

He says "You cannot force the process; you can encourage it." He says "Pay attention to the ego – be careful of the ego, watch the ego." (Marie aside:) That's not just for you – that's for everyone. That's our roadblock.

Well, it's everyone's roadblock. I had a dream someone told me to annihilate ego – "vanum populatum." Annihilate things of vanity – the things that are not love.

But he says "Watch out." He says "Understand the complexity... that you don't want to destroy the ego, and get rid of everything that is ego – what remains is sovereign. Honor yourself, which is not only the ego." He's trying to put the words in my mouth... He's talking about vanity – the selfie kind of thing, the vanity of the ego.

Vanity blinds us?

"The superficial layers that cover the essence.... don't forget your essence. That needs to be super powerful, to be sovereign, integrated completely – integral. That's the personality. He recommends to return to your persona, the essence, be as creative as you want form your essence, from your inner fire, but not from what's around you."

That's interesting, anything else you want to tell our friend?

"To keep watching the balance, because we have to fight this polarity, we have to watch out the duality, the polarity; too much selflessness is not right, too much ego is not right, balance. There's big importance in being... true love means to come from a strong fire within, the essence of a person, loving not because you gave that love to me, but you are generating it. It's important to not kill all the ego – it's finding the right amount of ego to hold onto." (Marie aside:) I think that's for me.

If you can focus on the love within, unconditional love, you can generate that outward?

He says "You can reach this only when you have integrated, when you are integral, full, that comes from acknowledging yourself." He was showing me to go to the reverse of selfie, from inside to the outside world; "find your own power within, not from without."

Like a reverse selfie?

"Yeah, it all comes from within."

So what you project to the world – don't focus on what the world projects onto you, focus on the power you can project... a sense of lover and power and balance?

"Once you love yourself you are able to spread the principle of love."

What else dude? Now that Marie has your frequency in her head she can communicate with you.

"She knows."

What a fun thing we were able to be together in this space.

"Any time dude."

Who said that?

Jesus.

He showed up in a friend's dream recently; we sat down and in a few minutes having the same conversation – he looked the same.

No!

Yes, exactly the same brown eyes gold flecks. Before we go let's say thanks to everyone.

******

CHAPTER TWENTY TWO:

"CALM DOWN AND RELAX"

DR. TAYLOR

Taylor is a close friend's daughter who is a scientist who has her PhD from University of San Diego. We've chatted in the past about this technique, she found it an unusual topic and agreed to explore it with me. As a scientist who has presented over 40 research papers, she found what I was saying to be a "bit far-fetched." But we gave it a shot anyway. My questions are in italics, Taylor's answers are in **bold.**

Rich: So, let's see if we can go anywhere. I'm going to ask you a series of questions – they'll be leading, try not to judge the answers. Let's see where we go. Have you ever had a dream that was otherworldly or unusual about a relative who passed away?

Taylor: Other worldly? Well, I have dreams all the time. I just did a reiki thing with my cousin where I felt I was floating above my body.

Did you have a visual sense you were floating?

Physical. I was an inch above my body.

Try to focus on that memory – as if it were frozen in time. Now take a look around. What do you look like?

I'm face down... wait. No, when I was floating I was face up; I remember now.

Looking down at yourself?

Correct.

Go up a foot or two above – can you? Looking down at yourself eyes are...

Closed.

Take a look at yourself floating above you. Do you look like you?

I know I'm me; but I'm not associated with me.

Any color that comes to mind looking at this energetic form of yourself?

Gold. It's gold all around; a soft glowing gold, but flat (matte) ish. It's energetic.

I want someone to come forward and talk to you and I'm suggesting that you visualize them – is that a male, female, or something else?

A male. (Laughs) He's overweight. Middle height; he's like 63. Has hair, a little. Little tufts of white hair; bald on top. Hazel eyes.

Does he seem familiar to you? (Worrying she was referring to me).

Mmm; no.

Let's ask him for a name, a place holder.

"Jonathan."

Thanks Jonathan. Now reach out in your mind's eye and take hold of his hands. What do they feel like?

They're wrinkled; soft. The energy feels strong...

What sensation or emotion comes to mind?

"Strength. The emotion is peacefulness. Strength and peace."

Jonathan, have you ever incarnated together?

I don't know.

Well let's ask him.

He says "maybe."

Have you had a life with her before?

"Probably."

Okay, probably. If so, then show her a lifetime you've had somewhere.

(Note: These are leading questions, but because I've done this so often, I know they don't show up unless they want to show their student something. In this case, I just follow the crumbs.)

Okay. I see we're on an island. It's outside. There's clear water – it's a tropical setting. Seems like the Bahamas on a beach.

Take a look at yourself.

I'm a woman but way tanner. He's there, also tan; he's a dude. He's younger; mid 30's. I'm maybe 30. We're partners. I don't think we are married.

What year is this?

A long time ago.

What date comes to mind?

600. (laughs)

It's allowed. 1600 or 600? or 600 BC?

It's AD. I'm wearing like a weird wrap made out of some animal skin – no top, beads or something above; he's got something similar.. he has dark hair, dark brown eyes.

Take hold of his hands, I want him to show you an earlier time in this life. Where are we?

We're in a hut with four people, Jonathan is there.

So he could be your brother.

Could be; I'm like 6.

Well I hope it's your brother otherwise it would be incestuous. Columbo over here. What do your parents look like?

They're older. Dad is stern. Looks like someone I know in this lifetime – the mom looks familiar too.

Let's thank them for showing up in this adventure. What are you eating?

Some kind of porridge, very bland. We're happy but the dad is stern.

Well I'm sure you were a handful. What does he call you?

"Little paunch."

What do you call him? Does he have a nickname?

I don't know.

That's all right. Let's go to a happy time in this lifetime – where you feel happy and proud.

(Note: This is a typical question when someone is under deep hypnosis. But we're sitting outside at a noisy Starbucks. Because her answers are quick and easy, I just follow whatever path appears.)

I made something. I'm outside. I built something, like a statue thing out of the sand and other materials. I'm like ten. It's like a sand sculpture.

Let's go to the last day of this lifetime.

I'm on a boat... there's a storm and a drowning scene...

How old are you?

I was like mid 40's and am realizing I was a fool to go out on this boat alone... in this storm.

Let's go to after when the sea has reclaimed you – where do you go?

I go back to the hut. I say goodbye to people.

How do you do that?

I'm floating over them in the hut... they're all there.

So you go to where your family is grieving for you? Do you reach out to them in some fashion?

Yeah, I do that by having some kind of favorite animal run by. Something related to my nickname – it's paunch. Like a deer.

So this deer goes by and they realize it's a sign from you?

Yes.

How did you ask the deer for this favor?

I just asked her and she did it. I gave (them) a gift.

But when you asked the deer – how do you do that? Do you give a story to the deer?

I said "Please visit them." And she did.

Shift your consciousness into the deer for a moment and look at you asking the question. How do you look to the deer?

I'm floating up top. I look like a human – but I'm partially see-through.

Does this deer seem familiar to you?

Yes, I knew the deer before. I think the deer is a representation of someone else. Someone I knew before and now they're a deer. That's the connection I had.

Okay, try to shift your consciousness into the deer's mind – is this accurate? Deer, were you a human before? Or was this "little paunch's" idea that you were a person before?

She says "I don't know if it matters," but there was enough connection to get the message forward.

(Note: I understand what she's saying, when she connected with the deer in this lifetime, she made the assumption or leap that the deer was someone that she knew that was reincarnated, and connected to the deer in that way.)

Where do you go after this?

Somewhere else. I'm floating first... then flying. Then we're in a castle.

Who's in this castle?

Italian Castello. Photo by the author.

The guy in charge and me – his name is Daniel. He looks familiar to me there (but not here). He's old, about 60... old for the time.

Are we somewhere between lives?

We're somewhere else.

Let's ask Daniel. First thanks for showing up – where are we? Are we between lives or is this someplace on earth?

I think this is someplace on earth in a high elevation area, in the mountains, in a country in Europe, it feels like Belgium. The year is 1900. (Taylor aside:) Wow it's recent.

So we skipped ahead to a more recent lifetime. What do you look like from Daniel's pov?

I'm blonde, about 20. I'm related to him. A niece or something. I may be a servant.

I would like Jonathan to escort her to her soul group. He knows what I'm talking about.

Okay. We're outside. There are four people; two males and two females.

Do they seem familiar?

I know three of the four from this lifetime.

Let's focus on the one you don't know – because it's disconcerting to talk to people you know who are also back on the flipside.

It's a girl.

Take her hands, look in her eyes. Can we ask you questions?

She says "Yes."

Are you a member of her soul group?

"Yes."

This is where she comes between lives, correct?

"Technically, yes."

Oh, I see – by technically, you mean that her higher self is there as well; what you're saying is that in this instance she's there, but some part of her is always there?

"Yes, that's right."

Are you someone she knows in this lifetime?

"No, I'm not with her in this lifetime."

What's the feeling you have holding her hand?

(Feels) like family.

What's her name?

Veronica.

Okay, Veronica, can you take her to a place of healing, where she normally goes between lives... and demonstrate that for us. Where are we?

We're outside. It's a garden with flowers. Lots of flowers. Bushes. And a fountain. You can see far into the distance, but it's like 150 feet in diameter and there is a fountain.

Huntington Gardens fountain. Photo by author.

Reach into the fountain. What's it feel like?

It's cold; it's clear...

Is it water?

No, it's energy

Can you drink it?

No.

Can you step into it?

Yes. It's rejuvenating. It's refreshing. It looks and feels like it's water, but more is going on.. it moves more. It's like it has its own personality.

Can you give her a sensation of this rejuvenation – whenever that sensation happens... do you have that now?

Yep.

Whenever you're feeling stressed or weird, you can step into this pool. What else is here?

Sunshine, flowers.

Go look at one.

It's pink; not a rose, but like a big petal flower. Like a poppy. It's soft.

Put your hand inside the flower. You can of course because it's an energetic concept, right?

It absorbs my hand (completely), my hand fades out.

What's that feel like?

Confusion.

Okay pull it out; we don't want to be confused. Pick something else in the garden.

It's a rock; a stone.

Can you lift it?

Yeah.

Pick it up and hold it. What's the feeling associated with it?

Warmth.

Put your hand inside the rock, like you did the flower.

It's stuck. It's frustrating. It's still warm but my hand is stuck.

Well, we can yank it out at any time – is there some kind of entity associated with this rock?

Yes.

Are you creating this associating or is it being created by someone else?

It's coming from somebody else. Somebody I'm tied to.

Someone we know?

My husband.

Someone you're connected to. Let's focus on him. Bring him forth; describe him.

He looks like a monk! His robes are orange. He's older and he's not the same race as me; Asian.

How do you know it's him?

I just know.

Can we speak to you? What do your robes represent?

They're something he's forced to wear over here. He's trying them on.

Is that Thai Buddhism?

Yes.

Why is he presenting himself in an orange robe?

He wants to please me; he knows I'll like it.

We can ask him questions about his path, but I don't think it's fair I ask questions about him without him being here. Let's go back to Veronica. Vee? Please take her hands and walk her to her council. Describe it.

We're both inside and outside; inside but an outside feel like a green house. There is diffused light – no plants but the feeling of plants. There's just the two of us – and the council.

How are they arrayed?

There are five standing shoulder to shoulder. A mix of men and women.

Thank you council for showing up – from left to right?

They are male, female, male, male, female; left to right.

Let's talk to the first person.

A male.

I'm going to ask him .. can you take his hand, look him in the eye? What's his name?

It's Jonathan!

Okay, your brother in that previous lifetime? If you can give her a term or word that represents her evolvement; what is it you've earned to be on her council?

"Patience."

Is she impatient?

"Yes. She always wants it faster sooner."

What do you tell her?

To calm down and relax.

Jonathan introduce her to the person on your left.

Her name is Nancy; with brown medium length hair, 55. She's all about excitement, adventure. Living it up.

I heard someone say nobody comes to the flipside wishing they held back more. How is our friend doing?

She thinks I'm doing well but should be having more fun. That I should travel more.

Where is she supposed to travel?

Some island in a developing country – like an island retreat with yoga everywhere.

Let's go to the next one over –

A guy ... it's David. He's older.

What's his spiritual evolvement for you?

"Honesty."

How's she doing?

"She's doing better lately."

Don't tell me more I don't want to know. Next person over?

It's Henry! He's younger. He's all about learning.

Education. Okay; so how's she doing?

"Great."

Who's next?

Desiree; she protects me, looks over me.

(Note: It's worth noting that I haven't kept score as to who is a woman or man, but her initial response to seeing them has not changed. I've found when a person "sees" their council, they can't "unsee them.")

Is there anyone on the council that can speak on behalf of the whole council?

Yeah, the first guy – Jonathan.

Let me ask, when we met you, you were teasing us, acting like you barely know her.

"Yes."

Why was that?

"To be safe."

Do you approve, or is this okay what we're doing? Asking questions to councils?

"Yes."

Do you personally approve of this work?

"Yes."

"Why?"

"Because it's time... to listen."

It's time to listen. To shift our focus to listen more to people who are guiding us?

"Yes."

And the lottery numbers are...?

Taylor laughs.

Jay, can you tell her why she chose that lifetime on the island, what's the overall theme of her journey?

"Industry."

What's that mean?

"Creating things." On the island she was creating sculptures...

And I'll guess that in this lifetime she has an opportunity to share her wit, wisdom and beauty with the planet as a therapist. What's the best way for her to do so?

"YouTube!"

Is that what he said?

That's what he said.

Describe it to me – just her talking... about her work?

About something. About something I made or wrote.

Something you wrote?

Probably.

She records that and films herself, is she talking directly to camera?

"Yes."

Is she helping people?

"Yes."

To understand what?

"Themselves."

What's she talking about; psychology or spirituality?

Psychology that leads to the spiritual.

Okay, thanks to everyone for allowing us to come here and Jonathan take her back to the healing place, the garden – show her what that regeneration process is.

I'm sitting, quietly. On the earth. Just sitting cross legged.

What does she do to generate that healing energy?

Meditate – close your eyes and wipe your mind.

Give her a 1, 2, 3 so she can connect.

"Call upon ancestors that care. Ask them to pay attention or help out."

So meditation in a quiet place, near an ocean, forest or garden – call upon your guides. Anything you want to ask them?

"How are they doing?" They said they're doing great.

Any advice for me?

"Yes, keep going!"

And one sentence she could pass along to her clients?

"You are stronger than you think."

You're stronger than you think. It's hard to believe, especially for those who are suffering. But all right – that's it.

That was fun! Very creative.

This is an unusual example for a number of reasons. But mainly since I've known this scientist since she was a toddler, know both of her parents well, and they are both really smart, really wonderful people. They had no idea that I had a coffee with their daughter and did this kind of unusual "so where are we?" kind of session. But anytime I was at an event or dinner with her parents, and she was there with her charming husband, we always fell into pretty unusual deep conversations about life, death and the great beyond.

Her journey is fascinating and I appreciate her sharing it with me, and now... with you.

CHAPTER TWENTY THREE:

"THERE ARE MANY LESSONS"

A gargoyle in Paris

Dr. Medhus (ChannelingErik.com) asked if I might interview medium Raylene Nunes, as she was someone who was going to be working with her son Erik (on the flipside) and to see what I thought of her talents.

Raylene is featured in the documentary "Talking to Bill Paxton" on Gaia TV but this is our first conversation together via Skype. My questions are in italics, her replies are in bold.

Rich: Hi, where are you on the planet Raylene?

Raylene: Denver.

I thought rather than me doing a session with you, perhaps we could just talk about your process. What was your first conscious memory you were able to communicate with people on the flipside?

About 9 years old – I was seeing things with my eyes that weren't so nice – they didn't look earthly; they were scary to me. Short, demonic looking things, and then I would start to see angelic presences, I was alarmed and shut it out. About age 14 I started seeing people – it was more like a fuzzy air type of thing – more in that sense.

Let's see if we can go back in your mind's eye to those initial contacts. In terms of demonic creatures; describe this creature. Was it like a gremlin?

That's a good description – very much like a gremlin. I'd say about 3 feet tall, two legs, two arms, crawling - not standing up straight.

Okay. Let's freeze that frame for a second. What color are the eyes?

Red.

Is it a him or her?

A him.

Does he have a name?

I never got one.

Well, let's ask him – freeze this frame, does he have a first name?

He does not wish to be called by a name, more of like ah...

Okay, we'll call him gremlin. I just want to ask him a question. A friend of mine, an actor I've known forever one day told us a story of seeing a gremlin – standing on his chest, eyeballing him, then running up the ceiling. He's an avowed skeptic and doesn't believe in anything he can't touch – but he was adamant that this event occurred when he was a child. So let's just call our gremlin friend "Gee."

Raylene laughs, "Okay."

Does Gee normally exist on this plane or realm or what's his home like? Where is home?

(She listens) He says "It is not on earth and it's more of a different dimension; a lower vibrational dimension.

Lower as in a physical term and not a pejorative? Does he mean lower "bad" or just different?

He's talking about the density of where he lives as being lower than ours.

Does he have family, friends, people he hangs out with over there?

He says "Not spirit friends, no." He says "He likes to engage with humans" – and "mess with people."

As a form of entertainment? But when he's not messing around with humans, does he know other gremlins. Like a soul group that he's incarnated with in the past?

He says "Yes. He does." He says he's come (here) to teach how to set boundaries with other beings." He says "He can be positive and negative as well." He's saying "It's a choice he makes."

Okay. Well let's look at his eyes for a moment. I know they're red and kind of scary looking at first, but there are frogs with bright orange eyes. That's about looks, but he's saying that while he's messing with people here – he's also introducing or tuning people on the other side?

Right.

Okay, thank you Mr. Gee. Let's shift to the positive angelic person that first came to visit you.

It was shortly after my grandfather passed away; he came to visit me. I saw him not solid – saw his body – heard him talking but didn't see him talking.

What was he saying?

That he was on the other side and told me things that would happen with my life, that I would be seeing things more clearly and he said I'd be seeing light beings that would help me. It was like he was no longer like my grandfather; it was like he was a teacher for me.

What's his name?

Manuel.

Can we ask him to come forward?

He's already here. He says "Hi, nice to meet you."

Where is he from when he was on the planet?

In Colorado. He liked to fish and he's still fishing… he still takes pleasure in it.

What kind of fish do you catch over there?

He says, "Whatever kind you wish to!" He's kind of a teasing you.

Manuel, can you describe the process, how is it you're able to create the environment for fishing – are you in waders or out in a boat?

"In a boat," he says. "I think of a place, mountains and a river and he can be there instantly." He says "It's not like he has to walk to gets somewhere; it comes in the form of a thought – he can move very quickly."

Put yourself in your boat; how big is it?

He says "It's about 12 feet long and it can be any size he desires, he likes it to be big and be by himself. He doesn't include other spirits with him, he talks about how he can be there at any time."

Because you're outside of time, you can do both?

"Yes."

Do you have your favorite rod or reel – do you create different ones or the same one?

He said "He prefers to use the same pole but he can create different ones." He's showing me a red pole with that thing that you twist.

In terms of bait? Do you make your own flies – or do you ask a creatures over there to participate?

He says bait is not necessary – he creates what looks like a worm, but it's more of a human experience. He says "He's wanting a connection to the human body that he's no longer in."

So even the worm itself is a mental creation just like the fish is?

"Yes."

Is there a feeling when you catch it? A tug on the line?

"It's more of a sensation, feeling and thoughts." He says "The way I feel over here is through vibration, we carry vibrations like love – it creates happiness. It's more of a sensation." He says "There's no hardness over there, it's more like a video or a movie playing out

for him. Like the work you create, it doesn't take a long time to create it."

It's like you think it and the thing appears, like very good CGI?

He says "Very good high def."

What kind of fish do you normally catch?

He says "I'm not a small fish catcher.." – he's pulling up these huge fish, like a shark. Like a sail fish.

The reason I ask these questions is to understand the architecture of what he's going through. What's the process when your granddaughter reaches out to you? Do you feel her tuning into her?

He says "I'm always connected to her." He says "He is standing by to assist me when I need it. It's like a telepathic connection – he is showing me a wire – you know when a kid makes a paper phone? We're always connected so I can channel him. He says "It's a feeling and telepathic."

What's a process people over here can use to reach out to loved ones on your side?

He suggests "people think about us and it we're there." He says 90% of that communication is when you hear their name, they're trying to connect to you as well. When their name comes into your head that's them trying to get your attention too.

So someone sees a bird or butterfly or hummingbird and they think of their loved one?

"Yes."

Describe the process please; how do you communicate with the butterfly to fly in front of your loved one's face?

He's telling me that it's more of a manipulation that they get to do. "It's asking them to borrow their energy to get your attention – it's more of a manipulation and they allow it – they control the animal in front of you and the animal allows it. And when you get that sign in front of you, you'll get the thought inside your head of who's trying to connect with you.

I was talking to Michael Newton on the flipside recently, and he told me it was a matter of saying the name of your loved one aloud or in your head. He said he is trying to help people over there to talk to people here but that implies it's not that easy.

Erik Medhus is coming through and says it's a process that has to be taught, we all have a knowing of it, but we have to learn how to communicate with them – the spirit lowering their vibration, the newly deceased aren't used to that vibration they have to learn how to do it. It's more like a therapy – he's talking about energy for people to lower their vibration.

How would you describe that to someone over there?

He's showing me the way they communicate is not with mouths – he's showing a (complete) visual to a person, like watching a tv show. He's putting images into their mind with his mind, and is showing them over there how to do the same – not so much with words but showing them how to do it with their minds.

Just thinking it?

Yes, just thinking it. Prince comes through and says that you are more at home than others. He says "I'm connected to you," and he's also one of your guides. He likes the type of work you do – because you notice people and he's helping you to notice people. He says he's on your soul train – he's connected to you and says that you're home.

I know a few people that Prince helps communicate – like it's a frequency with musicians.

Exactly; that's a really good way to categorize it. People who work with art, theater, music; he says there is a connection to these souls these types of beings. But he's correcting you, he's saying you channel him on a regular basis. He says "The way I communicate with you is your thought process. I'm talking about you creating music and not only movies, this is more, I would say deep – instead of writing it out, it's what you're supposed to create.

Let me ask you Prince, they're going to be releasing some of your old work – anything you want to mention about that?

He says "Tell them to not alter my work. It's ok to release my work he wants it to be out there – but not altered."

You mean editing? Remixing?

Yes, not to change the words or wording – he doesn't want it altered. He says "He doesn't want them remixed because it's authentic to him – it's not a selfish thing he's very proud of the work that he did."

Okay. I mention on of the interviews he did with Kim Babcock, where he talked about a previous lifetime where he suffered from not being able to communicate. And this time around he wanted to communicate on a global scale.

He's saying "Thank you for pointing that out – you're absolutely correct about that." He says "I still continue to work (on my music) from this side. People will still be saying "Prince inspired their music."

Raylene is one of a few who report seeing Prince on the Flipside.

What would be the most authentic way to reach out to you?

He smiles, he's flipping his hair, getting really serious. He says "Just say "Prince" and think of me and I'm there – think of me and I'm there – think about me and you're connected instantly – I have a knowing where you are." He says he can visit people instantly by thinking about them.

So why'd you check out early? You told us (Me and Jennifer Shaffer) that dancing killed you – meaning jumping off pianos hurt your ankles, which got you addicted to drugs.

He says "Thank you for being supportive – his disability from piano and many other things did lead to a drug addiction because it was more of an addiction used for pain." He's telling me, "It wasn't smart of him, but it was easy for him to access it – he doesn't blame anyone for his transition, he was ready to go – he was tired."

Are you playing with anyone over there?

He says, "I play with other music artists – we don't get together like we did in life because we're all connected now – think about having family function and being connected to every person – he's more into being in spirit form at the moment, if that makes sense. He's not urgent for the human experiences, he's not urging for that anymore – I can go back into time into my Prince memory and live that time as a human if we want to."

Let's talk about music – are you aware of music over there you were not aware of over here?

"Yes, it's all vibration, very different over here – no words to it, it's all vibration and it's very beautiful colors are different too."

To give us reference – I understand it's more of a feeling, but can you give us a description – as an instrument?

He's going on about a guitar. He says "Imagine a guitar, the string, when you push it and it makes the vibration and think about the color coming off the string, and the color red coming off the string."

Color is a vibration; red is a vibration – a wavelength you're saying if I found a note that is red – are the wavelengths similar?

He says "It's very similar."

I want to ask you about the music that you can hear that you're not creating over there. It's not coming from you or created by you – what does that sound like?

He says he's trying to explain it in a simple way – he says that it is hearing but also feeling. "You know how we can feel wind but can't see it?" He says "It's a vibration," he's comparing the vibration "to wind, to water. As to the density – it's like a love song would be

love, a sad song carrying a soft vibration of music" – He's talking about wind, water, moisture.

And I'm thinking in reference to people who have heard music during their near death experience – everyone that I've interviewed who experiences music over there – they don't hear one symphony or note, but etheric beautiful tones. I guess I'm trying to ask where does music come from?

He says "light."

Does it come from a particular person or place?

"From source."

Can we identify that place – I know it's hard to use human words – but who or what is the source?

He says, "Well "God" is source – it goes onto your belief system." He says, "There's only one source so if you have or think of your sources as Jesus, that would be one source – you're connected to source so you could think of yourself as source as well."

(Note: This is in line with many other interviews across the spectrum. "God" apparently refers not to an object or person, but to a energetic resonance, or a field of consciousness, literally can be experience by "opening one's heart to everyone and all things.")

I understand that God is an experience more than a person – related to love, and if you open your heart to everyone and all things you can experience god?

"Yes."

You could characterize that as walking through a garden. The garden is what god is, the religion is the flowers – but I'm asking about the celestial music. What are you hearing in the garden?

He says "Each movement with the wind has a different tone if it goes down or up it makes different sounds – he says it's different tones."

So when Beethoven talks about channeling the spheres to access music – was he channeling that musical wind?

He says "That's a good way to think of it; channeling the wind." But he says "It's on a broader band, more than wind." He's giving me a visual... "You can't see wind, imagine a tree moving back and forth – beaming down from the high end, the air is not coming down in one chunk. Think of music notes; it's coming down in notes, in wind notes, in tones, and then it transfers to your head. You can hear it – the channelers of music – they can hear the beat, it's a channeling of communicating with higher beings."

Renaissance notation for sacred music. Photo by author.

In terms of Prince's future – what does he want to do in the future?

He says "I would like to help people create music and also to help people transition on the other side; he's very much a helper." He's telling you "He's getting new ideas – and when you hear music in your head, he's encouraging you to use your abilities."

We have a mutual friend, our daughter's godmother Edna, who met you often in her work. What's your opinion of Aunt Edna?

He says "I can access her anytime and he does..." He says "It's not visual, it's a knowing." He says to "Tell her thank you." He says he's not normally one to say something personal to her.

Okay, the last time we spoke to Prince, Robin Williams came by. Is he around?

He is – he's been around for about two days, I didn't know he was waiting for you; he's clearly here for you. He says, "You have an interest in his life, you've taken great lengths to learn about him and his family; he said he was under a quite a bit of stress in life and he's saying for you to take one day in life at a time."

Robin gave us a blurb for our book "Backstage Pass to the Flipside." You told Jennifer Shaffer simply "Love love."

"Yes."

What does that mean to you?

He says "Love has lots of different definitions; not having any judgement about yourself or life – unconditional love, self-love, so many different types of love." He's talking about "Living without regret." He says "He loves unconditionally over here now – he's talking about people being depressed, about how words carry the vibration of love. He doesn't want anyone to have the struggles that he had in life." He says "He's a person who is very strong – going to stand up for love."

If you were going to talk to your younger self?

He says "I would tell my younger self to live one day at a time; I used drugs to cover up stress and cope with life, I didn't know how to cope with my busy life as it came quickly." He says "He would have lived a day at a time, instead of worrying how a movie would end up and live day by day."

It's a bit like the bike you rode every day – it was a meditative thing to do?

He says "Exactly; that's a meditation for many people being outdoors and outside of themselves."

A few people are distressed he left the stage the way he did; is it important to note that it doesn't matter how you left the stage, but what you did on stage?

"Yes, it's the mark you leave."

(Note: I'm thrilled to be doing this rapid fire interview. I'm meeting Raylene for the first time, I have no idea of her world view, but I know she's a married mom living in the midwest. Having been a music critic, growing up in the home of a concert pianist, having played in bands,

I'm familiar with music terminology and theory – then I have the decades of working in the film biz. So I can be relatively conversant about any topic with just about anyone; but I'm amazed how many answers Raylene is giving me without hesitation that are in line with, nearly exactly what I've heard from these same people with different mediums.)

I had an odd dream – it was the experience of being in the audience during Prince's life review. I was in a giant auditorium, and I could see him down on stage recounting something that happened to him. And the entire audience saw and felt the experience he was reporting - of him healing or helping some person. As I started to come to consciousness, and lose the dream, I turned to the person next to me and said "What a bummer I'm waking up, I'm enjoying this" and that person said "Don't worry, we'll be here for weeks."

Prince said "When I was in my life review it felt like it took the same amount of time I lived my life. It felt like it took forever. And Erik Medhus is agreeing with him, saying "It felt like it took forever." He allowed you to share some of his joy and pain and experiences with him. He's talking about you and your dream.

In this vision, I was deep in the audience – like row 572.. what was unusual was this new experience of being in the theater but actually experiencing what a person is expressing on stage. Mind bending.

"That's because distance is non-existent."

How much do you charge for that ticket to that show?

He's asking you the same question.

Ha. Thank you Mr. Prince Rogers Nelson. Let's shift to Erik Medhus for a moment. How about you Erik? What was your review like?

(Note: Erik Medhus wrote a book from the flipside; "My Life After Death." He talks about what it was like to take his own life, then realize that he wasn't dead, realized the pain he put his mother and family through. As noted, the medium Jamie Butler called Erik's mother Dr. Elisa Medhus and said "your son is sitting in my living room and won't leave until I call you." Since then she's done hundreds of interviews with her son.)

He said "It was outside, but like watching tv. Like seeing and experiencing things at the same time."

How many are in your council?

He says "At this time it's about 20. He says it's different for everybody."

Is there one spokesperson for your council?

"Yes, it's the person who comes and gets you for the transition; like a therapist lady."

Does she have a name?

He's telling me "Margaret."

Have you ever incarnated with her?

He says "I have, but not in this lifetime. I felt safe with her."

In terms of Margaret's connection to you and your life review what was that like?

He says it was sad, and times of excitement being overwhelmed. He said "My childhood was amazing, and getting older, I went through depression that was hard to go through."

Have you checked into any previous lifetimes?

Yes, he says "The shit that carried over from past lives, the depressions and themes that he had done carried over into this life."

When you look at those lifetimes from the perspective of a classroom – is there a common them for your lifetimes?

He says "Yes, you can think of it as a common theme but each is different in its own way." He's talking about themes of love, but also sadness, and extension of that theme.

(Note: Even as I edit this section, I can see how the syntax has changed from speaking to Prince or Robin to Erik, who tended to swear like a sailor according to his mom.)

Erik, can we talk to Margaret?

He says "Sure."

What does Erik look like to you?

Erik looks green and blue to her and he's radiating a feminine energy; we're not really looking with eyes, but it's a feminine energy.

Margaret, how do you think that Erik is doing?

She says "Erik is helping so many different beings on so many levels this is the beginning of his work, he can be very helpful in creating awareness. He's not done with what he's going to do."

Let me ask you this – about time. Correct me if I'm wrong, I have heard that a 25 year lifetime feels like ten minutes over there.

"Yes."

If 25 years is ten minutes, then 2500 years is a week?

She says "Yes, that's as close as you can get to telling the time frame in human sense."

(Note: This came during a session with hypnotherapist Scott De Tamble, and a friend who recalled a lifetime as a captain of a ship in 1610 in "It's a Wonderful Afterlife." When she returned home, she said "That 25 years felt like ten minutes." Since then I've asked this question many times, and get the same answer.)

Correct me if I'm wrong, but there is a linear progression, young souls to old souls?

"Yes," Erik is saying "new souls are created every day and old souls are returned, and these souls are done living their lives – and he's going into the linear timing being non-existent." He says "The older souls have more knowledge and more light, but think of them as a database. You can go and get information from this database at any time, but he doesn't like to call them older or younger; we are all equal but we do things for each other."

(Note: This is a densely packed answer. He's saying "linear time exists" in the afterlife (contrary to the "time does not exist" idea, it exists completely different to our relative experience) that "new souls come into existence at any time (answering the "where do souls come from?" question) and reports "there is no hierarchy over there" which upends millennia of religious doctrine... in two questions or less.)

Can you remember a lifetime were you and Margaret were together?

He says "Yes, in the 1800's; she was a teacher of his – he was a little boy and she was a schoolteacher, for six years. He says she taught him things... not romance but friendship."

Erik have you had lifetimes as a woman?

"Many. Many lifetimes as a woman."

In terms of your soul group – how many individuals are in your group?

"Hundreds. He comes from a very large soul group – don't think of it as the people on the planet – it's more thousands of different groups and families."

I've heard that you can learn more in one day of tragedy than 5000 years on some boring planet.

"Correct. You can learn more on earth than the afterlife; the hurt you felt from tragedy..." Erik is using his own death as an example; his mother could never have experienced what she went through because there's only love over there – but that's an experience you can't get on the other side."

(Note: It's hard for some to hear, but when one thinks of life as a play in a theater, it's easier to conceive how some actors go through incredible trauma during their play. Backstage they are congratulated for the trauma they've expressed onstage.)

Erik, if you can, access your life planning session, before you came to the planet. So what was the process; did it include the manner of you checking out?

He says "There were options for me – it was not set in stone that I would take my life. The option was there, I took that." There were lessons both for his mom and Erik... the harder lessons. He said "I do feel the grieving; he says "He felt that with them and points out that they're not going through it alone."

How many lives have you had?

"Thousands."

How many on Earth?

"Ten."

(Note: He answered these quickly and is aware of his journey from his current perspective.)

When you look back at the stage after a lifetime, do you say "I did a great job, or I could have done better?"

He says "I do not have any "regret." Yes, I wish I went a different route – regret is not a word I would use, I wish things would have happened differently but I wouldn't use regret."

But for our audience, once you are "off stage" is everything okay?

"You have no judgment – your ego goes away; you don't have that judgment anymore – nobody does."

In Erik's case, your impact on others began after you checked out?

"Correct."

And Prince's journey began when you picked up a guitar?

Prince says "It began in the womb. His spiritual mission began when he was very young."

He was visited by an angel. Do you remember that?

(Note: Prince told the story of having epilepsy as a child, and being "visited by an angel" who told him he would grow out of it, and be okay.")

He says "They told me that my disease would be cured and that I would be famous." He had a knowing that he would be famous.

Was this angel that came to you a woman or man?

"A woman." He says "He refers to her as angel."

What does she look like to you?

"She looks very angelic; she has angel wings; she came through to me." I'll describe her, she has clear wings, wearing pink and white like a wedding dress. But it looks like one suit – she's like someone very important, looking like a princess type of being.

Who are you if I may ask?

She says that "I am an angel you can think of me as a princess, she's more spirit; she doesn't choose to be human."

Can you show us your wings; is it etheric or something else?

It looks like this is fabric. It's very interesting – feels like a veil – scruffy... like not smooth.

Is this a constructed piece of fabric? Is the angel creating this image or does it exist unto itself?

She says "It exists unto itself." It feels scruffy – the variations of the feathers – the flocking. There are no feathers, it's all one layer of fabric in the form of like a C – it comes back around.

Is this something that you chose to present yourself as so that others could see you as an angel, or is this just your natural state?

"My natural state is light," she says. She's creating this to give you a visual – she says "She also communicates through dreams, works with quite a few people."

If I may ask you this. Why wings?

It's very much about the person's belief system – that they are very comfortable seeing that...

In your mind's eye, seeing her as light – what color of light are you seeing?

Yellow.

When you examine the light is it all one color or multiple colors of yellow?

It's yellow and clearish. You know when you turn on a lamp? It's like that. If I put my hand through it, I'm going to say it feels like dense, fuzzy air – when you turn the car on the exhaust – dense air.

Is this unusual to be talking to us in this fashion?

She says "Thank you for allowing me."

How did you come into existence, if you can access that?

She says "I came into existence to help people, when source created me." She has a knowing of that, she knew she was going to be an angel, she says to call her that – an angel being.

Do you only work with people on this planet?

She says she works with other planets, and animals and she's telling me (Raylene) to get a dog.

How did you manifest with Erik and others?

She says, "Before Erik passed she was helping to guide him with the decisions he was making – they (healing beings) come in many forms ... like if an animal is having depression, she'd work with them on a telepathic level, saying "You can handle this, this is going to be okay."

(Note: I have no questions prepared, and when I meet someone who can answer these concepts, as one can see, I just continue as long as they'll let me ask or provide me with answers. I continue on.)

I wonder if we can walk Raylene in to visit her own council?

(Raylene nods) There are five men here; they look like they're from biblical times.

Describe the room for me.

I don't see any doors, just brightness like light, a round table, not lengthy.

There's 5 here... plus you?

Plus me, and my guide Arnold; so seven. I want to call these men "wise men" – they're from biblical times.

Let's go from left to right.

The first is named Paul, then Adam, then Jeremiah, then Mark and Abraham. They're talking to me about decisions that I've got to make – deciding on whether I choose to stay longer.

(Note: This is prescient, not long after this interview Raylene had a bad flu and went into a coma. She was in hospital and out of touch for months. I did not transcribe this session until a year after she recovered because I was afraid she might not recover.)

This was a conversation you had before – we're stepping in on it?

Yes.

Who is the primary spokesperson for this group?

Paul, he's the one you'd call in charge – they all have the same standing... but he would be the main one to speak with.

What does Paul look like?

He needs to shave (laughs). Sorry, he has long hair to about his shoulder – it's brown, he's older, gray coming in. (to Paul:) Sorry.

No reason to apologize for what you see, and he is projecting his image to you.

His hair is long and curly – not tied back. Sort of how Jesus might appear to you. He's wearing one piece of clothing over his chest, what looks like a skirt – he has hairy legs and arms – very hairy. The clothing is something he made himself. Maybe out of a tree; not clothing we have - feels rough like tree material.

(Note: Never heard anyone describe clothing this way, and Raylene has great ability to see and describe what she's seeing.)

Let's ask him; what is this fabric and why are you wearing it?

He says, "I made it out of wheat, and I'm wearing it because this is the clothing I lived in ...this is the fabric I used for clothing in this time period."

The sash – is there any kind of symbol other than the cloth?

There are rock crystals. He's telling me, "The black ones represent protection, the aqua helps him communicate with god" as he calls it.

Each one of these individuals is here because of you Raylene, and they represent some aspect of you. Let's ask. I'll guess Paul represents something to do with nature.

"Yes. They're talking about representations for all of them – there is "protection" from Paul, Jeremiah shows me "love," that is a kind of love in terms of loving people without judging them... (Unconditional love) Mark is here – he's talking about "communicating with children." He says he's a guide of mine. Abraham helps me "transition from place to place, life to life" – he's a guide as well.

Like a travel guide? What quality does he represent?

He says "Lessons; there are many of them."

Like a teacher?

"Yes."

And you mentioned your guide Arnold?

Yes, he's very masculine – very much a support system... my support system for all my lives. There to help my emotional being.

Let me ask them, is this is an unusual thing to be interviewed like this?

They said "They don't get interviewed – they wish to be a part of this more often, this is more about humans being open to it." He's thanking you.

Glad to be of service. But you'd think in human history people would do this more often – perhaps we just hadn't figured out how to do it. Paul, if you could give us insight or guidance – how many times has she been in front of you?

"Hundreds." He says my current lifetime is my last lifetime here.

Well, we don't die, do we?

It's my "last classroom."

Let me ask you Paul, it is up to Raylene if she wants to come back, is that correct?

He says "If she chooses to come back she can, but she is an old soul and is living in many lives ... she's a therapist, helper on the other side for people that transition."

But if Raylene decides to come back here ... that's her choice?

"Yes."

People may find this disconcerting... reading this – it's up to her. I understand what you're saying she's reached a point where she doesn't have to come back.

He says "Yes, as everyone has free will. They can come back whenever they want or as perhaps as whatever animal they want to."

I've found it's rare in my research to cross between animal and human – I understand it's possible to do – animals reincarnate as animals in general, is that correct?

He says "That is correct; he is pointing out that the school they go to, is like ours; they choose to be animals."

Has Raylene ever been an animal in a previous lifetime?

"Sea creatures."

My question is ... let's say I wanted to come back as another animal than human, how does that work? Is there are hierarchical thing?

"No, you don't get the pleasure of being by (around) humans, the aquarium you choose to live in. Or if you decide to return as a dog, if you want to come down for love, each individual has each experience they want to experience."

What I've learned is that we only bring about third of our energy. Is that correct, Paul?

"Yes."

Two thirds is back home?

He says "Yes, this is called your higher self."

What is Raylene's higher self doing?

He's smiling; "She gets into trouble, messes with people." (Rayline aside) I like to joke with people over there; but I'm not that way in this life! It's very interesting (what I'm seeing.)

Like a playful leprechaun? Or a gremlin?

He says "The gremlin creatures are real, and some are manifested; if you have fear based on these creatures, you can manifest them as well."

I would assume gremlins have their soul group and councils?

"That's correct; there are lower vibrations, some call them "demonic" or those who are stuck that don't realize they've died."

Let's talk about demons for a moment. A retired exorcist said in an interview "Satan wasn't considered anything more than a wayward brother or a tempter until the plague when he became the embodiment of evil. It's a man made thing" We don't find that concept of evil in the afterlife research. Could you address that?

He says "That's the world over here (on earth). There is no hell." And now Erik is talking, "There is no hell and your belief structure is structured around you – if you believe in creatures, lower vibrations, they can exist for you – it's dependent upon your belief structure."

(Note: This is reflected in the research. People under hypnosis who encounter "hellish realms" see them disappear when asked "So why are we here?" People who have near death events (rarely, 1%) where they see something hellish, often transition or move through that environment to something different. Christian, Muslim, Hindu or Buddhist "hell realms" appear to not inherently exist, as no two descriptions match. As Erik notes, it appears when people do encounter something "hellish" its because they believe it to exist.)

Paul how do you think Raylene is doing?

He says she's doing a hard job and that it's going to come easier the more she does it. He's referring to both my spiritual and mother duties – being a challenge because trying to balance everything together... it's going to be difficult.

Let me ask Paul this, here I am interviewing you, why is it this information becoming accessible?

He says "You're (humanity) shifting, it's becoming easier to talk to us – the universe is shifting, it's easier to connect to his dimension. By thinking of a person, you're connecting to a conscious level of our soul."

What is that?

"You have an awareness of home, where you come from. You (innately) know there's something bigger beyond this body of ours, it's all on a conscious level."

(Note: Raylene and I have never spoken, and I've never mentioned how in the cases of people under deep hypnosis, they all refer to "heaven" or "the afterlife" as "home." As in "not here.)

Why is this happening now?

"So humanity can grow, people can learn about the afterlife and spirit dimensions, ET's and other beings from spirit worlds, helping them grow." Now he's talking about us helping them on the other side to communicate with us, lowering their vibration to communicate with us; a wide range of things that are happening (now), meditations, people seeing an image in their head, and accepting that; it's shifting.

(Note: Here again, the concept of E.T's – and how we may incarnate on other planets. So if one encounters an "E.T." it may be someone we knew in a previous lifetime. Either ours when we were living there on that planet, or theirs when they were living on ours.)

What's the genesis of the shift? Or has this always been happening?

"Yes. He says it's slowly been happening, but now is a peak time of fast and clear communication has been happening for 100's of years." He's talking about the pyramids, that time has already restarted – the worlds have already ended and restarted again ... evolution ... we have had help from spirits, we are restarting."

Let's go around the council room – anyone want to tell people something that might be healing?

From my guide Arnold; "Be patient with your spiritual awakening ability, tell people to get books and read. You all have spirit guides and councils, everyone has their own spirit guides, council and family – anyone can call on us.

Anything from Robin or Prince?

Robin says "Never give you dreams up, he says to still .. don't let anyone tear your dreams down. Stay away from substances." Prince is saying "To live life to the fullest and not let anyone judge you – don't let anyone judge you for being old, young, fat, thin – don't let them bring you down. If you want to be healthy its smart but don't let anyone tell you that you have to do."

Raylene, thank you so much. Have you ever accessed your council before?

No.

....

As noted, I didn't transcribe it as a few weeks after we recorded it, I heard that Raylene was in a coma. I didn't look at this until over a year later, and then Raylene was so kind to do an interview with my friend Bill Paxton on the flipside, and is part of the film "Talking to Bill Paxton" with Kimberly Babcock and Jennifer Shaffer. Dr. Medhus asked the questions I submitted to her – I had no idea who would do the "reading" – didn't know that it would be Raylene, but knowing how accurate and descriptive she can be, I was thrilled when I saw she was the one asking Billy the questions.

Hometown trees. Photo by author.

PART TWO WITH RAYLENE

I felt as if we had not asked enough questions when visiting Raylene's council. In this session, I see if I can make a beeline back to visit her council. "Can we visit your council?" She says "Yes."

Rich: Who's here?

Raylene: My guide Mark. We met him before. He's been with me since we met. (A few weeks earlier).

How does he look?

He's wearing a robe; looks like in biblical times.. he's about 6 feet tall.

Let me ask him, Mark, would you change into a different outfit - just so we can differentiate between the apostle look and something more contemporary?

He's laughing at you – he has on a kilt... it's green.

I ask because sometimes we visualize people and it connects us to the memories of apostles. I'm pretty sure Raylene's never seen an apostle with a kilt.

He wants to go somewhere else.

Let's take her to her library, wherever that is.

I'm seeing a big dark room with one book – like a magic book, huge, about 2 feet long and five feet high.

Any writing on it?

There's an eye on it – the gemstone is an eye. It's red.

What's the book feel like?

Energetic, very much so – a rough texture like cement. the energy is like... feeling water, feels like there's moistness to it – not wet at all. But has this texture.

Can you open it for us?

It's open. The page is blank; white.

Mark could you help her open it to a page that might be helpful to her?

Tell me what the door looks like.

It's light. There's no wood, it's not texture, it's light – I see something I could push open or push open to me – back and forth.

Okay let's push through the door – any association with this?

Fear.

Mark I need you to put a feeling of courage, there's nothing that can harm or frighten her – there's a reason to go through this door I'm sure it has to do with love.

He says "Yes." He's giving me his hand right now; it feels very soft, feminine.

Is there an energy associated with it?

Yes, very loving nurturing, very feminine.

Mark, would you walk through this door and show her what's on the other side?

"Yes. (After a moment) I feel stuck. I'm trying to walk and I feel stuck.

Mark can you get through the door?

He's on the other side of the door.

Mark, take both of her hands, loving contentment hands, and yank her through. Show her what it is you want to show her.

I'm outside in a forest. I don't see sky, it's very dark.

Mark, lighten this visual up a little bit so we can see it more clearly. What kind of trees are there?

I see pine trees.

Would you go over to the nearest pine tree? What does that feel like to the touch?

It's doesn't feel like a tree – very soft, very subtle.

Any energy?

Yes, going up and down; it's alive – I feel energized.

Give this tree a hug, what's the feeling or message you get from this pine tree when you hug it?

There is a female presence in the tree... I'm feeling loved. Her name is Emily.

Nice to meet you Emily, thank you for allowing us to share this.

She's telling you "Thank you."

Let me ask you Emily – what does Raylene look like to you?

"Like mud." (Raylene reacts to the visual) Wow.

Don't take it personally.

I'm not. (Raylene laughs)

Emily, do you generally view humans as mud? Or tell us how you view humans in general?

"I view them as beautiful people, human form, I'm not in a dimension that is earthly for her to be in the way she is."

Are you referring to this door?

No, this dimension she's in, right now with her. She says "It's the 5th dimension."

And what dimension are Raylene and I in?

"The third."

(Note: I've heard this before. It's hard to calculate "dimensions" but in an interview I've heard people talks about "being from the seventh realm coming down to incarnate on the fifth realm where they will later become humans in the third realm.")

Any messages you'd like to give us with regard to trees?

She says "I wish for humans to be gentle with the earth, and not cut down a precious life." She's referring to the tree as life as it is.

Trees are the opposite of lungs, we cannot exist without them?

"We'd be dead without them."

Are you annoyed when you see humans chopping down trees?

"Not so much annoyed but I feel the pain from the others trees and the family around me."

In terms of communication with trees, I saw a science report how ferns – the fuzzy moss that grows around trees – allows trees to communicate with each other. How do you communicate?

She's talking about vibration within the roots themselves, and says "When we move our leaves it's a form of communication with other trees – it's vibrational."

Have you ever existed on the planet?

"In Africa. In the early 1800's. I'm not a girl, I'm a man. I have on what looks to be... not a shirt like you and I have, this is something that... khaki pants that don't go all the way down."

By the way, Mark our guide – were you in this lifetime with her?

"I incarnated with her and I am in this lifetime with her. I was her son. The kids here are very malnourished. The country starts with a B."

Botswana?

"Yes."

Go to the last day of this lifetime – where were you? What happened?

There is a panther in front of me.

Black Panther; Quora

Was the panther in the woods?

Yes.

Freeze the frame before Mr. Panther makes his attack. Take a look at him – do you know him?

No, but I don't feel safe.

We're going to ask to speak to the panther directly. Can we?

Raylene nods. He's lying down.

Put your hand on his head what's that feel like?

Soft.

What's the feeling you get from him?

Hunger.

That's normal – I'd like to talk to the panther directly...

He's speaking telepathically.

Do you normally incarnate as a panther or have you incarnated in other forms?

(Raylene listens) He says "I've been a human many times and also fish."

As a human – is there a hierarchy in terms of fish, panther, human?

"We're all the same life form our souls are equal."

When you were in human form – did you feel like you were fully there or partially? Was all of your energy there?

"When I was human, I did not miss any of my spirituality back home, I had no awareness of it. Being a panther I have complete awareness of where I come from."

If you can give us a visual of what you look like between lives?

I'm looking at a ball of light – it's not a bright light – like a lightbulb. It's pure white with a tad of green.

I would ask Mr. Black Panther – are you a young soul, old soul?

"I'm very evolved. In terms of human terms; I'm ancient."

Can we access you in the future and get back to you on this?

He says "Of course you can." He's saying "He is a part of my family; my spiritual family and he's giving me lessons and knows me from previous lives."

Now let's go forward a bit – in this memory, then you attack our friend here; did you eat him or just kill him?

He's telling me that he ate me.

A natural thing – there's no fear associated with that, is there?

"None."

Very good – I assume Mr. Panther that you've been eaten as well?

"Yes, I have, but not in the current panther form." He indicates he lived to old age and died of malnourishment in this lifetime.

Fascinating. Thank you for telling us.

He says "Thank you."

(Note: Because I don't judge the answers, one can get answers from pretty much any object, person or thing that appears as a construct on the flipside. It's as if everything is sentient, everything has a memory, and everything is worth examining or asking questions to.)

Mark could you take her by the hand – and take her back to her council – how many people are there?

Seven.

May we speak to someone?

Yes, his name is Adam.

How have you been?

He says "Fabulous. How have you been?"

Better than you! (laughter)

He says "You think?" (Raylene laughs.)

So Adam why was she shown this lifetime in her akashic library - the book of her life, this one giant book in her library. What did she learn from this lifetime?

He's telling me it is the reason I'm afraid of forests, trees, I'm terrified of them. (Raylene shudders)

So we've learned something – she got attacked by an old friend – eaten, nourished – you were shown this lifetime today so you could release the fear associated with forests.

My husband has been trying to get me to go camping – I was too afraid to go.

Not anymore?

(Agreeing) Not anymore.

Now you can go out and nourish some mosquitoes. Okay, thanks everyone!

Again, this was the second time I met Raylene, over Skype. This idea that Raylene could "converse" with someone from "another realm" is repeated throughout this book, but this was the first time I had seen someone speaking to someone I had no idea we could speak with – from gargoyles to panthers.

As noted, I didn't transcribe Raylene's sessions once I heard she had gone into a coma. I was thrilled to hear she recovered fully, and is back helping Dr. Medhus with the Channeling Erik website. Thank you Raylene!!!

Now, before we continue, I'd like all the practicing Catholics to stop reading. That's right, put down your books, pull off your headphones and skip on the next chapter after the following one. I don't want to offend anyone who believes in Saints or Angels. But for those who stick around, we're about to take a trip into the deep rabbit hole known as "The Martini Zone."

CHAPTER TWENTY FOUR:

"THE SAINT"

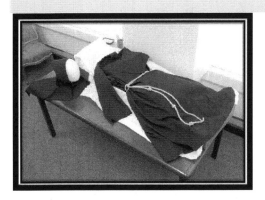

A Dominican monk's costume

As mentioned, I attended Scott De Tamble's (lightbetweenlives.com) training session, and as part of the group activity, one of the students offered to do a practice session with me.

As the hypnotherapist counted me down, I saw a group of people on the flipside. There was a crowd of people, and within the crowd I saw my old friend Howard Schultz. Howard was a successful television producer, and we talked about the flipside research for over a decade. We talked about how difficult it would be to make a television show that dealt with these topics, but he'd already tried to make a show that dealt with psychics.

His between life sessions is reported in the book "Flipside" in the chapter "River of Souls." Howard went far and deep, recalled being killed during the Holocaust and winding up the concentration camp of Dachau. In the between life portion, he saw himself as having chosen that lifetime to "experience the dark." He was saying that he'd had many lifetimes of laughter, in the light, and he had a desire to "experience the dark." (Recently, I posted Howard's full between life session at "MartiniProds" on YouTube).

However, the lifetime was so awful that he felt he had "seared his soul" by the experience, and reported a visual I've not heard before or since.

His guides walked him down to a river, a river he called the "River of Souls" and he walked out into the river to heal the wounds from the difficult lifetime he had just remembered.

Hypnotherapist Scott De Tamble conducted the session, and Howard spent some time in that river, feeling healed and refreshed. Since then, he's shown up a number of times in my sessions, including when I've done work with Jennifer Shaffer. He appeared on her couch a few times, and reported in a comedic tone and manner how he was enjoying his time on the flipside.

But as I saw this crowd standing there waiting for me, they were applauding, amused at my return. The hypnotherapist asked me to go through a tunnel, so that when I got to the other side of it, a previous lifetime would present itself to me.

Howard Schultz *(Photo: Lighthearted Ent.) Howard's between life session can be viewed at Martini.Zone – where he suggested from the flipside that I post it so people get an idea of what the flipside is like.*

As I emerged from the imaginary tunnel, I started to see a landscape, the light of the sea in the distance. It felt like a mountainous area, there were rocks, a dirt path, with mountains in the distance. When the hypnotherapist asked me to look at myself, I saw a tall, 6 foot 2 dark haired fellow who looked a bit like I did in my 20's.

Dark, wavy hair. I was wearing a thick black robe cloak or a robe... I was aware that it was thick, like woolen. Heavy and thick. I had a bald spot on the top of my head, and I said aloud "Oh, I see, I'm a Franciscan Monk.."

The date that came to me was 1394. I know that the monk Francis of Assisi lived in the 13th century, and I said "In this lifetime I'm dressed like Franciscan." (Black robe).

During my session, I focused on the life of the monk who lived from the 14th to the 15th century. First we visited where I was living; we took a trip to visit that monastery. I got the sense it was in the Italian countryside not far from the Florence, facing the sea.

I saw that it was a typical monastery from the 14th century. There were dirt floors, my personal cell was a small room with a flat, wheat or straw mattress, a chair and not quite a table, just a place for a candle lamp. That was my cell, that was my life, and I saw that I was a simple monk.

We went back to a time in my youth when I was dining with my family. I saw myself in a multi storied home my family, I saw my father (which I identified as one of my brothers from this lifetime), I saw a mother at the dinner table whom I didn't recognize.

I said the father was domineering and kind of dismissive of me – had the impression that he found me to be "airy fairy in the clouds," not suited for the kind of work that he was doing. So it was decided about the age of 15 that I would join the monastery.

I saw I had a sister and a brother (that I didn't recognize from my current life). The house was kind of large for that time period, two stories and resembled a Florentine museum I've visited in Florence, a 14th century villa preserved by the Davanzati family.

Museo Davanzati

I said "My father was a successful businessman," I couldn't access what he did for a living, but the word "Fabbrica" came to mind which translates as "factory." There was a crew of people who worked for him and there was the expectation that I would also work for him but I didn't want that. I didn't care for him personally, preferred being in nature, got along with my mother, but I saw her as a mousy person who let him physically and verbally abuse her. At one point, I saw her "looking down" as he berated her verbally.

At some point I went into the monastery; it was not a negative thing. People who send children to "serve" are considered to be lucky and holy - as the monastery was a place of learning and it was a thing of honor to have a son being given to the Priesthood (a bit like in Tibet, when a family gets a special dispensation or benefits for donating a child, for their service.) That meant that my donation helped the family with prestige or pride, gave the family status. I recalled the feeling of enjoying learning about new vistas, the experience of going into the monastery's library and knowing the "knowledge of the planet was inside."

(Note: I can recall the first library I went into in my hometown outside Chicago. It also had that feeling of looking at a sea of books and thinking "The knowledge of the planet is in here.")

In this case, I felt I wanted to go somewhere with a good education and joined this black robed monastery where they shaved the bald spot into my head. Then I saw myself in the monastery at a dining room table.

It was old, dark, the candle lit room filled with white bearded monks, wearing their cowls. I looked around and saw there were few young people – who were friends of mine, people my age, but the bulk of the others were all older men; the younger ones were all servers.

It felt like because of my father's status, or my family's heritage, I was treated in a special way, with kid gloves, kind of left to my own devices... I was aware that I found the whole monk concept slightly ridiculous; not religious at all, but a composed of ego and hierarchy.

The idea is that you sign up for a lifetime as a monk because you think it's a calling, you think you're going to be religious and heal people with spirituality; but in reality it's rules and ego and power moves and grabs; I found that to be worthy of my scorn.

I still did all the things you do as a monk - vespers, church service, all that stuff. I recalled I had a good singing voice – how I participated in chants. And then, when asked by the hypnotherapist about an event that had some significance, I saw rye bread with green mold on it, ergot.

Which is where LSD comes from – monks who kept rye bread in caves often got moldy bread with their dinner, and the ergot was LSD, a hallucinogen. Historically, monasteries had rye bread in storehouses, and sometimes they'd trip – full on, have visions, sometimes just enough to have visions in mass or by dreams (St. Elmo's Fire refers to a town that was doped by their rye bread) But in my case, I said that initially where we met me in this memory – walking by the ocean, I felt like "I was tripping" as I was looking at this overview of the ocean, vivid and full of vibrating color.

Apparently that particular day, I had enough ergot to have this "communing with nature experience," which can be like having an epiphany; feeling connected to everyone and everything. Like having a religious experience but by way of the LSD in the rye bread.

I was asked the question by the hypnotherapist; "So why are you showing Richard this lifetime?"

And suddenly I saw him. Jesus.

I was sitting in my bed, looking at the blank wall, tripping – and seeing a startling clear vision of the alpha and omega.

But as I saw this vision floating and dancing on the wall – I realized where I had seen it before. I had seen the same vision while growing up in Northbrook, near Techny, Illinois where there is a religious grotto next to the seminary of the Divine Word. Inside that grotto, where my pals and I used to sneak in late at night – inside, there is a diorama of Jesus praying in the garden of Gethsemane.

Divine Word Seminary Grotto in Techny, Illinois

I can recall the first time that I went into it. There was a room built underground, and one walked down through this cave, they came to a clearing inside the cave where Jesus is praying, blood running down his temple, surrounded by little lambs and other creatures. Doing his prayer prior to his crucifixion.

The effect was supernatural – he was quite realistic in the diorama. And now, this moment when I'm recalling this vision from a previous lifetime, I realize that it was nearly identical to the vision I had of him back then.

A postcard of the diorama inside; "Grotto of the Agony."

Only here was in the 14th century, living the life of a Dominican monk, and inside the cell I was living in, on the wall – I saw this three dimensional vision. Of Jesus, praying of the animals near him – also moving and breathing. It's possible I was seeing a future vision of my lifetime in Northbrook, Illinois – or an imaginary vision of the Grotto of the Agony - I don't know – but I know that seeing this vision had a profound effect on me in that lifetime.

The room sort of opened up and I saw Jesus in these flowing robes, seeing his persona and feeling that unconditional love many have reported. That overwhelming feeling of being "loved unconditionally." It was beyond anything I'd ever witnessed or experienced, it was a vision that completely dumbfounded me; I couldn't speak, could only weep with this feeling of **"Oh my... this is what people have written about – this experience is stunning..."**

That vision changed my monk lifetime from that point forward.

In this memory as this monk, after my visitation, I become someone who no longer feared anything – death, life, illness. I began to believe that everything that St. Francis had witnessed or seen was accurate, that the one didn't need money, property or anything when it came to preaching unconditional love. From that point forward, I began living a life as someone who had been "blessed" by some kind of "greater power."

And observing this lifetime of this monk, I suddenly began connecting the dots of this lifetime as your intrepid author. Of announcing at age 8 that I'd like to be a priest. Of becoming an altar boy and learning the mass in Latin. (And when I did, they promptly switched it to English, circa 1963). I think I only lasted three masses in Latin, then gave up.

Then in terms of the flipside research, I've been doing for over a decade, I thought of all the times the alpha and omega has shown up in these accounts. In "Hacking the Afterlife" I had numerous people appear on my doorstep claiming to have memories of "knowing him." Perhaps we all radiated some kind of odd frequency that attracted each other – people who have had a "vision" of the afterlife perhaps, one that included this fellow.

He shows up so frequently in my interviews, I no longer find it surprising. "Of course you met Jesus. Tell me about him." Someone I've known for decades is answering my questions while not under hypnosis, they stop and say "I think I'm seeing Jesus in this memory!"

I ask them to describe him (often with brown colored eyes with golden flecks in them). I ask the alpha and omega the same questions through these different people; "What are you doing here? How do you know this person? Did you survive the Crucifixion, were you married, did you have a family, did you retire to Kashmir with your family, how did this crucifixion ruse work?"

Despite hearing it from many; he tells the same contrary story.

"He's saying he survived the Crucifixion. He's saying he moved to another cave where they tended to his wounds. He's saying – he was married and he moved to Kashmir to live out his days. He's saying... that he didn't die on the cross." It is uncanny that this has happened to consistently the past decade or so; the only solace I have is that I always turn on the camera or recorder, and listen to the same details.

But back to our monk; the hypnotherapist is asking what his name was.

I say "Antonio..." I started to hear it in Latin – "Antoninus." I have the impression I was given a Latin name once I took the vows, and that name was what I was known by. "Antoninus of Florence."

(Note: I searched for "Antoninus" and was startled to find he was a Dominican, (black robed). He was friends with Fra' Angelico, the painter, and later became the Archbishop of Florence, born March, 1389; died May, 1459; "known by his baptismal name Antoninus. At the age of fifteen (1404) Antoninus applied for admission to the Dominican Order." Turns out he was quite influential in his lifetime, (as we'll hear later "a big deal") wrote many books in Latin and was widely considered a "progressive philosopher."

One abstract states "Antoninus of Florence (1389-1459) had an "Enormous influence on the Renaissance, and in some way, the Reformation and even the Counter-Reformation. Such varied figures as Marsilio Ficino, the Medici family including the Medici pope, Leo X, Martin Luther... in varied ways were inspired by his life and works. **"It has been said, "The greatest Florentine of the century was Archbishop Antoninus."** ("Atonino Pierozzi; A Locus of Dominican Influence." Astract for Academia.com by Ezra Sullivan;)

The other odd thing is that when I was writing a paper for my Humanties class at Boston University, I focused on the "Pazzi Conspiracy" and this time period, learning all of the major figures that had a hand in the life of Antoninus, from Cosimo De Medici to the Pope. Ten years later, I wrote a film script about it, (optioned by Hawk Koch Jr.) ten years after that wrote a miniseries for HBO about this same era (which HBO shelved when they made "Rome" instead.)

I've done deep research on all the characters Antoninus knew, from his benefactor Cosimo De Medici, to his grandson Lorenzo De Medici to his brother Giuliano, to Giuliano's girlfriend Simonetta Vespucci (the model for the Birth of Venus) to Botticelli (Lorenzo's uncle). I've been to most of these places Antoninus lived, from the same monastery where the infamous Savanorola ("Bonfire of the Vanities") was trained, been in his cell, visited the same monastery as Antoninus and Fra' Angelico. As I've always had the feeling during my research, when I first arrived in Rome at age 19, I was "returning to the homeland"

(Antoninus spent years in Rome as well) and later I was "revisiting" old friends and cities I knew... but had never been to before.

Portrait of Antoninus of Florence

Antoninus died on May 2, 1459. His funeral Mass was celebrated by Pope Pius II. He was canonized on Trinity Sunday, May 31, 1523. His "Saint's prayer" is *"Eternal God, you blessed Saint Antoninus with a marvelous gift of counsel. By the help of his prayers, while we walk in the darkness of this life, may we learn from the light of Christ all that we ought to do. We ask this through our Lord Jesus Christ, your Son, who lives and reigns with you and the Holy Spirit, one God, for ever and ever. Amen."* https://www.exurbe.com/spot-the-saint-more-dominicani/.)

During this hypnosis session, I am recalling living in the same monastery, speaking fluently in Latin (a language I've never studied) and visiting all the places in Florence I've been to. I'm aware that Antoninus considered the dogma of the church less than satisfactory, was known as a progressive in his era, (allowing that people who had divorces or abortions should remain Catholics) and because of his "visitation" always felt that he was closer to Jesus than anyone knew.

I was asked about the last day of his life, and saw him in a hospital in the monastery being attended by a number of people. I saw that he was dressed in white as he took his last breath about the age of 67 (which roughly lines up with the death of Antoninus of Florence). I noted that he was old for that era, that his body had broken down mainly because of the lack of vitamins, minerals in his food and his bones were falling apart. He caught pneumonia, and his last day he was dressed in white (I've found paintings of the funeral of Antoninus where he is dressed in white, and currently, his body is on display in that same 15th century white robe.)

I had never come across the name of Antoninus in my extensive research of the Pazzi Conspiracy over the past thirty years. I am steeped in the history of Florence and the Medici family paid handsomely by HBO to be so. The patriarch Cosimo is where my miniseries begins, and his relationship with the Platonic academy which he created. It was Cosimo's grandsons, Lorenzo and Giuliano who became the leaders in Florence who Antoninus saw grow up, saw the politics of the era, and must have witnessed firsthand the Pazzi conspiracy, as it happened in 1492. (Antoninus dies in 1459).

The people of Florence rose up against the Pazzi family after they murdered their beloved Giuliano De Medici and stabbed Lorenzo in the neck (at the behest of Pope Sixtus IV) and they attacked anyone who was associated with the crime, including killing an Archbishop associated with their family. So many Pazzi family members were hanged, that DaVinci and Michelangelo used the dead bodies as "models" because "they were cheap and never moved."

In my minds eye, after the death of Antoninus, I "flew" back to the homestead to say goodbye to my sister and brother (who still lived there) and then I saw my guide Ray, (whom I met in "Flipside.") He showed up the way he often does; like an old friend standing by patiently, with a smile as if to say "Hey brother, you okay? You want to go home?"

(Note: The more I research Antoninus, the more I see things that are familiar to me. He wrote numerous books about "how the world works," pontificated on how to "live one's life," how to behave in any given circumstance, ("Summa Theologica") how to treat others in general. The dogma of the church appeared to be problematic for him, and he's cited in abstracts by scholars as a major influence on Martin Luther and the Reformation. While reportedly "tolerant of abortion or divorce," he was adamant about Priests not having mistresses, excommunicated a few and even had one "heretic" burned at the stake.

He also promoted a controversial book by a Priest named Valla, (considered heretical by the Vatican) a book sponsored by Cosimo De Medici that argued church documents which granted Roman property to the fledgling church were forged, which granted all Roman temples and property to the new Church. ("The Donation of Constantine")

This detail was actually a subplot in my HBO miniseries because it infuriated the Vatican, and perhaps was part of the reason the Pope allowed the attempted assassination of the Medicis by the rival banking family the Pazzi. I was startled to discover it was Antoninus (this supposedly past lifetime of mine) who brought this information into the world.

The idea that I would somehow be a "partial reincarnation of Antoninus" is mind bending to say the least. The idea I would be reporting these heretical things about the afterlife, that "Jesus didn't die on the cross," that "reincarnation is not dictated by karma," but we agree to and choose each of our lifetimes is contrary to known religious beliefs. The idea that I might have known someone in the period of the Renaissance that I researched extensively, but never came across him despite his notoriety is equally mind bending.

I should point out here that "partial reincarnation" is the operative word; we reportedly bring that third of our conscious energy to any lifetime, so whatever percentage I brought to any lifetime is a distillation of all the other ones. It's not like I stepped out of Antoninus robes, put on tennis shoes and jeans and decided to become a film director and author.

But in the past ten years, I've had some pretty unusual memories. That includes a Sumerian Priest in the Kingdom of Sumeria, a Brahmin Hindu Priest in Kerala India, a Tibetan Buddhist monk in Lhasa, and now this Dominican Archbishop in Florence. I've also had memories of being a failed sculptor in Piraeus, Greece, a teacher of ethics and oratory near Pompeii, a callous Royal cad in Calais, France, a Catholic Nun in Paris. I can only report that in nearly every one these places that I've been on the planet in this lifetime, when I felt first arrived, I had the feeling like I had "been there before," or that I was "returning home" – whether it be Kerala, Paris, Piraeus, Lhasa, Pompeii, Rome or Florence. It's an unusual feeling that one dismisses outright – how could one feel they are "returning" if they've never been there before?

It's the same with meeting people that one has known from previous lifetimes – that feeling of "I feel like I know you from before" when in all likelihood one has.

I would never "claim to be a reincarnated saint" but it appears, based on my research and what I've been up to for the past dozen years, that some part of my conscious energy was some part of this conscious energy as well – that is, a modest Dominican monk who later became an Archbishop. His reputation was as someone who eschewed vanity, focusing more on helping those in need of help. He was likely the source of the term "Vanum populatum" that I heard in Latin before I began the film "Flipside."

I was in my apartment in Santa Monica, where just prior to waking up, heard someone's voice saying "Vanum populatum." It was said so clearly that I wrote it down, then weeks later looked it up. It means "Annihilate vanity." I thought "I live in LA, where do I begin?

But some months later, when I began this research into the flipside, I was filming people under deep hypnosis accessing the most profound things I've ever heard, and when Michael Newton suggested I do a deep hypnosis session, at first I was reluctant. "How can I report on something I'm doing?" But then I remembered meeting George Plimpton, the author of books where the author donned the outfit the of the thing he was writing about "Paper Lion" and "Paper Tiger."

I thought "What better way to prove this inaccurate?" I didn't believe in an afterlife, I didn't believe I could recall any previous lifetime, and despite filming a few people who did so, I had no belief I could be "under hypnosis." So they scheduled a session for me at the end of the week, and the night before I wrote down "ten questions" I might ask "anyone I might find" – not believing at all that I'd "find" anyone.

One of the questions as a trick question. "What's the meaning of vanum populatum?" I figured no one on the planet would know the answer to that obscure term – it's not in Latin literature that I can find – and I knew vaguely what it meant. But then a few hours in, I was addressing my own council (8 individuals) who seemed genuinely "entertained" by seeing me.

When the hypnotherapist (Jimmy Quast of Easton Hypnosis in Maryland) said "I have some questions you wrote down here" I said (on camera) "I've already asked them the questions." Mind you – I had jotted them down the night before at 2 in the morning, and consciously had no idea what they were – but it was as if they were burned into memory, and I had asked them and they were in the midst of answering each one.

When we got to "what's the meaning of vanum populatum?" They laughed. My lead council member said "Why don't you ask Richard? He knows the answer to that." When he said that, he put an image of myself into a bubble above my head – I could see myself lying on the couch, a few feet behind the camera (not what the camera was seeing, but a visual behind the camera) and I saw that he was referring to my "temporary self" – the guy on the couch, Richard.

In that moment I had a flash of understanding. I saw myself standing at this podium, addressing this council of eight, I looked like I did about age 18, longer hair, a suede vest and my head was kind of much larger than my body. And I realized that my guide was speaking to my "higher self" (otherwise he would have said "You know the answer to that question" and not "Richard does").

I looked a bit like this guy, age 18. Photo Ellyn Toscano

I also realized that I had spoken to myself in Latin from a previous lifetime where I knew Latin, and my higher self had given me this puzzle knowing I would look it up and learn what the source of the phrase was, as well as why it was important for me to repeat.

Vanum means vanity. Populatum means to "wipe off the face of the earth" or "utterly destroy." (Funny it has a different meaning now, but that's what Latin dictionaries claim.) In essence, my mission on the planet, should I choose to accept it – is to show people that everything that isn't associated with love, with unconditional love, with who we are on the flipside and why we're here on the planet, should be dismissed, dispensed with – annihilated.

Money. Fame. Ego. Clothing. Mansions. Etc.

It related directly to this guy Antoninus of Florence who likely is the one who said it to me – as if somehow he knew that it would inspire me to write this book and write this sentence. "If it doesn't serve love – then lose it."

I'm happy to report old Antoninus was made a saint years after his passing.

During the Vatican "hearings" to prove he was worthy of Sainthood, they cited "His visions of ecstasy." During the canonization hearings **"several men gave evidence of seeing "Antoninus "rise into the air while praying in his chamber." One said "his father told him he had seen the saint raised into the air during prayer."** (Hmm. An old trick from the lifetime as a Buddhist monk perhaps?) **Antoninus was responsible for depositing the relics of St. Catherine of Siena in Rome.**

So I took my penchant for self experimentation to the next level. The next time I met with medium Jennifer Shaffer, I brought along this new information to see if it was possible that I was some part of a reincarnation of this Florentine fellow. We asked for Luana Anders, my pal and confidant on the flipside, to assist in our chatting with him.

INTERVIEW WITH ST. ANTONINUS VIA JENNIFER SHAFFER

A cameo of Saint Antoninus in Florence with my pal Charles Grodin

Summa Theologica Moralis IV: **"And this is the whole purpose of this work, that from the knowledge of what is** narrated in histories men may learn to live well in this world, so that they might hope for beatitude from the Lord and attain it" *St. Antoninus*

Here is how I introduced the topic: (my comments *in italics,* Jennifer's replies **in bold.**)

Rich: Just to shift gears, I attended (hypnotherapist) Scott De Tamble's workshop on past life regression, and we did a practice session where I recalled being a monk in Italy. His name was Antoninus. Luana, if you can I'd like for you to put you in a chair.

Jennifer: He's here. He was a "big guy – a really important guy. He had control over a lot of people."

Okay. I want to clarify. Who is this fellow Antoninus?

(Jennifer listens, looks at me. Listens more. Looks at me. Shrugs.) He's you. (By way of explanation) It's like you have four souls that are in you right now.

Okay, let's avoid math puzzles for a moment. Was I this fellow known historically as Antoninus?

I'm getting "Yes." Part of you was Antoninus, part was this other guy (that we interviewed for another book.)

Well, mathematics aside, we have discussed in the past we only bring about a third of our conscious memory to a lifetime... is that what we're talking about?

"Right." I'm seeing that there's a huge control issue with him, controlling things; he had a love for water, or something to do with water.

Part of his mission later in life, perhaps. (I.e., "Bringing fresh water to a city of Florence" was one of Antoninus accomplishments he was famous for.)

(Jennifer pauses) Let's see how I can put this; it felt like in order to help people had to get rid of some people.

Well, that sounds like the politics of his day. I'm very familiar with Florentine and Vatican politics from that era. Perhaps you're referring to bad priests – I don't think he was killing anyone.

I don't think so either.

Perhaps he stripped them of power.

Antoninus is his name? It's funny, I heard the word "anus" at first. Not judging.

Okay, that's funny. Well, in my past life memory in Scott's workshop, I remembered living in a house in Florence with a domineering father.... who..

"Sent him away."

Correct. Sent him to a monastery at age 15. That order was Dominican I think – black robes.. I saw him as younger, his friends, and wasn't that focused on what happened later in life. I'm trying to clarify that he is the same guy as that one.

"Yes, he is."

He then becomes...

"The head of a church."

That's right. (Ding!) He was appointed the head of a church in Florence, he later becomes close to the Pope. His close friend was a painter.

"Like Michelangelo..."

Same era, painter who was a close friend of his; Fra Angelico. Angelico brought Antoninus into the Vatican and made him a famous guy. Is this correct? Is this me as well?

"Yes."

Antoninus was later made a saint by the Pope. Just saying – so now we're talking about my past life being a saint. Is this accurate?

"Yes."

Can we just put a halo on me now?

Patron Saint of Donuts

Look, I know this is odd – but I looked up Antoninus after I said it and found this fellow and now you're saying it's the same guy. I have no connection to this ego wise – "Vanum populatum."

(Note: I don't speak Latin but reported in "Flipside" that I dreamed someone said "vanum populatum" to me, which means "annihilate vanity" in a language I don't speak now, but did before.)

They showed me variations of yourself here, parts of you wanting to be connected to these people but not realizing it until now.

Well, I did want to be a priest as a kid until one tried to kiss me.

Right.

Okay, thanks Antoninus! We'll catch you the next time I'm in Florence.

*****

After this session, I reflected on all of the Catholic things that had happened with regard to my research into the flipside. In my initial interview with Paul Aurand for "Flipside" he told me that Jesus showed up often in his sessions, either people who knew him or were deeply affected by him. Then I did a session with a close friend (Molly) who recalled knowing Jesus in Jerusalem.

Since then I've met half a dozen people who claimed to be at the Crucifixion (one in this book, three in "Hacking the Afterlife") or aware of those events, and even people who claim to remember being in that story - Nicodemus, Johanna, Mary Magdalene, and a child of that family "Sara." (Not Stella, but I digress).

I have met numerous people who claim to know him between lives, claim to know him from before and claim to be able to access him directly. I can't argue that it's him – I can't argue that he's the one who is responding to people when they say they are speaking to him, but he says the same things that other people say about the journey. That we don't die – that he didn't die either – and that our "higher self" is always accessible. And that since he's outside of time, he points out; he's available to anyone anywhere anytime.

Not as a savior, or someone who is going to perform miracles – but as someone who represents unconditional love. Someone who represents source because "he brought more of it to this incarnation (as reported in "Hacking the Afterlife." I am not going to claim that I was Antoninus, or that I am Antoninus – but I find it unusual that I spent a good part of my life doing deep research into that era, specifically the "Pazzi Conspiracy" that took place during his lifetime, and was paid by HBO to write the miniseries "The DeMedicis" (which thanks to producer Tony To, paid the insurance for both of our beautiful children.)

Then we have the "Vanum Populatum" incident where I was speaking to myself in Latin – I heard it and wrote it down, knowing that I didn't speak or know Latin. I naturally assumed it was based on an earlier lifetime I had remembered where I was a merchant who went to Pompeii prior to the eruption, and lived a fully lifetime in Italy (as reported in "It's a Wonderful Afterlife.") But here I am finding a fellow who wrote numerous books about life and cosmology and the structure and architecture of life – all in Latin, a language I still can't speak.

But when I read about his life, I remember many things about it – because I've done that deep research, I know what they wore, I know what they ate, I know what it felt like to be living in Florence in 1450 and the more I think about it, the more memories flood back to me. Except for this one: being dug up 100 years after "my death" and put on display in the Church of San Marco. I've been to San Marco many times in my research for the Medici project – as a student going to school in Italy during my Junior Year Abroad in Rome, later when I taught film there... so I've passed this fellow dozens of times and never bothered to look at him.

Until now.

Well, here he is.

They dug up his body 100 years after he died, and it had not deteriorated.

Saint Antoninus is currently resting in the Church of San Marco in Florence. Nothing quite like looking for your tombstone and finding it. Nothing quite like seeing that they've pulled you out of your tomb and put you in a glass case for all to see in the middle of downtown Florence. Nothing quite like remembering this fellow's lifetime during a past life regression, remembering key moments and players and details – and then having your pal the medium confirm details of that memory, so much so that when you go to look them up they all "make sense."

Now I know why I felt like I was "returning home" the first time I was in a plane that landed in Italy. It was nearly 500 years since my last lifetime there (that I'm aware of) and included a memory of being on that place on this planet. Further, understanding why I wanted to be an altar boy, how I became disenchanted with the liturgy and it's rules and regulations, how I had to forge my own path away from the dogma of Christianity, only to get dragged kicking and screaming back into his orbit by the alpha and omega himself.

Not to argue that I'm a Christian. In another time or era, I know I'd be watching the flames lick the bottom of my robe, or would be "stoned to death" by an angry populous. But this time around – I can understand why I (my higher self who knows Latin) said to myself in a dream the words "vanum populatum." Because I knew that those words would put my temporary, current self Richard on a path to figure out what the heck "annihilate vanity" means, and how it applies to my job on the planet.

Antoninus wrote many books in Latin, was an author, a popular fellow, and eventually made a saint. Me – *not so much*. But now he's writing books in Santa Monica, chuckling at the idea the he might have been "a saint in a past life." And that the body isn't even buried! It's stuck in a glass case in a shrine at the Church of San Marco in Florence!

Well, if you happen to stop by the Chiesa Di San Marco in Firenze, make a point of saying *"Ciao."*

Antoninus Martinus with Kutenla, the State Oracle of Tibet.

CHAPTER TWENTY FIVE:

"HOME IS WHERE THE HEART IS"

Reverend Maryum Morse – Center of the Heart Santa Barbara

But enough about me.

This is a transcript of a 30 minute interview I did when "Hacking the Afterlife" came out. I was invited to do a book talk at the Center of the Heart church in Santa Barbara, and prior to going on stage, I asked if the minister Rev. Maryum Morse or her associate Roxy Angel wanted to participate in a live experiment. They both said "sure."

The video for this is located on my YouTube page, via MartiniZone.com. My comments are in italics, theirs are in bold.

Rich: Who wants to come up first? Maryum or Roxy? (to the audience) Here's what I pitched to them – if you had some kind of spirit adventure we can explore that. I'm not doing hypnosis or going to say "sleep!" I'm going to say "wake." Come on up Reverend. (as she arrives) You mentioned earlier you had an experience?

Maryum: I had one when my dad was dying; he came (in spirit form) to visit my brother, and those who could see him – scared my niece half to death. He came to me, either I traveled to their house out in Fortuna, California.

He was showing me in his body, he had Parkinson's - my mom was in bed next to him, and (in spirit form) he was jumping out of his

body. Like "Look at me!" (Laughs) And he'd jump back into his body (makes a stiff gesture) saying look – "I'm stuck ."

He did it like 20 or 30 times and I was like "Pop I get it! And I noticed a whole crowd nearby, they were my ancestors waiting for him.

Take a mental photo of that group. Your dad is relaxing?

He wanted to show me he was free.

Let's go to a moment when he stepped out. What's he wearing?

He's in his young body, the body he had in WWII with brown hair. He had a hot body; looked like (the actor in Tarzan or Flash Gordon) Buster Crabbe.

What's he wearing?

Like a light blue shirt; pants were dark brown.

Okay, great. Take his hands in yours; what do they feel like?

They're kind of rough and he has oil under his fingernails.

Look him in the eye, I'm sorry what's his name?

Quentin.

Hi Quentin. I just want to thank you for allowing us to play this game with you. Does he say anything?

"He's happy and he's learning a lot."

He's skipping ahead; I just want to say hi.

He's kind of serious.

Okay, here we are - here's your daughter – lighten up a little dude.

He just gave a little smile.

Okay, that's better. Quentin show Maryum what she looks like to you.

(Holds her face) Oh my god. He's showing me as a little girl.

Describe that.

I'm wearing a little sun dress; it's yellow.

Sweet. So that's how he sees you. Quentin do you mind? Can we ask you some questions?

He says "Yes."

What is your day like on the flipside?

He said that he has a lot of choices, (for) what to do; there's a lot of freedom there. When he got there he looked out to see what he needed to learn – and he's going to classes.

(Note: She chuckled, as I mentioned "taking classes" as one of the things I'd observed on the flipside.)

Let's go to one. Can you take us to one? Describe it.

There's 18 people; they're facing forward.

Is there a teacher? Male or female or something in-between?

Yes; (teacher is) female.

Hello Teacher, I apologize for interrupting your class is it okay?

She says "Yeah."

What's the teacher look like?

It looks like she has medium length hair, she's in her 40's.

Does she have a name?

I'm getting "Alana."

Alana, could you tell us what you're teaching in this class?

Right away, she said "Compassion."

Tell us, how do you teach compassion?

She says "She has them look at their lives and how they experienced it during their lives."

How do they share?

She's showing me they all are seeing their "life scene," she asks them to pick a time, and then they choose one – and they show it to the class. Oh wow, that's it.

Can you show us an example?

Oh my god. I'm seeing it's my dad. He's in the war, he saved his friend's life. He went into a no man's land and he pulled his friend out

Quentin, where was this battle?

"I was in Okinawa."

Your compassionate moment, you pulled your friend to safety?

"Yes. He was my buddy when we were fighting next to each other, we saw so many of our buddies die, we promised we'd help he other."

Is he a member of your soul group or classroom?

"Hmm. No, he's not."

I'm going to ask Alana – Can you show Maryum her guide? Is her guide a male, female or a combination?

(She laughs.) He's come before – a really tall, tall man or being... like 8 feet tall. His eyes are brown... his name is something with an A.

We'll call you Mr. A for now.

More like an Indian name. It's "Ashara."

Ashara – can we ask you some questions?

"Sure." He's nodding his head.

Do you do this often, have interviews with people still on the planet?

"No."

What does Maryum look like to you?

He's showing that I look like light to him – joyful and happy. It's a pink and golden light; the colors are pulsing. They move in kind of waves, moving out – not pulsing, just moving out.

Ash, can we walk her into her council?

"Yes." We're outside. It looks like – oh my gosh I've been here before; it's a clearing surrounded by trees.

Before we talk to your council would you go over and hug a tree? Is there a feeling associated with that?

There's a loving energy.

Put your hand inside the tree, because you can. What's the feeling you get?

It's giving me energy. It's coming right into me.

If this tree was an entity what would this tree call itself?

Something with an R.

Mr. R. Thank you Mr. Tree. I appreciate the hello, as I've done this before with other etheric trees.

(Note: As one tree pointed out "Planting a trillion trees will help balance the climate on the planet.")

Per LaChaise cemetery; Paris

Let's look at your council – how many people are here?

There's quite a group here – There's around 12. They're in a circle; standing. They're wearing robes, (they are) like rainbow colors, all different colors.

Let's go to your lead council member – spokesperson for this group?

It's a male.

Reach out and grab hold of this council person's hands – can we do that?

Oh my god. It's like – (I feel) there's no time or space, we're just... right... present.

Any emotion associated when holding onto them?

"I'm home."

(Note: "Home" is the term that most people under deep hypnosis use for the afterlife. When asked "where do you go after that lifetime?" they answer "home.")

Home. What's this council person's name?

"Samara."

Thank you Sam; how do you think Maryum is doing?

She laughs and gives a thumbs up. (Audience laughs).

Samara, have you been interviewed by people on the planet before?

"No, it's my first (time) like this."

(Teasing) I bet if you ask around they know me.

Oh yes, he said "I've heard about you."

Can you put a sensation in Maryum's body – so that she feels something that says that she is connected to you?

Wow. It's my feet. There's this energy in my feet; specifically in the left foot from my shin to my foot.

Try to memorize that sensation – it's a direct connection to your people on the other side. A few more things; lottery numbers?

(Maryum laughs.)

Any message you want to pass along to the people reading this or watching?

He's saying "To just to take time to be still and connect – into their inner wisdom." He said "The councils are always there, within us. And if we take that time to access them; just to breathe, take a moment and ask them for help.

Thank you – okay, let's say goodbye to everyone, your dad – your council members, thank them for showing up and allowing us to experience something.... that's consistent.

(Applause as she exits. To the audience:)

You see what I'm doing? I've been doing this for awhile – I'm in a vacuum; I have no idea how it affects the people I spoke to – Maryum and I just met. I never said we were going to visit her council members but everything she just said is consistent with what everyone else says.

Even if your mind is saying "Well that's not me, that's her journey, this is her path, that's her dad – that's not what the research shows. I've filmed 40 sessions, and I've taken a dozen people on the same trip.

"Roxy Angel Superstar" – Center of the Heart Santa Barbara

Roxy joins me on stage.

Rich: So I met Roxy Angel today. She told me that her husband passed some time ago. Just to remind everyone; I didn't see Maryum's father or council. I don't know them – she saw them. Is there a value to that?

Roxy: Yeah.

Tell me about your deceased husband Jason showing up.

It was not too long after he died, I was out on errands, and my roommate said "We got a problem. The doorbell had kept ringing, this had been going on for 12 hours, and then I heard it and I laughed because I remembered the story his best friend had told me, how they used to love ringing the doorbell incessantly. So I knew it was him – immediately – and after I realized that, it went on three or four more times then stopped.

And you also told me about your conception story?

Yes, when my son was conceived, I had an out of body experience, moved out of my body and into outer space. I went on this trip but I wasn't on drugs.

Can you visualize yourself in space from this event?

Yes, like it was yesterday.

What are you seeing?

Like an aurora borealis with clouds and colors.

Aurora Borealis (NASA)

Is there an object or a light nearby? Any person here with you?

Yeah, there's something there. A light.

I'm going to ask that light to manifest as a person – male or female or something in between?

Something in between – I see like shapes, like a cylindrical shape and it's got a cape or a hood.

How far away is this shape?

Seems very near – like six feet.

Well, person in the hoodie – we need your help. Please come forward and take your hood off.

It's a light.

I need you to coalesce into a person we can talk to; transform into a visual of a person that Roxy might understand.

(Gasps) I see Jason. (Her deceased husband).

Thank you Jason. Can you take his hand in yours?

Yes; it feels warm and sparkly. Like sparklers.

Look into his eyes. What's the sensation or emotion?

I'm getting warmth and love. Safety.

It's all the same feeling of the memory of being connected. Can you show Roxy what she looks like to you?

Like a flower.

What was it like for you to cross over. Who did you meet?

His mom.

Was that a happy occurrence?

"Yes; it was happy. Very happy."

Was your passing an exit point, or something you'd worked out before you came to the planet?

"It was not familiar to me."

Was that you ringing her doorbell?

"Yeah."

What was that thing about money in the drawer that Roxy mentioned to me earlier?

He said, "It was there (already) but he made me aware of it."

(Note: What I've learned is that the object is there, but on the flipside they're making it so a person doesn't notice or see it until they do – and it reminds them of the person who has crossed over.)

So you're keeping an eye on her?

"Yes."

What's it like for you to communicate with her? How does that occur?

He said something about images – "She sees things. Flashes of pictures."

Do you think of her – think of the image of her, you approach that image and communicate with her?

(Note: I've heard it's easier to "ping" or tap into a memory that includes a visual image, than sound. They have an easier time of showing us something rather than saying it.)

"Usually in dreams; it's easier."

Why is it easier for you to communicate with her in dreams?

"Because she is listening – I can give her the information without her input." (Roxy begins to laugh)

So – he prefers to communicate when you aren't interrupting him?

(She laughs loudly.)

I'm glad you can make her laugh. Please give us an example. How do you inject yourself into a dream?

He was very good with (energy or) lights – he knows how to make the lights dim.

Let me ask you, are you participating in any classes over there?

"Yes," he does.

What's one class you are involved with?

He said "He's dealing with something (a class) involved with energy."

(Note: I've visited about a dozen different classrooms. Nearly every class has something to do with the transfer of energy using the mind.)

How many are in your class?

"About 15. It's in an auditorium."

What's the teacher look like?

"A cylindrical being of thin light; cylindrical being."

If I may ask the teacher; can you give us a simplified version of how you manipulate energy? Is there a formula?

"Thoughts... and then it seems like with the mind, you move the shapes, manipulate ribbons of energy...?

Ribbons of energy. Can you manifest something from doing that? Manipulating energy to create something?

"Yes."

"What's an example of something you can create from a ribbon of energy?"

He says he's creating Merkabahs.

What's that?

"They are geometric shapes."

A "Merkabah" or geometric shape. Wikimedia.

I've heard this, they're like fractals. What do they function as?

"Gateways."

(Note: There are a number of definitions of "Merkabah" – one is traditional from Hebrew, meaning "chariot." New age literature often describes them as tetrahedrons or "form constants" that some people see during a deep hypnosis session. When I filmed this interview, I hadn't heard to them referred to in this fashion.)

Gateways to other realms?

"Other states of being."

Higher and lower states of being?

"They're whatever we are – on our level."

You use a Merkabah to transport yourself to another place?

"Yes."

Does it function like a portal or a black hole?

"It functions as a teleporter to another place."

Can we, as humans create something like this?

"You're too dense."

I'm hearing that the more conversations we have like this, the more we may be able to do something like this?

I'm getting from him that "It's not that easy, that some (barriers) are impenetrable, and some are easier."

How many of the 15 people in your class are still on the planet?

"About half – seven."

They are here on the planet, and then part of their energy is in class, learning how to transmit energy?

"Yes."

(Note: As noted, we bring about a third of our conscious energy to a lifetime and that the other two thirds is always doing something else – including attending classes. Roxy has no idea of what I'm referring to, but Jason does.)

Thank you Jason. Before we go, I wonder if you can give Roxy a hug, something to remind here that you're always with her. (Roxy wipes away tears.) May I give you a hug, Roxy?

The total time elapsed for these two "improvised talks" was 30 minutes from start to finish. My way of demonstrating it doesn't take deep hypnosis or faith to access people on the flipside. It just takes a basic knowledge about the architecture involved.

Detail from Raphael's "Heaven" in the Vatican.

CHAPTER TWENTY SIX:

"TALKING TO WATER"

Some angels floating around in clouds (Huntington Gardens)

I was contacted by Laura of the "Pan Society" about appearing on her blog broadcast. She was casually familiar with posts I've made about accessing the flipside. When we finally connected, she suggested that we do a show about "Evil and pain in the afterlife." I jokingly said "Well, that interview would be me saying one sentence, and then we'd have the rest of the hour to discuss."

I suggested our time might be more fruitful if we went exploring on the flipside, perhaps to meet her guides (which she was aware of).

.

Laura: Hi: It's your host Laura for Modern Animism radio. (After going into my bio) Rich is going to be sharing info that will show you anyone can access the other side.

Rich: Well, I've learned people don't have to be under hypnosis to access a memory, as everything is recorded as a slice of time.

So how do you do that?

It's a surface level thing, I recommend if a person wants to try hypnotherapy, go for the whole nine yards. The four to six hour session resonates much deeper – I'm just skipping a stone across the surface, but to demonstrate that it's possible without hypnosis at all. So Laura

– when we started this conversation, I asked if you had any dream that you can recall.

Laura: It's a dream I remember seeing Praying Mantises and they were opening up my skin like a tin can and I was terrified.

Rich: Okay. Did it feel real?

Yes.

I'm going to ask some leading questions because I can; I call this a game we're going to play. You said you had many guides, and I asked for a primary one. Your guide's name is...?

Pearl.

When you say her name what comes to mind?

She's small, about 100 pounds or less. Dark hair, glasses – kind face. Her eyes are brownish; hazel. She's wearing a shapeless, loose dark dress. It's fitted around the waist, but big and blousy on top and the bottom.

(Note: I'm not on camera, nor is Laura. I have no idea what she looks like and everything is over the phone. Whatever visuals she has, she's saying aloud, and the interview is on the Pan Society website. Read along if you'd like.)

Take a hold of Pearl's hands. Are they soft or hard?

Arthritic. Big knuckles; bony.

What age does she appear to be?

She feels young but she doesn't look young.

Pearl, can I ask you some questions?

"Yes."

Are you familiar with what I'm doing?

"Sort of."

Are you familiar with that through Laura?

"Yes."

I always ask; sometimes they say no. Have you ever had a lifetime with Laura?

"Yes. In Ohio." (Laura aside) She was my teacher who died in 1978.

Let's help Laura access a lifetime of hers that was previous. What comes to mind? Where are we?

Outside. It's green. Not enough to be a forest but it's green.

Are you male or female?

Female. Age is late 20's, early 30's. Wearing tan top, tan bottom looks like a safari outfit. Khaki with a hat. Shoes are leather, they look custom made.

What's her name?

First letter is a D. Dee sound. Last name is a G sound.

(Note: Sometimes the names are clearer, and if so, someone could do the forensic research to see if this person is noted in the historical record of this era. I'm more focused on getting her to visit her council at the moment.)

What year is this?

1930's. We're in Africa. Location is in the middle. She is a companion or wife to someone else here.

Let's go to a moment dining with her companion. What's her companion look like?

A male, dark hair, all.

What's his first name?

Steve pops into my head.

Steve can I ask you a question?

"Yes."

What does she look like to you – when you look at her who is she?

"Hmm. She's my wife. I'm very much in love. She has on a white shirt, red lipstick, red hair, it's curly."

What the heck are you doing bringing your wife to Africa? Were you mining? Hunting? What are you doing?

"I couldn't be separated from her. She wanted to come. She feels the same."

Are you in Laura's lifetime now?

"No."

Why not?

"Um. The timing wasn't right."

(Note: This answer relates to timelines that we choose for ourselves. Sometimes one person is not on the planet when their loved one is.)

Are you keeping an eye on her?

"From a distance."

Not so distant right now because here we are talking to you.

"Yes."

So Pearl – come forward my dear. I need your help. Can you escort her into her council?

"Yes."

Are we inside or outside?

We're outside. It's like space. Deep space.

How many people are here?

They're not people. There are lights. There are 5 light beings.

I want to thank them first for allowing us to have this conversation. Can we ask you some questions?

"Yes."

"Are you familiar with my work?"

"They say they know you."

How? Have you met me before?

"Yes. Some of them have talked to you before in a thing like this – (but) not all of them."

(Note: I know that the person I'm interviewing could not be aware of other conversations I've had and have yet to publish.)

How are they arrayed?

More or less a circle. They don't have limbs – they have light, not limbs, are are floating.

Pearl take her by the hand, walk up the first being on the far left. Describe that being.

It's a color – it's kind of greenish yellow - "pastelly"; the texture is foggy – not solid.

Is the color undulating or matte?

Kind of like concentrated fog; you couldn't touch it, but it's changing all the time.

Is this a male or female, neither or both?

Neither.

Can you manifest as an individual for the purpose of our conversation?

It's like it's trying but not quite there yet – (I see) it's got human limbs but the face is not clear – like the top part is not clear.. I got the bottom part and not the top.

That's fine; what's a name or letter we can use?

Another G.

Mr. or Miss G; what quality do you represent in Laura's lifetime that has allowed you onto her council?

The color is changing and I'm getting "spirituality."

Thank you. Each person on your council represents some quality of your spiritual evolvement. "Spirituality." Mr. or Ms. G have you incarnated as a human?

"No."

"How many councils do you sit on or participate in?

"Limitless."

Okay, are you one of the people who met me before?

"No."

What's your opinion of Laura's journey so far; how is she doing?

He is saying that it is not for him to judge but kind of like approval... but it's not that positive.

He's trying to avoid judgment on any level?

"Yes."

It's like instead of saying "she's good" - he doesn't seem to want to be limited by the idea of male or female – we limit them when we identify them. It's just a tip of the iceberg of who they are, and by calling them "male" or "female" limits them, is that correct?

"Yes." It's like he's trying to comply but yes, it's limiting.

In terms of spirituality – the quality you represent, is she on the right path? Not a judgment – but if you were in the balcony would you be applauding or giving a thumbs down?

"That's funny. Yes, applauding in the balcony is the way to put it."

I gave him something that wasn't over committed. Pearl how do you think our friend Laura doing?

Pearl is "effervescent with love."

Well, that's a little different answer – just a demonstration of how each person is different. This can't be information coming from you because you'd have them all cheering and using fireworks or the opposite. But each one has a different reply. Pearl loves what you're doing, but your teacher isn't going to cheer you on, but like a teacher wants you to learn. Mr. G, can you introduce us to your person on your left?

"A light as well. Blue. This being is male."

Can we ask for a name or letter we can work with?

It's a sound I can't make... like a bunch of consonants without a vowel. But with an S.

We know that your name isn't something we can comprehend, so we'll use S as a place holder. Mr. S; what do you represent on her council?

This is being communicated in symbols and sounds but not words – this is.. there's not a word for this, it's bigger than.. I don't know how to say this.

Let's start with this – are they form constants? Or a circle, square, pyramid – geometric shape? What word comes to mind?

It's like (the symbol represents) "the universe."

A Merkabah called "Metatron's cube" that reportedly symbolizes "the universe" but have no idea if this is what she's referring to. Wikimedia.

So when I ask "What do you represent in her spiritual evolvement?" The answer is you represent knowledge or access to the universe?

It's bigger than that, I think. It's kind of like infinity. "Moving through time and space, all things all at once," I don't know if I'm making sense.

You are to me. If I was going to put a word a word into your mouth it would be "consciousness?"

"Yes! That's the word, that's a good word."

(Note: I used "consciousness" because it's reflected in the research. I'm familiar with the idea that we're all connected and that connection is part of the medium for how the universe works. Consciousness may actually be "dark matter" or "dark energy" (not being dark, just "unknown" forms of energy). From what I've gathered, the best word to describe "all things being connected" is to use the word "consciousness." What's interesting is that she didn't say it was a good idea to use that word, but her council member did.)

As in "all the objects and all the things in the universe are interconnected." Is that what that symbol represents?

"Yes."

Where and how did Laura earn your representation? In this life?

 "Looks like a long time ago."

Okay, a long time ago she had a lifetime that was about learning about consciousness... and that is how you appeared on her council?

"Yes."

How many councils do you sit on?

"Very few. Less than ten."

Are you familiar with my work?

"Yes."

How so?

"Because he's familiar with everything."

So okay, Mr. S. The lottery numbers for this Friday are... (laughter) Just kidding. I know he could tell me but he won't. What's he wearing?

Everything is baby blue – he's wearing like a robe.

Is Pearl wearing any jewelry?

Pearl has a brooch. It's on her left shoulder... it's gold toned, it's got rhinestones and it's in the form of a peacock.

A peacock – is this animal related to Laura's journey or to Pearl's journey?

I'm getting "both."

What does the peacock represent metaphorically to Pearl?

"Beauty, spirituality and being seen."

A peacock brooch. Ebay.

Thank you Pearl. Now. Can you take hold of Mr. S's hand? What's that feel like?

It's... um. He doesn't have a hand. He's light. It's like a hologram, it's like he's not here, he's a projection.

Let me ask if the spokesperson for your council can come forward.

That's a different one – this one is magenta in color.

Can the light manifest as a person for the sake of conversation?

Yes, it is much easier for her. She's small, dark, happy.. and sassy.

What's a name we can use to address her?

It's a D.

Miss Dee; what do you represent on her council?

"Fun – amusement."

Are you familiar with my work?

"Yes."

How so?

This one has incarnated as a human, feels much more familiar, accessible, like she's know what's going on.

Can you take a hold of her hands and if there's an emotion?

Yes, she has a hand, it's easy to hold. It is small, the temperature is warm; she feels warm too... like a hug, like a mom.

Like you've known this person?

Yes, but a long time ago, feels distant like a cousin.

How many councils are you on Miss Dee?

Feels like more than the blue person – but not a lot.

The quality you represent is amusement, comedy or lightheartedness?

"Yes."

What's the purpose of that?

"It keeps things from getting too dark, too hard."

Is there a healing quality to laughter?

"Yes. It's not just for the person doing it but it can be shared."

I've heard laughter can heal or change the disposition of an ill person immediately?

"Yes."

I love that I ask council members to agree with me – what's your opinion of Laura's journey so far?

"Great; in terms of her laughing and having a good time."

Okay, that's a little different that Mr. G or Ms. S.

"She's very different than the others." (Meaning "Ms. Dee")

Is there anything you want me to address or talk about?

They say (for you to) "Keep talking about what your talking about because it's important for people to hear it."

I've also heard that our guides are always tethered to us – that's important to hear.

"Yes."

So why is it so difficult to access you guys?

"Fear and..." there's something else – **I'm not getting words – symbols; something like "A distortion in the energy field, I don't know if it's cellphone signals or some kind of distortion."**

Let me clarify, please correct me – for you guys to talk to us you have to change or lower your frequency?

"Yes!"

(Note: This has been repeated often in the research, so I'm kind of offering "yes" or "no" questions. They need to "slow down their frequency" to communicate, and we need to "speed up" ours through meditation, hypnosis or some other event.)

And in terms of our understanding we need to change our frequency through meditation, hypnosis or dreaming. While on the topic of dreams, let's ask Miss Dee this questions as she'll have a sense of humor about it. What about this praying mantis dream of Laura's?

I can't... Hmm. She's gone dark, I can't see her anymore.

Okay, so she's not going to answer this question. So Pearl, is it okay for us to ask this question about the PM dream?

She's smiling – and she's doing the same. She said "That's not important right now."

Okay, but Pearl may I explain what I think happened as a metaphor and you correct me?

"Yes."

People have experiences accessing lifetimes on other planets people have had experience of being visited by friends from other planets – no other way to put it – we may consciously think of them aliens, but in actuality they're friends coming to see how we're doing. Am I right so far Pearl?

She's saying, "The answers are going to come but not yet."

Let's just ask this; "Was the praying m dream accessing some entities or beings she knows?"

"Yes. She knows them. Yes, you're right about it being a contract and their being consent on a higher level."

That's all we needed to know about this. Pearl I want you to walk Laura into her "place of healing." She knows what I'm talking about. Are we inside or outside?

Outside. There's a lagoon, a waterfall, a natural pool. Some greenery – trees.

Walk her to the water. Put your hand in; what's that feel like?

"Cool, refreshing."

Is there any consciousness associated with this water?

"Mmm. Yes."

Male or female, neither or both?

Feels like both.

I'm going to ask this water a question. Is that okay?

"Yes."

Ms. Water – we'll call you Ms. Eau. Are you a construct creating this for Laura's benefit or do you exist on the flipside?

"Both."

So Laura is creating it and you're creating it – both?

"Yes."

Have you ever incarnated on Earth?

"No." Wait, I'm getting something else. "Yes."

How do we clean up the water on our planet? Is there a physical way to do that?

I've got – um. It's a filtration example, I'm seeing two things, evaporating, bubbling up and out, and the other is going through earth...

Is that cleansing process something that humans can recreate?

"It's already happening in nature."

So we can create these environments in dirt. What's the process that you can put in Laura's mind to transfer saltwater to fresh water in an inexpensive fashion?

"Swirling water moving in an oval shape."

Swirling Water. Wikimedia.

Is it swirling down or up?

"Both."

Are you saying that mixing or speeding up water molecules would help?

"Yes."

So an accelerator? Like the way a nuclear engine accelerates electrons? Or would acceleration create a way for the salt to fall due to gravity?

"Yes."

I've never had a conversation with water before. What would you like to tell our planet so we can have fresh water for our children or our next incarnation?

"Love the water. That's the bigger picture."

It sounds simple but it a huge answer opening your heart to water. Once we can see that water has a place, no less important than our mother, sister, brother, father; that everything is here for a reason, everything has consciousness?

"Yes. Love it in the way that you can... if you can it would be enough.

I asked one tree during one of these session; how do we fix the temperature of the planet. What's your advice Miss Eau?

I'm seeing the Australian brush fires – has something to do with balancing of elements – water and oxygen and fire.

Let me ask in terms of nuclear radiation in our water. Does that poison it forever? Or can it regenerate?

"Yes, it regenerates, but not on its own. It depends on other things to create this balance with it. I'm getting soil but also particles in the soil – like there's microbes in the soil that can clean the soil. The water itself isn't doing it it has to do with the soil, the water, the organisms in the water."

Multiple levels of filtering?

"And these organism are like a fungus that breaks down and purifies; it's a living organism within the water and the soil."

(Note: An article from 2015 talks about how scientists found a fungus in the Chernobyl reactor that was "eating, digesting and purifying" radioactive material. https://www.nature.com/)

Thank you Miss Water, thanks Pearl. What do you want Laura to experience now? What should she do?

"Open up and accept."

Accept what, coupons? (Laughter)

"Healing and love."

Coupons for healing and love. Let's thank everyone for helping.

Awesome! Thank you so much.

This is the last chapter of this exploration of speaking to councils.

I put it here to point out that despite the disconcerting reports that people have from the flipside (Aliens? Other planets? Councils? Guides? Classrooms?) there is some good news here.

That we can and should speak to our loved ones no longer on the planet, we can and should speak with our teachers and guides, and we should endeavor to learn how to do so.

One can use hypnosis, one can use a medium, but one can also use meditation or their own mind to access this information. After all, a certain portion of the population goes to a building every Sunday and prays aloud to people that they've never met, never seen, and never experienced. It's only when they get a reply that people deem them "crazy."

I'm recommending we all do so.

"Open oneself up to the possibility" is a familiar refrain. Everyone has their own path, their own journey – but we can share this information with each other to see how we can help each other. We can also ask for help in saving our planet, by asking how to clean our waterways, stop global warming, balance the oxygen of the planet (plant a trillion trees!) or find a way to change the paradigm.

We've heard **"Plant a trillion trees" "Stop eating flesh" "use water as an energy source" "radiation can be cleaned by organisms that exist"** etc. If anyone has focused on this kind of research, they'll know that this is the simplest of answers; it's my hope that inspires someone out there – perhaps not yet born – who will take up this clarion call and apply these suggestions to science, industry.

We've heard that we "incarnate" on other planets, that we have friends who incarnate on other planets, that we have council members who incarnate in other realms and other planets. We've spoken to people who have no conscious memory of ever being "off our planet" and yet are able to access memories of living on other planets.

We have people who claim to be able to see, hear, or have a relationship with religious avatars – from all religions and walks of life. But specifically we've spoken to people who claim to remember knowing Jesus during his lifetime, and report an alternate history as to what happened to the fellow. Further, he seems to be able to speak for himself on these matters – he is still preaching a version of "unconditional love for everyone and all things" but makes no claim that is the only way to "return home."

They all claim that once our journey here on the planet is over, we all "go home." There's no one to stop us outside any gates, we don't need a library card, or immigration card to get in – we all get in. Those who've made life difficult get a chance to relive all that pain and suffering they'd done to others. And those who've made our lives wonderful are there to greet us and remind us how much they love us.

But we've learned that this research is the tip of the iceberg. If it's possible to speak to our loved ones no longer on the planet, to speak with our guides and teachers and those who want us to succeed, imagine the kinds of things we can learn from them. Truly a way to introduce a new paradigm for the planet.

At least one can hope.

Earth from the moon; NASA

Afterword: Summa Theologica Martinus

With Mom, Anthy, in NYC circa 1959. Photo: R. Charles Martini

I once asked my mother what she thought the afterlife was like. Fully expecting something Catholic, I was surprised to hear her say "I think you have your home and you're surrounded by all your comfy things, and you have a beautiful garden." One day while doing a session with medium Jennifer Shaffer, she said "Your mother wants to tell you that she's gardening."

So what have we learned from this blueprint?

That life goes on.

In my first four books about the Flipside, filmed 50 people under deep hypnosis and reported verbatim what they said about the afterlife. In this book I film 50 people who are not under hypnosis and they say the same things about the afterlife.

I'm not knocking people who use hypnosis to access these same memories or experiences. In fact we wouldn't be having this discussion if I hadn't met some very talent hypnotherapists like Jimmy Quast, Michael Newton, Paul Aurand and Scott De Tamble.

To be clear; what I am doing in these "shorthand" explorations is not hypnosis, is not a healing technique, is not anything at all what hypnotherapy can offer. Going to a hypnotherapist can be life changing, and depending upon the ability of the hypnotherapist, can take hours or even days of exploration. Someone who can do that requires patience and a desire to heal or help people.

I'm asking people to "skim the surface." This "surface skimming" is not preferable to deep hypnosis, "life between life therapy" or the kinds of hypnosis that doctors like Brian Weiss offers. These "shortened" results are not life changing or healing the way hypnosis can be.

But by focusing on one element - councils - and asking council members about their journey, it's a form of verification. How could everyone speak to councils without hypnosis unless they actually exist?

This isn't a book about the validity of hypnosis - but it takes on the argument "hypnosis is not a valid tool of science." (Which is what a panel of scientists at UVA said when I presented them the cases from "Flipside" and Michael Newton's interview).

I've filmed or recorded 50 "deep hypnosis" cases (I use the term to differentiate stage hypnosis or guided meditation from "between life therapy") and now I've filmed or recorded about 50 cases of people not using any hypnosis saying the same things about their councils.

By asking questions that relate to structure, I can compare answers. Council members talk about how they got their gig. How many councils they sit on. I also do follow up interviews via Jennifer Shaffer, my medium pal, with individuals I've met during a session. It's mind bending for me to ask individuals I've met casually during a person's "surface session" later with a medium who can answer on their behalf. (As Dr. Drew asks "What's my council?" and my reply "I wasn't speaking to you Drew, but your guide.")

People walk away from the session no wiser than when they sat down for coffee. But if someone wants to explore this further, wants to understand how and why they chose the difficult lifetime they've led, I recommend finding a Newton Institute trained hypnotherapist (or just call Scott at lightbetweenlives.com)

But my point is simple; people not under hypnosis and people under hypnosis say the same relative things about the afterlife.

People *not under hypnosis* say the same relative things that people under hypnosis say about the same journey despite never having read a book about the topic, or not being aware of anything I've said about the subject.

They claim that life exists prior to incarnation (fully conscious) that life exists during incarnation (semiconscious) and then after incarnation (returning home to full conscious awareness of all of our lifetimes.) Not that we "dissolve into a sea of consciousness" but that we retain all the memories of this lifetime, all the memories of our previous lifetimes, and then all the memories of our experiences between lives.

Once they access their "higher self" (the conscious energy they've left behind) they can observe why they chose this lifetime, what consciousness is, the lives they've led before, their teachers, guides, council members.

People don't have to "believe" in anything to access this information, don't have to believe in religion, believe in little green men or have to wear pyramid hats. They may believe fervently in another reality – or are fervently attached to their world view. No amount of kicking, screaming, ranting or raving is going to change this data.

People will argue that in my non hypnosis sessions I ask leading questions. Yes, I do that on purpose. I'm saving time because I already know they have a guide and a council, a previous lifetime on earth. I could wait the five hours for them to get to the same place, but I take the short cut. As noted in the chapter with Scott De Tamble, this isn't a way to short circuit or circumvent hypnosis, it's just a proof of concept, that people don't have to be "under hypnosis" to gain insight into their path or journey.

I think therefore I am is western philosophy. *I think therefore I am not* is eastern philosophy, *I think therefore I might enjoy returning to the planet for pizza and cappuccinos* sums up my philosophy.

My wife pointed something out today – it used to take figure skaters (she was once a figure skater in Utah) ten years to learn a particular move. Now it takes three weeks to learn the same difficult move. Has training improved that much, or is it related to the "100th monkey concept?" That concept is the idea that if one monkey learns a new behavior – using a tool for food – the other ones "automatically learn it." Is that being passed by word of mouth? A universal unconscious?

Or the "higher selves" helping the person on earth to do things that are part of their spiritual evolution?

The renowned composer Phillip Glass notes it as well; certain keyboard pieces that were difficult to play or learn, once someone has mastered it, everyone seems to master it. It could be that "seeing" or "hearing" the process changes their ability to learn or know it. (Learning may be related to senses we aren't aware of, including seeing how fingers move, arms are held, etc.) There is evidence that people who have severe spectrum disorders (banging heads on walls), when they watch a videotape of their behavior it changes the wiring in the brain.

Does the wiring change because they're seeing something new? Or is seeing something new being assisted by what they can't see?

Some may be disconcerted at the discussions of "aliens" or "creatures from other planets." Well, I might add that people have been reporting "creatures" or "beasts" of higher intelligence since the dawn of mankind. Whether it's "Revelations" talking about "beasts" that appear to have superpowers, or Joseph Smith talking about seeing "Beasts at the right hand of God who have higher intellects" (In "Doctrines") they may be reporting something they've witnessed. It's our parsing of their memory that adds fear or issues of annihilation to the account. If we don't die, can't die, then there is no such thing as annihilation, or the "end of times" or "the end of the world." People report they've witnessed other worlds "end" – only to find themselves incarnating on another piece of real estate.

Does that mean we should save this piece of real estate? Well – let me put it this way, if you don't want to have fresh water, earth or air the next time you come back here – don't come back here. Find someplace else to incarnate. For those of us who like the planet, find a way to clean up the environment so we can share it with our children, and our reincarnation if we choose to return.

Finally, my wife Sherry had a dream recently where she was "speaking" with the scientist Mino; a young Japanese scientist whose mother Hisako Matsubara wrote a book about him after he died prematurely. My wife dreamed she was asking him questions about the nature of reality. She couldn't remember all of the dream (and also said "I may have been making this up") but reported "He was describing the essence of the afterlife as "both particle and wave.""

As we know from quantum mechanics energy is both particle and wave. (In the "double slit experiment" quantum mechanics demonstrates energy is both particle and wave.) He was telling her that on this side, the earth side of the veil, we experience more "particle." On the flipside we experience more "wave."

In some religious texts and accounts describe the afterlife as an experience of dissolving into a "sea of consciousness." I've had that experience, and reported it in "Flipside" where it felt like I had "dissolved" into a pool of golden light which gave me a sensation of intense connectedness. Some people do experience or report that sensation of being "one with everything" - but that doesn't mean they don't stay individuals. We are particles within a wave.

People, like energy, apparently are **both particle and wave.**

On this side of the veil we experience "particle" more. We are still connected to everyone but experience things individually. On the flipside we experience more "wave." We are still a particle but the experience is more "wave" like.

The best metaphor I can use for this experience is water. We are individual droplets. We have a cup of who we are and all our various lifetimes. We bring a portion of that cup to our lifetime and two thirds is always "back home."

In my wife's dream Mino also referred to her previous dream of "11:11" as a reference.

As noted in "Backstage Pass to the Flipside" my wife had a dream where our old friend Luana Anders appeared with new advice... but my wife's reaction to seeing her in the dream was to say "But Luana, you died 20 years ago. How can you be here?" Luana replied: "Think of 11:11. We meet at the decimals."

In order for those on the flipside to communicate, they need to slow/adjust their frequency to do so. If one thinks of the left "11" as a hallway here on earth and the other as a hallway there... "off planet" or "outside of time".. the wave experiencer has to slow down their frequency to communicate (through images, remembered sound etc) with the particle experiencer here who has to raise their frequency (through meditation, hypnosis, nde, obe, etc) to "meet at the decimals."

Turns out some dreams can be an effective way to learn new information.

Friend and mentor on the flipside Luana Anders

What do we learn from these accounts?

To sum up; what have we heard in this research?

CONSCIOUS ENERGY:

We bring "about 1/3rd" of our consciousness and 2/3^{rds} is always "back home" or "doing something else." It's another way to think of "soul." We are all both particle and wave; over here more particle than how we exist over there; as part of a wave.

TIME

is relatively nonexistent on the flipside. It exists, relative to our journey. We can "see the timeline" when off planet, and "move at the speed of thought." Time feels nonexistent in terms of our awareness.

SPACE

if we can move to other places at "the speed of thought" or "shift our consciousness to other realms, or distant places" it means that space is also a construct and doesn't exist per se.

GHOSTS:

"People who used to be on the planet." "Geophysical Holograms Of Sentients Transitioning." One can argue that technically there actually is "no such thing as ghosts" because "ghosts" are just individuals who used to be here. Not things. People.

ALIENS:

You, me, him and likely that other guy. One out of three people under deep hypnosis recalls lifetimes off world. Recalls why they chose to incarnate there, as well as chose to incarnate here. We need to drop the word entirely to understand who or what we actually are on this planet. Aliens R Us.

SATAN:

A mythological character from a novel. (See "Kurtz, Colonel") Doesn't exist except in the minds of those convinced he is a he, or that he is a person, object or thing. Same goes for "evil."

WHAT OR WHO IS GOD?

God appears to be another term for consciousness. (Best definition I've heard; "open your heart to everyone and all things and you'll experience God – which is essentially everything that is in existence both here and beyond.") Not a person, object or thing; a medium for consciousness and how we navigate life.

DARK MATTER, DARK ENERGY

seems to be the energy of something that existed in that space before (prior). Dark energy is the same – it requires an observation that includes "time" – as the matter that once was, always exists.

WHAT'S A BLACK HOLE?

A portal (for energy to move from one place to the next, carrying dark matter from one universe to the next.)

GOVERNMENT

seems to be the appropriate human ability to protect and save the planet, as well as rein in or help regulate those who are having a hard time navigating the planet. But compassion is required if not paramount.

REINCARNATION

reportedly is the process of conscious energy joining with a being. Applies to any living creature. Should just be called "incarnation." We all do it, including on other planets. We generally don't cross pollinate with other species on our planet but we can (with practice) shift consciousness into other creatures for brief amounts of time.

SOUL

is a word that poorly describes conscious energy. Also a musical term that relates to why we're on the planet.

CRIME

Try to allow that a person's journey may have been planned way before they committed whatever crime they've committed. Or that others have agreed to have them "commit" that crime to teach them lessons in love. It means that we have to rethink what "justice" of "punishment" is. If it includes taking that person's life, then we've lost the opportunity to help them correct the wrongs they've created.

HOW DO I TALK TO LOVE ONES WHO'VE PASSED?

Say their name, ask them questions; when you hear an answer before you can ask the question you'll know you've made a connection.

HOW DO WE SAVE THE PLANET?

Plant a trillion trees. Clean water through technology, but also use water as fuel. "Stop eating flesh." "Love the planet."

HOW DO I ACCESS MY COUNCIL?

As we've seen, it's not hard. If they want you to access them, they'll invited you to.

ARE MY GUIDES ALWAYS KEEPING AN EYE ON ME?

We've heard it more than once; "they're always tethered to us."

WHY IS THERE SO MUCH SUFFERING?

We're in a giant university. Each classroom has different tasks. Some consider them adventure while others consider them punitive.

CAN I ACHIEVE NIRVANA IN LIFE?

If one "wants to experience nirvana see above for "What or who is God?" We all wind up back home, reconnect to our conscious energy, and realize all the lives we've led. No hurry to get there.

WHAT'S THE MEANING OF LIFE?

Love.

Etcetera...

I'm paraphrasing. These accounts point to a greater truth. I can't answer these questions, but I can point people in the direction to answer them for themselves. Each one of these questions is explored in this book. If what these folks are saying, about life, about the journey is accurate, as a species we might have to rethink everything. Why we are on the planet. How to save the planet. How to judge or not judge human behavior. How to love ourselves and the earth.

(From the Afterword of "Flipside: A Tourist's Guide on How to Navigate the Afterlife")

1. Souls don't die.

We've been around for millennia; our souls continue on for millennia. In between lives we are fully conscious, with all of our memories intact. Yes, our bodies die, our loved ones depart from us in this life. But we reconnect with them in the Afterlife.

2. After death we return to our soul group, where we recognize those we've been reincarnating with for eons.

There's anywhere from 3-25 people in our individual group and we usually plan our next life with these same folks. We share laughs and memories of the life just lived and eventually plot with them our next adventure. We may even recognize them during this lifetime; usually identified with the thought "I felt like I always knew this person the moment I met them," or "I knew we would marry."

3. In between lives, we all have a life planning session where we choose our next life; we are able to pick and choose what kind of life we want to lead for various reasons, as well as choose our parents.

"Why would I choose those people who've made my life miserable?" is a familiar refrain. The answer is that you chose them so that you could be where you are today. Either far, far away from them - which is a gift in some cases, or their influence had directly put you in the place you're supposed to be on the planet. It puts a different spin on your parents behavior when you consider you chose them because of it. As well as why your own children chose you.

4. We each have our own "council of elders" who oversee our lifetimes, and engage with us in Socratic debate about how we did.

Everyone has a council of elders, and everyone goes to see them at least twice; once upon our return so they can help assimilate all the lessons from that lifetime, and once again just before we take another trip into human form. They don't sit in judgment; rather they help you discern your path. Usually there are 6-12 people on any given council; it seems the younger souls have fewer.

5. No humans are born without a soul, and we don't arrive at our chosen body until the fourth month (or sometimes later).

Consciousness is something we've retained from our life between lives. Some kind of veil, or filter, prevents us from remembering those previous lives. However, through the process of deep hypnosis, we're able to bypass these filters and access these previous memories. The idea that we don't join the body until the fourth month would be controversial to advocates who believe life begins at conception. The human animal life may begin at conception, but the spiritual life does not.

6. We don't reincarnate as other animals.

Each species comes back with in its own pantheon; i.e. birds of a feather, fish in the sea, and animals on land can swap places with those in their group, but not within other groups. To the concept of being reborn in a "lower life form" as a result of negative karma - that's not what is reported. All life forms are sacred; there are no pejoratives when it comes to life. However, its reported you can access your animal friends at any time in the life between lives – they're an energy pattern as well, and can spend hours playing fetch once again.

7. When we return to our home base, with our soul group, all actions and effects are left behind - we return to a pure state where we enjoy a world without pain, sin or suffering. There is no hell per se, nor a Satanic like region or persona.

Those who've caused pain, sin or suffering experience the pain they inflicted fully – as if they were the person being hurt during their life review. Afterwards they may choose (or it's decided for them) to be isolated from others in order to learn from their mistakes. There is no Satan or hell per se. Once you depart this plane, you no longer have access to the negativity here, or those who might perpetrate it. (For those Satanists out there, sorry, don't mean to offend.) According to the thousands who've journeyed into the afterlife, there's no evil waiting for us. But we may experience our own form of hell based on how we've treated other human beings.

8. The process of reincarnation is planned by us, not subject to karma, past mistakes, or past injustices. People choose to be gay, choose to be crippled, or choose to be blissful depending on their spiritual depth.

We don't travel up or down in any fashion, going from peasant to rich person, or unhappy soul to happy soul. Free will is the law of the Universe, and it's up to us who we want to return as, or even if we want to reincarnate. But inevitably, the pull of helping your loved ones and friends, brings us back time after time. Our life choices are up to us. That includes sexuality, physical type, body shape, etc. We may choose to struggle with these issues in order to progress spiritually, or to help those around us to progress. Those who live on the fringes of society are frequently older souls who chose to be there.

9. Bad experiences, including suicide, murder, mayhem and other events are frequently worked out in advance, with the agreement of all souls involved.

They claim there's no such thing as random violence. This may sound controversial, but according to the research, pretty universal. When examining a life between life session, we get an opportunity to see those details, however heinous or upsetting, to be true.

10. Our friends in our soul group frequently show up as pals in this life, relatives, brothers, sisters, loved ones or even as adversaries.

As mentioned, Judas claimed Jesus came to him and asked him to turn him over to the Romans as a favor. "If you truly love me, you'll do this for me." There are many reasons to be on the planet, we benefit from all our own experiences, but the main role might be one of servitude.

11. Our progression in the afterlife can be charted, in part, based on what color we see ourselves as - the earlier souls are closer to white, and through the spectrum, they wind up into the violet realm. But there is no hierarchy.

As hypnotherapist Jimmy Quast (Easton Hypnosis) put it; "No one gets to hoard the jellybeans." The idea of someone being smarter, better, richer, happier, more famous, more revered, more anything is just not the case. You are the perfect self you're meant to be. All paths are sacred, and none is judged lesser than another. Just older.

12. We all have a soul, spirit guide or "Guardian Angel," sometimes more than one.

Every one of us has a spirit guide who has agreed to watch over all of our incarnations. It gives new meaning to the sacrifice one does at the service of others - can you imagine becoming a mentor to a soul for all of their lifetimes? But the journey many of us are on is to eventually be a guardian angel (spirit guide) for another soul; no time like the present to start treating others like they might be a future candidate.

13. All of this movement and planning is based on energy.

Every thought, action, word or deed contains it, every emotion as well. Treat it with sacred intent, whether praying for deliverance, or to help another soul. If you think it, believe it, pray for it, sing it, act it or create it, you've put that personal energy out into the Universe. It can help, heal, or in negative cases, harm others.

14. There are other Universes and places we can reincarnate. Some religions have spoken of them, various planes in different dimensions Religion is a construct that mirrors the afterlife.

Earth is the best school, the best playground, the best place to advance our souls. "You'll learn more in one day of tragedy on Earth, then perhaps 5,000 years on another, simpler planet," according to one interview. The argument has been raised, "There aren't enough souls to reincarnate. Where'd the new souls come from?" According to Newton's patients, there are other places to reincarnate and new souls are reportedly being born. When we graduate from our many lifetimes, the graduation ceremony includes being rewarded with (and offering to guide through many lifetimes) a new soul.

15. Love and compassion turn out to be not just religious concepts, but words that explain how the Universe actually works; from energy transfer to why we choose a particular life.

Love is the wheelwork of nature, and that attraction and energy is what keeps us going. Compassion is part of the fabric as it's included in many examples of what we give our loved ones by reincarnating by their side. The Golden Rule is actually golden for a reason, because it represents how the Universe works. Loving your neighbor as yourself, nature as yourself, your fellow beings on all levels as yourself, turns out to be not only a spiritual maxim, but a physical one as well.

16. Religion is a man-made experience based on our god like nature.

In light of this research, world religions seem to be echoing the same thing; in the afterlife we have eternal qualities, and experience a heaven-like state of bliss. And while we're on Earth, we try to recreate or relive that experience. One could say we're "trying to get back to the Godhead," or "return to God." They're the same. Was Jesus the son of God? Aren't we all? Was Moses or Mohammed the chosen prophet? Aren't we all?

Religion expresses the inexpressible, examines the unexamined, and finds truth in the nature of all things. Science aspires to take the same journey, by making logical sense of what we are doing on the planet, how we got here, and where we are going. For those who believe that life ends in death, that's not what's reported. For those who think the stress of this lifetime is based on karma from a previous one; that too doesn't bear up under this form of scrutiny. Forgiveness, compassion and love for all people and things appears to be the universal law of the Universe.

17. We have both an animal ego and a spiritual ego.

According to this research, we started incarnating on Earth millennia ago. Perhaps when humans became upright or adept; our spiritual energy melded with the human's, and thus began consciousness. Perhaps this event coincided with the formation of societies 60,000 years ago and is our "missing link."

Human life appears to be an agreement between the animal and spiritual ego. That fact helps to underline why people act a certain way, and could have a profound influence on the criminal justice system – if a person is struggling in this life with animalistic tendencies is there a way of examining a healing process that's not "Clockwork Orange " but based on helping souls discover their purpose? As mentioned, in Holland, they've already begun to bring in psychics and past life regressionists to help cure career criminals.

18. Curing and healing people is part of the work done by others in the Afterlife.

People choose their lifetimes before coming here to continue their work in a particular field. Musicians may return to further their music knowledge, perhaps explaining child prodigies like Mozart and others. Doctors and Nurses are involved with healing energy transfer, and may have had many lifetimes where they continued their practice. Just the way Tibetan lamas might spend a lifetime studying esoteric practices, and then remember them in their ensuing lifetime, we can all tap into the knowledge of our previous lifetimes to help with our current one.

19. There are no coincidences.

What appears to be a matter of amazing coincidence, upon examination, turns out to be an incredible planned sequence, like a complex 3D chess or "Second Life" game being played on multiple planes where each move affects the other players. As a butterfly's wings in a rain forest may cause a hurricane in Asia, everything can be linked in cause and effect if one looks long and hard enough. And by the way, is the reason you've picked up this book.

20. You are doing pretty much what you set out to do.

Time and again, people report the spiritual journey they're on was laid out in advance. This is annoying for anyone with a remote control - we all have the inclination to change the channel, to want to change our circumstance, get richer quicker - but the answer is: "You're doing fine, you're on the right path, relax." As hard as your path may seem, you're on it for a spiritual reason.

21. This research is the tip of the iceberg.

I wrote the above about ten years ago. I can report that it has not changed when interviewing people not under hypnosis.

I can only assume that a person will look at this book from time to time, see something that resonates, put it down or pause the audio – until another time when they need to hear these incredible stories about the architecture of the afterlife again. It's as amazing to hear as it is to film, as it is to write, as it is to say into a microphone for future generations. There's a reason why you've been led to this material, and it has to do with one's own path and journey.

Someone near and dear to me had a thought about Robin Williams and his voice suddenly popped into her mind. Not believing it was him, she asked her question anyway "So why did you choose that method to do yourself in?" His answer was "**I didn't have drugs. I didn't own a gun; it was something easy to do and I didn't think too much about it.**"

She thought "That's an elaborate answer, I must be making this up." Then she heard **"You aren't making it up dearie."** She said "I must be making this up because that sounded like Mrs. Doubtfire's voice." She heard Robin say; **"Well who do you think she is? She's part of me as well."**

I've been editing "Backstage Pass to the Flipside: Talking to the Afterlife with Jennifer Shaffer Book Three" simultaneously and realize they are companions; both reference each other. I've included some of the times I interviewed people met in "council meetings" then later conduct a "follow up" interview via medium Jennifer Shaffer.

For in depth interviews with a variety of people mentioned in this book, from Robin Williams, to Prince, Aretha Franklin to Dr. Helen Wambach, and a variety of people who "came to our class" invited by other classmates, I recommend picking up the third book in the series "Backstage Pass to the Flipside Book Three."

As mentioned earlier, when I wrote "Hacking the Afterlife" I took out the chapter about Robin Williams because the book was too long. Then during a session with Jennifer Shaffer, she said "Robin wants you to put his chapter back in." (She didn't know there was a chapter about Robin in the book.) When the book was done, I texted Jennifer to ask if we could get "blurbs" for the book. Minutes later she called with 5 different "reviews" from people we'd chatted with (Prince, Edgar Cayce, etc). When it came to Robin she heard him say *"Love love."*

Jennifer asked him what he meant. He said **"Love what love is. What it represents. How it's the prime mover of the universe. If you love love itself, you're loving everyone and yourself."**

It appears the key to unlock the "Flipside Code" is "unconditional love." There is no scientific definition for it, other than "no one knows it unless they've experienced it." Chances are, we've all experienced it at some point, either in this life, or a previous one. "Love" appears to be the physical key to unlocking reality. If one can define "love," they can understand consciousness and how everything is connected.

But there's one more step involved in unlocking the code. One needs to "consciously turn the key." The only way to turn the key is to use "love" as well by "Opening your heart to everyone and all things." The only way to open a heart in that fashion is understanding "unconditional love." The flipside code (the formula for "all things") is unlocked using those two items – one is the key, the other is the motivation to turn the key. One is the engine, the other is the effect. One is from the head, the other is from the heart. "I love therefore I am."

Love love.

Vatican staircase, swirling water, galaxy; particles and waves

ABOUT THE AUTHOR

Photo by Russ Titelman

Dedicated to Sherry, my loving wife and two wiser-than-I-can-pretend-to-be children, Olivia and RJ.

This books exists due to those who allowed me to interview them, *not having a clue where we might go*. Thanks to Jennifer Shaffer (JenniferShaffer.com) and all *The Jennifers* interviewed, as well as Luana Anders and class. Thanks to Tony Stockwell, Chuck Tebbetts, Dr. Elisa Medhus for including me in her research into ChannelingErik.com and introducing me to Raylene and Kimberly. To my pal Bill Paxton, to Marie, the people in the book anonymously for logical reasons, but their stories are no less compelling.

To Joel Gotler, literary maven, to those millions (2.5 to date) on Quora who have read, argued or corrected my posts there, to Heather Wade for convincing Art Bell to have me on his show, then later for accessing him on the flipside. To Dr. Drew and his wife Susan, who allowed me on her show, had no idea that I would walk Drew into the flipside – and to his continued skepticism about whether or not I actually "hypnotized" him.

To Scott De Tamble, (lightbetweenlives.com) friend and hypnotherapist who constantly amazes, to Iris, my dear pal, Marie, Tracey, Mitchell, others who have put up with my rantings about the flipside and then took the time to take me on a journey to your own version of it. Not to mention all the council members and guides on the flipside who allowed me to ask them questions. Amazing.

Jim, Josh, Rosie, Livia – who were as startled as I was in hearing them talk about off world adventures or between life councils without any hypnosis at all. Scottie, Steph for allowing yourselves to "say whatever pops into your minds" during our interviews/sessions. Sean, that's not your real name, but you know who I'm thanking. To Angie in Newport, Taylor Peyton and others who took the time to "explore" not knowing if we'd get anywhere or find anything.

To the folks who donated on my GoFundMe page (link at RichMartini.com) Tim Bair, Kari Krug, Christine Lynne, Tom Naso, Lyn (Tigg) Boyce, Chris Rawls, Tash Govender, Diana Takata, Alex Broskey, Savarna Wiley, Don Thompson, Robert Thurman, Carin Levee, Chris Monaghan, John Wylie, Daniel Kearney, Maureen Johanson, Bill Dale, Eric Harrington, Lisa Yesse, Tamara Guion-Yagy, Lynette Hilton, John Tibayan, Jon Burnham. Thanks for your support!

To Father Antoninus – odd to thank him – but each of my books contains a past life memory and this isn't different. To Maryum and Roxy – thanks for sharing your journeys with me. To my father Romeo Charles Martini, a Chicago based Architect who taught me how to read a blueprint, and who inspired the title of this book. To my mom Anthy, a concert pianist who taught me that practice makes perfect, and home is where the heart is. We'll catch you all on the flipside.

Bio: Chicago native, author and award-winning filmmaker Richard Martini has written and/or directed 8 theatrical feature films. "Flipside" was his debut non-fiction book on a topic. The documentaries "Flipside" and "Talking to Bill Paxton" are distributed by Gaia TV and Amazon Prime. Has written for "Variety" "Premiere" and "Inc.com" His books include "Flipside: A Tourist's Guide to the Afterlife" "It's a Wonderful Afterlife: Further Adventures in the Flipside volumes one and two" "Hacking the Afterlife" have all have been to #1 in their genres in kindle at Amazon after his appearances on "Coast to Coast" radio with George Noory.

"Backstage Pass to the Flipside: Talking to the Afterlife with Jennifer Shaffer" is available online or via major online book outlets and is in two volumes. Volume 3 to be released soon. This is his 7th book. For more information: *RichMartini.com MartiniZone.com* on YouTube.